Cinema Censorship and the Law

by Jeremy Geltzer

Also by Jeremy Geltzer

Dirty Words and Filthy Pictures: Film and the First Amendment

Latino Hollywood

Race Films: 50 Years of Independent African American Cinema

Behind the Scenes: A Child's Guide to Film History

Charlie's Little Tramp: The Life of Charlie Chaplin

Oscar Micheaux: A Self-Made Man

Cinema Censorship & the Law

Table of Contents

1

Introduction

From its roots as a nickelodeon attraction to emergence as a multi-million dollar business and internationally recognized art form, the American film industry has an untold history. For over 100 years laws and court decisions have influenced what movies could be made and what state regulators had the power to censor.

What might be self-evident today—that motion pictures and electronic media are a valid and potent means of communication—was not always so clear. Just ten years after emerging from Edison's research and development laboratory in Menlo Park, NJ, motion pictures broke out to become an American obsession. In 1896, the old-fashioned on-screen smooch of May Irwin and John C. Rice in *The Kiss* caught audiences' interest, and the Lumière brother's *Arrival of a Train* scared patrons out of their seats. By 1907 nickelodeon theaters offered epics, such as Kalem's *Ben-Hur* (1907) and Georges Méliès' *20,000 Leagues Under the Sea* (1907); animation, such as Edison's *The Teddy Bears* (1907); and exciting thrillers ripped-from-the-headlines, such as Lubin's *The Unwritten Law: A Thrilling Drama based on the Thaw-White Tragedy* (1907).

Amid this great expansion, Chicago passed a film censorship ordinance. The 1907 law made it illegal to exhibit a motion picture without first clearing it with the Chief of Police and obtaining a permit. Jake Block, a local theater, owner challenged the law. It was a valiant move for the entrepreneur-qua-reluctant free speech advocate. But the system wasn't ready to understand the flickering silent image as speech. Judge James H. Cartwright unflinchingly supported the local law, writing: "The purpose of the ordinance is to secure decency and morality in the moving picture business." (*Block v. Chicago*, 87 N.E. 1011, 1013 [Ill. 1909]).

But the motion picture industry continued to grow stronger. Even operating from a position of vulnerability against the multiplying ranks of municipal morality police and state censors, filmmakers kept pushing. One year after *The Birth of a Nation* (1914) charged across America, the Supreme Court chimed in. The High Court snubbed their noses at the attractive nuisance of cinema. The Mutual decisions of 1915 set aside all doubt: movies were not embraced within the First Amendment's guarantees of free expression.

Filmmakers retrenched and turned to self-regulation and industry organization. It would not be mainstream Hollywood that challenged the status quo. The job was left for independent and international producers. What happened was interesting: initially, the law had influenced which films would be permitted. As the medium grew more sophisticated, motion pictures began to influence judicial interpretation of the First Amendment. In 1952 motion pictures were brought under Constitutional protection with the *Miracle* decision.

The decision had vast cultural impact. Within 100 years, the freedom of speech evolved from a narrow restriction on the federal government to combat possible abuse of silencing contrary political opposition to a more inclusive understanding. The medium of motion pictures played an important role in guiding the courts to a broader interpretation of the First Amendment. By 1968, non-verbal symbolic speech or expressive conduct was recognized in *United States v. O'Brien*, 391 U.S. 367 (1968). Draft card destruction, flag burning, and pointed profanity could be protected. But the law was not all-of-a-sudden an anything goes free-for-all. When the Free Speech Coalition protested Measure B, the Los Angeles Safer Sex In the Adult Film Industry Act, as a violation of free speech, the argument didn't fly. The measure passed in 2012. Revenge porn was criminalized in Texas, Oregon, and Vermont; does this violate the First Amendment? Should Cyberbulling be protected? Panhandling has been positioned as expressive conduct, but are topless panhandlers in Times Square? (Jacob Gershman, "Are Topless Panhandlers Covered by the First Amendment?" in *The Wall Street Journal Law Blog*, August 21, 2015). Letting the weeds grow in your front lawn is not expressive (Jack Bouboushian, "Unkempt Weeds Aren't Art, Seventh Circuit Says," in *Courthouse News Service*, September 29, 2015) but is snapping a shot of a ballot-selfie? (Kristine Guerra, "Ballot Selfie Law Faces Scrutiny from Federal Judge," in *USA Today*, October 14, 2015).

While the general progression of case law charts a course toward greater expressive rights, this journey unfolded in fits and starts. As the primary sources in *Cinema Censorship and the Law* will demonstrate, the early decades saw political censorship upheld by the courts, in the examples of Margaret Sanger and Robert Goldstein. Mid-century, as the Civil Rights era was dawning, Southern censors were still strictly regulating images of African Americans on the screens of theaters. Even when the pendulum swung the other way and the Porno Chic was seen in mainstream media there were limits, as seen in the *Extreme Associates* case.

Motion pictures-makers played an important role in broadening the idea of what can be considered speech and expressive conduct in America. Some aspects might seem silly at first glance—condoms, bare breasts, and selfies, but the real issue is: how far are we willing to allow the state to regulate behavior?

Cinema Censorship and the Law should raise provocative and intensely personal questions. On one hand, we must recognize the benefits of free expression, in terms of educating, informing, entertaining. But the countervailing forces of regulation deserve equal consideration. Especially in our increasingly wired and interconnected electronic world, there is a strong case for protecting people, particularly children, from harmful, unwanted or inappropriate content.

2

Film is Not Speech

Harry Aitken at Mutual Film's Milwaukee Headquarters.

Motion pictures in America began as a sideshow attraction, a cheap amusement that entertained working class audiences and children. By 1905, nickelodeon theaters threw open their doors in neighborhoods across America. A new industry was emerging and the original inventors, such as Thomas Edison, the American Mutoscope and Biograph Company, and Vitagraph, were challenged by entrepreneurial newcomers such as Marcus Loew, William Fox, Carl Laemmle, and Adolph

Zukor. As the new medium developed, a corporate and industrial framework took shape. Initially, the cartel of original power players, which would come to be known informally as the Edison Trust and incorporated as the Motion Picture Patents Company ("M.P.P.C.") holding company and the General Film distribution company, insisted that exhibitors purchase only their films. Contemporary advertisements described a picture's subject and theater owners would buy the movies sight unseen. *The Great Train Robbery* (1903) was sold as individual scenes. The exhibitor could elect how long the narrative would run; an additional stand-alone scene of an outlaw shooting directly into the lens was offered as supplementary material. It could be placed at the beginning or the end of the program—or wherever the projectionist elected to run the shot. By 1905 more complex multi-scene narratives were sold at a single price; a 15-meter reel of film could cost as much as $25.00. If the print was properly cared for it could be projected 300 times.

This system benefited motion picture producers but was difficult for exhibition outlets to maintain. As film technology evolved from single shot actualities to multi-scene narratives, theater programs had to be changed more often, requiring more money to buy new films.

Into this environment, a new system emerged: the film exchange. *Mutual v. Ohio* described the new process. "[F]ilms are shipped to exchanges and by them rented to exhibitors, and the exchanges are described as nothing more or less than circulating libraries or clearing houses. And one film serves in many theatres from day to day until it is worn out." (*Mutual v. Ohio*, 236 U.S. 230, 241 (1915), internal quotation marks omitted). Film exchanges were the middlemen, buying from manufacturers and renting to exhibitors cutting the General Film Company out of the equation.

To build a client base, film exchanges advertised in trade journals, mailed leaflets, and hired salesmen to promote the medium. If New York was the production capital, Chicago became a key distribution hub. The Second City was a gateway to the Midwest, and numerous exchanges opened to service the country. By 1906, Chicago teemed with over 15 exchanges, including Eugene Cline & Company, William Swanson & Company, William B. Moore's Stereopticon & Film Exchange, a M.P.P.C.-licensed outlet George Kleine Optical, and a coalition of independent producers called the International Projecting and Producing Company.

In 1906, Harry E. Aitken (1877-1956) and his brother Roy incorporated the Western Film Exchange based in Milwaukee, WI. Western was a successful venture, rapidly expanding to open branch offices in Chicago, St. Louis, and Joplin, MO. Harry Aitken became a power player in the second phase of film industry development in the U.S. In the first phase, Edison and his confederation of inventors perfected and popularized the entertainment medium. But these pioneers were reluctant to change. Through the General Film Company, Edison's Trust demanded that theaters buy films; furthermore, they were reluctant to make movies longer than one reel. In addition the Trust demanded a royalty or subscription from every outlet that used their patented equipment, this license fee was on top of the sale price.

The Aitkens' film exchange made it cheaper for theater owners to rent films, and so more exhibitors got in the game. More theaters opened, demanding more films. Film programs became more ambitious, adding story films, animated shorts, and newsreels.

But Harry Aitken had even greater ambitions. He negotiated exclusive output deals with the film industry's leading producers: establishing partnerships with Majestic Studios (D.W. Griffith), Keystone Studios (Mack Sennett), and Kay Bee Studios (Thomas Ince). Any theater that wanted to show a Griffith thriller, a Keystone comedy, or an Ince western had to rent from Mutual.

Mutual took especial pride in their newsreel unit, which delivered timely current events reports to theaters and supplemented entertaining story films. When municipal regulations and administrative licensing held up the business of film distribution, Aitken decided to challenge the system. *Mutual Film Corp. v. Industrial Commission of Ohio* and *Mutual Film Corp. of Missouri v. George H. Hodges, Governor; Charles H. Sessions, Secretary of State; John S. Dawson, Attorney General; and W. D. Ross, State Superintendent of Public Instruction of the State of Kansas*, were the first cases to consider film and the First Amendment. These cases rose to the Supreme Court and would set the stage for the next half century.

Harry K. Thaw arrives in San Francisco after cross country drive. Copyright, 1915, Mutual Weekly.

Scene from a Mutual Newsreel featuring socialite-turned-scandal celebrity Harry K. Thaw (1915)

MUTUAL FILM CORPORATION v. INDUSTRIAL COMMISSION OF OHIO

Supreme Court of United States
236 U.S. 230 (1915)
Argued January 6-7, 1915
Decided February 23, 1915
Appeal from the District Court of the United States for the Northern District of Ohio

***239** MR. JUSTICE McKENNA, after stating the case as above, delivered the opinion of the court.

Complainant directs its argument to three propositions: (1) The statute in controversy imposes an unlawful burden on interstate commerce; (2) it violates the freedom of speech and publication guaranteed by § 11, art. 1, of the constitution of the State of Ohio;[1] and (3) it attempts to delegate legislative power to censors and to other boards to determine whether the statute offends in the particulars designated.

It is necessary to consider only §§ 3, 4 and 5. Section 3 makes it the duty of the board to examine and censor motion picture films to be publicly exhibited and displayed

***240** in the State of Ohio. The films are required to be exhibited to the board before they are delivered to the exhibitor for exhibition, for which a fee is charged.

Section 4. "Only such films as are in the judgment and discretion of the board of censors of a moral, educational or amusing and harmless character shall be passed and approved by such board." The films are required to be stamped or designated in a proper manner.

Section 5. The board may work in conjunction with censor boards of other States as a censor congress, and the action of such congress in approving or rejecting films shall be considered as the action of the state board, and all films passed, approved, stamped and numbered by such congress, when the fees therefor are paid shall be considered approved by the board.

By § 7 a penalty is imposed for each exhibition of films without the approval of the board, and by § 8 any person dissatisfied with the order of the board is given the same rights and remedies for hearing and reviewing, amendment or vacation of the order "as is provided in the case of persons dissatisfied with the orders of the industrial commission."

The censorship, therefore, is only of films intended for exhibition in Ohio, and we can immediately put to one side the contention that it imposes a burden on interstate commerce. It is true that according to the allegations of the bill some of the films of complainant are shipped from Detroit, Michigan, but they are distributed to exhibitors, purchasers, renters and lessors in Ohio, for exhibition in Ohio, and this determines the application of the statute. In other words, it is only films which are "to be publicly exhibited and displayed in the State of Ohio" which are required to be examined and censored. It would be straining the doctrine of original packages to say that the films retain that form and composition even when unrolling and exhibiting to audiences, or, being ready for

***241** renting for the purpose of exhibition within the State, could not be disclosed to the state officers. If this be so, whatever the power of the State to prevent the exhibition of films not approved — and for the purpose of this contention we must assume the power is otherwise plenary — films brought from another State, and only because so brought, would be exempt from the power, and films made in the State would be subject to it. There must be some time when the films are subject to the law of the State, and necessarily when they are in the hands of the exchanges ready to be rented to exhibitors or have passed to the latter, they are in consumption, and mingled as much as from their nature they can be with other property of the State.

It is true that the statute requires them to be submitted to the board before they are delivered to the exhibitor, but we have seen that the films are shipped to "exchanges" and by them rented to exhibitors, and the "exchanges" are described as "nothing more or less than circulating libraries or clearing houses." And one film "serves in many theatres from day to day until it is worn out."

The next contention is that the statute violates the freedom of speech and publication guaranteed by the Ohio constitution. In its discussion counsel have gone into a very elaborate description of moving picture exhibitions and their many useful purposes as graphic expressions of opinion and sentiments, as exponents of policies, as teachers of science and history, as useful, interesting, amusing, educational and moral. And a list of the "campaigns," as counsel call them, which may be carried on is given. We may concede the praise. It is not questioned by the Ohio statute and under its comprehensive description, "campaigns" of an infinite variety may be conducted. Films of a "moral, educational or amusing and harmless character shall be passed and approved" are the words of the statute. No exhibition, therefore, or "campaign"

***242** of complainant will be prevented if its pictures have those qualities. Therefore, however missionary of opinion films are or may become, however educational or entertaining, there is no impediment to their value or effect in the Ohio statute. But they may be used for evil, and against that possibility the statute was enacted. Their power of amusement and, it may be, education, the audiences they assemble, not of women alone nor of men alone, but together, not of adults only, but of children, make them the more insidious in corruption by a pretense of worthy purpose or if they should degenerate from worthy purpose. Indeed, we may go beyond that possibility. They take their attraction from the general interest, eager and wholesome it may be, in their subjects, but a prurient interest may be excited and appealed to. Besides, there are some things which should not have pictorial representation in public places and to all audiences. And not only the State of Ohio but other States have considered it to be in the interest of the public morals and welfare to supervise moving picture exhibitions. We would have to shut our eyes to the facts of the world to regard the precaution unreasonable or the legislation to effect it a mere wanton interference with personal liberty.

We do not understand that a possibility of an evil employment of films is denied, but a freedom from the censorship of the law and a precedent right of exhibition are asserted, subsequent responsibility only, it is contended, being incurred for abuse. In other words, as we have seen, the constitution of Ohio is invoked and an exhibition of films is assimilated to the freedom of speech, writing and publication assured by that instrument and for the abuse of which only is there responsibility, and, it is insisted, that as no law may be passed "to restrain the liberty of speech or of the press," no law may be passed to subject moving pictures to censorship before their exhibition.

***243** We need not pause to dilate upon the freedom of opinion and its expression, and whether by speech, writing or printing. They are too certain to need discussion—of such conceded value as to need no supporting praise. Nor can there be any doubt of their breadth nor that their underlying safeguard is, to use the words of another, "that opinion is free and that conduct alone is amenable to the law."

Are moving pictures within the principle, as it is contended they are? They, indeed, may be mediums of thought, but so are many things. So is the theatre, the circus, and all other shows and spectacles, and their performances may be thus brought by the like reasoning under the same immunity from repression or supervision as the public press — made the same agencies of civil liberty.

Counsel have not shrunk from this extension of their contention and cite a case in this court where the title of drama was accorded to pantomime; [1a] and such and other spectacles are said by counsel to be publications of ideas, satisfying the definition of the dictionaries — that is, and we quote counsel, a means of making or announcing publicly something that otherwise might have remained private or unknown, — and this being peculiarly the purpose and effect of moving pictures they come directly, it is contended, under the protection of the Ohio constitution.

The first impulse of the mind is to reject the contention. We immediately feel that the argument is wrong or strained which extends the guaranties of free opinion and speech to the multitudinous shows which are advertised on the bill-boards of our cities and towns and which regards them as emblems of public safety, to use the words of Lord Camden, quoted by counsel, and which seeks to

***244** bring motion pictures and other spectacles into practical and legal similitude to a free press and liberty of opinion.

The judicial sense supporting the common sense of the country is against the contention. As pointed out by the District Court, the police power is familiarly exercised in granting or withholding licenses for theatrical performances as a means of their regulation. The court cited the following cases: *Marmet v. State*, 45 Ohio, 63, 72, 73; *Baker v. Cincinnati*, 11 Ohio St. 534; *Commonwealth v. McGann*, 213 Massachusetts, 213, 215; *People v. Steele*, 231 Illinois, 340, 344, 345.

The exercise of the power upon moving picture exhibitions has been sustained. *Greenberg v. Western Turf Ass'n*, 148 California, 126; *Laurelle v. Bush*, 17 Cal. App. 409; *State v. Loden*, 117 Maryland, 373; *Block v. Chicago*, 239 Illinois, 251; *Higgins v. Lacroix*, 119 Minnesota, 145. See also *State v. Morris*, 76 Atl. Rep. 479; *People v. Gaynor*, 137 N.Y.S. 196, 199; *McKenzie v. McClellan*, 116 N.Y.S. 645, 646.

It seems not to have occurred to anybody in the cited cases that freedom of opinion was repressed in the exertion of the power which was illustrated. The rights of property were only considered as involved. It cannot be put out of view that the exhibition of moving pictures is a business pure and simple, originated and conducted for profit, like other spectacles, not to be regarded, nor intended to be regarded by the Ohio constitution, we think, as part of the press of the country or as organs of public opinion. They are mere representations of events, of ideas and sentiments published and known, vivid, useful and entertaining no doubt, but, as we have said, capable of evil, having power for it, the greater because of their attractiveness and manner of exhibition. It was this capability and power, and it may be in experience of them, that induced the State of Ohio, in addition to prescribing penalties for immoral exhibitions, as it does in its Criminal

***245** Code, to require censorship before exhibition, as it does by the act under review. We cannot regard this as beyond the power of government.

It does not militate against the strength of these considerations that motion pictures may be used to amuse and instruct in other places than theatres — in churches, for instance, and in Sunday schools and public schools. Nor are we called upon to say on this record whether such exceptions would be within the provisions of the statute nor to anticipate that it will be so declared by the state courts or so enforced by the state officers.

The next contention of complainant is that the Ohio statute is a delegation of legislative power and void for that if not for the other reasons charged against it, which we have discussed. While administration and legislation are quite distinct powers, the line which separates exactly their exercise is not easy to define in words. It is best recognized in illustrations. Undoubtedly the legislature must declare the policy of the law and fix the legal principles which are to control in given cases; but an administrative body may be invested with the power to ascertain the facts and conditions to which the policy and principles apply. If this could not be done there would be infinite confusion in the laws, and in an effort to detail and to particularize, they would miss sufficiency both in provision and execution.

The objection to the statute is that it furnishes no standard of what is educational, moral, amusing or harmless, and hence leaves decision to arbitrary judgment, whim and caprice; or, aside from those extremes, leaving it to the different views which might be entertained of the effect of the pictures, permitting the "personal equation" to enter, resulting "in unjust discrimination against some propagandist film," while others might be approved without question. But the statute by its provisions guards against such variant judgments, and its terms, like other

***246** general terms, get precision from the sense and experience of men and become certain and useful guides in reasoning and conduct. The exact specification of the instances of their application would be as impossible as the attempt would be futile. Upon such sense and experience, therefore, the law properly relies. This has many analogies and direct examples in cases, and we may cite *Gundling v. Chicago*, 177 U.S. 183; *Red "C" Oil Manufacturing Co. v. North Carolina*, 222 U.S.380; *Bridge Co. v. United States*, 216 U.S. 177; *Buttfield v. Stranahan*, 192 U.S. 470. See also *Waters-Pierce Oil Co. v. Texas*, 212 U.S. 86. If this were not so, the many administrative agencies created by the state and National governments would be denuded of their utility and government in some of its most important exercises become impossible.

To sustain the attack upon the statute as a delegation of legislative power, complainant cites *Harmon v. State*, 66 Ohio St. 249. In that case a statute of the State committing to a certain officer the duty of issuing a license to one desiring to act as an engineer if "found trustworthy and competent," was declared invalid because, as the court said, no standard was furnished by the General Assembly as to qualification, and no specification as to wherein the applicant should be trustworthy and competent, but all was "left to the opinion, finding and caprice of the examiner." The case can be distinguished. Besides, later cases have recognized the difficulty of exact separation of the powers of government, and announced the principle that legislative power is completely exercised where the law "is perfect, final and decisive in all of its parts, and the discretion given only relates to its execution." Cases are cited in illustration. And the principle finds further illustration in the decisions of the courts of lesser authority but which exhibit the juridical sense of the State as to the delegation of powers.

Section 5 of the statute, which provides for a censor

***247** congress of the censor board and the boards of other States, is referred to in emphasis of complainant's objection that the statute delegates legislative power. But, as complainant says, such congress is "at present non-existent and nebulous," and we are, therefore, not called upon to anticipate its action or pass upon the validity of § 5.

We may close this topic with a quotation of the very apt comment of the District Court upon the statute. After remarking that the language of the statute "might have been extended by descriptive and illustrative words," but doubting that it would have been the more intelligible and that probably by being more restrictive might be more easily thwarted, the court said: "In view of the range of subjects which complainants claim to have already compassed, not to speak of the natural development that will ensue, it would be next to impossible to devise language that would be at once comprehensive and automatic."

In conclusion we may observe that the Ohio statute gives a review by the courts of the State of the decision of the board of censors.

Decree affirmed.

[1] "Section 11. Every citizen may freely speak, write, and publish his sentiments on all subjects, being responsible for the abuse of the right; and no law shall be passed to restrain or abridge the liberty of speech, or of the press. In all criminal prosecutions for libel, the truth may be given in evidence to the jury, and if it shall appear to the jury that the matter charged as libelous is true, and was published with good motives, and for justifiable ends, the party shall be acquitted."

[1a] *Kalem v. Harper Bros.*, 222 U.S. 55 (1911).

MUTUAL FILM CORP. OF MISSOURI v. HODGES

Supreme Court of United States
236 U.S. 248 (1915)
Argued January 6-7, 1915
Decided February 23, 1915

***249** Appellant, which we shall call complainant, it being such in the court below, is a Delaware corporation and the defendants are officers of the state of Kansas.

The bill attacks the validity of a law of Kansas censoring moving picture films, and prays an injunction against its enforcement. The relief was denied and the bill dismissed. This appeal was then allowed.

The bill alleges that complainant is engaged in local and interstate commerce in the renting, leasing, selling, and delivery of "films" in the state of Kansas and other states, which films have been and now are being used in the motion picture show business in Kansas, as well as elsewhere.

It is alleged that a film 'may be a scenario of an original story or theatrical production, conceived by a writer or author. This is a sketch of a plot, or chief incidents of a libretto or play, a drama, a prose or poetical composition, depicting human life and conduct on a stage. It may be also a reproduction of animated objects, scenery, picturesque views or animals, and is descriptive, educational, instructive, as well as amusing.'

The manner of the production of a film is stated, and that there are in the state about five hundred moving

***250** picture theaters using the films, and each theater uses an average of three films a day.

That a revenue in the shape of a tax of $2 is attempted to be imposed upon each film censored, which means a tax of $6 per day on the films sold, rented, or used in each show, approximating $3,000 per day on the picture show business in the state, and making a total revenue of $40,000 for the first three months from the beginning of the enforcement of the act, and thereafter a revenue of thousands of dollars to be imposed as a tax upon films printed and produced in Kansas.

That the act places a tax of about $300 a week on the films rented, hired, and shipped into the state for the period of three months, and about $6,000 for the first year, and means thereafter a tax on the interstate commerce business of complainant, a similar tax to be imposed on all films produced and printed and sent into Kansas.

That upon the films brought into the state the

duty of censorship is imposed upon the state superintendent of public instruction, thereby attempting to place in him the exclusive power of censorship of all films sent into the state for use in the state, and the power to review and stamp with his approval the films used, shipped, or rented or sent into the state; and the act provides that no film shall be exempt until a fee of $2 be paid, and that all fees shall be paid into the state treasury and credited to the general fund of the state. That on account of the way the business is conducted, complainant and other film exchanges must necessarily bear the expense of censorship, otherwise the amount of the charges therefor would be necessarily doubled or trebled.

The bill attacks the law for various reasons, having foundation, it is alleged, in the provisions of the Federal and state Constitutions, which may be summarized as follows: The prohibition upon the state to lay an import or export duty; or to abridge the privileges and immunities

***251** of citizens of the United States, the statute of the state offending in this as it places an embargo and prohibition upon citizens of other states in transacting a lawful business in Kansas. The statute violates the Bill of Rights of the United States and of the state of Kansas, as it deprives of life, liberty, and property without due process of law, and particularly of the freedom to say, write, or publish whatever one will on any subject, 'being only responsible for all abuse of that liberty,' and that there can be no abuse until it is judicially determined.

It is alleged that the attorney general of the state threatens to enforce the act, although it seems to be charged that he is without the means to do so, and arrests have been made on information filed in one of the courts of the state.

The answer of defendants asserts in elaborate allegations the necessity of the act and of the censorship of films; that it is not primarily a revenue measure, but is an exercise in good faith of the police power of the state for the protection of the public morals, and that 'the legislature, in its unimpeachable wisdom, believed that uncensored pictures were detrimental to the morals and perversive of true education.' In denial of any grievance of complainant under the act the answer alleges the following: 'Answering still further, defendants allege that this complainant has no interest in the act of the Kansas legislature complained of, nor does the complainant exhibit pictures to the people of Kansas in moving picture shows, or elsewhere, nor does the complainant come directly under the provisions of said act, nor can the complainant, as a Delaware corporation licensed to do business in the state of Missouri, transact interstate business within the state of Kansas either with or without the payment of an inspection fee under the act complained of, nor is the complainant liable to any criminal prosecution under the act complained of, but only the persons,

***252** firms, partnerships, companies, and corporations which actually do exhibit pictures uncensored within the state of Kansas in violation of the act. And defendants further allege that upon its own showing this complainant has brought only mere moot questions into this honorable court.'

A hearing upon an interlocutory or temporary injunction was waived and the case heard upon its merits, one judge only sitting, the parties agreeing thereto.

Affidavits in support of the bill were filed. One of them was by an exhibitor of films within the state, and showed the number of theaters owned by him, the number of films received by him and the price paid therefor, and that they were manufactured elsewhere than in Kansas. It affirmed that he never exhibited nor has he ever seen exhibited indecent, immoral, obscene, or sacrilegious pictures or films; that among the films exhibited by him is a film known as the 'Mutual Weekly,' which consists of photographs of events of current interest throughout the world. A list of the subjects represented is given.

An affidavit of one of the managers of the complainant was also filed, giving an account of the production of the films and their distribution. After a detail of this by complainant and by other 'film exchanges' renting out films in the state, and which operate independently of complainant, it is said:

'In my opinion the only possible method of continuing the rental of film in the state of Kansas, if the proposed censorship law were to go into effect, would be for the film exchanges to procure the approval required by statute. There are a large number of motion picture exhibitors in the state of Kansas—about five hundred (500). I do not believe it would be in any wise practicable for the exhibitors themselves to procure the approval of the different films. In the first place, the same subjects are rented from different film exchanges and are shown in ***253** different theaters concurrently. No exhibitor would be in a position to know whether the subject had been approved or not, without submitting the same to the superintendent of public instruction. The result would be that in almost every case each reel of film received by an exhibitor on rental for exhibit would have to be sent to Topeka for approval, because the exhibitor would not, at his peril, exhibit the same.

'The film exchange, on the other hand, could, with less difficulty than the exhibitor, ascertain whether a film had been approved or not, because the film exchange itself handles large quantities of films, and at least as to its own produce could keep track of the approval or nonapproval thereof, therefore making it absolutely necessary for this complainant, or the other film exchanges, to submit before renting out their films to their patrons in Kansas the films for approval.

'In the second place, in my opinion, no exhibitor would consent to pay the censoring charge on any particular reel or reels of film, because he would insist that the film be rented out to some other exhibitor in Kansas before him, so that someone else should pay the tax.' * * * [Argument of Counsel from pages 253-256 intentionally omitted]

***256** MR. JUSTICE McKENNA, after stating the case as above, delivered the opinion of the Court.

Necessarily the first factor to be considered is the law of the state. It is entitled, 'An Act Regulating the Exhibiting or Using of Moving Picture Films or Reels; Providing and Regulating the Examination and Approval of Moving Picture Films and Reels, and Fixing Penalties for the Violation of This Act, and Making an Appropriation for Clerical Help to Carry This Act into Effect.' [Laws 1913, chap. 294, p. 504.]

The following are its provisions: On and after the 1st of April, 1913, it shall be unlawful to exhibit or use any moving picture film or reel unless the same shall have been examined

***257** and approved by the superintendent of public instruction. Films used in institutions of learning are exempt from the provisions of the act. It is made the duty of such officer to examine the films or reels intended for exhibition, and approve such as he shall find to be moral and instructive, and to withhold his approval from such as tend to debase or corrupt the morals. His approval is to be stamped in writing upon the films or reels approved. He is to keep a record of examinations made by him, noting those approved and those not approved, stating the reasons for the latter. A charge of $2 is to be made for each examination. He is given the power and authority to supervise and regulate the display of all moving picture films or reels in all places of amusement or elsewhere within the state, to inquire and investigate, and to have displayed for his benefit to aid him in his investigation, those which are intended to be displayed, and shall approve such as shall be moral and proper, and disapprove such as are sacrilegious, obscene, indecent, or immoral, or such as tend to corrupt the morals. His disapproval of any film or reel may be reviewed by a commission consisting of the governor, attorney general, and secretary of state, and if they, or a majority of them, find the film or reel fit for exhibition, it shall be approved. It is the duty of every person exhibiting or permitting to be exhibited any film or reel within the state to furnish the superintendent of instruction, if he require it, a description of such film or reel and a description of its scenes and purposes, and to exhibit and display it for his examination and approval. Any person exhibiting or permitting to be exhibited any unapproved film or reel shall be guilty of a misdemeanor, and each liable to suit and separate fines.

It will be observed that the law makes only exhibitors or those permitting exhibitions of unapproved films liable to the penalties of the act, and, as we have seen, it is alleged by the defendants that as complainant is in neither

***258** class, it has no standing to attack the statute. To this complainant replies that its sales are interfered with, and invokes, as sustaining its right to complain, *Savage v. Jones*, 224 U.S. 501, 56 L. ed. 1182, 32 Sup. Ct. Rep. 715. This may be; but complainant, by asserting such right, cannot enlarge the character of the statute, or give to it an operation which it does not have--cannot, for instance, make the importation of films into the state an offense under it, and not their exhibition, which only it punishes--cannot, therefore, make the act an interference with interstate commerce instead of what it is--an exercise of the police power of the state upon things within the state. Nor can it make any difference that the 'exchanges' can more conveniently submit the films for approval than exhibitors can.

The opinion in No. 456 [236 U.S. 230 , 59 L. ed. -- 35 Sup. Ct. Rep. 387] becomes applicable here.

SUPREME COURT HOLDS CENSORSHIP LAW IS O. K.

The Mutual Film Corporation Lost Its Suit Against Kansas Motion Picture Censorship.

Washington, Feb. 24.—The United States supreme court yesterday afternoon held that the Ohio and Kansas moving picture censorship laws are constitutional.

The validity of the Ohio and Kansas moving picture censorship laws was challenged by the Mutual Film corporation and the Mutual Film company. The Mutual Film corporation is a Virginia corporatian and has an executive office in New York. Its business is mostly that of selling films to film exchanges and its operates an exchange in Detroit, Mich., which does business in western Ohio. The Mutual Film company is an Ohio corporation and it purchases films from the Mutual Film corporation and distributes them among exhibitors in Ohio, Pennsylvania, West Virginia and Kentucky and maintains exchanges in Cleveland, Columbus and Cincinnati.

The Kansas law is practically identical with the Ohio law except that the Kansas statute confers censorship authority on the state superintendent of instruction while the Ohio law confers this authority upon a board of censors acting under the industrial commission of the state.

The Ohio statute provides that no film shall be exhibited by an exhibitor until it shall have been approved by the censor, a charge of $1 a reel being exacted for each film censored when the film is of a certain length and $2 when it is of other lengths. The law provides:

"Only such films as are in the the judgment and discretion of the board of censors of a moral, educational or amusing and harmless character shall be passed and approved by such board."

A criminal penalty is provided for those who violate the law by exhibiting motion pictures without the approval of the board.

In both the Ohio and Kansas cases the lower federal courts were asked to prevent the enforcement of the law by injunctions and in both cases the application for injunction was denied. Thereupon appeals were taken to the supreme court.

The film companies challenged the validity of the statutes on three important grounds:

That they interfered with interstate commerce.

That they violated the constitutonal principle of freedom of publication.

That the Ohio law contravened the constitution of Ohio by delegating legislative power to the board of censors.

Great Bend Tribune, February 24, 1915

Indeed, this case was argued conjointly with that, and submitted on the same briefs. It is here contended that the Kansas statute has the same invalidity and for the same reasons as it was contended there that the statute of Ohio had. We need not, therefore, repeat the reasoning. It establishes that both statutes are valid exercises of the police power of the states, and are not amenable to the objections urged against them--that is, do not interfere with interstate commerce nor abridge the liberty of opinion; nor are they delegations of legislative power to administrative officers.

Decree affirmed.

3

Birth Control & Treason

Margaret Sanger in *Birth Control* (1917)

After *Mutual v. Ohio* determined that state and municipal administrators could censor motion pictures without running against First Amendment free speech protections, a network of regional regulators sprang up, quickly crisscrossing the country.

Chicago was the first city to systematically enforce film regulations, enacting an ordinance in 1907. In 1911, Pennsylvania became the first state to license and approve motion pictures.

Ohio approved legislation in 1913, which stood up to scrutiny by the Supreme Court in *Mutual*. New York City, the center of the film universe, mandated oversight in 1913 as well. Maryland followed in 1916 and Kansas in 1919. In 1921-2 New York State, Florida, and Virginia all entered the arena. By the end of the decade Atlanta, Birmingham, Memphis, Minneapolis, Providence, Seattle, and St. Louis among other municipalities were viewing, approving, cutting, and censoring motion pictures. Charging exchanges an import tax and each exhibitor an exhibition fee, states and cities could fill their coffers while protecting the morals of their communities.

The legal rationale for film censorship was well established. Since movies were regarded as "shows" and "spectacles" like a circus or carnival, licensing was historically justified. Theater licensing had been widely practiced and unquestioned during the nineteenth century and even earlier. Courts upheld theater licensing as a method to control inappropriate, racy or politically charged performances as a valid exercise of the state's police power in the interest of public safety. The *Mutual* decision extended this line of reasoning to motion pictures, holding that film was not part of the press and therefore unprotected, outside the realm of privileged speech.

Even political speech, communications closest to the core of constitutional protections, was subject to state censorship. Margaret Sanger (1879-1966) was an early guiding light of the Women's movement. Working as a nurse on New York's Lower East Side, Sanger combined feminist ideas with practical medical knowledge. On October 16, 1916 she opened the first birth control clinic in the U.S. Nine days later, police raided the clinic and arrested her. Tried and convicted, she served 30 days in prison. Sanger appealed, but her conviction was upheld.

Seeking to spread the word of her mission, Sanger wrote, directed, produced, and starred in a biopic depicting her struggle to educate the poor on family planning. The polemical picture was simply entitled *Birth Control* (1917). George H. Bell, New York City's Film Commissioner, attempted to block the film but liberal minded Judge Nathan Bijur stood by Sanger's film. It was an incredible victory for free speech and the First Amendment. But the triumph was brief. Six weeks later Bijur's decision was overturned and the picture was banned.

Sanger's picture may have been censored but her message grew stronger. Not so for Robert Goldstein (1883-?). Goldstein was a tailor/costumer working in Los Angeles (see *Wood Lumber v. Moore*, 191 P. 905, 908 [Sup. Ct. Cal, 1920]). Joseph Henabery, the actor who portrayed Abraham Lincoln in *The Birth of a Nation* (1915), recalled in his memoir that

Goldstein traded his craft services for a financial interest and participation in Griffith's epic film. The actor remembered that "Goldstein got a tremendous award for taking a chance." (Joseph Henabery and Anthony Slide, *Before, In, and After Hollywood: The Autobiography of Joseph E. Henabery* [Lanhan MD, The Scarecrow Press; 1997], 83).

With his windfall, Goldstein produced his own film based on the American Revolution. But it was the wrong picture for the wrong time. As the U.S. was gearing up to enter World War I, Goldstein's scenes of horrific acts committed by the British against the colonists were seen by the courts as seditious propaganda. Goldstein's *The Spirit of '76* (1917) was branded as treasonous, a violation of the Espionage Act of 1917. *The Spirit of '76* was confiscated and the producer sentenced to a ten year prison term. The man was destroyed and to this day *The Spirit of '76* remains a lost film.

Not long after *The Spirit of '76* debacle, on April 14, 1917, the Federal Government formed the Committee for Public Information (C.P.I.) to monitor and administer war propaganda. In the aftermath of Goldstein's case, moguls like Jesse Lasky, Carl Laemmle, and Marcus Loew were far more cooperative with state agents. In return for the government's pledge to limit interference, the commercial film industry would "volunteer" its production resources and distribution networks for state services. Stars participated in Liberty Bond drives and short subjects were produced to reflect C.P.I. positions. A precedent was set: the government and the film industry would align to provide mutual support. (See Frank Manchel, *Film Study: An Analytical Bibliography* [Rutherford, Fairley Dickinson University Press, 1990), 223-225]. This alliance would prove important in future war efforts.

Lois Weber directed *Scandal* (1915) with her husband Phillips Smalley, their first film for Universal Pictures. The film dealt with the consequences of gossip mongering.

MESSAGE PHOTOPLAY CO. v. BELL, COMMISSIONER OF LICENSES

Supreme Court, New York County
100 Misc. 267 (N.Y. Misc. 1917)
Special Term, June, 1917

***268** BIJUR, J.

This is a motion for a temporary injunction to restrain the commissioner of licenses from revoking the license of a theatre because of the proposed production thereat of a moving picture known as "Birth Control." No question is raised concerning the general power of the commissioner to issue and revoke licenses. Greater N.Y. Charter, §§ 641, 642, added by Laws of 1914, chap. 475. For the purposes of this motion also, the implied definition of the function of the commissioner, contained in chapter 3, article 2, section 41, of the Code of Ordinances of the City of New York, as amended to July 16, 1916, may be accepted. That section reads as follows: "The inspectors of the department of licenses * * * shall report to the commissioner any offense against morality, decency or public welfare * * *." It is conceded by the plaintiff that the discretion of the commissioner, exercised in a proper case, may not be interfered with by the courts merely because the latter may not agree with the commissioner's reasoning or judgment. It is not claimed on behalf of the commissioner, however, that the discretion conferred upon him may be exercised without any reasonable basis of fact, or, as it is frequently phrased, "arbitrarily exercised." Such exercise would be subject to review and correction by the courts in an appropriate proceeding. *People ex rel. Lieberman v. Vandecarr*, 199 U.S. 552, 562; *People ex rel. Schwab v. Grant*, 126 N.Y. 473, 482; *People ex rel. Lodes v.*

***269** *Dept. of Health*, 189 id. 187, 194; *Ormsby v. Bell*, 171 A.D. 657.

The question is, therefore, whether there is any valid or reasonable basis for the commissioner's opinion that the play is "against morality, decency or public welfare." Plaintiff admits that the commissioner is acting in good faith.

On the other hand, I think I may say that it is conceded on behalf of the commissioner that there is nothing indecent or obscene in any of the pictures in the sense in which those words are usually understood, that is to say, they contain nothing which might ordinarily be regarded as prurient or directly "suggestive." The scenario of the play may be briefly summarized as follows: It presents a number of pictures showing the poverty and misery frequently associated with the presence of large families of children among the poor. It illustrates the sufferings of one or more women to whom childbirth means serious danger to life. It then presents pictures of comfort among the rich where smaller families are supposed to obtain. Intermingled with these are pictures of Mrs. Sanger acting as a nurse. She is strongly tempted to advise some of the suffering poor women on the subject of birth control, but refrains from giving such information because it is forbidden by law. Penal Law, § 1142. Finally, she concludes to defy the law and opens a clinic to disseminate information on this subject. There is then portrayed a movement undertaken by persons of means who engage detectives to suppress her efforts. The clinic established by Mrs. Sanger is exhibited crowded by poor women. Thereupon the police, instigated by the association referred to, place Mrs. Sanger under arrest, and she is finally shown in prison after conviction for violating the law. No suggestion or hint of the methods or means looking to a violation of the law or for facilitating birth control is anywhere contained in the proposed

***270** exhibition. It may perhaps be inferred from the pictures that the rich violate the law by employing contraceptive methods of which the poor are ignorant; that there is a certain amount of hypocrisy on the part of those who lend their active support to the enforcement of this law, and that Mrs. Sanger is actuated by high and unselfish motives in condemning and even in violating it. This inference is illustrated by touches which I presume are intended to lend to the performance greater dramatic color.

The objections to the exhibition as presented on behalf of the commissioner may, I think, fairly be summed up as follows: First, that it deals with a subject which is in itself immorally suggestive; second, that it advertises the existence of contraceptive methods or means, and substantially announces that Mrs. Sanger is familiar therewith; third, a subject of this kind is not fit for treatment in a public moving picture theatre; fourth, that the performance encourages violation of the law. Taking up the last objection first, I can find no sound basis for it. The result of the exhibition is to show Mrs. Sanger punished for a violation of the law. There is no encouragement for others to follow the same course, nor is it even hinted that violence or defiance of the law should be indulged in to nullify its provisions or for the relief of those who may have suffered its penalties. It has been suggested that it is unmoral to present Mrs. Sanger, a violator of the law, as a "heroine;" but the use of this catch phrase, borrowed from the language of the "border drama," must not divert us from a just appraisal of the performance. It cannot be fairly said that she is presented in the play as a martyr, though that might be permissible. If any one with a saving sense of humor had proposed to call the play "The Way of the Transgressor Is Hard," the title would

***271** have been perhaps more truly descriptive. Broadly considered, the criticism that this performance encourages violation of the law might be addressed with equal force to an exhibition of the exploits of John Brown or a narrative of the career of William Lloyd Garrison. As to the argument that the exhibition advertises either the subject of birth control or Mrs. Sanger's activities — while of course it is true that any form of publicity must necessarily have that effect — it does not seem to me to be possible in a judicial sense to distinguish the publicity here afforded from that contained in the very law itself. Moreover, apart from other and fundamental considerations to which I presently shall advert, the subject and Mrs. Sanger's connection therewith have been so voluminously and recently exploited without restriction in the daily press that this or similar exhibitions are but an afterglow compared with the glaring light of publicity which has thus previously been thrown upon them.

The objection that the matter is not of a character fit for treatment at a public moving picture exhibition seems to me to lie rather to the good taste of the promoters of the picture than to any legal impropriety in the play itself. The subject is plainly one in which the public has an interest, and concerning which two conscientious and opposite views are and may properly be held. As, therefore, the public welfare may be affected by the dominance of the one or the other view, it is both appropriate and lawful that the matter be publicly considered, provided the presentation be free from gratuitous or obtrusive uncleanliness. In that respect I am unable to distinguish substantially the presentation in this proposed exhibition from one in words at public meetings. It may also be argued with much plausibility that a discussion or presentation of a subject of this kind should be limited to persons

***272** engaged in certain professions or of a certain age, although the precise line of demarcation would be rather difficult to draw. Any extended consideration of this branch of the question is rendered fairly academic by the proposal of plaintiff to limit admission to the performance to adults only. Viewed as other than an ordinary dramatic entertainment, the exhibition is merely a pictured argument against an existing law. As such, it deals with an undoubtedly great problem of life, in which our citizenship as a whole has the right to take an active interest. It is possible that a certain and perhaps not altogether prudish sense of delicacy may be offended, or a natural disinclination to consider frankly an unpleasant subject may be shocked into activity by this exhibition; but that does not warrant the suppression of a prosaic public performance. It is true that unclean minds may find unclean suggestion in the discussion of any subject which involves the relations of the sexes. The same possibility exists even in necessary everyday conversations on such matters. It lies dormant in hundreds of the classics of literature and art; in pictures, books, operas and plays open to every one, even in Holy Writ.

The welfare of the community, however, cannot be limited by a standard based upon the possible misconceptions of persons with perverted tastes. It may not be inept to recall the passage from Mill on Liberty, in the course of which, while discussing freedom of speech, he cites the case of Socrates, who was convicted of "immorality" as a "corrupter of youth." The pictures suggest nothing erotic or obscene; neither the subject of birth control nor the course of its advocates or opponents is presented in "high colors" nor with undue exaggeration, but rather in a measured and dispassionate tone. I think that a valuable analogy

***273** and guide as to the law applicable to this case is to be found in the many decisions which deal with the extent of the police power of the state; such for example, as *Lochner v. New York*, 198 U.S. 45, revg. People v. Lochner, 177 N.Y. 145, and also Matter of Jacobs, 98 N.Y. 98, 114. In the prevailing opinion in the Lochner case, in the Federal Supreme Court, at page 56, occurs the significant phrase: "It must, of course, be conceded that there is a limit to the valid exercise of the police power by the State. * * * Otherwise * * * The claim of the police power would be a mere pretext — become another and delusive name for the supreme sovereignty of the State to be exercised free from constitutional restraint." And the question is thus there posed: "Is this a fair, reasonable and appropriate exercise of the police power of the State, or is it an unreasonable, unnecessary and arbitrary interference with the right of the individual to his personal liberty? * * *" From this standpoint, it seems to me that there is nothing in the exhibition proposed to be given which warrants or calls for the exercise for any censure or censorship on the part of the commissioner, and that the performance is beyond his power to interdict. Viewed from another angle, however, my conclusion appears to be strongly fortified. It is needless to speak of the importance of freedom of speech in a republic like ours.

The value of that institution in a democratic government has been accentuated by the result of our political experiment in which public opinion has become perhaps the dominant factor. So keen an observer as Lord Bryce has devoted an entire part of his classic, "The American Commonwealth," to a consideration of the value and influence of public opinion in our government. In discussing two dangers to which a government thus influenced may be exposed, he says: "One

***274** — the smaller one — yet sometimes troublesome, is the difficulty of ascertaining the will of the majority. * * * The other danger is that minorities may not sufficiently assert themselves. Where a majority has erred, the only remedy against the prolongation or repetition of its error is in the continued protests and agitation of the minority, an agitation which ought to be peaceably conducted, carried on by voice and pen, but which must be vehement enough to rouse the people and deliver them from the consequences of their blunders." Under the same head, again, he cites the strength of popular government (after comparing it to a pyramid — the very emblem of stability), and adds: "It has no need to fear discussion and agitation." Assured freedom of speech insures resort to discussion as to the sole necessary means to reform. The solvency of American institutions is based largely upon the flexibility of the popular life and of the institutions under which it exists. The abiding conviction on the part of every citizen that he may freely express his opinion and advocate any peaceable means of reform is in itself the greatest preventive of the use of force or of temptation to violent and subversive change. Indeed, it is probably the decisive factor in reconciling us (as Lord Bryce intimates) to willing submission to the iron discipline of war, and to according to our administrative officers in times of crisis an almost absolute power. We know that when the need has passed the people may safely and freely demand the recall of that power to its proper source. De Tocqueville, in his "Democracy in America" (Pt. III, chap. 21), says: "Although the Americans continually modify or abrogate some of their laws, they are far from evidencing revolutionary passions." This observation is accurate, but not complete.

To my mind the learned author has overlooked the

***275** fact that in the very statement of the phenomenon he was including its cause. Had he said: "Because the Americans continually modify their laws they are far from showing revolutionary passions," he would have apprehended one of the truths which accounts for the evenness of our national existence. Comparatively paradoxical as it may appear, the soundness and the serenity of our communal life rest upon the absence of rigidity in our system of law and upon the opportunity for the facile change of such of our institutions as are not absolutely fundamental. Compared with the importance of guarding the commonwealth against even the possibility of disturbing the foundation of our social solidity by unduly limiting the vital right of free speech, the contention that the exhibition here complained of might be construed as immoral, seems to me to be negligible. I think that the performance which the commissioner of licenses has sought to interdict may not properly be interpreted as more than an attempt to present a dramatic argument in favor of the change of an existing law; that while its form, its force and its good taste may furnish ground for an honest difference of opinion, there is nothing in it which can reasonably be viewed as "against morality, decency or public welfare." It affords, therefore, no basis for the exercise of any discretion on the part of the commissioner. It is a measured and decent exercise of the right of free speech, guaranteed by our constitutions, essential to our national well-being, and, as such, beyond the power of the commissioner of licenses to forbid.

Motion granted.

MESSAGE PHOTOPLAY CO. v. BELL, COMMISSIONER OF LICENSES

Appellate Division of the Supreme Court of New York, First Department
179 App. Div. 13 (N.Y. App. Div. 1917)
Decided July 13, 1917

LAUGHLIN, J.

This is a suit in equity for a permanent injunction to the same effect as the temporary injunction contained in the injunction order from which the appeal is taken. The plaintiff shows by its complaint and affidavits, among other things, that it is engaged in manufacturing and producing motion picture films and in leasing and selling them; that it has manufactured and produced the motion picture film "Birth Control" and has arranged to produce the same at the Park

***15** Theatre and has at great expense advertised the presentation thereof; that the film consists of various episodes in the life of one Margaret H. Sanger, showing how, in the course of her duties as a nurse, she became interested in the subject; that performances are to be limited to adults and have been so advertised; that the film had been viewed by persons of repute and standing in the community who had expressed their views in favor of its production and had been passed by the national board of review and that the film contains no scenes which are lewd or lascivious or disgusting in thought, nature or character, or that in any manner tend to create degenerate influences upon the morals or arouse the thoughts or emotions to indecent conclusions; that prior to the day on which the film was to be first presented the defendant notified the licensee that he had had the picture reviewed by representatives of his department and by citizens whose judgment he valued, and had received and fully considered their reports, and that in his judgment the exhibition was immoral, indecent and directly contrary to public welfare, and that in view of the pending war a plan to limit birth control should not be made a part of amusement, entertainment or recreation in the metropolis, and that for those reasons the exhibition should not be given in a licensed theatre, and if given, action would be taken against the licensee of the theatre under the authority vested in him by the charter and Code of Ordinances of the city. The plaintiff contends that the film is not indecent, immoral or contrary to public welfare and that the reasons assigned by defendant for refusing to permit the exhibition are arbitrary, unjust, unreasonable, unwarranted and confiscatory in their nature and in violation of law and interfere with the freedom of contract. It is charged that the licensee of the theatre will not, in view of defendant's action, permit the production and that other licensees have notified plaintiff that they will not allow its production for the same reason and that plaintiff has no adequate remedy at law.

On the part of the defendant affidavits made by the deputy commissioner of licenses and by others who viewed the photo-play, known as "Birth Control," on the afternoon of May 5, 1917, the day before it was to be produced at the Park Theatre,

***16** set forth in full the headings and subheadings that were thrown on the screen in connection with the pictures and state that in their opinion the play tends to ridicule the public authorities and the provisions of section 1142 of the Penal Law forbidding the dissemination of contraceptive knowledge, and that the dissemination and advertising of such methods for the prevention of conception offends in the extreme against the public welfare and that the play is not alone immoral in teaching people to prevent conception, but that it is entirely opposed to public welfare in that it is a propaganda to limit the production of children and is also against the public welfare in that it distinctly raises a class issue, setting before the public the squalor, poverty and ignorance of the poor, owing to their lack of information with respect to the prevention of conception, and the luxury and small families of the rich due to their ability to acquire from physicians knowledge and means of preventing conception and also depicts the wealthy as contributing funds for the prosecution of those who attempt to enlighten the poor and lowly with respect to birth control and for the avowed purpose of maintaining the poor as the servant and laboring classes, and that in their opinion the dissemination of knowledge of contraceptive methods to all classes of persons, married and unmarried, would tend to immorality. Other affidavits were presented by defendant including one by himself, showing that Mrs. Sanger was tried and convicted for maintaining a clinic in Brooklyn for the dissemination of information on the subject of birth control and that she has served her sentence of one month and that her sister and husband have also been convicted for the distribution of literature in support of her propaganda for birth control. The defendant states in his affidavit that in his judgment the film tends to teach immorality and is entirely opposed to the public welfare, and that the film has for its main purpose the exploitation of Mrs. Sanger who was persistent in violating the law, and tends to bring into disrespect the officials in charge of the enforcement of the criminal statutes against the dissemination of contraceptive methods; that the film clearly advertises that conception may be controlled and that Mrs. Sanger knows how it may be prevented and how childbirth may be controlled;

***17** that a propaganda of this character is, in his opinion, contrary to public welfare and would, through indiscriminate publicity and discussion, cause an increase of immorality and would bring to the attention and knowledge of young unmarried people that there are safeguards which may be used to prevent conception, and would have a tendency to arouse class hatred, as it tends to show that the rich have small families and favor the poor having large families. Some of the pictures and subheadings depict Mrs. Sanger as a nurse attending an under-nourished woman who is exhausted from having too many children and is surrounded by squalor and in bed, in labor pains and about to give birth to a child, while there are several of her small children half-starved, emaciated and ill-clad about her, and the birth of her child shows the doctor warning the woman not to have another child, and shows her pleading with him to instruct her with respect to birth control, and that he refuses the advice on the ground that the law forbids it, and shows her then pleading with Mrs. Sanger for like information, and depicts the same woman resorting to malpractice to avoid the birth of a child, from which she dies, and shows that these were the circumstances which led Mrs. Sanger to inaugurate her propaganda for birth control. The picture further depicts her distributing pamphlets apparently containing prescriptions to prevent conception, and her arrest and trial and conviction; and the final picture shows her behind prison bars serving her sentence, with the subtitle "No matter what happens, the work shall go on." It is not claimed that the means of preventing conception are stated or in any manner conveyed; but that there are such means known to Mrs. Sanger is clearly represented. This is a sufficient summary of the respective claims for the purposes of the appeal.

It is contended in behalf of the respondent that the purpose of the motion picture is to create public sentiment in favor of the repeal of the statute prohibiting the dissemination of information with respect to birth control, and that it has a constitutional right to agitate the repeal of a statute. We are not concerned with the freedom of speech guaranteed by the Constitution (Art. 1, § 8). We have to do with the question

***18** of revoking a license, which is not property but merely a temporary permit to conduct a business that would be unlawful without it. (*People ex rel. Lodes v. Department of Health*, 189 N.Y. 187.) This action necessarily rests on a concession that the plaintiff has no constitutional or other right, on the theory of freedom of speech or of the public press or otherwise, to give public exhibition of the film in question at an unlicensed theatre; for if it has, then the defendant's revocation of the license will not affect its rights and could not be enjoined, for on that theory no license was required. (See *Matter of Whitten*, 152 App. Div. 506.) It has been, however, authoritatively settled that it is not only competent for the Legislature of the State to require a license for public theatrical and motion picture exhibitions, but also to censor such productions in order that they may be regulated and controlled in the interest of morality, decency and public safety and welfare. (*Mutual Film Corporation v. Ohio Industrial Commission*, 236 U.S. 230; *Mutual Film Corporation v. City of Chicago*, 224 Fed. Rep. 101; *Matter of Franklin Film Mfg. Corporation*, 253 Penn. St. 422; *Buffalo Branch, Mutual Film Corporation v. Breitinger*, 250 id. 225; *Block v. City of Chicago*, 239 Ill. 251; *Matter of Ormsby v. Bell*, 218 N.Y. 212. See, also, *Matter of Stubbe v. Adamson*, 220 N.Y. 459.) It is not necessary to consider the power of the Legislature in the premises, but only the authority delegated by it to the defendant. By section 641 of the Greater New York charter (Laws of 1901, chap. 466), as added by chapter 475 of the Laws of 1914, the Legislature delegated to the commissioner of licenses, by very broad and comprehensive language, authority to grant and revoke licenses, as follows:

"The commissioner of licenses shall have cognizance and control of the granting, issuing, transferring, renewing, revoking, suspending and canceling: * * *

"4. Of all licenses in relation to theatres and concerts now issued under the provisions of sections fourteen hundred and seventy-three, fourteen hundred and seventy-four, fourteen hundred and seventy-five and fourteen hundred and eighty-three of the Greater New York charter, by the police commissioner. * * *

"The commissioner of licenses is hereby vested with all

***19** the powers and functions now exercised in relation to licenses by (1) the mayor pursuant to the Code of Ordinances of the City; * * * (4) by the police commissioner in relation to theatres and concerts; * * *."

By section 31 of article 2 of chapter 3 of the Code of Ordinances of the City of New York, adopted during 1916, the commissioner of licenses was authorized, among other things, to regulate and control all motion-picture theatres, and he is directed to appoint such inspectors as may be necessary to enable him to carry out the provisions of that article; and by section 41 the inspectors appointed by him are required, among other things, to investigate the character of exhibitions in motion-picture theatres, and to report to the commissioner any offense "against morality, decency or public welfare committed in said exhibitions." The form of license granted by the commissioner is not given in the record, but section 2 of article 1 of chapter 3 of the Code of Ordinances provides that said licenses "shall be uniform and may, in the discretion of the commissioner, contain provisions and conditions which, in his judgment, may be essential for the welfare and benefit of the people of and visitors to the city." (See Cosby's Code Ord. [Anno. 1917] pp. 38, 41, 42, 32, 33.) These statutory provisions and ordinances, the validity of which are not and could not well be questioned, necessarily delegate to the commissioner authority to issue and to revoke licenses according to his judgment and discretion, to be exercised, of course, in good faith and impartially and conscientiously according to what he believes to be in the interest of morality or decency or public safety or public welfare. It is not the judgment and discretion of those who are interested in exploiting a film commercially, as is the plaintiff, or of citizens generally, or even the courts, but that of the commissioner only, that is called into action. The commissioner, however, must not abuse the discretion vested in him by acting capriciously or arbitrarily, or on false information and without reasonable ground for apprehending that the public morality or decency or safety or welfare will be endangered; but the extent of inquiry collaterally by the courts with respect to his action is whether there is reasonable ground upon which such apprehension may honestly rest in the exercise of a fair and legal

***20** discretion, and if not, the court may require him to act or enjoin him from acting; but if the question be doubtful and there be room for an honest difference of opinion, then the matter must be left to the official to whom the Legislature has delegated authority, and his action in refusing to grant a license, or in revoking one granted, cannot be annulled or controlled collaterally as by mandamus or injunction. (*People ex rel. Schwab v.Grant*, 126 N.Y. 473; *Matter of Ormsby v. Bell*, supra; *People ex rel. Rota v.Baker*, 136 App. Div. 7; *Genesee Recreation Co. v. Edgerton*, 172 id. 464; *People ex rel. Cumisky v. Wurster*, 14 id. 556; *People ex rel. Ritter v. Wallace,* 160 id. 787; *People ex rel. Lodes v. Department of Health*, supra; *People ex rel. Peixotto v. Board of Education*, 212 N.Y. 463; *Matter of Franklin Film Mfg. Corporation*, supra; *People ex rel. Van Norder v. Sewer Commission*, 90 App. Div. 555; *Bainbridge v. City of Minneapolis*, 131 Minn. 195; for decisions in which the same rule is stated but mandamus was issued, see *People ex rel. Empire City Trotting Club v. State Racing Comm.*, 190 N.Y. 31; *People ex rel. Cosby v. Robinson*, 141 App. Div. 656.) There is no evidence that the threatened action of the defendant is in bad faith, and it must, therefore, be presumed that he is acting honestly in the exercise of fair and impartial discretion and judgment. (*City of Buffalov. Hill*, 79 App. Div. 402.) The merits of the action should not be determined on conflicting affidavits, nor should a temporary injunction issue in such case against the official in whom the law has vested the duty of acting in the premises. (See *Matter of Whitten*, supra; *Genesee Recreation Co. v. Edgerton*, supra; *People ex rel. Ritter v. Wallace*, supra.) I am of opinion that it has not been shown that the threatened action of the commissioner will, if consummated, constitute an abuse of the discretion vested in him, or that it will be capricious and arbitrary or founded upon erroneous information, or that he has not reasonable ground to apprehend that public morality or decency or the public welfare will be endangered by the presentation of this motion picture film. It is immaterial that the plaintiff proposes voluntarily to restrict admission to adults, for that action it may change at any time and admit all those whom the law permits to attend motion picture shows. The nature of the subject dealt with by

***21** this motion picture in itself is evidence that there is room for an honest opinion on the part of the defendant that the presentation of the photo-play will be injurious to public morality, decency and welfare. The Legislature has declared it to be against the public interests to have contraceptive information disseminated. It is not too much to say of this record, in addition to the other things which have been alluded to, that it fairly appears that the concentration of the minds of those in attendance at such a production on this question of birth control for a considerable period of time — for the film is long — may engender a desire to obtain the information, of the existence of which they are thus assured, and lead to violations of the law. I am of opinion that the action of the commissioner is justified both in the interests of public decency and public welfare. I think that the rule of ejusdem generis should not be applied in construing the ordinance; but without the ordinance and by virtue of the statute conferring upon the commissioner authority to grant and to revoke licenses, he necessarily has a broad discretion in the interests of public welfare. He would surely have the right to forbid, under pain of revocation of the license, a production that would by reflecting upon race or religion, inflame or incite part of the community to disorder. He would in time of war be authorized, and it would be his duty, to prevent any exhibition at a licensed theatre that might be to the prejudice or disadvantage of the State or nation. The exercise of such authority would be well within the police power of regulation for the public welfare.

It follows, therefore, that the order should be reversed, with ten dollars costs and disbursements, and the motion denied, with ten dollars costs.

CLARKE, P.J., SMITH, PAGE and SHEARN, JJ., concurred.

Order reversed, with ten dollars costs and disbursements, and motion denied, with ten dollars costs.

UNITED STATES v. MOTION PICTURE FILM "THE SPIRIT OF '76"

District Court S.D. California

252 F. 946 (1917)

Decided November 30, 1917

BLEDSOE, District Judge. The facts developed in this proceeding show that this photoplay, "The Spirit of '76," attempts to portray some of the more important phases of the American War for Independence, and special scenes, like Paul Revere's Ride, the signing of the Declaration of Independence, and the like, are given particular mention and prominence. In addition—and these are the parts of the film inveighed against—scenes purporting to illustrate the Wyoming Valley Massacre are shown. A British soldier is pictured impaling on a bayonet a baby

Robert Goldstein directs Jack Cosgrove as Adda Gleason looks on in *The Spirit of '76* (1917)

lying in its cradle and then whirling it around his head so impaled. Other unspeakable atrocities committed by British soldiers, including the shooting of harmless women, the dragging off, sometimes by the hair of the head, of young American girls, etc., are exhibited.

Because of adverse criticism and objection, before the scheduled initial performance a private exhibition of the picture was had, attended by divers local and governmental representatives. At this performance none of the objectionable features above mentioned were shown, and in consequence no open objection to the proposed run of the play was voiced. Immediately following this preliminary presentation, though, the director, Goldstein, inserted into the film in appropriate places the scenes of the Wyoming Massacre just referred to, and proceeded to show them at the ensuing evening performance. This he did, he says, "to excite the audience" and attract greater attention to his production.

The film is owned by a corporation, but seems to be and to have been managed by Goldstein, the man who wrote the scenario and who has "produced" the picture. As is usual in such cases, a good many thousands of dollars, probably in excess of $100,000, have been expended in the work of such production.

I have listened very carefully to the statement of Mr. Scott, counsel for the stockholders in the film company, and I sympathize with them for having made an investment in this film with no knowledge of its true character. The various stockholders, of course, I do not know, and, in consequence, cannot know their attitude toward the presentation of this film. I have given careful consideration to the suggestion made by counsel with respect to the possibility, and even probability, of financial losses inuring to the stockholders—perhaps of some considerable consequence. Bearing all this in mind, however, and assuming that they and their associates are going to suffer some considerable loss, this court at this time is in no mood to weigh the financial losses of a few individuals as against possible detriment to the United States of America. If it be that some will have to suffer loss, yet it is only a financial loss, and, at worst, will be only a fractional part of the loss that others are going to have to suffer—some even of their lives—because of the war in which we are now engaged.

History is history, and fact is fact. There is no doubt about that. At the present time, however, the United States is confronted with what I conceive to be the greatest emergency we have ever been confronted with at any time in our history. There is now required of us the greatest amount of devotion to a common cause, the greatest amount of co-operation, the greatest amount of efficiency, and the greatest amount of disposition to further the ultimate success of American arms that can be conceived, and as a necessary consequence no man should be permitted, by deliberate act, or even unthinkingly, to do that which will in any way detract from the efforts which the United States is putting forth or serve to postpone for a single moment the early coming of the day when the success of our arms shall be a fact and the righteousness of our cause shall have been demonstrated.

We are engaged in a war in which Great Britain is an ally of the

United States. It is a fact that we were at war with Great Britain during the Revolutionary times, and whatever occurred there is written upon the page of history and will have to stand, whomsoever may be injured or hurt by the recital or recollection of it. But this is no time, in my judgment (this is the thought that controls me in this matter), whatever may be the excuse, whether it be a financial return or otherwise, for the exploitation of those things that may have the tendency or effect of sowing dissension among our people, and of creating animosity or want of confidence between us and our allies, because so to do weakens our efforts, weakens the chance of our success, impairs our solidarity, and renders less useful the lives we are giving, to the end that this war may soon be over and peace may soon become a thing substantial and permanent with us. I am in no mood, either, particularly after having listened to the testimony of this man Goldstein, to consider the suggestion that the film be returned, and so much of it be permitted to be exhibited as has not met with special objection.

It is a fair inference from the circumstances, considering the hearing had in Chicago, the objections then made, the language used in characterizing its scenes of atrocity as being "reprehensible" and as evidencing "malice," that the disposition and purpose of the whole play in its deeper significance is to incite hatred of England and England's soldiers. And it is not at all necessary that it should be shown to have such effect; it is enough if it is calculated reasonably so to excite or inflame the passions of our people, or some of them, as that they will be deterred from giving that full measure of co-operation, sympathy, assistance, and sacrifice which is due to Great Britain, simply because of the fact that Great Britain, as an ally of ours, is working with us to fight the battle which we think strikes at our very existence as a nation.

Ordinarily the exploitation of such harmless, in one sense, highly inspiring, in another sense, scenes as Paul Revere's Ride, which is one of the most beautiful things in history, could not be detrimental or distasteful to anybody. Ordinarily it could be put on in such a way as to be a source of unending delight and gratification to any man, be he American or be he English; but that is not the point. There are interspersed in this play those things which tend to appeal to the passions of our nature, which tend to arouse our revenge and to question the good faith of our ally, Great Britain, and to make us a little bit slack in our loyalty to Great Britain in this great catastrophe or emergency. Therefore, as I say, this is no time or place for the exploitation of that which, at another time or place, or under different circumstances, might be harmless and innocuous in its every aspect. It is like the "right of free speech," upon which such great stress is now being laid. That which in ordinary times might be clearly permissible, or even commendable, in this hour of national emergency, effort, and peril, may be as clearly treasonable, and therefore properly subject to review and repression. The constitutional guaranty of "free speech" carries with it no right to subvert the purposes and destiny of the nation.

In addition, this man, by his own admission, knew that these things—the bayoneting of the babe and the like—had been severely criticized and were inhibited. He knew that objection had been made to them. He knew, just as well as he knows we are sitting here now, that the private presentation of this film on last Tuesday morning was for the purpose of seeing if there was anything objectionable in it. To fit it for such private presentation it was gone over by him with a fine tooth comb, no doubt; but immediately thereafter a sedulous effort was indulged in by him to insert those things which would tend to "excite" and to create a prejudice against Great Britain. This demands an inquiry into the ultimate motives and purposes of this man, and no doubt justifies other and different action against him. But in any event, referring to the special problem now before us, and considering only the harm not to come to us, I feel that I can do no less than to say that, so far as it is within the power of this court, this thing has got to stop.

I have no disposition, of course, to confiscate any one's property. There may come a time and place where this play, devoid of some of its horror, which never ought to be in it at any time, and devoid of its immorality, which is and ought to be shocking to any man who possesses a respectable quantum of decency in his makeup, devoid of those things, the time may come when it could be put on, and put on entertainingly and refreshingly before an audience of American people. The fact is, however, that the film is of such a character that it can be used to our national disadvantage in time of national emergency, and this cannot be allowed. If the result be to bring a loss upon those who are financially interested, so be it. It is merely a loss they must sustain because of the unwisdom they have demonstrated in trusting their financial affairs to one who possesses such a slight modicum of appreciation of the eternal fitness of things as does this man who is presenting and claiming the right to present this picture at this time.

The motion for the return of the film will be denied without prejudice. It will be held in the possession of the marshal until such time as, under changed conditions, it may properly be presented, and the district attorney is directed to prepare for the court a warrant for the seizure of the original, which is within the jurisdiction of this court, as shown by the testimony given here, and that will be put in the same place and kept under the same surveillance.

GOLDSTEIN v. UNITED STATES

Circuit Court of Appeals, Ninth Circuit

258 Fed. 908 (1919)

Decided May 26, 1919

In Error to the District Court of the United States for the Southern Division of the Southern District of California; Benjamin F. Bledsoe, Judge.

Robert Goldstein was convicted, under Act June 15, 1917, of knowingly, willfully, and unlawfully attempting to cause insubordination, disloyalty, mutiny, and refusal of duty in the military and naval forces of the United States during war, and he brings error. Affirmed.

The plaintiff in error was convicted on two counts of an indictment, the first of which charged as follows: "That throughout the period of time from the 6th day of April, in the year of our Lord one thousand nine hundred and seventeen, to the day of the finding and presentation of this indictment, the United States has been at war with the Imperial German government, and that during said period of time one Robert Goldstein, whose full and true name other than as herein stated is to the grand jurors unknown, hereinafter called defendant, in the city of Los Angeles, state of California, and within the Southern Division of the Southern District of California and within the jurisdiction of this honorable court, did, on the 28th day of November, in the year of our Lord one thousand nine hundred and seventeen, knowingly, willfully and unlawfully attempt to cause insubordination, disloyalty, mutiny, and refusal of duty, in the military and naval forces of the United States in the manner following, that is to say:

"That at the time and place aforesaid, the said Robert Goldstein did present to the public at Clune's Auditorium Theater, a certain motion picture play, entitled and known as 'The Spirit of '76,' which said motion picture play was designed and intended to arouse antagonism, hatred, and enmity between the American people, and particularly the American military and naval forces, against the people of Great Britain, and particularly against the military and naval forces of Great Britain at a time when, as the defendant then and there well knew, the government of Great Britain with its military and naval forces was an ally of the United States in the prosecution of the war as aforesaid against the Imperial German government; that among the scenes so presented in said motion picture play, 'The Spirit of '76,' there was, at the time and place aforesaid, presented to the public in said picture the scene of a soldier of Great Britain whirling an American infant around on the point of his bayonet, and the scene of British soldiers in the act of shooting and bayoneting helpless and defenseless American women and children and dragging American women and children by their hair and capturing and carrying away young American girls, and many other scenes of like character, all of which were designed and intended and were being used for the purpose of causing insubordination, disloyalty, mutiny, and refusal of duty in the military and naval forces of the United States."

There was a demurrer to each count of the indictment for its failure to state an offense against the laws of the United States, and a motion to quash which specifically pointed out the absence of allegation showing the proximity

of military or naval forces of the United States, or that they could be affected thereby. The demurrer and the motion were overruled.

Crittenden Thornton, of San Francisco, Cal., for plaintiff in error.

Robert O'Connor, U. S. Atty., and W. F. Palmer, Sp. Asst. U. S. Atty., both of Los Angeles, Cal.

Before GILBERT, MORROW, and HUNT, Circuit Judges.

HUNT, Circuit Judge (after stating the facts as above). The demurrer and the motion to quash raised the question whether or not either count of the indictment alleged an offense against the United States.

[1] We will first consider the count which charges an attempt to cause insubordination and disloyalty or refusal of duty. The statute, Act of June 15, 1917, is clear and simple in its language. Whoever, when the United States is at war, shall willfully cause, or attempt to cause, insubordination, disloyalty, mutiny, or refusal of duty in the military or naval forces of the United States, shall be punished as provided. The question of the truth or falseness of the thing done by the person who, when the state of war exists, attempts to cause disloyalty or any of the other conditions enumerated, is not the essence of the inquiry. Enacted as the statute was while the country was at war, the evident, underlying purpose of its language was to prevent any willful attempt to engender feelings of lack of fidelity to the United States among the military or naval forces or any attempt made with evil mind to cause any disobedience to lawful authority in the military or naval forces; and the statute should always be read in the light of the purpose of its enactment.

It is clear that an attempt to create disloyalty may be by showing a picture to the public, as well as by uttering speech or publishing a writing. The picture might be a truthful representation of an historical fact, and yet the nature of it, the circumstances surrounding the exhibition thereof, the time, the occasions when the public exhibitions are had, may well tend to show whether the picture would naturally, in the light of great events, be calculated to foment disloyalty or insubordination among the naval or military forces. In time of peace, a picture purporting to show incidents of a war fought more than a hundred years before, and exhibiting soldiers of a foreign country bayoneting helpless American women and children, might arouse but ordinary interest. But, if it has come about that a war is being fought by the United States and in the war the cause of the United States is allied with that of the foreign country whose soldiers are pictured as murdering American women and children, and if, at the time the United States is enforcing draft laws and raising a large army and navy to fight the common enemy of the two allied countries, it seems but reasonable to say that the exhibition of such a picture is calculated to arouse antagonisms and to raise hatred in the minds of some who see it against the ally of the United States, and as a probable effect to put obstruction in the way of the necessary co-operation between the allied countries against the enemy, and to undermine an undivided sentiment for the United States and to encourage disloyalty and refusal of duty or insubordination among the military and naval forces. Schenck v. United States, 249 U. S. 47, 39 Sup. Ct. 247, 63 L. Ed. 470.

[2] Nor, in an attempt of the character indicated, is it necessary that the picture exhibited should actually be seen by soldiers and sailors already enlisted. Millions of men within the provisions of the conscription act and subject to call were in the military and naval forces throughout the country and were part of the public. The exhibition to the public at a public place, if given with the evil intent described, is sufficient. In Coldwell v. United States, 256 Fed. 805, 168 C. C. A. 151, the Court of Appeals for the First Circuit considered an objection to an indictment wherein it did not appear that the persons whom the defendant was alleged to have addressed were in the military or naval forces of the United States. The court said:

> "The act makes it an offense to willfully 'attempt to cause insubordination, disloyalty, mutiny or refusal of duty in the military or naval forces of the United States,' or to 'willfully obstruct the recruiting or enlistment service of the United States,' and its language is broad enough to include statements calculated to produce these results, when made in the presence of persons who are not in the military or naval forces of the United States, provided they are willfully made and with the intent set out in the act."

[3] The second count also charges a violation of the Espionage Act, in that it specifically alleges that the defendant, in the aid of the German Government, had control of and was willfully using the film as a means to violate section 3 of title 1 of the Act of June 15, 1917, c. 30, 40 Stat. 219 (Comp. St. 1918, § 10212c), the Espionage Act, in the manner as fully described in the first count of the indictment. The first count is referred to and drawn into the body of the second count by reference to the motion picture play "The Spirit of '76," and it is charged that it was designed and intended for use and was used as the means of violating section 3 of title 1, Act of June 15, 1917, c. 30, and title 11, § 22 (Comp. St. 1918, §§ 10212c, 10212i). When considered with the first count incorporated within it, we think the second count is sufficient.

We believe that the issues under the counts were properly for the jury, and, as the evidence upon which the verdict was predicated is not in the record, we must accept the verdict as sustained by the evidence.

The judgment is affirmed.

Under Espionage Act.

GOLDSTEIN IS FOUND GUILTY.

Film Producer is Convicted by Jury on Two Counts.

Much Affected by Verdict; will Ask a New Trial.

Twenty-two Years and Heavy Fine Maximum Penalty.

Robert Goldstein, promoter and exhibitor of the film, "The Spirit of '76," was found guilty last night on the first and second counts of the grand jury indictment charging him with violation of the Espionage A[illegible]

REVIVE 'SPIRIT OF '76,' FILM BARRED IN 1917

Goldstein, Who Produced It, Got Ten-Year Prison Term Under Espionage Act.

TO BE SEEN AT TOWN HALL

4

The Production Code

A series of scandals rocked the entertainment world in the second decade of the 20th Century. The standard of social conduct was quickly evolving from highly conservative values of Victorian propriety and strict Edwardian etiquette to a more carefree attitude. The new normal was a jarring shift. Sex, suicide, divorce, and rape made the headlines.

Hollywood certainly seemed to be a den of inequity. In 1918, the biggest movie star in the world, Charlie Chaplin, rushed into a marriage with 17-year old Mildred Harris when she claimed to be pregnant. Turns out that she wasn't pregnant until returning from their wedding night. America's Sweetheart, Mary Pickford, had developed an onscreen persona as clean and wholesome as a fresh snowfall. Off screen, the starlet was not quite as innocent. In a 1920 celebrity swap, Pickford divorced her first husband, Owen Moore, and married Douglas Fairbanks three weeks later. It was not a good year for the Pickfords. Mary's brother Jack, a star in his own right, was caught cheating by his wife, the beautiful Olive Thomas, a former nude model. Olive committed suicide—by overdosing on Jack's syphilis medication in a scandal that truly packed a one-two-three punch (adultery, suicide, and VD). Finally, the following year, screen funny man Roscoe "Fatty" Arbuckle was implicated in the rape and manslaughter of a starlet during a wild alcohol-soaked party in San Francisco—during the Prohibition Era.

The film industry was not the only area of entertainment that appeared to be riddled with corruption. The 1919 Chicago White Sox-Cincinnati Reds World Series was revealed to be a set up. Eight players were implicated in the fix, which went to trial as *People of the State of Illinois v. Edward V. Cicotte, et. al* (Indictment No. 23912, 1921). On July 29, 1921 after a brief deliberation, the Cook County jurors returned a verdict of not guilty. The scandal would go unpunished by the judicial system (an internal advisory board would later ban for life eight players involved in the incident).

Baseball team owners were as worried about their bottom line as well as damage to the reputation of America's Favorite Past Time. They decided to institute a level of organization and oversight to the sport. Judge Kenesaw Mountain Landis had been appointed to the U.S. District Court for the Northern District of Illinois by Theodore Roosevelt. Landis was a hard-hitting jurist: in 1907, he handed down a $24,000,000 judgement against Standard Oil and John D. Rockefeller (reversed on appeal to the 7th Circuit). Landis was equally strict when faced with draft dodgers and conscientious objectors during World War I. He handed out the maximum sentence to over 100 men who refused to fight. But even more importantly, Landis was a die hard baseball fan. On November 12, 1920, Landis accepted a $50,000 stipend to serve as the first Commissioner of Baseball (he remained on the bench).

Similarly, the film industry was looking for a representative whose credentials were respectable. They found the perfect advocate in Will H. Hays. Hays served as the chairman of the Republican National Committee from 1918-1921, supporting GOP candidate Warren Harding's bid for the White House. When Harding was elected president, Hays was rewarded with the Cabinet-level position of Postmaster General. Needing a Washington insider to vouch for film industry independence and deflect any censorship legislation emerging on the Hill, Adolph Zukor, Louis B. Mayer, Jack Warner, Samuel Goldwyn, and representatives from Fox Films and Universal offered Hays the job as Chairman of the newly formed Motion Pictures Producers and Distributors Association (M.P.P.D.A.).

The timing was right. Filmmakers need a trustworthy voice to address concerns over morality, which might have repercussions in the financial community. And Hays needed a speedy exit. A year into Harding's administration, the Teapot Dome scandal was beginning to break. This scandal--regarded before Watergate as the worst U.S. political imbroglio--concerned a bribery incident over oil reserves in Wyoming and California. Hays allegedly received contributions to the GOP in exchange for favorable government contracts. Secretary of the interior Albert Bacon Fall was indicted for taking bribes. Hays jumped at the opportunity to get out of Washington, and become spokesman for Hollywood's newfound moral conscience. In 1924, Hays resigned from his political post and headed West.

As president of the M.P.P.D.A., Hays reached out to and coordinated with moral authorities across the nation. His aim was to woo regional regulators and create an alliance of friendly film agencies. Hays sought the cooperation and input of key outspoken moralists and cultural commentators, including Rev. Wilbur Crafts, super-intendant of the International Reform Bureau, Canon William Sheafe Chase, President of the New York Civic League and rector of Christ Church in Brooklyn, and publisher Martin Quigley along with Quigley's righthand man, Joseph Breen. Breen would later join the M.P.P.D.A. as the division's chief enforcer

The M.P.P.D.A.'s goal was to prevent the spread of governmental censorship. Regional regulators remained in place but through various methods, such as a list of Don't and Be Carefuls, a Formula, and finally a Production Code, an uneasy balance was achieved between filmmakers and morally minded state censors.

The original femme fatale, Theda Bara in *Cleopatra* (1917)

WHEREAS, on March 26, 1923, a Resolution was unanimously adopted by the members of the Motion Picture Producers & Distributors of America, Inc., to intensify their efforts to carry out the purpose of the Association, which Resolution, signed by the members of the Association and others, was as follows:

"The Resolution passed at the Annual Meeting of the Motion Picture Producers & Distributors of America, Inc., on March 26 1923, to be signed by the members of this Association and by such others interested in motion pictures, as will by so doing signify their willingness to aid in carrying out the purposes of the Association.

"WHEREAS the undersigned corporations engaged in the production and (or) distribution of motion pictures are members of the Motion Picture Producers & Distributors of America, incorporated March 11, 1922, under the laws of the State of New York, 'to foster the common interest of those engaged in the motion picture industry in the United States by establishing and maintaining the highest possible moral and artistic standards in motion picture production; by developing the educational as well as the entertainment value and the general usefulness of the motion picture; * * * *;' and

"WHEREAS the several member companies of this Association have made a sincere and earnest effort to attain to these objectives in the pictures produced during this period, and

"WHEREAS since last May additional companies have been admitted to membership in this Association and desire thus formally to put themselves on record concerning these objects, and all members desire formally to reaffirm these purposes, and

"WHEREAS the citizens of twenty-three states, recognizing the efforts which the Association is making in this regard, have defeated, repealed or withheld legislation designed to censor motion pictures by political machinery and have placed the responsibility for the character of pictures squarely upon the industry, and

"WHEREAS individuals and societies the country over and the national citizen organizations of the Committee on Public Relations have expressed their confidence in the good faith and the ability of the industry to correct at the source such faults as exist, and to accomplish the purposes of the Association, and are cooperating with the industry to this end, and have sent to the Association this day a memorial of appreciation of this Association's efforts and accomplishments, and

"WHEREAS the future freedom of the industry from both political and unofficial censorship and the success of the Association's efforts and the industry's welfare depend entirely upon the ability of the industry to discharge this responsibility,

"NOW THEREFORE BE IT RESOLVED that this Association and every member of it hereby reaffirms the determination 'to establish and maintain the highest possible moral and artistic standards in motion picture production and to develop the educational as well as the entertainment value and the general usefulness of the motion picture ' and

"BE IT FURTHER RESOLVED that every effort be made to induce those companies which are not members of this Association to conform to these standards, and

"BE IT FURTHER RESOLVED that this Resolution shall be signed by the several members of this Association and such other companies, directors, scenario writers and others, who will by so doing signify their willingness to aid in this effort, and

"BE IT FURTHER RESOLVED that the President of this Association be requested to advise those interested of this determination on the part of the Association to merit the faith reposed in it, to thank them for their cooperation, and to request them to continue to cooperate to the end that motion pictures may attain to their greatest usefulness" and

WHEREAS, on June 19, 1924, the following Resolution was passed by the Board of Directors of the Motion Picture Producers & Distributors of America, Inc.,

"WHEREAS, the members of the Motion Picture Producers & Distributors of America, Inc., in their continuing effort 'to establish and maintain the highest possible moral and artistic standards of motion picture production' are engaged in a special effort to prevent the prevalent type of book and play from becoming the prevalent type of picture; to exercise every possible care that only books or plays which are of the right type are used for screen presentation; to avoid the picturization of books or plays which can be produced only after such changes as to leave the producer subject to a charge of deception; to avoid using titles which are indicative of a kind of picture which could not be produced, or by their suggestiveness seek to obtain attendance by deception, a thing equally reprehensible; and to prevent misleading, salacious or dishonest advertising;

"NOW, THEREFORE, BE IT RESOLVED by the Board of Directors of the Motion Picture Producers & Distributors of America, Inc., that said Association does hereby reaffirm its determination to carry out its purposes above set out; and does hereby repledge the best efforts of the members of the Association to that end; and does hereby further declare that they will not produce or promote the production, distribute or promote the distribution, exhibit or promote the exhibition, or aid in any way whatsoever in the production, distribution or exhibition by the members of this Association or by companies subsidiary to said members or by any other person, firm or corporation producing, distributing or exhibiting pictures, of any picture or pictures by whomsoever produced, distributed or exhibited, which because of the unfit character of title, story, exploitation or picture itself, do not meet the requirements of this preamble and resolution or hinder the fulfillment of the purposes of the Association set out herein" and

WHEREAS, on July 21, 1924, the Board of Directors of the Association of Motion Picture Producers, Inc., (California) passed a similar Resolution approving the Resolution of the Board of Directors of the Motion Picture Producers & Distributors of America, Inc., of June 19, 1924, and

WHEREAS, the policy outlined by the foregoing and other similar Resolutions by the Motion Picture Producers & Distributors of America, Inc., has resulted in the steady improvement in the quality of pictures, both morally and artistically, and

WHEREAS, further to definitize the purpose of the Association in this regard and to promote the further progress and development of pictures, both from the moral and artistic standpoint, the following Resolution was unanimously adopted on June 8, 1927, by the Association of Motion Picture Producers, Inc., (California):

"WHEREAS the purposes of the Motion Picture Producers & Distributors of America, incorporated March 11, 1922, under the laws of the State of New York, 'to foster the common interest of those engaged in the motion picture industry in the United States by establishing and maintaining the highest possible moral and artistic standards in motion picture production, by developing the educational as well as the entertainment value and the general usefulness of the motion picture,' is the high ideal towards which the members of the Association of Motion Picture Producers, Inc., have been consistently striving, and

"WHEREAS the standards of production, including theme, treatment, acting, construction, lighting and photography, have constantly improved, and

"WHEREAS in addition to increasing the entertainment value of pictures, the 'educational and general usefulness ' of pictures have been given thought, to the end that they are now serving in the religious, civic, educational, medical and scientific fields, and

"WHEREAS municipal, state and federal officials by refusing to further limit and burden the industry have expressed their approval of its development, and

"WHEREAS the large and powerful civic, educational, social, religious and commercial organizations of the country have expressed their confidence in us and are supporting us in our opposition to unjust attacks, and

"WHEREAS the developing foreign market has not only given us a further outlet for our product but has made of us a diplomatic and commercial agent for our Government and for our own nationals and for every government whose history, literature, nationals, and locale we use in pictures, and

"WHEREAS the confidence placed in us and our responsibility to the public which we serve is realized, and

"WHEREAS the experience of these years of cooperative effort has indicated further responsibilities,

"NOW THEREFORE BE IT RESOLVED that the Association of Motion Picture Producers, Inc., cooperating with the Motion Picture Producers & Distributors of America, Inc., exercise even greater care in the production of pictures, and

"BE IT FURTHER RESOLVED that those things which are included in the following list shall not appear in pictures produced by the members of this Association, irrespective of the manner in which they are treated:

"1. Pointed Profanity--by either title or lip--this includes the words God, Lord, Jesus, Christ (unless they be used reverently in connection with proper religious ceremonies), Hell, S.O.B., damn, Gawd, and every other profane and vulgar expression however it may be spelled;

"2. Any licentious or suggestive nudity--in fact or in silhouette; and any lecherous or licentious notice thereof by other characters in the picture;

"3. The illegal traffic in drugs;

"4. Any inference of sex perversion;

"5. White slavery;

"6. Miscegenation (sex relationships between the white and black races);

"7. Sex hygiene and venereal diseases;

"8. Scenes of actual child birth--in fact or in silhouette;

"9. Children's sex organs;

"10. Ridicule of the clergy;

"11. Willful offense to any nation, race or creed; and

"BE IT FURTHER RESOLVED that special care be exercised in the manner in which the following subjects are treated, to the end that vulgarity and suggestiveness may be eliminated and that good taste may be emphasized:

"1. The use of the Flag;

"2. International Relations (avoid picturizing in an unfavorable light another country's religion, history, institutions, prominent people and citizenry);

"3. Religion and religious ceremonies;

"4. Arson;

"5. The use of firearms;

"6. Theft, robbery, safe-cracking and dynamiting of trains, mines, buildings, et cetera (having in mind the effect which a too-detailed description of these may have upon the moron);

"7. Brutality and possible gruesomeness;

"8. Technique of committing murder by whatever method;

"9. Methods of smuggling;

"10. Third Degree methods;

"11. Actual hangings or electrocutions as legal punishments for crime;

"12. Sympathy for criminals;

"13. Attitude toward public characters and institutions;

"14. Sedition;

"15. Apparent cruelty to children and animals;

"16. Branding of people or animals;

"17. The sale of women, or of a woman selling her virtue;

"18. Rape or attempted rape;

"19. First night scenes;

"20. Man and woman in bed together;

"21. Deliberate seduction of girls;

"22. The institution of marriage.

"23. Surgical operations;

"24. The use of drugs;

"25. Titles or scenes having to do with law enforcement or law enforcement officers;

"26. Excessive or lustful kissing, particularly when one character or the other is a 'heavy'."

NOW, THEREFORE, BE IT RESOLVED, that the Board of Directors of the Motion Picture Producers & Distributors of America, Inc., do hereby approve and confirm the said Resolution so adopted by the said Association of Motion Picture Producers, Inc., (California) on June 8, 1927, above set out and do hereby re-pledge the best efforts of the members of this Association to carry out the purposes of said Resolution, and

BE IT FURTHER RESOLVED, that the Board of Directors of the Motion Picture Producers & Distributors of America, Inc., do hereby approve and reaffirm the Resolution of this Board passed on June 19, 1924, as hereinabove in the preambles to this Resolution set out, and re-pledge the best efforts of the members of this Association to carry out all of the purposes set out in said Resolution passed on June 19, 1924.

TO INSURE FURTHER the faithful performance of the provisions of this Resolution, the undersigned hereby agrees to be responsible that such provisions are faithfully carried out by the company with which he is connected.

____

____

____

____

____

____

____

____

____

____

Concerning the Character of Pictures

A Pledge

ASSOCIATION OF MOTION PICTURE PRODUCERS, INC.
5504 Hollywood Blvd.
Los Angeles, Calif.

Educational Studio
E. H. Allen

F. B. O. Studios, Inc.
Edwin King

First National Pictures, Inc.
A. L. Rockett

First National Pictures, Inc.
Ned Marin

Fox Film Corporation
Sol Wurtzel

Samuel Goldwyn, Inc.
Samuel Goldwyn

Samuel Goldwyn, Inc.
Abraham Lehr

Harold Lloyd Corporation
William R. Fraser

Metro-Goldwyn-Mayer Corporation
Louis B. Mayer

Metro-Goldwyn-Mayer Corporation
Irving G. Thalberg

Metropolitan Pictures Corporation
Wm. Sistrom

Paramount Famous Lasky Corporation
B. P. Schulberg

Paramount Famous Lasky Corporation
J. J. Gain

Hal Roach Studios, Inc.
Hal E. Roach

Hal Roach Studios, Inc.
Warren Doane

Mack Sennett Studio
J. A. Waldro

United Artists Studio Corporation
Joseph M. Schenck

United Artists Studio Corporation
M. C. Levee

Universal Pictures Corporation
Henry Henigson

Warner Bros Pictures, Inc.
Jack L. Warner

Chadwick Productions
I. E. Chadwick

On June 8, 1927, an important resolution was unanimously adopted by the Association of Motion Picture Producers, Inc., (California). This action followed the adoption of a resolution similar in principle by the national organization, the Motion Picture Producers & Distributors of America, Inc. Furthermore, the chief executives of each of the member companies of the two Associations agreed in writing to be responsible for the faithful performance of the provisions of this resolution.

Following this action, the organized industry pledged itself to the United States government to the faithful observance of its own formula by proposing and agreeing to the incorporation of the content of the resolution as Rule 21 of the industry's Practice Code, adopted in October, 1927, at the Trade Practice Conference For The Motion Picture Industry conducted by the Federal Trade Commission.

These pledges were based on a thorough study of what should and should not be done by a most representative committee of studio executives, which incorporated its conclusions in the resolutions.

In view of these guaranties to ourselves, the public and the government, it is important that every person employed by our companies, who has anything to do with the nature and quality of the themes and action in the photoplays produced by them, shall be thoroughly informed concerning the provisions of this pledge and be held accountable for its observance.

Aid, by way of information concerning the probable public reaction to a given theme, sequence or treatment, may be obtained through the Studio Relations Department of the Association, which has a representative in each member studio. This machinery has been set up by the members of the Association for their own protection and its cooperation should be sought whenever there is any question about the advisability of using any proposed material, before money is wasted in making footage that will inevitably be eliminated before the picture is released.

With the advent of the sound and talking picture, the failure of any responsible person to use every means to ascertain the acceptability of themes, sequences, treatment and dialogue may easily lead to most serious consequences and financial losses.

The resolution follows:

"WHEREAS the purposes of the Motion Picture Producers & Distributors of America, incorporated March 11, 1922, under the laws of the State of New York, 'to foster the common interest of those engaged in the motion picture industry in the United States by establishing and maintaining the highest possible moral and artistic standards in motion picture production, by developing the educational as well as the entertainment value and the general usefulness of the motion picture,' is the high ideal towards which the members of the Association of Motion Picture Producers, Inc., have been consistently striving, and

"WHEREAS the standards of production, including theme, treatment, acting, construction, lighting and photography, have constantly improved, and

"WHEREAS in addition to increasing the entertainment value of pictures, the 'educational and general usefulness' of pictures have been given thought, to the end that they are now serving in the religious, civic, educational, medical and scientific fields, and

"WHEREAS municipal, state and federal officials by refusing to further limit and burden the industry have expressed their approval of its development, and

"WHEREAS the large and powerful civic, educational, social, religious and commercial organizations of the country have expressed their confidence in us and are supporting us in our opposition to unjust attacks, and

"WHEREAS the developing foreign market has not only given us a further outlet for our product but has made of us a diplomatic and commercial agent for our Government and for our own nationals and for every government whose history, literature, nationals and locale we use in pictures, and

"WHEREAS the confidence placed in us and our responsibility to the public which we serve is realized, and

"WHEREAS the experience of these years of cooperative effort has indicated further responsibilities,

"NOW THEREFORE BE IT RESOLVED that the Association of Motion Picture Producers, Inc., cooperating with the Motion Picture Producers & Distributors of America, Inc., exercise even greater care in the production of pictures, and

"BE IT FURTHER RESOLVED that those things which are included in the following list shall not appear in pictures produced by the members of this Association, irrespective of the manner in which they are treated:

1. Pointed Profanity—by either title or lip—this includes the words, God, Lord, Jesus, Christ (unless they be used reverently in connection with proper religious ceremonies), Hell, S.O.B., damn, Gawd, and every other profane and vulgar expression however it may be spelled;
2. Any licentious or suggestive nudity—in fact or in silhouette; and any lecherous or licentious notice thereof by other characters in the picture;
3. The illegal traffic in drugs;
4. Any inference of sex perversion;
5. White slavery;
6. Miscegenation (sex relationships between the white and black races);
7. Sex hygiene and venereal diseases;
8. Scenes of actual child birth—in fact or in silhouette;
9. Children's sex organs;
10. Ridicule of the clergy;

11. **Wilful offense to any nation, race or creed; and**

"BE IT FURTHER RESOLVED that special care be exercised in the manner in which the following subjects are treated, to the end that vulgarity and suggestiveness may be eliminated and that good taste may be emphasized:

1. **The use of the Flag;**
2. **International Relations (avoid picturizing in an unfavorable light another country's religion, history, institutions, prominent people and citizenry);**
3. **Religion and religious ceremonies;**
4. **Arson;**
5. **The use of firearms;**
6. **Theft, robbery, safe-cracking and dynamiting of trains, mines, buildings, et cetera (having in mind the effect which a too-detailed description of these may have upon the moron);**
7. **Brutality and possible gruesomeness;**
8. **Technique of committing murder by whatever method;**
9. **Methods of smuggling;**
10. **Third Degree methods;**
11. **Actual hangings or electrocutions as legal punishments for crime;**
12. **Sympathy for criminals;**
13. **Attitude toward public characters and institutions;**
14. **Sedition;**
15. **Apparent cruelty to children and animals;**
16. **Branding of people or animals;**
17. **The sale of women, or of a woman selling her virtue;**
18. **Rape or attempted rape;**
19. **First night scenes;**
20. **Man and woman in bed together;**
21. **Deliberate seduction of girls;**
22. **The institution of marriage;**
23. **Surgical operations;**
24. **The use of drugs;**
25. **Titles or scenes having to do with law enforcement or law enforcement officers;**
26. **Excessive or lustful kissing, particularly when one character or the other is a 'heavy.'"**

To assure, further, the faithful performance of the provisions of this Resolution, the undersigned hereby agrees to be responsible that such provisions are faithfully carried out by the studio with which he is connected.

Christie Film Company
Al E. Christie

Cecil B. deMille Pictures Corporation
Cecil B. deMille

Cecil B. deMille Pictures Corporation
Louis M. Goodstadt

"4. The use of firearms;

"5. Theft, robbery, safe-cracking, and dynamiting of trains, mines, buildings, etc. (having in mind the effect which a too-detailed description of these may have upon the moron);

"6. Brutality and possible gruesomeness;

"7. Technique of committing murder by whatever method;

"8. Methods of smuggling;

"9. Third-degree methods;

"10. Actual hangings or electrocutions as legal punishment for crime;

"11. Sympathy for criminals;

"12. Attitude toward public characters and institutions;

"13. Sedition;

"14. Apparent cruelty to children and animals;

"15. Branding of people or animals;

"16. The sale of women, or of a woman selling her virtue;

"17. Rape or attempted rape;

"18. First-night scenes;

"19. Man and woman in bed together;

"20. Deliberate seduction of girls;

"21. The institution of marriage;

"22. Surgical operations;

"23. The use of drugs;

"24. Titles or scenes having to do with the law enforcement or law-enforcing officers;

"25. Excessive or lustful kissing, particularly when one character or the other is a 'heavy':"

RESOLVED, That the execution of the purposes of this resolution is a fair trade practice.

\- - - - -

*The above list of signatory obligators has been augmented since the adoption of the resolution by the affiliation with Motion Picture Producers and Distributors of America, Inc., of the following companies:

The Caddo Company, Inc.,
Electrical Research Products, Inc.,
RCA Photophone, Inc.,
Sono-Art Productions, Inc.,

Printed in U. S. A.

WHEREAS, for the purpose of further establishing and maintaining the highest possible moral and artistic standards in motion pictures, the following companies, members of the Motion Picture Producers and Distributors of America, Inc., to wit:

Bray Productions, Inc.,
Chadwick Productions,
Christie Film Company, Inc.,
Cecil B. de Mille Pictures Corporation,
Distinctive Pictures Corporation,
Eastman Kodak Company,
Educational Film Exchanges, Inc.,
First National Pictures, Inc.,
Fox Film Corporation,
D. W. Griffith, Inc.,
Inspiration Pictures, Inc.,
Buster Keaton Productions,
Kinogram Publishing Corporation,
Metro-Goldwyn-Mayer Distributing Corporation,
Paramount Famous Lasky Corporation,
Principal Pictures Corporation,
Producers Distributing Corporation,
Pathe Exchange, Inc.,
RKO Distributing Corporation,
Hal Roach Studios,
Joseph M. Schenck Productions, Inc.,
Talmadge Producing Corporation,
United Artists Corporation,
Universal Pictures Corporation,
Vitagraph, Inc.,
Warner Bros. Pictures, Inc.,

*

and the Association of Motion Picture Producers, Inc., of California, which consists of the following companies, to wit:

Christie Film Company, Inc.,
Cecil B. de Mille Productions, Inc.,
Educational Studios, Inc.,
First National Productions Corporation,
Fox Film Corporation,
Samuel Goldwyn, Inc.,
Harold Lloyd Corporation,
Inspiration Pictures, Inc.,
Metro-Goldwyn-Mayer Corporation,
Metropolitan Pictures Corporation,
Paramount Famous Lasky Corporation,
Pathe Exchange, Inc.,
RKO Studios, Inc.,
Hal Roach Studios, Inc.,
Mack Sennett, Inc.,
Sound Studios, Inc.,
United Artists Studio Corporation,
Universal Pictures Corporation,
Warner Bros. Pictures, Inc.,
Jack White Comedy Corporation,
Asher, Small & Rogers, Inc.,
Kane Productions, Inc.,
Sam E. Rork, Inc.,

have adopted the following formula with reference to the selection and rejection of certain story material for picturization:

"RESOLVED, That those things which are included in the following list shall not appear in pictures produced by the members of this Association, irrespective of the manner in which they are treated:

"1. Pointed profanity—by either title or lip—this includes the words 'God,' 'Lord,' 'Jesus,' 'Christ' (unless they be used reverently in connection with proper religious ceremonies), 'hell,' 'damn,' 'Gawd,' and every other profane and vulgar expression however it may be spelled;
"2. Any licentious or suggestive nudity—in fact or in silhouette; and any lecherous or licentious notice thereof by other characters in the picture;
"3. The illegal traffic in drugs;
"4. Any inference of sex perversion;
"5. White slavery;
"6. Miscegenation (sex relationships between the white and black races);
"7. Sex hygiene and venereal diseases;
"8. Scenes of actual childbirth—in fact or in silhouette;
"9. Children's sex organs;
"10. Ridicule of the clergy;
"11. Willful offense to any nation, race or creed:

And be it further

"RESOLVED, That special care be exercised in the manner in which the following subjects are treated, to the end that vulgarity and suggestiveness may be eliminated and that good taste may be emphasized:

"1. The use of the flag;
"2. International relations (avoiding picturizing in an unfavorable light another country's religion, history, institutions, prominent people, and citizenry);
"3. Arson;

INTER-OFFICE MEMO

To MR. HAYS

Date September 10, 1928

From C.E.M.

Since dictating the attached memorandum on September 7, I have talked with you about the subject, and desire to supplement further by reference to three recent Tiffany pictures the suggestion contained in the memorandum; namely, that some way must be found to stop the distribution and exhibition by our member companies of pictures made by non-member companies which violate the "don'ts".

The Tiffany-Stahl picture, STORMY WATERS, was rejected entirely by the Ohio Board of Censors. The following selections from the eliminations by other censorship boards indicate the reasons for the rejection:

Reel 2: Sub-title, "You must have been pretty drunk not to have remembered getting married."
Reel 3: Scene showing Lola's legs as she slips in bath.
Scene in the dance at table where Lola wiggles her body suggestively for entertainment of ship's crew, and all views of men's faces as they register reaction to the girl's dancing.
Reel 4: Scene of girl wiggling and thumbing nose.
Reel 5: Entire scene of Lola kneeling between Captain Steele's knees with her arms on his legs.
Indecent action of girl's lips directly following sub-title, "You think so - well, you ain't seen nothing yet."
Scene of girl thumbing nose.
Reel 6: Sub-title, "I never married you - that was a lot of apple sauce."
In row boat, indecent action of lips and scene of thumbing nose.

The Tiffany picture, THE HAUNTED SHIP, is offensive chiefly because of violations of the standards of the industry regarding extreme brutality: It also contains offensive scenes of a Chinaman handling a white girl. The eliminations include:

Scene where skipper strikes man in the face who is chained and helpless.
Views of dancer in dive moving body suggestively.
Sub-title, "Keep your slimy hands off me," and accompanying scene of sailor mauling girl.
Views of boy being strung up by sailors.
Views of skipper lashing boy with whip.
View of skipper's brutal face and sub-title, "Cry for mercy as your mother did."
Also sub-title, "You are going up and then down to Hell".

The Tiffany picture, LINGERIE, appears to be what its name implies. The most offensive sub-title is the following, which appears twice:

"Je vous aime - voulez-vous coucher avec moi?"

Among the other eliminations are:

Reduce footage where soldier is struggling with"Lingerie".
Cut out scene of girl's legs shown through transparent negligee.
Cut out underlined words in sub-title: "Madame is granting the little girl a vacation and wishes you a delightful affair."
Cut to three feet each all scenes where soldier kisses "Lingerie" as they sit in chair.
Where couple is seated on piano bench, cut out scenes where man bends woman back in his arms and kisses her.
Cut out sub-title "Be careful, my husband is in the next room", and "He's harmless - he can not move, hear or speak."
Cut out all scenes where man is in woman's bedroom.

These instances are submitted to reinforce the suggestion that some formula ought to be found for requiring non-member companies to have their films reviewed by the Association and amended if necessary to avoid violations of the "don'ts", and that only the pictures so reviewed be distributed by our member companies and affiliated theatres.

I am not unmindful of the legal difficulties that might follow the suggestion that "the motion picture trust is trying to prevent our pictures being shown", etc. But I believe some of these non-member companies, particularly Tiffany, are deliberately making pictures that are over the border line of good taste and definitely violate the "don'ts". From a public relations standpoint, it would be fine to be obliged to defend a law suit occasioned by our insisting that these non-member companies live up to the standards the Association has adopted for its own members.

C.E.M.

INTER-OFFICE MEMO

Date September 7, 1928

To MR. HAYS

From C.E.M.

Recently we saw in the projection room the French picture, THE MODEL OF MONTMARTRE, which is to be released by Paramount. A considerable number of deletions had already been made, but there remained in the picture two sequences at the artists ball in Paris which violate the nudity clause of the don'ts. In one instance a semi-nude woman is shown riding astride a man's shoulders. The other is a flash of the nude torso of a woman.

Last Friday, in Portland, as indicated in my daily report, I saw the Tiffany-Stahl picture, A GRAIN OF DUST, which has in it five violations of the profanity dont's, and some very salacious bedroom scenes. Also, at lease one salacious title.

The picture was shown at the Empire Theatre, which is controlled by Publix. When the most salacious scene came on the screen, there were audible gasps from a number of those in my vicinity in the audience, and a dozen or more women left the theatre, several of them taking children along with them.

For some time, I have been wondering whether we ought not to give serious thought to the question of devising some sort of consultation service in this office for our member companies in the case of foreign and non-member pictures, which would correspond to the service rendered by Colonel Joy on the coast during the production of our own pictures.

CEM

5

Ecstasy & The Outlaw

With the Production Code in place, studio executives were obliged to tread lightly in certain areas. Gone were "God Damns" on the lips of aviators in the battle scenes of *Wings* (1927). Banished f were the titillating sin and redemption stories of Cecil B. DeMille's crowd pleasers like *Male and Female* (1919). Eliminated were the racially charged thrillers that had stampeded across America in the wake of as D.W. Griffith's *The Birth of a Nation* (1915). With the counsel of M.P.P.D.A. President Will Hays, studio motion pictures were sanitized and cleaned up. Movies were positioned as morally uplifting for audiences and as safe investments for financiers.

Motion pictures were still outside the protections of the First Amendment but the Production Code Administration worked to keep Hollywood on the straight and narrow and prevent the further spread of regional censors. Challenges to the status quo would not come from mainstream Hollywood producers but from foreign filmmakers and uncompromising independents.

Exploiting the sophisticated themes of female sexual longing, adultery, and male impotence, Gustav Machatý wrote and directed a film entitled *Ecstasy*. Produced outside Prague in 1932, the film starred a young Viennese beauty named Hedwig Kiesler. In the film, the girl marries an older husband who is unable to perform on their wedding night. Leaving the unconsummated marriage she is introduced to a hunky worker on her father's farm. The sparks fly at first sight and they end up snuggling close under the covers on a dark and stormy night. The girl's face glows with orgasmic satisfaction as audiences witnessed the first film depicting female sexual satisfaction.

Ecstasy fascinated and scandalized. Louis B. Mayer, the most prudish and proper of studio executives, caught an express steamer to Europe where he immediately signed the starlet, transforming her into Hedy Lamarr. Machatý followed them to MGM where he served as an uncredited B-unit director on several studio tentpoles, including *The Good Earth* (1937) and *Madame X* (1937) before heading to Poverty Row to direct *Jealousy* (1945) for Republic Pictures. Aribert Mog played Hedwig's strapping lover. Mog chose to stay in the European film industry, where he became a strident Nazi supporter and Aryan film star. He died while fighting on the Eastern Front near the Polish border in 1941. Hedy maintained her beautiful but slightly scandalous edge in her Hollywood films, appearing as the seductive native girl Tondelayo in *White Cargo* (1942) and the biblical femme fatale in Cecil B. DeMille's *Samson and Delilah* (1949).

Ecstasy had the censors worked up. It was the mid-1940s before a highly edited version of the film would be cleared for showings in U.S. theaters. Around that time, a new challenge was emerging from America's foremost independent filmmaker.

Howard Hughes had inherited a fortune but demonstrated his own innovative skill with radio, aviation, and mechanical devices at an early age. He excelled in business but it was Hollywood that attracted the young entrepreneur. Hughes was only 22 years old when he produced *Two Arabian Nights* (1927); the film claimed a Best Director Academy Award. He followed up with a series of hard-hitting pictures, including *The Racket* (nominated for Best Picture, 1928), *Hell's Angels* (nominated for Best Cinematography, 1930), and *The Front Page* (nominated for Best Picture, 1931).

Hughes began upsetting the authorities with the violence he portrayed in *Scarface: The Shame of a Nation* (produced 1931, released 1932). He knowingly pushed the censors, telling his production team "Screw the Hays Office... make it as exciting, as grisly as possible." (Gregory D. Black, *Hollywood Censored: Morality Codes, Catholics, and the Movies* [Cambridge University Press: UK, 1994], 126). *Scarface* captured gangland violence, and was even more explosive than the barrage of gunfire unleashed in *The Public Enemy* (1931) and *Little Caesar* (1931), two Warner Bros. films produced during the same period. The difference between the films was clear: while James Cagney was delivered to his mother as a lifeless carcass in the final scene, and Edward G. Robinson was gunned down on the steps of a church, Paul Muni's ruthless gangster was glorified, uncompromising, and only killed off after much debate with the censoring committee.

If *Scarface* agitated the morality police, Hughes's *The Outlaw* was calculated to cause outrage. *The Outlaw* was a fetish-western that featured the object of Hughes's obsession: Jane Russell. Hughes was infatuated with Russell's well proportioned figure and ample cleavage and he kept it on display throughout the picture. The engineering-prodigy-turned producer even put his mechanical skill to use, designing a brassiere to hoist Russell's assets to his desired position. She claimed the bra was too uncomfortable to ever wear. Still, Russell is seen bending over throughout the picture, tussling in the hayloft, and pouting sensually at the camera.

Hughes completed *The Outlaw* in 1941 but refused to make the PCA's requested cuts. He challenged the system, and throwing the resources of the Hughes Tool Company behind litigation, helped to wear down the P.C.A. during a 5 year long battle of attrition. Hughes did not prevail but his lawsuit helped burn through the M.P.A.A.'s resources, making it vulnerable to the next major challenge.

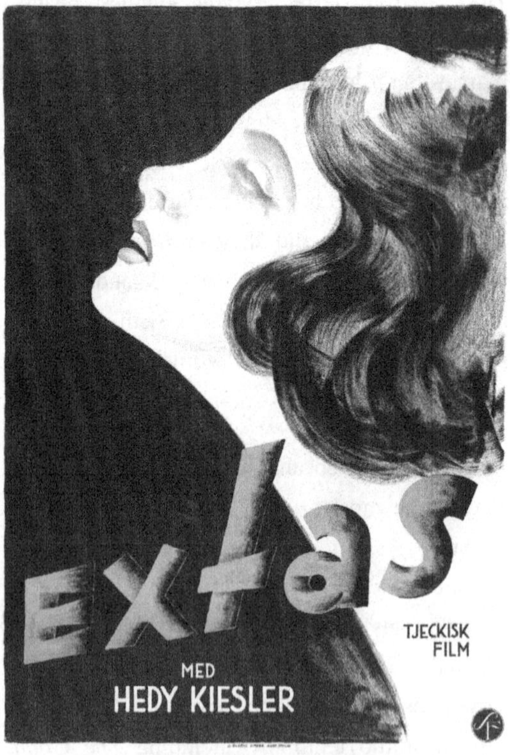

EUREKA PRODUCTIONS, INC. v. LEHMAN, Governor of New York

17 F.Supp. 259 (1936)
District Court, S. D. New York
Decided December 14, 1936

***260** MANTON, Circuit Judge.

This application is for a preliminary injunction before a court convened pursuant to section 266 of the Judicial Code, as amended (28 U.S.C. § 380 [28 U.S.C.A. § 380]), to restrain the defendants, state officials, from interfering with the exhibition, within the state of New York, of a film entitled "Ecstasy." Decision is to be determined upon a summons and complaint, answer and affidavits for and against the motion.

The complainant alleges it purchased this film from the Elekta Film Corporation of Prague, Czecho-Slovakia, with exclusive rights to its distribution, exploitation, and exhibition; that a print of that film was imported into the United States. The film, after it was screened and exhibited before customs officials as provided by section 305 of the Tariff Act of 1930, 46 Stat. 688 (19 U.S.C.A. § 1305), was admitted as an import December 5, 1935. Subsequently, the Motion Picture Division and the Commissioner of Education of the state of New York refused the complainant's application for a permit to exhibit the film within the state because it was indecent and immoral and would tend to corrupt morals. Article 43 of the Education Law (Consol.Laws, c. 16), § 1082.

This refusal to grant a permit is challenged because it is claimed to encroach upon federal power over foreign commerce in violation of the Constitution (article 1, § 8). It is also contended that by legislation the federal government has spanned the entire field of regulation, thereby superseding state legislation in accordance with Article 6 of the Constitution. The argument is made that, since the federal authorities admitted the film, determining it not to be immoral within section 305 of the Tariff Act of 1930, its exhibition within a state may not later be prohibited by the state authorities.

We need not consider the defendants' contention that the film is not the same article which was received in foreign commerce, since it was re-edited after entry into the United States to make it adaptable to American audiences, for we think that censorship by statutory regulation in the state of New York constitutes no burden upon foreign commerce. The licensing provision of the state statute applies equally to all films sought to be exhibited within the state. It is intended merely to regulate their local use. *Pathe Exchange v. Cobb*, 202 App.Div. 450, 195 N.Y.S. 661, affd. 236 N.Y. 539, 142 N.E. 274. Whether it be interstate or foreign commerce, the validity of a state statute is to be determined by its practical effect. *Baldwin v. G. A. F. Seelig, Inc.*, 294 U.S. 511, 55 S.Ct. 497, 79 L.Ed. 1032; *Corn Products Ref. Co. v. Eddy*, 249 U.S. 427. 39 S.Ct. 325, 63 L.Ed. 689, but cf. *DiSanto v. Penn.*, 273 U.S. 34, 47 S.Ct. 267, 71 L. Ed. 524. This state regulation of a strictly local use can hardly be said to burden foreign commerce. In regulating the local exhibition of films, the state exercises its police power after the article has lost its character as an import and consequently does not invalidly interfere or conflict with the exercise of federal power. *Mutual Film Corp. v. Industrial Comm.*

of Ohio, 236 U.S. 230, 35 S.Ct. 387, 390, 59 L.Ed. 552, Ann.Cas.1916C, 296; *Fox Film Corp. v. Trumbull*, 7 F.(2d) 715 (D.C.Conn.). In the *Mutual Film Corp.* case, supra, motion pictures were shipped in interstate commerce and an Ohio state statute dealt with their censorship for exhibition in Ohio. The court said: "The censorship, therefore, is only of films intended for exhibition in Ohio, and we can immediately put to one side the contention that it imposes a burden on interstate commerce. * * * It is only films which are `to be publicly exhibited and displayed in the state of Ohio' which are required to be examined and censored. It would be straining the doctrine of original packages to say that the films retain that form and composition even when unrolling and exhibiting to audiences, or, being ready for renting for the purpose of exhibition within the state, could not be disclosed to the state officers. * * * There must be some time when the films are subject to the law of the state, and necessarily when they are in the hands of the exchanges, ready to be rented to exhibitors, or have passed to the latter, they are in consumption, and mingled as much as from their nature they can be with other property of the state."

See, also, *Mutual Film Co. v. Industrial Comm. of Ohio*, 236 U.S. 247, 35 S.Ct. 393, 59 L.Ed. 561; *Mutual Film Co. v.*

***261** *Hodges*, 236 U.S. 248, 35 S.Ct. 393, 59 L.Ed. 561.

We cannot accept the argument that the character of foreign commerce persists through the exhibition of the film in the state after its arrival. If, after a film passes in interstate commerce into a second state for exhibition, the regulatory laws of that second state are enforceable, we think the same applies to a foreign film after its arrival and readiness for distribution and exhibition. All films, domestic and foreign, offered for exhibition in the state of New York, are subject to uniform regulations by the provisions of the statute. The statute did not deal differently with foreign films. All are required to meet the same standard of decency and morality.

Various actions of the federal law (section 305 of the Tariff Act of 1930, Title 19 U.S.C.A. § 1305; Title 18 U.S. C.A. §§ 396, 512, 405, 406, 407) are relied on as supporting the contention that Congress intended to regulate exclusively the exhibition of films and that the state cannot interfere. Undoubtedly, in a conflict between federal and state legislation, the former is superior. *Oregon-Washington R. & Nav. Co. v. Washington*, 270 U.S. 87, 46 S.Ct. 279, 70 L.Ed. 482. We need not consider whether Congress could regulate the exhibition of films within a state, for it is clear that it has not undertaken to do so. Section 305 of the Tariff Act of 1930 regulates the admission of films into the United States and provides for their seizure and forfeiture. Section 245 of the Criminal Code, as amended (18 U.S.C.A. § 396),. makes it a crime to enter or cause to be brought into the United States or to knowingly deposit with any express company or other common carrier an obscene or lewd film. These statutes have the same scope and application as provisions relating to prize-fight films. 37 Stat. 240, 18 U.S.C.A. § 405. In *Weber v. Freed*, 239 U.S. 325, 36 S.Ct. 131, 60 L.Ed. 308, Ann.Cas.1916C, 317, it was held that Congress could validly prohibit the importation of these films. To the objection that Congress had exceeded its power since it actually meant to regulate the subsequent exhibition of these films, the court said that it could not inquire into the motives of Congress and that, if the objection was sustained, federal power over foreign commerce would be destroyed wherever an imported article was designed for subsequent use. The purpose of Congress was to supplement and aid state legislation, leaving the matter of local exhibition for determination by the states. *United States v. Johnston* (D. C.) 232 F. 970.

Congress, therefore, did not seek to supersede the police power of the state, and the judgment of the federal officers in admitting the film did not prevent the state officers from arriving at a different judgment when it came to the exhibition of the film and the granting of a license therefor.

The motion is denied.

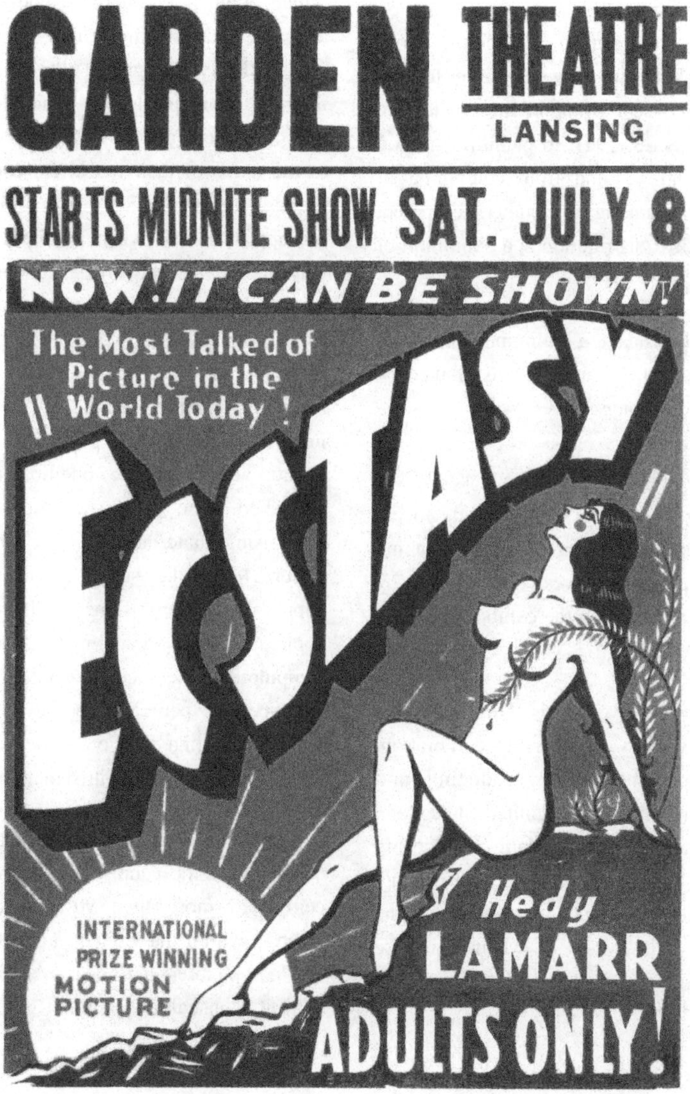

HUGHES TOOL CO. v. MOTION PICTURE ASS'N OF AMERICA, INC.

66 F. Supp. 1006 (1946)
District Court, S. D. New York.
Decided June 14, 1946

***1007** BRIGHT, District Judge.

By this motion, plaintiff seeks an injunction pendente lite, restraining defendant from revoking, or taking any steps looking to, the revocation of the seal of approval granted by defendant on May 23, 1941, to plaintiff's motion picture "The Outlaw," and from combining or conspiring with or among its members to prevent or impair plaintiff's distribution and exhibition of such picture.

Upon notice to defendant, a preliminary stay until the determination of this motion was granted by Judge Leibell, restraining

***1008** defendant and its officers and agent from (1) revoking or taking any steps looking to the revocation of that seal of approval, and (2) taking any action in respect to the advertising used by plaintiff in connection with the exhibition of said motion picture.

The complaint states two claims. The first is that defendant, a voluntary membership corporation, is composed of the major producing and distributing companies in the United States, and has a close and effective working relationship with all but 5% of the remaining producing, distributing and exhibiting companies in the motion picture industry, all of whom comprise more than 95% of the producers, distributors and exhibitors in the industry. Under its constitution and by-laws, there has been created within its organization, a Production Code Administration and an Advertising Code Administration, alphabetically designated PCA and ACA, to impose upon production and distribution of motion pictures a system of censorship according to the terms of their respective codes. The PCA requires the submission of a completed film to it for approval, and when required deletions and changes have been made, issues its seal of approval. Non-member cooperating affiliated producers may also submit their pictures to the PCA for the same purpose and with the same result. The right to void the seal and to require its immediate surrender is granted to the defendant for any violation of the conditions under which it is issued. One of the conditions is that all advertising material used in exploiting motion pictures shall be submitted to the ACA for approval. The provisions of the code shall be applied to all advertising material submitted, with scrupulous fairness, equality and impartiality, and an appeal is permitted to the president of the defendant from a decision of the Administrator of the ACA rejecting submitted material.

It is further alleged that the defendant by its rigid control over the supply of motion pictures, has compelled more than 90% of the exhibiting theatres within the United States to exhibit only "sealed" pictures and no others, and to refuse to exhibit "unsealed" pictures under economic coercion and threat of having their supply of "sealed" pictures entirely shut off, in consequence of which more than 90% of all exhibiting theatres refuse to exhibit pictures which do not have defendant's seal.

It is further alleged that plaintiff's motion picture department, under the name of "Hughes Productions," is a member in good standing of the defendant, is bound by its constitution, by-laws and regulations, in respect to all pictures it produces, by the conditions under which the seal of approval is granted, and that all advertising and publicity material used in publicizing its pictures must be submitted to the ACA for approval.

In 1941, plaintiff produced "The Outlaw," submitted it to the PCA for a seal, and such a seal was issued on May 23, 1941, after certain frames had been trimmed from the picture. In 1945 plaintiff contracted with the United Artists Corporation, distributor and former member of the defendant, for the general public release of "The Outlaw," under a contract which required plaintiff to deliver to United Artists the motion picture, "and as a condition precedent to the delivery will have procured a seal" from the defendant.

The advertising campaign material caused to be prepared by plaintiff was submitted to the ACA for approval between November 1945 and February 1946, and it rejected an outdoor poster, a number of pen and ink drawings, and six photographs. Plaintiff appealed to the defendant's president, who, on March 29, 1946, affirmed the rejection of the bulk of the material except as to the photographs.

It is further alleged that the resolutions establishing the ACA are unlawful, coercive and ineffective as an improper delegation of authority by defendant's board of directors; and in that they afford no adequate appeal from the capricious, discriminatory and unreasonable rejection of its advertising; by reason of all of which plaintiff has been deprived of its property without due process of law.

Plaintiff further claims that it has been damaged by the discrimination, arbitrary action, and total lack of impartiality of the ACA and the president; and that the rejection of certain advertising, referring to

***1009** prior censorship difficulties with local authorities, was unlawful and in violation of the First Amendment to the Constitution of the United States. Because of the rejection of this advertising, plaintiff states it has been greatly damaged in the sum of $1,000,000.

The second claim set forth is framed under the Sherman Anti-Trust Act, 15 U.S. C.A. §§ 1-7, 15 note. It is alleged that the defendant and its members (of which plaintiff was one) entered into an agreement and conspiracy to hinder and suppress competition in the interstate sale, distribution and showing of motion picture films, and to create a monopoly in the production and distribution of motion pictures of members and cooperating affiliated non-members; and by reason of the economic control centered in the seal, they have coerced and compelled a virtual totality of motion picture producers to submit all stories, scripts, and completed motion picture films and their titles, to its PCA for seal of approval, without which motion picture films cannot be shown in more than 90% of the motion picture theatres; by means of which producers are compelled to avoid controversial film treatment of social, political, economic, educational and public matters of importance, in contravention of the guarantee of free speech contained in the First Amendment of the Constitution of the United States; and in compelling all advertising matter used in the exploitation of motion pictures to conform to specific standards adopted and enforced by the defendant.

'THE OUTLAW' IS BANNED

State Regents Uphold Esmond Ruling Against Hughes Film

"The Outlaw," Howard Hughes's film saga of the old West based on the adventures of Billy the Kid, was banned from theatres in this State yesterday by the State Board of Regents. Meeting at the State Office Building, the Regents denied the producer's appeal from a preliminary ban by Irwin Esmond, director of the State Motion Picture Division.

The Regents also sustained Mr. Esmond's ruling that, if four scenes and bits of dialogue found objectionable by the reviewers were deleted from the film, the picture would be licensed. No comment could be obtained from Mr. Hughes's representatives in New York yesterday on whether the decision would be obeyed or an appeal be taken to the Appellate Division of the Supreme Court.

The picture, which is estimated to have cost between $2,000,000 and $3,000,000, was finally approved by the Hays censorship office for the movie industry last May after Mr. Hughes yielded to demands that he eliminate shots of Jane Russell, star of the film, leaning forward over a mirror.

It is claimed that as a result of such combination and conspiracy, there is withheld from the public a large body of information, knowledge and understanding of such controversial topics against the wishes of individual producers, distributors and exhibitors, and to the great detriment of the public; owners of motion picture theatres are compelled to refuse to accept any pictures for exhibition which do not bear the seal of approval; all non-member producers are compelled to obtain a seal under economic threat of finding more than 90% of the theatres barred to them; producers, distributors and exhibitors are compelled to conform their advertising to defendant's arbitrary, discriminatory and preconceived notions of public propriety; a private censorship is imposed upon the industry, by which defendant has assumed quasi-governmental functions and police powers which may properly be exercised only by governmental agencies; and the legitimate business of many independent producers, distributors and exhibitors have been restrained and controlled, in violation of the Sherman Anti-Trust Act, 15 U.S.C.A. §§ 1-7, 15 note, and Clayton Act, 38 Stat. 730, by reason of defendant's group boycott of producers, distributors and exhibitors, who do not obtain the seal of approval.

These, it is claimed, subject plaintiff to the penalty of revocation of the seal for the use of any rejected advertising material, and thus cause a breach of plaintiff's contract with United Artists, and restrain the effective distribution of "The Outlaw." It is further claimed that the system of private censorship thus imposed is unconstitutional and unlawful in that the by-laws and regulations are arbitrary and discriminatory and afford no fair, lawful or adequate trial or appeal, thus depriving plaintiff of his property rights without due process; and the banning by defendant of the film treatment of certain controversial topics and the prohibition of certain advertising and mention of prior censorship constitute a continuing conspiracy in violation of plaintiff's rights guaranteed by the First Amendment. It asks damages in the sum of $5,000,000.

These broad allegations have not been sustained by proof of facts.

"The Outlaw" is claimed to be a story built on the saga of Billy the Kid, and apparently is a glorified "Western," featuring to some extent the escapades of Billy, and those of a tough girl Rio, in a western frontier town, who uses, among other attractions, a gun and a pitchfork with considerable lethal intent.

In 1940 the final shooting script of the picture was submitted to the PCA and a number of suggestions as to changes were accepted. The finished picture was presented in March, 1941, other suggestions were made and in part adopted, but the deletions were still insufficient to bring the

***1010** picture in conformity with the production code, and defendant refused to issue a certificate of approval. Appeal was taken to defendant's board of directors, and after repeated screening in the presence of the board and the removal of additional footage from the controversial scenes, it was agreed between the parties that, upon the excision of additional footage, the certificate of approval would issue. On May 23, 1941, that was done, and the certificate provided in part:

"Dear Mr. Hughes:

"The attached certificate of approval is issued, upon the condition that its acceptance by you, binds you, as producer, and/or your distributor, and any and all other agents of yours, and your assigns, and successors, to the following terms and conditions: * * *

"(3) That any and all advertising and publicity matter, including material for press books, still photographs, poster and lobby card designs, and trailers, used in any manner in connection with the advertising and exploitation of this picture, shall be submitted for approval to the Advertising Advisory Council of the Motion Picture Producers and Distributors of America, Inc., and that only such advertising or publicity material or trailers, approved by such Council shall be used in advertising and exploiting the picture hereby approved, and

"(4) That, in addition to any other applicable penalties, the Production Code Administration reserves the right to void this Certificate, at any time hereafter, for any violation of the conditions set forth herein and/or of the violation of any of the rules and regulations promulgated by the Board of Directors of the Motion Picture Producers & Distributors of America, Inc."

The crux of the present dispute is a narrow one, and relates only to the alleged rejection of certain advertising matter which plaintiff's president describes as "only a small portion of the advertising with which the film is to be launched."

Plaintiff's papers reveal that it has not complied with the terms of the certificate in so far as advertising is concerned. In 1943, at San Francisco, the advertising, which had not even been submitted to defendant, was of such a character as to incur the condemnation of public authorities and its consequent withdrawal. Other undenied instances are shown which reveal that plaintiff's president has sought and still seeks to arrogate to himself the decision of what advertising should be indulged in, regardless of the contract above quoted, and of the rules and regulations of the association of which his production company was a member.

The advertising now in controversy in substance consists of pictures, cuts, and lithographs of the lady Rio, featuring more her breasts, legs and positions than the saga of Billy the Kid, and using the words "Exactly as it was filmed — Not a Scene Cut."

This advertising was submitted by plaintiff to the ACA for approval in December 1945. It consisted of still photographs, newspaper advertising, and art work for proposed posters. There were 202 stills submitted, 187 were approved, I was rejected and the remaining 14 were returned for retouching. Plaintiff appeals with respect to only 6 of these 14, and defendant's president reversed the decision of the Administrator of the ACA, and they are no longer the subject of discussion.

Twenty-six newspaper advertisements were approved. As to 20 others which were returned for correction, plaintiff appealed and the rejection was sustained. Eight of the advertisements were pen and ink drawings, in which the breasts of the star were emphasized and exposed. The Administrator of the ACA suggested that these drawings could be rendered unobjectionable by a slight retouching, that is, by the raising of the blouse a fraction of an inch, which plaintiff refused to do. Others were rejected because they showed a man and woman together in hay in a compromising horizontal position. Another was rejected because it exposed too much bosom and carried the line: "What are the two great reasons for Jane Russell's rise to stardom?" Eleven others were rejected because they contained what the Administrator terms was a false and misleading statement — "Exactly as filmed — not a scene

***1011** cut." Four others were rejected because they contained the word "censored" displayed across the figure of the star with her anatomy exposed. There was also rejected the use of a type line, "How would you like to tussle with Russell?" These rejections were all sustained on appeal to defendant's president.

A photostat of a painting of the star, from which it was proposed to prepare a poster 8'8" × 14'5" was submitted, and after it was retouched, was accepted. Later finished posters were submitted, which the Administrator states did not reproduce the painting but knowingly and indecently emphasized the star's breasts, they were rejected, and the rejection sustained on appeal.

Since these rejections and the appeal therefrom, and prior to the commencement of this action, plaintiff's advertising agent has submitted 8 additional newspaper advertisements, which have been approved; and United Artists, its distributing agent, has submitted 11 pages of material for a "press book" and various other pieces of miscellaneous display material, all of which have been approved.

It is further shown, without dispute, that plaintiff is now using not only rejected advertising material, but also material which has never been submitted to the defendant, both in newspapers and on sign displays, and has even released the picture which caused trouble for it in San Francisco in 1943. Late in April, 1946, it is alleged, and not denied, a sky-writing airplane wrote the words "The Outlaw" in the sky over Pasadena, and then made two enormous circles with a dot in the middle of each.

The appeal from the action of the Administrator of the ACA, was to defendant's president in accordance with its by-laws. Upon that appeal, plaintiff was represented by counsel, and had full opportunity to present its argument and contentions.

It is not necessary for a determination of this motion that I pass upon whether or not the rejections of the advertisements because of the exposure of too much anatomy, or because of the use of the expressions mentioned, were wrong or otherwise. They certainly were not arbitrary or discriminatory. Concededly, one of the purposes for which defendant was organized was to establish and maintain the highest possible moral and artistic standards in motion picture production. That was in part in response to objections voiced in press and otherwise throughout the United States to the kind of pictures which appeared from time to time in the theatres, and to some of the advertisements used in the promotion of pictures. I shall not interfere with the carrying out of that purpose, particularly in favor of one whose sole object is a selfish one.

Nor will I hold that the processes offered by defendant for submission to it of proposed advertising, and for its examination and approval or rejection, are of such a character that they do not present a fair opportunity for consideration, honest decision, and full and complete representation, nor that such trial and appeal were either perfunctory, useless or illusory. The results obtained by plaintiff as to this very picture completely disprove any such contention. The seal of approval was granted liberally, it now appears. Governmental authorities in several communities subsequently required further deletions. And the disapproval of pictures of the star was not final; they were returned for correction. There is no evidence of discrimination against plaintiff. If anything, there is shown a desire to cooperate. That plaintiff's president was not satisfied with the results proves nothing other than that he would not be satisfied unless he had all of his own way.

As to the use of the words, "Exactly as it was filmed — not a scene cut," I can see no fair reason for interfering with their rejection. They are not true. Even if plaintiff in this case is in a position to invoke the First Amendment relating to freedom of speech, and of that I have grave doubt, he can hardly succeed where the speech which has been rejected is not the truth. It is shown without dispute, both by plaintiff's own affidavit as well as by those submitted in opposition to this motion, that after the completed film was submitted to the defendant in 1941, prior and subsequent to which portions of the original film had been cut at defendant's request,

***1012** deletions were required and made of additional objectionable footage and dialogue by censoring authorities in New York, Pennsylvania, Ohio, Maryland, Massachusetts, San Francisco and Chicago.

Plaintiff alleges that its inability to use these words, which it claims is a vital part of his advertising campaign, will cause him great loss. The papers submitted do not bear this out. It does not appear that the raising of the blouse or the lowering of the skirt on the star a small fraction of an inch, or the correction of the recumbent position of the man and woman, or the elimination of the words relating to censorship, will so terribly affect plaintiff's box office receipts. To the contrary, the papers show that in Richmond and Norfolk, Virginia and Atlanta, Georgia, where Loews refused to use the objectionable advertising submitted by plaintiff, plaintiff's own claim is that the showing of "The Outlaw" broke all box office records.

Plaintiff asks the court to restrain defendant from interfering with its right to publish the truth. A necessary basis for any such restraint would be that he is seeking to publish the truth. The defendant does not here seek to invade the plaintiff's right of free speech and press. It seeks only to deny plaintiff's right to do whatever he sees fit under the defendant's seal of approval. If plaintiff insists upon its so-called rights, whatever they may be, it may do so; but it cannot insist that it do it with defendant's approval, or under conditions which the public may believe is with the defendant's approval.

'THE OUTLAW' IS BANNED

Film Producer Group Withdraws Its Approval Over Hughes Ads

Special to THE NEW YORK TIMES.

HOLLYWOOD, Sept. 8—The general tightening of morals censorship in Hollywood, in which there has been a marked increase lately, hit Howard Hughes' much-discussed production "The Outlaw" today. After permitting the Jane Russell Western film to play for over a year, the Motion Picture Producers Association, on a technicality, ordered it withdrawn from the country's principal theatres within a week.

Joseph I. Breen, the association's production code administrator, sent notice to Mr. Hughes that the association's certificate of approval granted in May, 1941, had been withdrawn because of Mr. Hughes' failure to submit his advertising for association approval. This advertising has been peppered with words like "sexational."

HOLLYWOOD, Calif., Sept. 8 (AP) —Howard Hughes, referring to the Motion Picture Association as "the Hays office," issued a statement saying:

"The only thing I have to say about 'The Outlaw' is this—

"The censors may not like it, but the public does.

"The Hays office is assuming the position of dictator in the selection of the public's entertainment."

There is not shown here any refusal or threatened refusal on the part of any exhibitor to exhibit without the seal. There is not shown here the refusal on the part of any distributor to distribute without the seal. Plaintiff already has distribution and exhibition. Not one instance is shown where either distribution or exhibition has been refused because of the absence of a seal, or because a seal once granted has been cancelled. Plaintiff's distributor, the United Artists, is not a member of the defendant and is not bound by its rules. And the papers submitted show beyond any question of a doubt that many pictures without the defendant's seal are being exhibited throughout the country.

Plaintiff's real complaint seems to be that because he claims to have invested $2,000,000, and that "The Outlaw" is the only picture which it has produced since 1941 and its entire status as a producer is at stake on this one production, the defendant's "threat (which the papers show it has not made) to revoke the seal" must be gauged on the basis of the financial loss that may be involved and of plaintiff's capacity to go on producing motion pictures. It overlooks the fact that all of this danger, if any there may be, is being caused by its obvious and admitted violation of its contract with the defendant. It is perfectly willing to accept the benefit of the seal which it says will give it entry into all of the 18,000 theatres in the United States, but is is not willing to accept the conditions under which it may operate with the seal. That part of its contract which will result in profit to it is good; that part which requires it to restrain its advertising is bad. I know of no law which authorizes a party to accept the good in a contract and reject what he does not like. It cannot have its cake and eat it too. If it wishes to retain the seal, it must be on the condition that it adhere to the agreement under which it holds and has used it.

This would only seem to be fair and equitable to the defendant, organized in part, to the knowledge of the motion picture public, to keep pictures decent and morally acceptable. By the issuance of its seal, which is shown on every motion picture approved by it, the public is led to understand that that picture has defendant's approval. In addition, the picture being approved, the public may properly assume that the advertisement and promotional matter of the picture is likewise approved. The blame for improper, salacious or false advertisement is, therefore, placed as much at the door of the defendant as of the producer. There is no reason for subjecting the defendant to this criticism caused solely by the action and arbitrary conduct of the plaintiff.

This motion is denied for the following reasons, among others:

***1013** 1. The agreement under which plaintiff holds the seal is the beginning and end of this controversy. It is either wholly good or wholly bad. If it is good, plaintiff cannot retain part and reject the balance. Certainly it is not unilateral.

2. If it is bad because defendant allegedly is engaged in a combination in violation of the Sherman Act, then this court should not lend its injunctive process to uphold any part of it.

3. That some of the defendant's members, who distribute motion pictures, have agreed that they will not "release, distribute or promote the release or distribution or in any way, directly or indirectly, make available for release or distribution, any motion picture which has not theretofore been approved," is not, in my opinion, a violation of the Act. The purpose of the approval is in furtherance of the proper purpose of the defendant to censor pictures which it may consider are not up to the highest possible moral and artistic standards. Defendant, I believe, owes that duty to the public. Even if it does not, it holds itself out as so doing, and the obligation is the same. If there is any restraint in such a proper purpose, it is a reasonable one.

4. The contract under which the seal of approval was granted, and upon which plaintiff now so strenuously relies, is not inherently invalid or illegal. That being so, it is enforceable, even though one of the parties to it is violating the Sherman Act. *Connolly v. Union Sewer Pipe Co.* 184 U.S. 540, 549, 551, 22 S.Ct. 431, 46 L. Ed. 679; *Small Co. v. Lamborn & Co.*, 267 U.S. 248-252, 45 S.Ct. 300, 69 L.Ed. 597; *The Charles E. Wisewall, D.C.*, 74 F. 802; *Standard Oil Co. v. Markham, D.C.*, 61 F. Supp. 813-815.

5. However, if the seal contract can be said to be illegal because of the alleged illegal character of the defendant and the alleged combination and conspiracy among its members, plaintiff cannot in the same breath enforce it and attack it. Both parties to it would seem to be in pari delicto, and in such a case, the court will not lend its aid to either; it will leave them as it finds them. *Northwestern Oil Co. v. Socony Vacuum Oil Co.*, 7 Cir., 138 F.2d 967-971, certiorari denied 321 U.S. 792, 64 S. Ct. 790, 88 L.Ed. 1081; *Eastman Kodak Co. v. Blackmore*, 2 Cir., 277 F. 694-698. This principle, of course, would have no application if it may be said that plaintiff in entering into the contract was laboring under economic compulsion or duress, as it is called. But I find no evidence of that.

6. That there may some time be a violation of the Sherman Act, either by a combination of the defendant and its members to prohibit exhibition or distribution of plaintiff's picture, or because of the agreements between the distributor members above quoted, that they will not distribute or aid in the distribution of unsealed pictures, does not, in my opinion, affect the present question. Those possible acts, anticipated by plaintiff, have done nothing to bring about the present controversy. It arises solely by reason of the seal agreement and plaintiff's conduct with reference thereto. The violation of the Sherman Act, if any, in other words, is not the cause nor the means by which this case has been brought about. The violation has not occurred, nor damaged plaintiff in any respect, which would seem to be a pre-requisite to enable plaintiff to recover under the provisions of that law. Title 15 U.S. C.A. § 15. The possibility of damage in the future is most speculative; plaintiff's picture has been produced, distributed, and is now being exhibited. No alleged violation of the Sherman Act has caused the situation now confronting the court. No combination or conspiracy in which the defendant is involved produced it. It arises only from the relationship between plaintiff and defendant, crystalized in the contract between the two of them. Defendant has not breached that contract, and there is no evidence that it intends to do so. Before plaintiff could suffer any damage under the facts shown here, there must occur at least two further acts — a cancellation of the seal, and an exclusion from exhibition, or a cancellation by the United Artists of its distributing contract. Even if the latter should occur, there are, so the papers show, at least three other distributors who are not members of the defendant.

7. The situation in which plaintiff finds itself can be remedied in two ways. This

***1014** court may grant the injunction sought, which will either perpetuate an illegal contract, or permit plaintiff to enforce what he likes and reject the balance. This will hold out to the public the approval by the defendant of something it does not approve.

Or it may be remedied by plaintiff doing what it contracted to do. I cannot see any reason why this court should do an inequity to satisfy one who clearly violates its contract. I cannot bring myself to believe that the defendant will cancel its seal if the plaintiff carries out fairly its part.

8. This entire controversy has been precipitated by the act of plaintiff. It has not only violated the terms under which it obtained the seal, both before and since the submission of the disputed

advertising to the defendant, but it claims the right so to do, even though it requires the recognition of another part of the contract it is violating. Its compliance with the contract does not involve very much on its part. An examination of the various exhibits persuades me that the whole matter is a trivial one, a tempest in a teapot. In fact, it seems more an effort on the part of the plaintiff to add this case and its peregrinations through the courts as additional publicity and advertising in promotion of the picture.

9. Finally, it is contended that, "So long as the illegal combination and present use of the seal persists, plaintiff is bound * * * to make every effort to retain the seal. * * * When, upon final decision of the merits of the suit, * * * the use of the seal as the mechanism of the unlawful combination is terminated, the economic coercion to which plaintiff is now subject will be at an end. Plaintiff will then be free * * * to compete in the motion picture field unrestricted by the need to conform to defendant's seal requirements. Only then is it right to require the surrender of the seal. Until then to penalize plaintiff for refusing to do so is the equivalent of depriving it of the protection of the anti-trust laws."

If the seal will not be required at the end of this litigation, why is it required now? The conclusion to be drawn is obvious. Plaintiff obviously wants to prolong the present status until its picture has run its life, it will have received the profit from its exhibitions, and will no longer require the seal; and all this in opposition to defendant, under its seal of approval, and in violation of its contract. That is too naive. If plaintiff wishes to retain the seal of approval, it must comply with its agreement and with the conditions upon which the seal was granted.

The motion is, therefore, denied, and the stay granted by Judge Leibell vacated. Settle order on notice.

The Outlaw
HERE'S WHY THIS THRILLING NEW PICTURE HAS BEEN KEPT OFF THE SCREEN FOR TWO YEARS!
O.K. BOYS, THAT'S IT!
HUGHES DIRECTOR
1944-HOWARD HUGHES, WORLD FAMOUS FLYER AND MOTION PICTURE PRODUCER, COMPLETES HIS PICTURE THE OUTLAW.
HOWARD HUGHES DISCOVERED JEAN HARLOW, PAUL MUNI, GEORGE RAFT, AND PAT O'BRIEN. NOW, IN THE OUTLAW, HE PRESENTS HIS SENSATIONAL NEW STAR DISCOVERY— JANE RUSSELL
JUNE, 1944-THE OUTLAW WORLD PREMIERE IS HELD AT SAN FRANCISCO. THE PICTURE BREAKS EVERY EXISTING RECORD!! HELD OVER FOR 8 WEEKS! PLAYS TO MORE THAN 300,000 PEOPLE!!
TIVOLI
THE OUTLAW
THE OUTLAW IS TRIGGER-FAST ACTION COMBINED WITH DARING SENSATION TOO STARTLING TO DESCRIBE!
THEN...THE OUTLAW IS BANNED BY THE CENSORS! BUT RATHER THAN CUT A SINGLE SCENE FROM THE FILM, HOWARD HUGHES WITHDRAWS IT FROM THE THEATRES OF THE WORLD.
CENSORED!
I'M GOING TO FIGHT THIS BATTLE TO THE FINISH AND MAKE SURE THAT THE PUBLIC SEES MY PICTURE EXACTLY AS I MADE IT!
THE OUTLAW
INTRODUCIN JANE RUSSELL
DARING! THRILLING! FAST MOVING!
CLOSED BY CENSORS
THANK YOU, MR. HUGHES
NOW, AT LAST, AFTER A TWO YEAR'S FIGHT WITH THE CENSORS HOWARD HUGHES BRINGS YOU HIS DARING PRODUCTION THE OUTLAW...EXACTLY AS IT WAS FILMED...NOT A SCENE CUT...AND INTRODUCING A NEW STAR, JANE RUSSELL

6

Southern Censorship

While film licensing agencies stretched across the United States, Southern censors were particularly active in the 1940s and 1950s. The moralizing movie administrators of Memphis, TN, Atlanta, GA, and Marshall, TX serve as examples of how local government officials were able to use regional bias to constrict and constrain the freedom of expression. In the decade before the Civil Rights movement, the movies that most concerned these Southern city censors centered on race issues.

The Memphis Board of Film Censors was established by Mayor E.H. "Boss" Crump. Boss Crump built a political machine that controlled the region for decades; after serving as commissioner of various departments, he was elected Mayor of Memphis in 1910. The following year he established the film board to restrict motion pictures, plays, and other public exhibitions deemed "immoral, lewd, or lascivious." But the administrators were mostly lax. Records indicate they halted the Sam Lucas-starring version of *Uncle Tom's Cabin* (1914). They felt that the leading actor, an African American man, might cause a racial disturbance. But little else was abridged by the Memphis agency, possibly because censors in neighboring states had already left their mark on movies distributed in the River City region.

Then in 1927, Lloyd T. Binford was appointed Chairman of the Memphis Board of Censors. Binford was given a small tin badge and relished his position as the city's moral spokesman. Film exhibitors in Memphis suddenly experienced a much more difficult regime. In his first year on the job Binford banned Cecil B. DeMille's *King of Kings* (1927) because he objected to the film's portrayal of Jews. Unwilling to give up on long held principles and prejudices, Binford saw motion pictures as a potentially destabilizing force that needed to be regulated and controlled. In 1940 he banned MGM's *Cabin in the Sky* and encouraged an amendment to the city's motion picture code that was ratified in 1943: "Now, Therefore, Be It Resolved, that hereafter no moving picture shall be exhibited at any moving picture theater catering to white or to white and colored audiences in which an all negro cast appears or in which roles are depicted by negro actors or actresses not ordinarily performed by members of the colored race in real life" (*The Pittsburgh Courier*, September 15, 1956).

Black talents vanished from Memphis screens. Lena Horne was cut from *Ziegfield Follies of 1946* and *Till the Clouds Roll By* (1946). Pearl Baily was removed from *Variety Girl* (1947) and Duke Ellington, Cab Calloway, Nat King Cole were expunged from short subjects. The term "Binfordized" became known in the film industry for aggressive censoring—the June Allyson comedy *Sailor Takes a Wife* (1945), was banned because a black servant showed resentment toward a white character. In 1947, Binford banned a Hal Roach kiddie comedy, *Curley* (1947). This cut would help tip the scale. Change was on the horizon but for now the city censor had the upper hand.

Binford's triggers were well known. By contrast, Atlanta's city censor Christine Smith could be more unpredictable. Smith took office in 1945. Unlike the Memphis film regulator, who seemed to feel threatened by images on the screen, Smith appeared to genuinely enjoy the movies. She praised Olivier's *Henry V* (1944) and Powell and Pressburger's *The Red Shoes* (1948) (Harold H. Martin, *Atlanta and Environs, Vol. 3 1940-1976* [The University of Georgia Press, Atlanta; 1987], 411). But when a cycle of racially-charged melodramas were released by Hollywood, Smith pushed back. After viewing *Lost Boundaries* (1949), a film focusing on an African American doctor passing for white, she slapped a ban on the picture. Her reasoning: "it is contrary to the public good." ("*Lost Boundaries* Faces Atlanta Ban," in *The New York Times*, August 21, 1949).

But when another "race passing" picture came to town, Smith championed the film. *Pinky* was approved with minimal cuts. Commented Smith: "I know this picture is going to be painful to a great many Southerners. It will make them squirm, but at the same time it will make them realize how unlovely their attitudes are." ("*Pinky* Paves Way in Atlanta Opening," in *Brooklyn Daily Eagle*, November 18, 1949).

The censors of Marshall, TX were less understanding. When W.L. Gelling, the manager of the local Paramount Theater, projected *Pinky*, he was jailed and fined. Eric Johnson, the President of the M.P.A.A. and successor to Will Hays, supported an appeal but the outlook was grim. The ban on *Pinky* was upheld by the Texas Supreme Court. The court was still not ready to accept film on an equal footing with the press. Wrote Judge Tom L. Beauchamp: "We cannot concede that the motion-picture industry has emerged from the business of amusement and become propaganders of ideas entitling it to freedom of speech." ("*Pinky* Ban Upheld by Court in Texas," in *The New York Times*, January 31, 1952).

Gelling v. Texas would be the final film of the era where the censors held the upper hand. Within months the decision would be overturned upon review by the Supreme Court. But before then motion pictures would have to become speech. The movies needed a *Miracle*.

UNITED ARTISTS CORP. v. BOARD OF CENSORS OF CITY OF MEMPHIS

225 S.W.2d 550 (1949)
Supreme Court of Tennessee
Decided December 17, 1949

NEIL, Chief Justice.

* * *

***551** The censorship boards of Memphis and Shelby County act under the authority of Chapter 54 of the Private Acts of 1921, as amended by Chapter 394 of the Private Acts of 1929, and Sections 1131-1139 of the Memphis Municipal Code, also Chapter 403 of the Private Acts of 1947, which authorized the censoring of pictures outside the City of Memphis.

The Board of Censors, following a private exhibition of the picture, wrote the following letter to the United Artists:

"Commission Government "Memphis, Tenn. "August 9 1947 "United Artists Corporation "St. Louis, Missouri

"Gentlemen:

"The Memphis Board of Censors passes 'The Marauders' and the Bebe Daniels Picture, but I am sorry to have to inform you that it is unable to approve your 'Curley'

***552** picture with the little negroes as the south does not permit negroes in white school nor recognize social equality between the races even in children.

"Yours truly "/s/ Lloyd T. Binford Chairman"

Upon the receipt of this letter the petitioners filed a joint petition in the circuit court seeking a review of the action of the Board of Censors. The petition alleged that the Board had banned the picture without legal authority, (1) that the Private Acts under which it acted were unconstitutional in that they denied to petitioner the right of freedom of speech and due process, (2) that it acted "solely on the ground that members of the colored race appear therein", (3) that in refusing to approve the picture for exhibition it was not supported by any fact and was "illegal, capricious and arbitrary", and "contravenes any authority purportedly delegated to or vested in said Boards", and hence was in derogation of the "due process", and "equal protection of the laws", as guaranteed by the constitution of Tennessee and of the United States.

* * *

The petition sets forth in detail the several ordinances of the city and the resolutions by the Quarterly Court of Shelby County, conferring authority upon the Board, and alleges that no authority is given said Board to ban any picture from publication on account of race or color; that its authority, if any, extends only to censorship of pictures which are "immoral, lewd or lascivious", and that the picture, "Curley", in no wise falls under the ban of the statute or city ordinances.

The letter from the Board to United Artists is claimed to constitute all of the proceedings before the Board with respect to the motion picture "Curley".

* * *

***553** The trial judge sustained the defendants' motion and dismissed the petition, principally upon the grounds (1) that the statutes and ordinances complained of "are limited in their scope and are applicable only to local exhibitors," ...[and] (3) that the action of the Board of Censors, consisting of the letter addressed to United Artists was "advisory only" and was coram non judice and did not present a justiciable controversy.

The trial court declined to allow the film to be exhibited before him, to which action an exception was taken. The case was heard and disposed of as under the common law writ of certiorari.

The assignments of error (eleven in number) need not be stated in detail. The determinative questions may be stated, under the following sub-heads, as they appear on the petitioners' brief, the contention being made (1) "Censorship of Talking Motion Pictures Is Unconstitutional Per Se", (2) "Action of Board of Censors in Particular Case Is Illegal and Unconstitutional Even Though Censorship Is Not Unconstitutional Per Se" * * *

Able counsel for the appellants have cited many cases in which the courts have dealt with the propositions relating to freedom of speech and of the press. We are in no wise in disagreement with the appellants as to the fundamental principles announced in these decisions, and especially with the insistence that there is no authority in the law "To use race or color as the sole legal basis for censorship of talking-motion pictures". The trial judge pretermitted consideration of the constitutional guarantee of free speech because in his opinion the statutes and ordinances assailed by the appellants did not apply to them in that they were not exhibitors, and furthermore the letter of the Board to United Artists was only advisory and was coram non judice.

***554** We think the constitutionality of these statutes and ordinances cannot be questioned on the grounds of their abridgment of the right of "freedom of speech" except by someone who has the right to speak and is denied the privilege of speaking. The gist of the present action is that the statutes and ordinances herein assailed constitute an abridgment not of their right to speak but of the right of third persons to speak and who are not parties to this cause. In the instant case no exhibitors of moving pictures in Memphis, to whom these ordinances and statutes apply, are claiming that they are denied "freedom of speech" or the right to contract with the petitioners.

* * *

We think in all fairness to the Board of Censors the appellants should have asked for a final hearing and made a request for a reply as to whether their action was a finality before resorting to legal proceedings. We do not mean to say that this was a prerequisite to their right to institute this suit, but it indicates an indifference to whether it was final or "advisory".

***

***555** The Federal decision more directly in point is *Tad Screen Advertising v. Oklahoma Tax Com.*, 10 Cir., 126 F.2d 544, 548, in which the Court said: "It is well settled that a producer or manufacturer who ships motion picture films from one state to exhibitors in another state to be exhibited by the latter is engaged in interstate commerce. But when an article that has been transported in interstate commerce has arrived at a destination and is there held for use or disposal, it passes under the protection of state law and becomes subject to the taxing and police power of the state."

* * *

Our final conclusion is that "if * * * the power to accomplish by contract what is here claimed were to be upheld, all lines of demarcation between national and state authority would become obliterated". [233 U.S. 16, 34 S.Ct. 580.] This was the statement

***556** by Chief Justice White in Browning v. City of Waycross, supra, and it is equally true in the instant case.

Under the admitted facts of this case, and the authorities cited, the appellants are subject to Code Section 4128, and not having complied with its provisions the suit is not maintainable in the Courts of Tennessee

* * *

All assignments of error are overruled and the judgment of the trial court is affirmed.

All concur.

Memphis Movie Censor Accused Of Illegality In Banning Film

KNOXVILLE, Tenn., Oct. 4 (U.P.)—The Memphis Board of Censors, headed by white-haired Lloyd T. Binford, was accused of unconstitutionally banning a movie showing Negro and white children in school together when "Our Gang" comedies played there for years.

Counsel for Hal Roach Studios, producers of the picture, "Curley," which was banned in Memphis in 1947, laid the charge before the Tennessee Supreme Court. Roach and United Artists Corp., the distributors, appealed from a lower court ruling upholding the Memphis Board's action.

Atty. Hamilton Little told the black-robed justices that "Curley" is the same type family comedy as the "Our Gang" movies, whose standing cast includes Negro and white children playing together.

"Curley" he described as a film in which an attractive young teacher gains the affections of her pupils through her athletic prowess.

Binford forbade the showing of "Curley" in Memphis because he said it violates Southern segregation laws.

The courts, Little said, have held that censorship of any kind may not be based on race or religion. He acknowledged, however, that the plaintiffs were proceeding on the assumption that Southern segregation laws are valid, but said there is no law preventing anyone from "protesting against an idea. One should have the right. . . to disseminate the expression of ideas," he asserted.

Little criticized Circuit Judge Floyd Henderson who dismissed the plaintiff's previous petition for a writ of certiorari in January, 1948, ruling that both complainants are out-of-state corporations and not local Memphis exhibitors.

As such, Henderson ruled, they had no controversy against the board's action.

Little said the Circuit Court refused even to witness a showing of the movie because it was not "concerned with the soundness of the reasons assigned" by the censorship board.

The Anniston Star, October 4, 1949

RD-DR CORPORATION et al. v. SMITH et al.

183 F.2d 562 (1950)
United States Court of Appeals Fifth Circuit
Decided July 14, 1950

***562** HUTCHESON, Chief Judge

Plaintiffs, two corporations engaged, one in the business of producing, the other in the business of distributing, motion pictures, brought this suit to restrain the enforcement of the provisions of the code and censorship ordinance of the City of Atlanta, and for a judgment declaring its provisions unconstitutional and void.

The claim was not narrowly based upon the particular terms of the particular ordinance, the particular manner of its enforcement, or the particular motion picture subjected to censorship. It was based broadly upon the claim that, under the due process clause of the Fourteenth Amendment, as extended in recent decisions of the Supreme Court to include freedom of speech, of the press and of assembly,[1] "motion pictures are a medium of communication, entitled as part of the press," to complete freedom and protection from censorship by any state or political subdivision.

Defendants moved to dismiss the complaint on the authority of *Mutual Film Corp. v. Ohio Indemnity Co.*, 236 U.S. 230, 35 S.Ct. 387, 59 L.Ed. 552, holding that "the exhibition of moving pictures is a ***563** business pure and simple, originated and conducted for profit like other spectacles and not to be regarded as the press of the country, or as organs of public opinion within the constitutional meaning of freedom of speech and publication". Their motion was sustained, the complaint was dismissed, and plaintiffs have appealed.

Here they admit that the judgment finds support in the cited case and that unless it is disregarded by us as no longer authoritative, the judgment must be affirmed. They urge upon us, however, that in the present state of the decisions expanding "the first amendment rights as limitations upon the states and advancing them to a preferred position in our constitutional scheme", it must be taken for granted by us that, given an opportunity to do so, at least a majority of the Supreme Court, as now constituted, will overrule it, and we should, therefore, give it the anticipatory coup de grace.

Proceeding on the apparent assumption that this court is, or ought to be, in agreement with appellant's view that the decision was, and is, erroneous, and that it, therefore, ought to, and will be, overruled, appellants' arguments tend to beg the question, fall short in convincing exposition.

Considered each by itself and as a whole, the bits of evidence relied on by appellants to support their claim that the Supreme Court is prepared, by extending the 14th Amendment to include motion pictures, to nationalize the motion picture industry and thus remove it from state and local control, fall far short of doing so. Indeed, if, as appellants seem to contend, we must decide this appeal, not by determining for ourselves whether the *Mutual Film* case was correctly decided and, therefore, is still the law, but by shrewd guessing whether it will be able to muster a majority in the Supreme Court this would not avail them. For we think it plain that if anything can be said to have clearly emerged from the struggle to extend the Fourteenth Amendment as an instrument of nationalism by striking down all state regulatory power, it is, that whatever individual judges may say in dissent, the court, as now constituted, will not overrule, or in any manner depart from, the holding in the *Mutual Film Corporation* case but will fully reaffirm it.

* * *

***565** We cannot agree with appellants that it is any part of our duty to consult crystal ball gazers or diviners or to do the gazing and divining for ourselves in order to base a decision on a prophesy. Our duty is in accordance with the long settled and still controlling principles of judicial decision, despite vigorously announced views of individual judges to the contrary, to determine not how, if we were legislators we would write the law, but how, in accordance with the principles governing judicial decision, including Stare Decisis, and the adjudicated cases, which make up the law, it must be written.

Coming then to the decision of this case, in that spirit, and guided by those principles, we are in no doubt that the law was correctly laid down in the opinion under attack and that the views there expressed ought not to be receded from.

Further, while we are prepared to concede to appellants that one or more of the judges may be found to be in agreement with them, we find nothing in the stream of tendency in the opinions of courts of last resort, state and federal, taken singly and as a whole, which at all supports the view broadly announced here, that the Fourteenth Amendment paralyzes all state supervisory control of moving picture exhibitions.

We particularly disagree with, and dissent from, the view they thus in substance advance: that moving pictures have now emerged from the business of amusement into instruments for the propagation of ideas and, therefore, like newspapers, freedom of assembly, freedom of speech, must be regarded as within the protection of the Fourteenth Amendment; that censorship of moving pictures by states or local communities is contrary to the new enlightenment and the trend of the new national opinion; and that the Mutual Film decision, standing in the way is now antiquated and tottering to its fall, and should be decently and finally interred.

* * *

To put it still another way, it would seem that when appellants assert that a controlling precedent like this one should be overruled, on the ground that what the predecessors of the present court decided was not the Constitution but merely the gloss they had put on it, the question should be seriously put to them. "Who is putting the gloss on the Constitution? Is it the earlier judges who concluded, in the *Mutual Film* case, that exhibitions and spectacles like moving pictures are not protected by the Fourteenth Amendment from state supervisory control, or is it the present appellants who assert that they are?

To quote from Mr. Morrison's fine article, note 2, supra: "No matter how desirable the results might be, it is of the essence of our system that the judges must

***566** stay within the bounds of their constitutional power. Nothing is more fundamental — even the Bill of Rights. To depart from this fundamental is, in Mr. Justice Black's own words, 'to frustrate the great design of a written constitution.'"

The judgment below was right. It is affirmed.

Memphis Bans Movie

Memphis, Tenn., Aug. 20.—Th Memphis censor board today ban ned "Lost Boundaries," a movi dealing with racial problems.

" 'Lost Boundaries' couldn't pla in the South," censor board chair man Lloyd T. Binson said. "I deals with social equality betwee whites and negroes in a way that i not practiced in the South. W banned it for that reason."

'Lost Boundaries' Gets Atlanta Ban

Presentation of "Lost Boundaries" has been banned in Atlanta, Ga., by the city's movie censor.

In banning Louis deRochemont's movie, Miss Christine Smith, the censor, said she had "no particular reason."

According to the Associated Press, Miss Smith said she had the power to ban the movie if she thought it detrimental to "good order, good health or good morals."

"Memphis Bans Movie" in *The Gaffney Ledger,* August 25, 1949; "*Lost Boundaries* Gets Atlanta Ban" in *The Portsmouth Herald,* August, 20 1949.

GELLING v. STATE

247 S.W.2d 95 (1952)
Court of Criminal Appeals of Texas
Decided January 30, 1952.

***95** BEAUCHAMP, Judge.

* * * The facts of the case are without dispute. The name and character of the picture exhibited are immaterial. The objection which was lodged against the picture by the Board of Censors is immaterial to the discussion of this case, because it is not claimed that they abused the discretion lodged in them, but the contention is made that the ordinance was invalid and the reasons relied upon are the basis for this opinion.

* * * Much of the discussion in appellant's brief has been along the line of contentions made in other cases which have been before several courts in recent years

***96** and may be denominated as an eloquent plea that this court overrule the holding of the Supreme Court of the United States in *Mutual Film Corp v. Industrial Commission of Ohio*, 236 U.S. 230, 35 S.Ct. 387, 59 L. Ed. 552, decided in 1915. After careful consideration of this case and many of the cases which have followed and referred to it, particularly those cited by appellant, we have come to the conclusion that the most logical and positively correct expression is found in the case of *RD-DR Corporation et al. v. Smith* et al., 5 Cir., 183 F.2d 562, opinion by Chief Judge Hutcheson of the U.S. Court of Appeals, New Orleans. Having so concluded, we content ourselves with following that opinion after first stating some of the contentions made in appellant's brief.

The brief reviews the evidence of appellant and calls attention to his statement that the picture involved had been reviewed by both Life and Look, magazines that are sold and distributed in Marshall. Apparently the position is that since this was done there is no point in barring the picture, regardless of what it may be. The position is taken, further, that the motion picture to the extent that it partakes of the features of the magazines in the field of entertainment and education, is entitled to the same protection as the press and entitled to the same freedom. On the subject and in behalf of this position, I doubt if we could find or that there may be presented a stronger argument than that in appellant's brief. Most of it has been discussed and referred to in other reported cases, but there is one feature that especially attracts our attention as being new and different. The extent of the investment in the show houses and in equipment and fixtures approximate $100,000, which is a substantial investment in property and building. The thought is that this investment indicates a permanence and removes a fear discoverable in the *Mutual* case as to the responsibility of the exhibitors. An examination of the *Mutual* case does not impress us that the court was moved to any degree by such a fear. Even in 1915 the position of the motion picture seems to have been well established. Further answer to the interesting discussion on this subject is not called for.

Neither do we find in the reported cases "that there is an indication" in recent Supreme Court decisions "that there has been a shift of emphasis in the court's attitudes." The opinions of the several Federal District Courts and Appellate Courts speaking on the subject have not pointed out a discoverable change of sentiment helpful to appellant in the question. We pretermit discussion of the several cases placed in appellant's brief and confine our thinking, chiefly, to Judge Hutcheson's opinion in *RD-DR Corporation et al. v. Smith et al.*, supra.

The question discussed in that opinion is based on what appears to be the same contention made by appellant in his brief in the instant case, that is that the *Mutual Film Corporation v. Industrial Commission of Ohio*, supra, has either been superseded or that the drift of the opinions of the Supreme Court has been so far from the position taken by that court in 1915 that we cannot rely upon the opinion in that case as controlling in the case now before us. As we view the brief it is conceded by appellant that the *Mutual* case is in point and decisive and that it sustains the position of the state in the instant case. Such would be our conclusion even in the absence of any such admission. However much we have been enlightened by the brief, we are not in accord with the conclusions which it asks us to reach. The Supreme Court of the United States may extend the Fourteenth Amendment to include motion pictures, and thus nationalize the industry and remove it from state and municipal control, but we are not expecting this until it has done so, and certainly will not yield that important function on behalf of the state and the municipality until we are forced to do it. We respect the decisions of that great court to the extent that we do not feel that we should speculate on a change of sentiment and a reversal of its sound opinions of so long standing. To engage in guessing what the court is going to do next is not to follow its decisions as contemplated

***97** by the oath which the members of this court take. We do not hesitate to comply with that oath when the decisions of that court have been given. We are firmly entrenched in our position that we should not depart from its decisions even if we were faced with uncertainties, a fact we do not admit. We find that the Supreme Court has frequently had opportunity to reconsider its holding in the *Mutual* case and that it has consistently refrained from doing so.

As stated by Judge Hutcheson in the opinion referred to, we see no useful purpose in reviewing the several attacks which have been made and which have failed to secure any modification of the holding in the *Mutual* case. We think the opinion was an expression of the law, a correct interpretation of the Fourteenth Amendment as applied to the matter before the court at that time, and we find no reasonable ground for a change of the application even at this distant day. We cannot concede that the motion picture industry has emerged from the business of amusement and become propagators of ideas entitling it to freedom of speech. If in fact circumstances have developed surrounding the industry whereby television can bring to the youth of our cities, and even of rural areas, matters which are improper and even though magazines of a type are circulated through the U.S. Mails which present ideas derogatory to the proper development of good citizens, yet we cannot concede that this has divested the municipal authorities of a right to regulate such subjects. If some are exposed to evil, if evil it be, there is within such fact no argument that other and all evil should be strewn in the path of our youth. The desire of a great industry to reap greater fruits from its operations should not be indulged at the expense of Christian character, upon which America must rely for its future existence. Every boy and every girl reaching manhood or womanhood is, to an extent, the product of the community from which he comes. If the citizens of that community are divested of all power to surround them with wholesome entertainment and character building education then their product will go forth weak indeed. If the community surrenders its power voluntarily, if the state does, then we may expect our Federal Government to move into fields with which it should not be encumbered and in which it cannot best serve. Our loyalty to our government is based on an appreciation for its efficiency. We cherish the history of a Federal Government which has been based on a constitution as solid as the rocks and whose constancy is not shifted by the changing winds. It is the duty of this court, and of all courts, to follow the mandates and stay within the powers of our constitutional provisions. This is fundamental. To speculate on its meaning, to predict a change in the attitudes of the court toward it, is contrary to our ever thinking...The judgment of the trial court is affirmed.

'Pinky' Banned Again!

BIRMINGHAM, Ala. — Determined to keep its reputation of being one of the South's worst spots insofar as political administration is concerned with race relations, Birmingham Friday officially banned the motion picture "Pinky."

20th Century-Fox Wins Battle to Show Uncut Production of 'Pinky'

WASHINGTON, D. C.—The Supreme Court's decision this week that the Twentieth Century-Fox film, "Pinky," could not be censored on the basis of its message opens the road for the film to be shown in communities whose censorship boards have banned it.

Spyros P. Skouras, president of Twentieth Century-Fox, made the following statement: "We are naturally elated over the Court's decision in again upholding freedom of expression as evidenced in Twentieth Century-Fox' production of 'Pinky.'

"We were certain that the industry's right to examine in the form of entertainment social customs and the relations between groups would be upheld.

"This opinion is shared by the majority of American audiences who have thus far attended showings of 'Pinky' throughout the United States in numbers far exceeding 25 million."

Starring Jeanne Crain and Ethel Waters, the film tells the problems of a light-skinned colored girl who "passes" while away from her home in the South.

"*Pinky* Banned Again!" in *The Pittsburgh Courier,* February 4, 1950; "20th Century-Fox Wins Battle," in *The Pittsburgh Courier,* June 14, 1952.

7

The *Miracle* Decision

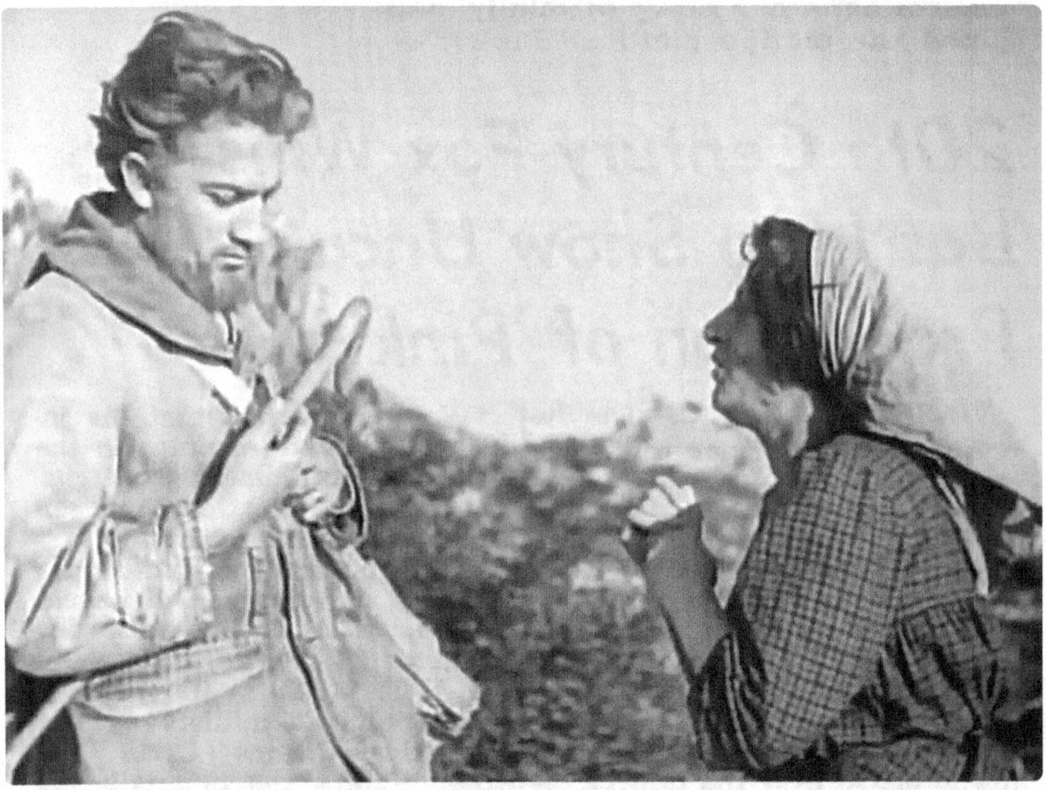

In 1952, *The New York Times* announced "Freedom of the Screen." The U.S. Supreme Court reversed *Burstyn v. Wilson*, and the *Miracle* decision finally brought motion pictures within the protections of the First Amendment and free expression. But it was not the first time the paper used the headline. Twenty years earlier the *Times* had printed that same headline.

In a short article buried on page 14, *The New York Times* covered the story of Chicago Mayor William Emmett Dever's desire to see a boxing film, heavyweight champ Jack Dempsey versus

Tommy Gibbons. "Mayor Dever of Chicago said the other day that if the pictures of the fight between Mr. Dempsey and Mr. Gibbons at Shelby could be exhibited lawfully in the city he would like to go and see them." ("Freedom of the Screen," in *The New York Times*, September 5, 1923). Two days later the *New York Clipper* reported "Chicago Judge Compares Picture Censorship with 'Freedom of Press.'" The fistic film unspooled, a less-than-thrilling 15-round grudge match that Dempsey won by unanimous decision.

But Harry M. Fisher, the circuit court judge for Cook County who cleared the Dempsey-Gibbons picture, was idealistic about the movies. He wrote, "The time will come when…censorship will be a thing of the past. The [film] industry presents far too great and wonderful a vista, educationally and from a standpoint of wholesome entertainment." (*New York Clipper*, September 7, 1923). But the Mid-western jurist also had a realistic understanding of the era, stating that Americans were as addicted to censorship as the ancient Romans. He cleared the way for Mayor to see the fistic film but the freedom of the screen headline was two decades premature.

In the time between Judge Fisher's decision and the Supreme Court's *Miracle* ruling, filmmakers continued to test the boundaries of film licensing laws.

Arthur Mayer was born and raised in Demopolis, AL, deep in the heart of film censorship territory. By the mid-1930s he formed a partnership with a Polish immigrant named Joseph Burstyn to import provocative international pictures to U.S. theaters. They first ran into trouble with a French film entitled *Remous* (1935). Retitled *Whirlpool* aka *Whirlpool of Desire* for American audiences, the film promised sophisticated and titillating thrills. *Remous* was banned in New York State in a case entitled *In the Matter of Arthur Mayer and Joseph Burstyn v. James Byrne*, 256 App. Div. 431 (N.Y. 1939). The set back did not dissuade these avid cineastes. Mayer and Burstyn continued to deliver interesting art films to American theaters, including Renoir's *The Lower Depths* (1936), Gance's *Louise* (1939), and Rossellini's *Rome, Open City* (1946). In 1948 Mayer and Burstyn dissolved their partnership.

Looking for his next project, Burstyn found a Italian omnibus film that caught his eye. *L'Amore* originally played with two sections: the first, *The Human Voice* (1930), was directed by Jean Cocteau and the second, *The Miracle*, directed by Roberto Rossellini. Burstyn replaced Genet's segment with two featurettes, Marcel Pagnol's *Jofroi* (1936) and Jean Renoir's *A Day in the Country* (1936). He retitled the multi-part picture *Ways of Love*.

Burstyn could never have guessed that his sensuous art film would change the course of

American cinema. *Ways of Love* divided audiences. The New York Film Critics Circle voted the picture Best Foreign Language Film for the year. The Legion of Decency condemned the film. From the pulpit of St. Patrick's Cathedral, Cardinal Francis Spellman urged all Catholics to boycott the film ("Spellman Urges Miracle Boycott," in *The New York Times,* January 8, 1951), while Bosley Crowther, the *New York Times* lead film reviewer championed the picture (Bosley Crowther, "A Crucial Issue," in *The New York Times*, February 25, 1951).

New York's Regents banned *The Miracle* and Burstyn enlisted a lawyer named Ephraim London. It was London's first major First Amendment case. The attorney argued all the way to the Supreme Court, and in a surprising turn of events, prevailed over the censors. London managed to demonstrate that motion pictures could be communicative expression and speech such that the medium should be recognized and protected under the First Amendment. Regulation was not entirely banished; film censorship could still exist, but a ban based on sacrilege alone could not stand. There was more work to be done to realize true freedom of the screen, but Ephraim London managed to take the first step in the journey.

For London, this was the beginning of the story. The attorney became one of America's foremost First Amendment advocates. He returned to the Supreme Court to clear *Lady Chatterley's Lover* in *Kingsley International Pictures v. Regents of New York* and *Les amants* in *Jacobellis v. Ohio.* Before the 2nd Circuit London continued to champion European art films in *United States v. One Carton Positive Motion Picture Film Entitled 491* and *United States v. 35mm Motion Picture Film Entitled Language of Love*. In the 5th circuit he represented *Empire Pictures Distributing Company v. City of Fort Worth* on behalf of *...And God Created Women.* In Tennessee London fought for a film entitled *Women of the World* in *Embassy Pictures Corp. v. Hudson.* Ephraim London's work would continue paving the way for broader rights and free expression.

But for Joseph Burstyn, *The Miracle* was a swan song. The distributor discovered one more important film talent, picking up rights to Stanley Kubrick's first feature film, *Fear and Desire* (1953). But 18 months after his victory with *The Miracle*, Burstyn boarded a plane bound for Paris. He was heading to the City of Lights to scout for his next foreign film, but died en route ("Burstyn, Film Man, Dies on Sea Flight," in *The New York Times*, November 30, 1953). Burstyn's former partner, Arthur Mayer, continued to push for film freedom as a principal figure at Kingsley International Pictures, a distributor that figures prominently in the next chapter of film and the First Amendment.

JOSEPH BURSTYN, INC. v. WILSON

343 U.S. 495 (1952)

Supreme Court of United States

Argued April 24, 1952

Decided May 26, 1952

Appeal form the Court of Appeals of New York

***497** MR. JUSTICE CLARK delivered the opinion of the Court.

The issue here is the constitutionality, under the First and Fourteenth Amendments, of a New York statute which permits the banning of motion picture films on the ground that they are "sacrilegious." That statute makes it unlawful

"to exhibit, or to sell, lease or lend for exhibition at any place of amusement for pay or in connection with any business in the state of New York, any motion picture film or reel [with specified exceptions not relevant here], unless there is at the time in full force and effect a valid license or permit therefor of the education department. . . . [Footnote 1]"

The statute further provides:

"The director of the [motion picture] division [of the education department] or, when authorized by the regents, the officers of a local office or bureau shall cause to be promptly examined every motion picture film submitted to them as herein required, and unless such film or a part thereof is obscene, indecent, immoral, inhuman, sacrilegious, or is of such a character that its exhibition would tend to corrupt morals or incite to crime, shall issue a license therefor. If such director or, when so authorized, such officer shall not license any film submitted, he shall furnish to the applicant therefor a written report of the reasons for his refusal and a description of each rejected part of a film not rejected in toto. [Footnote 2]"

Appellant is a corporation engaged in the business of distributing motion pictures. It owns the exclusive rights to distribute throughout the United States a film produced in Italy entitled "The Miracle." On November 30, 1950, after having examined the picture, the motion picture division of the New York education department,

***498** acting under the statute quoted above, issued to appellant a license authorizing exhibition of "The Miracle," with English subtitles, as one part of a trilogy called "Ways of Love." [Footnote 3] Thereafter, for a period of approximately eight weeks, "Ways of Love" was exhibited publicly in a motion picture theater in New York City under an agreement between appellant and the owner of the theater whereby appellant received a stated percentage of the admission price.

During this period, the New York State Board of Regents, which by statute is made the head of the education department, [Footnote 4] received "hundreds of letters, telegrams, post cards, affidavits and other communications" both protesting against and defending the public exhibition of "The Miracle." [Footnote 5] The Chancellor of the Board of Regents requested three members of the Board to view the picture and to make a report to the entire Board. After viewing the film, this committee reported to the Board that, in its opinion, there was basis for the claim that the picture was "sacrilegious." Thereafter, on January 19, 1951, the Regents directed appellant to show cause, at a hearing to be held on January 30, why its license to show "The Miracle" should not be rescinded on that ground. Appellant appeared at this hearing, which was conducted by the same three-member committee of the Regents which had previously viewed the picture, and challenged the jurisdiction of the committee and of the Regents to proceed with the case. With the consent of the committee, various interested persons and

***499** organizations submitted to it briefs and exhibits bearing upon the merits of the picture and upon the constitutional and statutory questions involved. On February 16, 1951, the Regents, after viewing "The Miracle," determined that it was "sacrilegious," and for that reason ordered the Commissioner of Education to rescind appellant's license to exhibit the picture. The Commissioner did so.

Appellant brought the present action in the New York courts to review the determination of the Regents. [Footnote 6] Among the claims advanced by appellant were (1) that the statute violates the Fourteenth Amendment as a prior restraint upon freedom of speech and of the press; (2) that it is invalid under the same Amendment as a violation of the guaranty of separate church and state and as a prohibition of the free exercise of religion; and, (3) that the term "sacrilegious" is so vague and indefinite as to offend due process. The Appellate Division rejected all of appellant's contentions and upheld the Regents' determination. 278 App.Div. 253, 104 N.Y.S.2d 740. On appeal the New York Court of Appeals, two judges dissenting, affirmed the order of the Appellate Division. 303 N.Y. 242, 101 N.E.2d 665. The case is here on appeal. 28 U.S.C. § 1257(2).

As we view the case, we need consider only appellant's contention that the New York statute is an unconstitutional abridgment of free speech and a free press. In *Mutual Film Corp. v. Industrial Comm'n*, 236 U.S. 230 (1915), a distributor of motion pictures sought to enjoin the enforcement of an Ohio statute which required the prior approval of a board of censors before any motion

***500** picture could be publicly exhibited in the state, and which directed the board to approve only such films as it adjudged to be "of a moral, educational or amusing and harmless character." The statute was assailed in part as an unconstitutional abridgment of the freedom of the press guaranteed by the First and Fourteenth Amendments. The District Court rejected this contention, stating that the first eight Amendments were not a restriction on state action. 215 F. 138, 141 (D.C.N.D. Ohio 1914). On appeal to this Court, plaintiff in its brief abandoned this claim and contended merely that the statute in question violated the freedom of speech and publication guaranteed by the Constitution of Ohio. In affirming the decree of the District Court denying injunctive relief, this Court stated:

"It cannot be put out of view that the exhibition of moving pictures is a business pure and simple, originated and conducted for profit, like other spectacles, not to be regarded, nor intended to be regarded by the Ohio constitution, we think, as part of the press of the country or as organs of public opinion. [Footnote 7]"

In a series of decisions beginning with *Gitlow v. New York*, 268 U.S. 652 (1925), this Court held that the liberty of speech and of the press which the First Amendment guarantees against abridgment by the federal government is within the liberty safeguarded by the Due Process Clause of the Fourteenth Amendment from invasion by state action. [Footnote 8] That principle has been

***501** followed and reaffirmed to the present day. Since this series of decisions came after the *Mutual* decision, the present case is the first to present squarely to us the question whether motion pictures are within the ambit of protection which the First Amendment, through the Fourteenth, secures to any form of "speech" or "the press." [Footnote 9]

It cannot be doubted that motion pictures are a significant medium for the communication of ideas. They may affect public attitudes and behavior in a variety of ways, ranging from direct espousal of a political or social doctrine to the subtle shaping of thought which characterizes all artistic expression. [Footnote 10] The importance of motion pictures as an organ of public opinion is not lessened by the fact that they are designed to entertain as well as to inform. As was said in *Winters v. New York*, 333 U.S. 507, 333 U.S. 510 (1948):

"The line between the informing and the entertaining is too elusive for the protection of that basic right [a free press]. Everyone is familiar with instances of propaganda through fiction. What is one man's amusement, teaches another's doctrine."

It is urged that motion pictures do not fall within the First Amendment's aegis because their production, distribution, and exhibition is a large-scale business conducted for private profit. We cannot agree. That books, newspapers, and magazines are published and sold for profit does not prevent them from being a form of expression whose liberty is safeguarded by the First Amendment. [Footnote 11]

***502** We fail to see why operation for profit should have any different effect in the case of motion pictures.

It is further urged that motion pictures possess a greater capacity for evil, particularly among the youth of a community, than other modes of expression. Even if one were to accept this hypothesis, it does not follow that motion pictures should be disqualified from First Amendment protection. If there be capacity for evil it may be relevant in determining the permissible scope of community control, but it does not authorize substantially unbridled censorship such as we have here.

For the foregoing reasons, we conclude that expression by means of motion pictures is included within the free speech and free press guaranty of the First and Fourteenth Amendments. To the extent that language in the opinion in *Mutual Film Corp. v. Industrial Comm'n*, supra, is out of harmony with the views here set forth, we no longer adhere to it. [Footnote 12]

To hold that liberty of expression by means of motion pictures is guaranteed by the First and Fourteenth Amendments, however, is not the end of our problem. It does not follow that the Constitution requires absolute freedom to exhibit every motion picture of every kind at all times and all places. That much is evident from the series of decisions of this Court with respect to other

***503** media of communication of ideas. [Footnote 13] Nor does it follow that motion pictures are necessarily subject to the precise rules governing any other particular method of expression. Each method tends to present its own peculiar problems. But the basic principles of freedom of speech and the press, like the First Amendment's command, do not vary. Those principles, as they have frequently been enunciated by this Court, make freedom of expression the rule. There is no justification in this case for making an exception to that rule.

The statute involved here does not seek to punish, as a past offense, speech or writing falling within the permissible scope of subsequent punishment. On the contrary, New York requires that permission to communicate ideas be obtained in advance from state officials who judge the content of the words and pictures sought to be communicated. This Court recognized many years ago that such a previous restraint is a form of infringement upon freedom of expression to be especially condemned. *Near v. Minnesota ex rel. Olson*, 283 U.S. 697 (1931). The Court there recounted the history which indicates that a major purpose of the First Amendment guaranty of a free press was to prevent prior restraints upon publication, although it was carefully pointed out that the liberty of the press is not limited to that protection. [Footnote 14] It was further stated that "the protection even as to previous restraint is not absolutely unlimited. But the limitation has been recognized only

***504** in exceptional cases." Id. at 283 U.S. 716. In the light of the First Amendment's history and of the Near decision, the State has a heavy burden to demonstrate that the limitation challenged here presents such an exceptional case.

New York's highest court says there is "nothing mysterious" about the statutory provision applied in this case:

"It is simply this: that no religion, as that word is understood by the ordinary, reasonable person, shall be treated with contempt, mockery, scorn and ridicule. . . . [Footnote 15]"

This is far from the kind of narrow exception to freedom of expression which a state may carve out to satisfy the adverse demands of other interests of society. [Footnote 16] In seeking to apply the broad and all-inclusive definition of "sacrilegious" given by the New York courts, the censor is set adrift upon a boundless sea amid a myriad of conflicting currents of religious views, with no

***505** charts but those provided by the most vocal and powerful orthodoxies. New York cannot vest such unlimited restraining control over motion pictures in a censor. Cf. *Kunz v. New York*, 340 U.S. 290 (1951). [Footnote 17] Under such a standard the most careful and tolerant censor would find it virtually impossible to avoid favoring one religion over another, and he would be subject to an inevitable tendency to ban the expression of unpopular sentiments sacred to a religious minority. Application of the "sacrilegious" test, in these or other respects, might raise substantial questions under the First Amendment's guaranty of separate church and state with freedom of worship for all. [Footnote 18] However, from the standpoint of freedom of speech and the press, it is enough to point out that the state has no legitimate interest in protecting any or all religions from views distasteful to them which is sufficient to justify prior restraints upon the expression of those views. It is not the business of government in our nation to suppress real or imagined attacks upon a particular religious doctrine, whether they appear in publications, speeches, or motion pictures. [Footnote 19]

Since the term "sacrilegious" is the sole standard under attack here, it is not necessary for us to decide, for example,

***506** whether a state may censor motion pictures under a clearly drawn statute designed and applied to prevent the showing of obscene films. That is a very different question from the one now before us. [Footnote 20] We hold only that, under the First and Fourteenth Amendments, a state may not ban a film on the basis of a censor's conclusion that it is "sacrilegious."

Reversed.

Footnotes

1. McKinney's N.Y. Laws, 1947, Education Law, § 129.

2. Id., § 122

3. The motion picture division had previously issued a license for exhibition of "The Miracle" without English subtitles, but the film was never shown under that license.

4. McKinney's N.Y.Laws, 1947, Education Law, § 101; see also N.Y.Const., Art. V, § 4.

5. Stipulation between appellant and appellee, R. 86.

6. The action was brought under Article 78 of the New York Civil Practice Act, Gilbert-Bliss N.Y.Civ.Prac., Vol. 6B, 1944, 1949 Supp., § 1283 et seq. See also McKinney's N.Y.Laws, 1947, Education Law, § 124.

7. 236 U.S., at 244, 244

8. *Gitlow v. New York*, 268 U.S. 652, 268 U.S. 666 (1925); *Stromberg v. California*, 283 U.S. 359, 283 U.S. 368 (1931); *Near v. Minnesota ex rel. Olson*, 283 U.S. 697, 283 U.S. 707 (1931); *Grosjean v. American Press Co.*, 297 U.S. 233, 297 U.S. 244 (1936); *De Jonge v. Oregon*, 299 U.S. 353, 299 U.S. 364 (1937); *Lovell v. Griffin*, 303 U.S. 444, 303 U.S. 450 (1938); *Schneider v . State*, 308 U.S. 147, 308 U.S. 160 (1939).

9. See *Lovell v. Griffin*, 303 U.S. 444, 303 U.S. 452 (1938).

10. See Inglis, *Freedom of the Movies* (1947), 20-24; Klapper, *The Effects of Mass Media* (1950), passim; Note, *Motion Pictures and the First Amendment*, 60 Yale L.J. 696, 70708 (1951), and sources cited therein.

11. See *Grosjean v. American Press Co.*, 297 U.S. 233 (1936); *Thomas v. Collins*, 323 U.S. 516, 323 U.S. 531 (1945).

12. See *United States v. Paramount Pictures, Inc.*, 334 U.S. 131, 334 U.S. 166 (1948): "We have no doubt that moving pictures, like newspapers and radio, arc included in the press whose freedom is guaranteed by the First Amendment."

It is not without significance that talking pictures were first produced in 1926, eleven years after the *Mutual* decision. Hampton, *A History of the Movies* (1931), 382-383.

13. E.g., *Feiner v. New York*, 340 U.S. 315 (1951); *Kovacs v. Cooper*, 336 U.S. 77 (1949); *Chaplinsky v. New Hampshire*, 315 U.S. 568(1942); *Cox v. New Hampshire*, 312 U.S. 569 (1941).

14. *Near v. Minnesota ex rel. Olson*, 283 U.S. 697, 283 U.S. 713-719 (1931); see also *Lovell v. Griffin*, 303 U.S. 444, 303 U.S. 451-452 (1938); *Grosjean v. American Press Co.*, 297 U.S. 233, 297 U.S. 245-250 (1936); *Patterson v. Colorado*, 205 U.S. 454, 205 U.S. 462 (1907).

15. 303 N.Y. 242, 258, 101 N.E.2d 665, 672. At another point, the Court of Appeals gave "sacrilegious" the following definition: "the act of violating or profaning anything sacred." Id. at 255, 101 N.E.2d at 670. The Court of Appeals also approved the Appellate Division's interpretation: "As the court below said of the statute in question, 'All it purports to do is to bar a visual caricature of religious beliefs held sacred by one sect or another. . . .'" Id. at 258, 101 N.E.2d at 672. Judge Fuld, dissenting, concluded from all the statements in the majority opinion that "the basic criterion appears to be whether the film treats a religious theme in such a manner as to offend the religious beliefs of any group of persons. If the film does have that effect, and it is 'offered as a form of entertainment,' it apparently falls within the statutory ban regardless of the sincerity and good faith of the producer of the film, no matter how temperate the treatment of the theme, and no matter how unlikely a public disturbance or breach of the peace. The drastic nature of such a ban is highlighted by the fact that the film in question makes no direct attack on, or criticism of, any religious dogma or principle, and it is not claimed to be obscene, scurrilous, intemperate or abusive." Id. at 271-272, 101 N.E.2d at 680.

16. Cf. *Thornhill v. Alabama*, 310 U.S. 88, 310 U.S. 97 (1940); *Stromberg v. California*, 283 U.S. 359, 283 U.S. 369-370 (1931).

17. Cf. *Niemotko v. Maryland,* 340 U.S. 268 (1951); *Saia v. New York*, 334 U.S. 558 (1948); *Largent v. Texas*, 318 U.S. 418 (1943); *Lovell v. Griffin*, 303 U.S. 444 (1938).

18. See *Cantwell v. Connecticut*, 310 U.S. 296 (1940).

19. See the following statement by Mr. Justice Roberts, speaking for a unanimous Court in *Cantwell v. Connecticut*, 310 U.S. 296, 310 U.S. 310 (1940): "In the realm of religious faith, and in that of political belief, sharp differences arise. In both fields, the tenets of one man may seem the rankest error to his neighbor. To persuade others to his own point of view, the pleader, as we know, at times, resorts to exaggeration, to vilification of men who have been, or are, prominent in church or state, and even to false statement. But the people of this nation have ordained in the light of history, that, in spite of the probability of excesses and abuses, these liberties are, in the long view, essential to enlightened opinion and right conduct on the part of the citizens of a democracy."

"The essential characteristic of these liberties is, that, under their shield, many types of life, character, opinion and belief can develop unmolested and unobstructed. Nowhere is this shield more necessary than in our own country, for a people composed of many races and of many creeds."

20. In the *Near* case, this Court stated that "the primary requirements of decency may be enforced against obscene publications." 283 U.S. 697, 283 U.S. 716. In *Chaplinsky v. New Hampshire*, 315 U.S. 568, 315 U.S. 571-572 (1942), Mr. Justice Murphy stated for a unanimous Court: "There are certain well defined and narrowly limited classes of speech, the prevention and punishment of which have never been thought to raise any Constitutional problem. These include the lewd and obscene, the profane, the libelous, and the insulting or 'fighting' words -- those which, by their very utterance, inflict injury or tend to incite an immediate breach of the peace."

But see *Kovacs v. Cooper*, 336 U.S. 77, 336 U.S. 82 (1949): "When ordinances undertake censorship of speech or religious practices before permitting their exercise, the Constitution forbids their enforcement."

MR. JUSTICE REED, concurring in the judgment of the Court.

Assuming that a state may establish a system for the licensing of motion pictures, an issue not foreclosed by the Court's opinion, our duty requires us to examine the facts of the refusal of a license in each case to determine

***507** whether the principles of the First Amendment have been honored. This film does not seem to me to be of a character that the First Amendment permits a state to exclude from public view.

MR. JUSTICE FRANKFURTER, whom MR. JUSTICE JACKSON joins, concurring in the judgment of the Court; MR. JUSTICE BURTON, having concurred in the opinion of the Court, also joins this opinion.

A practised hand has thus summarized the story of "The Miracle": [Footnote 2/1]

"A poor, simple-minded girl is tending a herd of goats on a mountainside one day when a bearded stranger passes. Suddenly it strikes her fancy that he is St. Joseph, her favorite saint, and that he has come to take her to heaven, where she will be happy and free. While she pleads with him to transport her, the stranger gently plies the girl with wine, and when she is in a state of tumult, he apparently ravishes her. (This incident in the story is only briefly and discreetly implied.)"

"The girl awakens later, finds the stranger gone, and climbs down from the mountain not knowing whether he was real or a dream. She meets an old priest who tells her that it is quite possible that she did see a saint, but a younger priest scoffs at the notion. 'Materialist,' the old priest says."

"There follows now a brief sequence -- intended to be symbolic, obviously -- in which the girl is reverently sitting with other villagers in church. Moved by a whim of appetite, she snitches an apple from the basket of a woman next to her. When she leaves the church, a cackling beggar tries to make her share

***508** the apple with him, but she chases him away, as by habit, and munches the fruit contentedly."

"Then, one day, while tending the village youngsters as their mothers work at the vines, the girl faints and the women discover that she is going to have a child. Frightened and bewildered, she suddenly murmurs, 'It is the grace of God,' and she runs to the church in great excitement, looks for the statue of St. Joseph, and then prostrates herself on the floor."

"Thereafter she meekly refuses to do any menial work, and the housewives humor her gently, but the young people are not so kind. In a scene of brutal torment, they first flatter and laughingly mock her, then they cruelly shove and hit her and clamp a basin as a halo on her head. Even abused by the beggars, the poor girl gathers together her pitiful rags and sadly departs from the village to live alone in a cave."

"When she feels her time coming upon her, she starts back towards the village. But then she sees the crowds in the streets; dark memories haunt her; so she turns towards a church on a high hill and instinctively struggles towards it, crying desperately to God. A goat is her sole companion. She drinks water dripping from a rock. And when she comes to the church and finds the door locked, the goat attracts her to a small side door. Inside the church, the poor girl braces herself for her labor pains. There is a dissolve, and when we next see her sad face, in close-up, it is full of a tender light. There is the cry of an unseen baby. The girl reaches towards it and murmurs, 'My son, My love, My flesh!'"

"The Miracle"--a film lasting forty minutes--was produced in Italy by Roberto Rossellini. Anna Magnani played the lead as the demented goat-tender. It was first shown at the Venice Film Festival in August, 1948,

***509** combined with another moving picture, "L'Umano Voce," into a diptych called "Amore." According to an affidavit from the Director of that Festival, if the motion picture had been "blasphemous," it would have been barred by the Festival Committee. In a review of the film in *L'Osservatore Romano,* the organ of the Vatican, its film critic, Piero Regnoli, wrote:

"Opinions may vary, and questions may arise--even serious ones--of a religious nature (not to be diminished by the fact that the woman portrayed is mad [because] the author who attributed madness to her is not mad). . . . [Footnote 2/2]"

While acknowledging that there were "passages of undoubted cinematic distinction," Regnoli criticized the film as being "on such a pretentiously cerebral plane that it reminds one of the early d'Annunzio." The Vatican newspaper's critic concluded: "we continue to believe in Rossellini's art, and we look forward to his next achievement." [Footnote 2/3] In October, 1948, a month after the Rome premiere of "The Miracle," the Vatican's censorship agency, the Catholic Cinematographic Centre, declared that the picture "constitutes in effect an abominable profanation from religious and moral viewpoints." [Footnote 2/4] By the Lateran agreements and the Italian Constitution, the Italian Government is bound to bar whatever may offend the Catholic religion.

However, the Catholic Cinematographic Centre did not invoke any governmental sanction thereby afforded. The Italian Government's censorship agency gave "The Miracle" the regular nulla osta clearance. The film was freely shown throughout Italy, but was not a great success. [Footnote 2/5] Italian movie critics divided in opinion. The critic for II Popolo, speaking for the Christian Democratic Party, the Catholic

***510** party, profusely praised the picture as a "beautiful thing, humanly felt, alive, true and without religious profanation as someone has said, because, in our opinion, the meaning of the characters is clear, and there is no possibility of misunderstanding." [Footnote 2/6] Regnoli again reviewed "The Miracle" for *L'Osservatore Romano*. [Footnote 2/7] After criticising the film for technical faults, he found "the most courageous and interesting passage of Rossellini's work" in contrasting portrayals in the film; he added: "Unfortunately, concerning morals, it is necessary to note some slight defects." He objected to its "carnality" and to the representation of illegitimate motherhood. But he did not suggest that the picture was "sacrilegious." The tone of Regnoli's critique was one of respect for Rossellini, "the illustrious Italian producer." [Footnote 2/8]

On March 2, 1949, "The Miracle" was licensed in New York State for showing without English subtitles. [Footnote 2/9] However, it was never exhibited until after a second license was issued on November 30, 1950, for the trilogy, "Ways of Love," combining "The Miracle" with two French films, Jean Renoir's "A Day in the Country" and Marcel Pagnol's "Jofroi." [Footnote 2/10] All had English subtitles. Both licenses

***511** were issued in the usual course after viewings of the picture by the Motion Picture Division of the New York State Education Department. The Division is directed by statute to "issue a license"

"unless [the] film or a part thereof is obscene, indecent, immoral, inhuman, sacrilegious, or is of such a character that its exhibition would tend to corrupt morals or incite to crime." N.Y. Education Law, § 122. The trilogy opened on December 12, 1950, at the Paris Theatre on 58th Street in Manhattan. It was promptly attacked as "a sacrilegious and blasphemous mockery of Christian religious truth" [Footnote 2/11] by the National Legion of Decency, a private Catholic organization for film censorship, whose objectives have intermittently been approved by various non-Catholic church and social groups since its formation in 1933. [Footnote 2/12] However, the National Board of Review (a non-industry lay organization devoted to raising the level of motion pictures by mobilizing public opinion, under the slogan "Selection Not Censorship") [Footnote 2/13] recommended the picture as "especially worth seeing." New York critics on the whole praised "The Miracle"; those who dispraised did not suggest sacrilege. [Footnote 2/14] On December 27, the critics selected the "Ways of Love" as the best foreign language

***512** film in 1950. [Footnote 2/15] Meanwhile, on December 23, Edward T. McCaffrey, Commissioner of Licenses for New York City, declared the film "officially and personally blasphemous" and ordered it withdrawn at the risk of suspension of the license to operate the Paris Theatre. [Footnote 2/16] A week later, the program was restored at the theatre upon the decision by the New York Supreme Court that the City

***513** License Commissioner had exceeded his authority in that he was without powers of movie censorship. [Footnote 2/17]

Upon the failure of the License Commissioner's effort to cut off showings of "The Miracle," the controversy took a new turn. On Sunday, January 7, 1951, a statement of His Eminence, Francis Cardinal Spellman, condemning the picture and calling on "all right-thinking citizens" to unite to tighten censorship laws, was read at all masses in St. Patrick's Cathedral. [Footnote 2/18]

The views of Cardinal Spellman aroused dissent among other devout Christians. Protestant clergymen, representing

***514** various denominations, after seeing the picture, found in it nothing "sacrilegious or immoral to the views held by Christian men and women," and, with a few exceptions, agreed that the film was "unquestionably one of unusual artistic merit." [Footnote 2/19]

In this estimate, some Catholic laymen concurred. [Footnote 2/20] Their opinion is represented by the comment by Otto L. Spaeth, Director of the American Federation of Arts and prominent in Catholic lay activities:

"At the outbreak of the controversy, I immediately arranged for a private showing of the film. I invited a group of Catholics, competent and respected for their writings on both religious and cultural subjects. The essential approval of the film was unanimous."

"There was indeed 'blasphemy' in the picture -- but it was the blasphemy of the villagers, who stopped at nothing, not even the mock singing of a

***515** hymn to the Virgin, in their brutal badgering of the tragic woman. The scathing indictment of their evil behavior, implicit in the film, was seemingly overlooked by its critics. [Footnote 2/21]"

William P. Clancy, a teacher at the University of Notre Dame, wrote in The Commonweal, the well known Catholic weekly, that "the film is not obviously blasphemous or obscene, either in its intention or execution." [Footnote 2/22] The Commonweal itself questioned the wisdom of transforming Church dogma which Catholics may obey as "a free act" into state-enforced censorship for all. [Footnote 2/23] Allen Tate, the well known Catholic poet and critic, wrote:

"The picture seems to me to be superior in acting and photography but inferior dramatically. . . . In the long run, what Cardinal Spellman will have succeeded in doing is insulting the intelligence and faith of American Catholics with the assumption that a second-rate motion picture could in any way undermine their morals or shake their faith. [Footnote 2/24]"

At the time "The Miracle" was filmed, all the persons having significant positions in the production -- producer, director, and cast -- were Catholics. Roberto Rossellini, who had Vatican approval in 1949 for filming a life of St. Francis, using in the cast members of the Franciscan

***516** Order, cabled Cardinal Spellman protesting against boycott of "The Miracle":

"In The Miracle men, are still without pity because they still have not come back to God, but God is already present in the faith, however confused, of that poor, persecuted woman, and since God is wherever a human being suffers and is misunderstood, The

Miracle occurs when at the birth of the child the poor, demented woman regains sanity in her maternal love. [Footnote 2/25]"

In view of the controversy thus aroused by the picture, the Chairman of the Board of Regents appointed a committee of three Board members to review the action of the Motion Picture Division in granting the two licenses. After viewing the picture on Jan. 15, 1951, the committee declared it "sacrilegious." The Board four days later issued an order to the licensees to show cause why the licenses should not be cancelled in that the picture was "sacrilegious." The Board of Regents rescinded the licenses on Feb. 16, 1951, saying that the "mockery or profaning of these beliefs that are sacred to any portion of our citizenship is abhorrent to the laws of this great State." On review the Appellate Division upheld the Board of Regents, holding that the banning of any motion picture "that may fairly be deemed sacrilegious to the adherents of any religious group ... is directly related to public peace and order," and is not a denial of religious freedom, and that there was "substantial evidence upon which the Regents could act." 278 App.Div. 253, 257, 258, 260, 104 N.Y.S.2d 740, 743, 744-745, 747.

The New York Court of Appeals, with one judge concurring in a separate opinion and two others dissenting,

***517** affirmed the order of the Appellate Division. 303 N.Y. 242, 101 N.E.2d 665. After concluding that the Board of Regents acted within its authority and that is determination was not "one that no reasonable mind could reach," id. at 250-255, 256-257, 101 N.E.2d 665, 667-671, the majority held, first, that "sacrilegious" was an adequately definite standard, quoting a definition from Funk & Wagnalls' Dictionary and referring to opinions in this Court that, in passing used the term "profane," which the New York court said was a synonym of "sacrilegious"; second, that the State's assurance

"that no religion . . . shall be treated with contempt, mockery, scorn and ridicule . . . by those engaged in selling entertainment by way of motion pictures"

does not violate the religious guarantee of the First Amendment, and third, that motion pictures are not entitled to the immunities from regulation enjoyed by the press, in view of the decision in *Mutual Film Corp. v. Ohio Industrial Comm'n*, 236 U.S. 230. Id. at 255-256 [argument of counsel -- omitted], 236 U.S. 258-260, 260 U.S. 260-262, 101 N.E.2d 670-674. The two dissenting judges, after dealing with a matter of local law not reviewable here, found that the standard "sacrilegious" is unconstitutionally vague, and, finally, that the constitutional guarantee of freedom of speech applied equally to motion pictures, and prevented this censorship. 303 N.Y. 242, 264, 101 N.E.2d 665, 675. Both State courts, as did this Court, viewed "The Miracle."

Arguments by the parties and in briefs amici invite us to pursue to their farthest reach the problems in which this case is involved. Positions are advanced so absolute and abstract that, in any event, they could not properly determine this controversy. See *Ashwander v. Tennessee Valley Authority*, 297 U.S. 288, 297 U.S. 341, 297 U.S. 346-348. We are asked to decide this case by choosing between two mutually exclusive alternatives: that motion pictures may be subjected to unrestricted censorship, or that they

***518** must be allowed to be shown under any circumstances. But only the tyranny of absolutes would rely on such alternatives to meet the problems generated by the need to accommodate the diverse interests affected by the motion pictures in compact modern communities. It would startle Madison and Jefferson and George Mason, could they adjust themselves to our day, to be told that the freedom of speech which they espoused in the Bill of Rights authorizes a showing of "The Miracle" from windows facing St. Patrick's Cathedral in the forenoon of Easter Sunday, [Footnote 2/26] just as it would startle them to be told that any picture, whatever its theme and its expression, could be barred from being commercially exhibited. The general principle of free speech, expressed in the First Amendment as to encroachments by Congress, and included as it is in the Fourteenth Amendment, binding on the States, must be placed in its historical and legal contexts. The Constitution, we cannot recall too often, is an organism, not merely a literary composition.

If the New York Court of Appeals had given "sacrilegious" the meaning it has had in Catholic thought since St. Thomas Aquinas formulated its scope, and had sustained a finding by the Board of Regents that "The Miracle" came within that scope, this Court would have to meet some of the broader questions regarding the relation to the motion picture industry of the guarantees of the First Amendment so far as reflected in the Fourteenth. But the New York court did not confine "sacrilegious" within such technical, Thomist limits, nor within any specific, or even approximately specified, limits. It may fairly be said that that court deemed "sacrilegious" a self-defining term, a word that carries a well known, settled meaning in the common speech of men.

***519** So far as the Court of Appeals sought to support its notion that "sacrilegious" has the necessary precision of meaning which the Due Process Clause enjoins for statutes regulating men's activities, it relied on this definition from Funk & Wagnalls' Dictionary: "The act of violating or profaning anything sacred." But this merely defines by turning an adjective into a noun and bringing in two new words equally undefined. It leaves wide open the question as to what persons, doctrines or things are "sacred." It sheds no light on what representations on the motion picture screen will constitute "profaning" those things which the State censors find to be "sacred."

To criticize or assail religious doctrine may wound to the quick those who are attached to the doctrine and profoundly cherish it. But to bar such pictorial discussion is to subject non-conformists to the rule of sects.

Even in *Mutual Film Corp. v. Ohio Industrial Comm'n*, 236 U.S. 230, it was deemed necessary to find that the terms "educational, moral, amusing or harmless" do not leave "decision to arbitrary judgment." Such general words were found to "get precision from the sense and experience of men." Id. at 236 U.S. 245, 236 U.S. 246. This cannot be said of "sacrilegious." If there is one thing that the history of religious conflicts shows, it is that the term "sacrilegious" -- if by that is implied offense to the deep convictions of members of different sects, which is what the Court of Appeals seems to mean so far as it means anything precisely -- does not gain "precision from the sense and experience of men."

The vast apparatus of indices and digests, which mirrors our law, affords no clue to a judicial definition of sacrilege. Not one case, barring the present, has been uncovered which considers the meaning of the term in any context. Nor has the practice under the New York law contributed light. The Motion Picture Division of the Education Department does not support with explanatory

*520 statements its action on any specific motion picture, which we are advised is itself not made public. Of the fifty-odd reported appeals to the Board of Regents from denials of licenses by the Division, only three concern the category "sacrilegious." [Footnote 2/27] In these cases, as in others under the Act, the Board's reported opinion confines itself to a bare finding that the film was or was not "sacrilegious," without so much as a description of the allegedly offensive matter, or even of the film as a whole to enlighten the inquirer. Well equipped law libraries are not niggardly in their reflection of "the sense and experience of men," but we must search elsewhere for any which gives to "sacrilege" its meaning.

Sacrilege, [Footnote 2/28] as a restricted ecclesiastical concept, has a long history. Naturally enough, religions have sought to protect their priests and anointed symbols from physical injury. [Footnote 2/29] But history demonstrates that the term is hopelessly vague when it goes beyond such ecclesiastical definiteness and is used at large as the basis for punishing deviation from doctrine.

Etymologically, "sacrilege" is limited to church-robbing: sacer, sacred, and legere, to steal or pick out. But we are

*521 told that "already in Cicero's time it had grown to include in popular speech any insult or injury to [sacred things]." [Footnote 2/30] "In primitive religions [sacrilege is] inclusive of almost every serious offence even in fields now regarded as merely social or political. . . ." [Footnote 2/31] The concept of "tabu" in primitive society is thus close to that of "sacrilege." [Footnote 2/32] And in

"the Theodosian Code the various crimes which are accounted sacrilege include -- apostasy, heresy, schism, Judaism, paganism, attempts against the immunity of churches and clergy or privileges of church courts, the desecration of sacraments, etc., and even Sunday. Along with these crimes against religion went treason to the emperor, offences against the laws, especially counterfeiting, defraudation in taxes, seizure of confiscated property, evil conduct of imperial officers, etc. [Footnote 2/33]"

During the Middle Ages the Church considerably delimited the application of the term. St. Thomas Aquinas classified the objects of "sacrilege" as persons places, and thing. [Footnote 2/34] The injuries which would constitute

*522 "sacrilege" received specific and detailed illustration. [Footnote 2/35] This teaching of Aquinas is, I believe, still substantially the basis of the official Catholic doctrine of sacrilege. Thus, for the Roman Catholic Church, the term came to have a fairly definite meaning, but one, in general, limited to protecting things physical against injurious acts. [Footnote 2/36] Apostasy, heresy, and blasphemy coexisted as religious crimes alongside sacrilege; they were peculiarly in the realm of religious dogma and doctrine, as "sacrilege" was not. It is true that Spelman, writing "The History and Fate of Sacrilege" in 1632, included in "sacrilege" acts whereby

"the very Deity is invaded, profaned, or robbed of its glory. . . . In this high sin are blasphemers,

*523 sorcerers, witches, and enchanters. [Footnote 2/37]"

But his main theme was the "spoil of church lands done by Henry VIII" and the misfortunes that subsequently befell the families of the recipients of former ecclesiastical property as divine punishment.

To the extent that English law took jurisdiction to punish "sacrilege," the term meant the stealing from a church, or otherwise doing damage to church property. [Footnote 2/38] This special protection against "sacrilege," that is, property damage, was granted only to the Established Church. [Footnote 2/39] Since the repeal less than a century ago of the English law punishing "sacrilege" against the property of the Established Church, religious property has received little special protection. The property of all sects has had substantially the same protection as is accorded non-religious property. [Footnote 2/40] At no time up to the present has English law known "sacrilege" to be used in any wider sense than the physical injury to church property. It is true that, at times in the past, English law has

***524** taken jurisdiction to punish departures from accepted dogma or religious practice or the expression of particular religious opinions, but never have these "offenses" been denominated "sacrilege." Apostasy, heresy, offenses against the Established Church, blasphemy, profanation of the Lord's Day, etc., were distinct criminal offenses, characterized by Blackstone as "offences against God and religion." [Footnote 2/41] These invidious reflections upon religious susceptibilities were not covered under sacrilege as they might be under the Court of Appeals' opinion. Anyone doubting the dangerous uncertainty of the New York definition, which makes "sacrilege" overlap these other "offenses against religion," need only read Blackstone's account of the broad and varying content given each of these offenses.

A student of English lexicography would despair of finding the meaning attributed to "sacrilege" by the New York court. [Footnote 2/42] Most dictionaries define the concept in the limited sense of the physical abuse of physical objects. The definitions given for "sacrilege" by two dictionaries published in 1742 and 1782 are typical. Bailey's defined it as

"the stealing of Sacred Things, Church Robbing; an Alienation to Laymen, and to profane and common Purposes, of what was given to religious Persons, and to pious Uses. [Footnote 2/43]"

Barclay's said it is "the crime of taking any thing dedicated to divine worship, or profaning any thing sacred," where "to profane" is defined "to apply any thing sacred to common uses. To be irreverent to sacred persons or things." [Footnote 2/44] The

***525** same dictionaries defined "blasphemy," a peculiarly verbal offense, in much broader terms than "sacrilege," indeed in terms which the New York court finds encompassed by "sacrilegious." For example, Barclay said "blasphemy" is "an offering some indignity to God, any person of the Trinity, any messengers from God, his holy writ, or the doctrines of revelation." [Footnote 2/45] It is hardly necessary to comment that the limits of this definition remain too uncertain to justify constraining the creative efforts of the imagination by fear of pains and penalties imposed by a necessarily subjective censorship. It is true that some earlier dictionaries assigned to "sacrilege" the broader meaning of "abusing Sacraments or holy Mysteries," [Footnote 2/46] but the broader meaning is more indefinite, not less. Noah Webster first published his American Dictionary in 1828. Both it and the later dictionaries published by the Merriam Company, Webster's International Dictionary and Webster's New International Dictionary, have gone through dozens of editions and printings, revisions and expansions. In all editions throughout 125 years, these American dictionaries have defined "sacrilege" and "sacrilegious" to echo substantially the narrow, technical definitions from the earlier British dictionaries collected in the Appendix, post, p. 343 U.S. 533. [Footnote 2/47]

***526** The New York Court of Appeals' statement that the dictionary "furnishes a clear definition," justifying the vague scope it gave to "sacrilegious," surely was made without regard to the lexicographic history of the term. As a matter of fact, the definition from Funk & Wagnalls' used by the Court of Appeals is taken straight from 18th Century dictionaries, particularly Doctor Johnson's. [Footnote 2/48] In light of that history, it would seem that the Funk &

***527** Wagnalls' definition uses "sacrilege" in its historically restricted meaning, which was not, and could hardly have been, the basis for condemning "The Miracle." If the New York court reads the Funk & Wagnalls' definition in a broader sense, in a sense for which history and experience provide no gloss, it inevitably left the censor free to judge by whatever dogma he deems "sacred" and to ban whatever motion pictures he may assume would "profane" religious doctrine widely enough held to arouse protest.

Examination of successive editions of the Encyclopaedia Britannica over nearly two centuries up to the present day gives no more help than the dictionaries. From 1768 to the eleventh edition in 1911, merely a brief dictionary-type definition was given for "sacrilege." [Footnote 2/49] The eleventh edition, which first published a longer article, was introduced as follows:

"the violation or profanation of sacred things, a crime of varying scope in different religions. It is naturally much more general and accounted more dreadful in those primitive religions in

***528** which cultural objects play so great a part, than in more highly spiritualized religions where they tend to disappear. But wherever the idea of sacred exists, sacrilege is possible. [Footnote 2/50]"

The article on "sacrilege" in the current edition of the Encyclopaedia Britannica is substantially the same as that, in the 1911 edition.

History teaches us the indefiniteness of the concept "sacrilegious" in another respect. In the case of most countries and times where the concept of sacrilege has been of importance, there has existed an established church or a state religion. That which was "sacred," and so was protected against "profaning," was designated in each case by ecclesiastical authority. What might have been definite when a controlling church imposed a detailed scheme of observances becomes impossibly confused and uncertain when hundreds of sects, with widely disparate and often directly conflicting ideas of sacredness, enjoy, without discrimination and in equal measure, constitutionally guaranteed religious freedom. In the Rome of the late emperors, the England of James I, or the Geneva of Calvin, and today in Roman Catholic Spain, Mohammedan Saudi Arabia, or any other country with a monolithic religion, the category of things sacred might have clearly definable limits. But in America, the multiplicity of the ideas of "sacredness" held with equal but conflicting fervor by the great number of religious groups makes the term "sacrilegious" too indefinite to satisfy constitutional demands based on reason and fairness.

If "sacrilegious" bans more than the physical abuse of sacred persons, places, or things, if it permits censorship of religious opinions, which is the effect of the holding below, the term will include what may be found to be "blasphemous." England's experience with that treacherous word should give us pause, apart from our

***529** requirements for the separation of Church and State. The crime of blasphemy in Seventeenth Century England was the crime of dissenting from whatever was the current religious dogma. [Footnote 2/51] King James I's "Book of Sports" was first required reading in the churches; later all copies were consigned to the flames. To attack the mass was once blasphemous; to perform it became so. At different times during that century, with the shifts in the attitude of government towards particular religious views, persons who doubted the doctrine of the Trinity (e.g., Unitarians, Universalists, etc.) or the divinity of Christ, observed the Sabbath on Saturday, denied the possibility of witchcraft, repudiated child baptism or urged methods of baptism other than sprinkling, were charged as blasphemers, or their books were burned or banned as blasphemous. Blasphemy was the chameleon phrase which meant the criticism of whatever the ruling authority of the moment established as orthodox religious doctrine. [Footnote 2/52] While it is true that blasphemy prosecutions

***530** have continued in England -- although in lessening numbers -- into the present century, [Footnote 2/53] the existence there of an established church gives more definite contours to the crime in England than the term "sacrilegious" can possibly have in this country. Moreover, the scope of the English common law crime of blasphemy has been considerably limited by the declaration that "if the decencies of controversy are observed, even the fundamentals of religion may be attacked," [Footnote 2/54] a limitation which the New York court has not put upon the Board of Regents' power to declare a motion picture "sacrilegious."

In *Cantwell v. Connecticut*, 310 U.S. 296, 310 U.S. 310, Mr. Justice Roberts, speaking for the whole Court, said:

"In the realm of religious faith, and in that of political belief, sharp differences arise. In both fields, the tenets of one man may seem the rankest error to his neighbor."

Conduct and beliefs dear to one may seem the rankest "sacrilege" to another. A few examples suffice to show the difficulties facing a conscientious censor or motion picture producer or distributor in determining what the New York statute condemns as sacrilegious. A motion picture portraying Christ as divine--for example, a movie showing medieval Church art--would offend the religious opinions of the members of several Protestant denominations who do not believe in the Trinity, as well as those of a non-Christian faith. Conversely, one showing Christ as merely an ethical teacher could not but offend millions of Christians of many denominations. Which is "sacrilegious"? The doctrine of transubstantiation, and the veneration of relics or particular stone and wood embodiments of saints or divinity, both sacred to

***531** Catholics, are offensive to a great many Protestants, and therefore, for them, sacrilegious in the view of the New York court. Is a picture treating either subject, whether sympathetically, unsympathetically, or neutrally, "sacrilegious"? It is not a sufficient answer to say that "sacrilegious" is definite, because all subjects that in any way might be interpreted as offending the religious beliefs of any one of the 300 sects of the United States [Footnote 2/55] are banned in New York. To allow such vague, undefinable powers of censorship to be exercised is bound to have stultifying consequences on the creative process of literature and art -- for the films are derived largely from literature. History does not encourage reliance on the wisdom and moderation of the censor as a safeguard in the exercise of such drastic power over the minds of men. We not only do not know, but cannot know, what is condemnable by "sacrilegious." And if we cannot tell, how are those to be governed by the statute to tell?

It is this impossibility of knowing how far the form of words by which the New York Court of Appeals explained "sacrilegious" carries the proscription of religious subjects that makes the term unconstitutionally vague. [Footnote 2/56] To stop short of proscribing all subjects that might conceivably be interpreted to be religious, inevitably creates a situation whereby the censor bans only that against which

***532** there is a substantial outcry from a religious group. And that is the fair inference to be drawn, as a matter of experience, from what has been happening under the New York censorship. Consequently the film industry, normally not guided by creative artists, and cautious in putting large capital to the hazards of courage, would be governed by its notions of the feelings likely to be aroused by diverse religious sects, certainly the powerful ones. The effect of such demands upon art and upon those whose function is to enhance the culture of a society need not be labored.

To paraphrase Doctor Johnson, if nothing may be shown but what licensors may have previously approved, power, the yea-or-nay-saying by officials, becomes the standard of the permissible. Prohibition through words that fail to convey what is permitted and what is prohibited for want of appropriate objective standards, offends Due Process in two ways. First, it does not sufficiently apprise those bent on obedience of law of what may reasonably be foreseen to be found illicit by the law-enforcing authority, whether court or jury or administrative agency. Secondly, where licensing is rested, in the first instance, in an administrative agency, the available judicial review is in effect rendered inoperative. On the basis of such a portmanteau word as "sacrilegious," the judiciary has no standards with which to judge the validity of administrative action which necessarily involves, at least in large measure, subjective determinations. Thus, the administrative first step becomes the last step.

***533** From all that has been said, one is compelled to conclude that the term "sacrilegious" has come down the stream of time encrusted with a specialized, strictly confined meaning, pertaining to things in space, not things in the mind. The New York Court of Appeals did not give the term this calculable content. It applied it to things in the mind, and things in the mind so undefined, so at large, as to be more patently in disregard of the requirement for definiteness, as the basis of proscriptions and legal sanctions for their disobedience, than the measures that were condemned as violative of Due Process in *United States v. Cohen Grocery Co.*, 255 U.S. 81; *A. B. Small Co. v. American Sugar Refining Co.*, 267 U.S. 233; *Connally v. General Construction Co.*, 269 U.S. 385; *Winters v. New York*, 333 U.S. 507; *Kunz v. New York*, 340 U.S. 290. This principle is especially to be observed when what is so vague seeks to fetter the mind and put within unascertainable bounds the varieties of religious experience.

APPENDIX TO OPINION OF MR. JUSTICE FRANKFURTER [Omitted without implication] * * *

Footnotes

2/11 Crowther, "The Strange Case of The Miracle,'" *Atlantic Monthly*, April, 1951, pp. 35, 36-37.

2/2. *L'Osservatore Romano*, Aug. 25, 1948, p. 2, col. 1, translated in part in *The Commonweal*, Mar. 23, 1951, p 592, col. 2.

2/3. Ibid.

2/4. *N.Y. Times*, Feb. 11, 1951, § 2, p. 4, cols. 4-5.

2/5. *Time*, Feb.19, 1951, pp. 60-61.

2/6. *Il Popolo*, Nov. 3, 1948, p. 2, col. 9, translated by Camille M. Cianfarra, *N.Y. Times*, Feb. 11, 1951, § 2, p. 4, col. 5.

2/7. *L'Osservatore Romano*, Nov. 12, 1948, p. 2, cols. 3-4.

2/8. Ibid.

2/9. "The Miracle" was passed by customs. To import "Any obscene lewd, lascivious, or filthy . . . motion-picture film" is a criminal offense, 35 Stat. 1088, 1138, 18 U.S.C. (Supp. IV) § 1462, and importation of any obscene "print" or "picture" is barred. 46 Stat. 590, 688, 19 U.S.C. § 1305. Compare the provision, "all photographic-films imported . . . shall be subject to such censorship as may be imposed by the Secretary of the Treasury." 38 Stat. 114 151 (1913), 42 Stat. 858, 920 (1922), repealed 46 Stat. 590, 762 (1930). See Inglis, *Freedom of the Movies*, 68.

2/10. *Life*, Jan. 15, 1951, p. 63; Sat.Rev. of Lit., Jan. 27, 1951, pp. 28-29.

2/11. *N.Y. Times*, Dec. 31, 1950, p. 23, col. 4.

2/12. Inglis, *Freedom of the Movies*, 120 et seq.

2/13. Id. at 74-82.

2/14. Howard Barnes, *N.Y. Herald Tribune*, Dec. 13, 1950, p. 30, cols. 1-3: "it would be wise to time a visit to the Paris in order to skip [The Miracle']. . . . Altogether it leaves a very bad taste in one's mouth."

Bosley Crowther, N.Y. Times, Dec. 13, 1950, p. 50, cols. 2-3: "each one of the [three] items . . . stacks up with the major achievements of the respective directors. . . . ['The Miracle'] is by far the most overpowering and provocative of the lot."

N.Y. Times, Dec. 17, 1950, § 2, p. 3, cols. 7-8: "a picture of mounting intensity that wrings the last pang of emotion as it hits its dramatic peak . . . vastly compassionate comprehension of the suffering and the triumph of birth."

Wanda Hale, *N.Y. Daily News*, Dec. 13, 1950, p. 82, cols. 1-3: "Rossellini's best piece of direction since his greatest, "Open City." . . . artistic and beautifully done by both the star and the director."

Archer Winsten, *N.Y. Post*, Dec. 13, 1950, p. 80, cols. 1-3: "Magnani's performance is a major one and profoundly impressive. This reviewer's personal opinion marked down the film as disturbingly unpleasant and slow."

Seymour Peck, *N.Y. Daily Compass*, Dec. 13, 1950, 3, cols. 3-5: "The Miracle' is really all Magnani. . . . one of the most exciting solo performances the screen has known."

Alton Cook, *N.Y. World-Telegram*, Dec. 13, 1950, p. 50, cols. 1-2: "[The Miracle' is] charged with the same overwrought hysteria that ran through his 'Stromboli.' . . . the picture has an unpleasant preoccupation with filth and squalor . . . exceedingly trying experience."

Time, Jan. 8, 1951, p. 72, cols. 2-3: "[The Miracle'] is second-rate Rossellini despite a virtuoso performance by Anna Magnani."

Newsweek, Dec. 18, 1950, pp. 93-94, col. 3: "strong medicine for most American audiences. However, it shows what an artist of Rossellini's character can do in the still scarcely explored medium of the film short story."

Hollis Alpert, Sat.Rev. of Lit., Jan. 27, 1951, pp. 28-29: "Pictorially the picture is a gem, with its sensitive evocation of a small Italian town and the surrounding countryside near Salerno. . . . Anna Magnani again demonstrates her magnificent qualities of acting. The role is difficult. . . ."

"But my quarrel would be with Mr. Rossellini, whose method of improvisation from scene to scene . . . can also result in extraneous detail that adds little, or even harms, the over-all effect."

2/15. *N.Y. Times*, Dec. 28, 1950, p. 22, col. 1.

2/16. Id., Dec. 24, 1950, p. 1, cols. 2-3.

2/17. *Joseph Burstyn, Inc. v. McCaffrey*, 198 Misc. 884, 101 N.Y.S. 2d 892.

2/18. *N.Y. Times*, Jan. 8, 1951, p. 1, col. 2. The Cardinal termed "The Miracle" "a vile and harmful picture," "a despicable affront to every Christian" ("We believe in miracles. This picture ridicules that belief"), and finally "a vicious insult to Italian womanhood." As a consequence, he declared: "we, as the guardians of the moral law, must summon you and all people with a sense of decency to refrain from seeing it and supporting the venal purveyors of such pictures. . . ."

Id. at p. 14, cols. 2-3.

For completeness' sake, later incidents should be noted. Picketers from the Catholic War Veterans, the Holy Name Society, and other Catholic organizations -- about 1,000 person in all during one Sunday -- paraded before the Paris Theatre. Id. Dec. 29, 1950, p. 36, col. 3; Jan. 8, 1951, p. 1, col. 2; Jan. 9, 1951, p. 34, col. 7; Jan. 10, 1951, p. 22, col. 6; Jan. 15, 1951, p. 23, col. 3. A smaller number of counter pickets appeared on several days. Id., Jan. 10, 1951, p. 22, col. 6; Jan. 20, 1951, p. 10, cols. 4-5. See also id. Jan. 23, 1951, p. 21, col. 8; Jan. 25, 1951, p. 27, col. 7.

The Paris Theatre on two different evenings was emptied on threat of bombing. Id., Jan. 21, 1951, p. 1, cols. 2-3; Jan. 28, 1951, p. 1, cols. 2-3. Coincidentally with the proceedings before the New York Board of Regents which started this case on the way to this Court, the Paris Theatre also was having difficulties with the New York City Fire Department. The curious may follow the development of those incidents, not relevant here, in the N.Y. Times, Jan. 21, 1951, p. 53, cols. 4-5; Jan. 27, 1951, p. 11, col. 3; Feb. 6, 1951, p. 29, col. 8; Feb. 10, 1951, p. 15, col. 8; Feb. 15, 1951, p. 33, col. 2.

2/19. Excerpts from letters and statements by a great many clergymen are reproduced in the Record before this Court, pages 95-140. The representative quotations in the text are from letters written by the Rev. H. C. DeWindt, Minister of the West Park Presbyterian Church, New York City, R. 97, and the Rev. W. J. Beeners of Princeton, New Jersey, R. 98, respectively.

2/20. Catholic opinion generally, as expressed in the press, supported the view of the Legion of Decency and of Cardinal Spellman. See, for example, The [New York] *Catholic News*, Dec. 30, 1950, p. 10; Jan. 6, 1951, p. 10; Jan. 20, 1951, p. 10; Feb. 3, 1951, p. 10; Feb. 10, 1951, p. 12, and May 19, 1951, p. 12; Commonweal, Jan. 12, 1951, p. 351, col. 1; The [Brooklyn] Tablet, Jan. 20, 1951, p- 8, col. 4;id. Jan. 27, 1951, p. 10, col. 3; id. Feb. 3, 1951, p. 8, cols. 3-4; Martin Quigley, Jr., "The Miracle' -- An Outrage"; The [San Francisco] Monitor, Jan. 12, 1951, p. 7, cols. 3-4 (reprinted from Motion Picture Herald, Jan. 6, 1951); The [Boston] Pilot, Jan. 6, 1951, p. 4. There doubtless were comments on "The Miracle" in other diocesan papers which circulate in various parts of the country, but which are not on file in the Library of Congress or the library of the Catholic University of America.

2/21. Spaeth, "Fogged Screen," *Magazine of Art*, Feb., 1951, p. 44; N.Y. Herald Tribune, Jan. 30, 1951, p. 18, col. 4.

2/22. Clancy, "The Catholic as Philistine," *The Commonweal*, Mar. 16, 1951, pp. 567-569.

2/23. *The Commonweal*, Mar. 2, 1951, pp. 507-508. Much the same view was taken by Frank Getlein writing in *The Catholic Messenger*, Mar. 22, 1951, p. 4, cols. 1-8, in an article bearing the headline: "Film Critic Gives Some Aspects of The Miracle' Story: Raises Questions Concerning Tactics of Organized Catholic Resistance Groups in view York." See also "Miracles Do Happen," *The New Leader*, Feb. 5, 1951, p. 30, col. 2.

2/24. *N.Y. Times*, Feb. 1, 1951, p. 24, col. 7.

2/25. Id., Jan. 13, 1951, p. 10, col. 6; translation by Chworowsky, "The Cardinal: Critic and Censor," *The Churchman*, Feb. 1, 1951, p. 7, col. 2.

2/26. That such offensive exploitation of modern means of publicity is not a fanciful hypothesis, see *N.Y. Times,* April 14, 1952, p. 1, col. 4.

2/27. *In the Matter of "The Puritan,"* 60 N.Y.St.Dept. 163 (1939); In the Matter of "Polygamy," 60 N.Y.St.Dept. 217 (1939); In the Matter of "Monja y Casada -- Virgen y Martir" ("Nun and Married -- Virgin and Martyr"), 52 N.Y.St.Dept. 488 (1935).

2/28. Since almost without exception "sacrilegious" is defined in terms of "sacrilege," our discussion will be directed to the latter term. SeeBailey, Universal Etymological English Dictionary (London, 1730), "Sacrilegious" -- "of, pertaining to, or guilty of Sacrilege"; Funk & Wagnalls' New Standard Dictionary (1937), "Sacrilegious" -- "Having committed or being ready to commit sacrilege. Of the nature of sacrilege; as, sacrilegious deeds."

2/29. For general discussions of "sacrilege," see Encyclopaedia of Religion and Ethics (Hastings ed., 1921), "Sacrilege" and "Tabu"; Rev. Thomas Slater, A Manual of Moral Theology (1908), 226-230; The Catholic Encyclopedia (1912), "Sacrilege", and Encyclopaedia Britannica, "Sacrilege."

2/30. Encyclopaedia Britannica (1951), "Sacrilege."

2/31. Ibid.

2/32. See Encyclopaedia of Religion and Ethics (Hastings ed., 191), "Tabu."

2/33. Encyclopaedia Britannica (1951), "Sacrilege."

2/34. St. Thomas Aquinas, Summa Theologica, part II-II, question 99. The modern Codex Juris Canonici does not give any definition of "sacrilege," but merely says it "shall be punished by the Ordinary in proportion to the gravity of the fault, without prejudice to the penalties established by law. . . ." See Bouscaren and Ellis, Canon Law (1946), 857. 2 Woywod, A Practical Commentary on the Code of Canon Law (1929), par. 2178, 477 478, thus defines sacrilege: "Sacrilege consists in the unworthy use or treatment of sacred things and sacred persons. Certain things are of their nature sacred (e.g., the Sacraments); others become so by blessing or consecration legitimately bestowed on things or places by authority of the Church. Persons are rendered sacred by ordination or consecration or by other forms of dedication to the divine service by authority of the Church (e.g., by first tonsure, by religious profession)."

2/35. After his method of raising objections and then refuting them, St. Thomas Aquinas defends including within the proscription of "sacrilege," anyone "who disagree[s] about the sovereign's decision, and doubt[s] whether the person chosen by the sovereign be worthy of honor" and "any man [who] shall allow the Jews to hold public offices." Summa Theologica, part II-II, question 99, art. 1.

2/36. Rev. Thomas Slater, S. J., A Manual of Moral Theology (1908), c. VI, classifies and illustrates the modern theological view of "sacrilege":

Sacrilege against sacred persons: to use physical violence against a member of the clergy; to violate "the privilege of immunity of the clergy from civil jurisdiction, as far as this is still in force"; to violate a vow of chastity.

Sacrilege against sacred places: to violate the immunity of churches and other sacred places "as far as this is still in force"; to commit a crime such as homicide, suicide, bloody attack there; to break by sexual act a vow of chastity there; to bury an infidel, heretic, or excommunicate in churches or cemeteries canonically established; or to put the sacred place to a profane use, as a secular courtroom, public market, banquet hall, stable, etc.

Sacrilege against sacred things: to treat with irreverence, contempt, or obscenity the sacraments (particularly the Eucharist), Holy Scriptures, relics, sacred images, etc., to steal sacred things, or profane things from sacred places; to commit simony; or to steal, confiscate, or damage willfully ecclesiastical property. See also The Catholic Encyclopedia, "Sacrilege."

2/37. Sir Henry Spelman, The History and Fate of Sacrilege (2d ed., 1853), 121-122. Two priests of the Anglican Church prepared a long prefatory essay to bring Spelman's data up to the date of publication of the 1853 edition. Their essay shows their understanding also of "sacrilege" in the limited sense. Id. at 1-120.

2/38. 2 Russell, Crime (10th ed., 1950), 975-976; Stephen, A Digest of the Criminal Law (9th ed., 1950), 348-349. See 23 Hen. VIII, c. 1, § III; 1 Edw. VI, c. 12, § X; 1 Mary, c. 3, §§ IV-VI.

2/39. 7 & 8 Geo. IV, c. 29, § X, which the marginal note summarized as "Sacrilege, when capital," read: "if any Person shall break and enter any Church or Chapel, and steal therein any Chattel . . . [he] shall suffer Death as a Felon." This statute was interpreted to apply only to buildings of the established church. Rex v. Nixon, 7 Car. & P. 442 (1836).

2/40. 7 & 8 Geo. IV, c. 29, § X, was repealed by 24 & 25 Vict., c. 95. The Larceny Act and the Malicious Injuries to Property Act, both of 1861, treated established church property substantially the same as all other property. 24 & 25 Vict., c. 96, § 50; e. 97, §§ 1, 11, 39, superseded by Larceny Act, 1916, 6 & 7 Geo. V, c. 50, § 24.

2/41. Blackstone, bk. IV, c. 4, 41-64.

2/42. Compare the definitions Of "sacrilege" and "blasphemy" in the dictionaries, starting with Cockeram's 1651 edition, which are collected in the Appendix, post, p. 343 U.S. 533.

2/43. Bailey An Universal Etymological English Dictionary (London, 1742), "Sacrilege."

2/44. Barclay, A Complete and Universal English Dictionary (London, 1782), "Sacrilege."

2/45. Id., "Blasphemy."

2/46. Thomas Blount, Glossographia (3d ed., London, 1670).

2/47. Webster's Compendious Dictionary of the English Language (1806): "Sacrilege" -- "the robbery of a church or chapel." "Sacrilegious" -- "violating a thing made sacred."

Webster's American Dictionary (1828): "Sacrilege" -- "The crime of violating or profaning sacred things; or the alienating to laymen or to common purposes what has been appropriated or consecrated to religious persons or uses." " Sacrilegious" -- "Violating sacred things; polluted with the crime of sacrilege."

Webster's International Dictionary (G. & C. Merriam & Co., 1890): "Sacrilege" -- "The sin or crime of violating or profaning sacred things; the alienating to laymen, or to common purposes, what has been appropriated or consecrated to religious persons or uses." "Sacrilegious" -- "violating sacred things; polluted with sacrilege; involving sacrilege; profane; impious."

Webster's New International Dictionary (G. & C. Merriam Co., 1st ed., 1909): "Sacrilege" -- "The sin or crime of violating or profaning sacred things; specif., the alienating to laymen, or to common purposes, what has been appropriated or consecrated to religious persons or uses." "Sacrilegious" -- "Violating sacred things; polluted with, or involving, sacrilege; impious." Repeated in the 1913, 1922, 1924, 1928, 1933 printings, among others.

Webster's New International Dictionary (G. & C. Merriam Co.,2d ed., 1934): "Sacrilege" -- "The crime of stealing, misusing, violating, or desecrating that which is sacred, or holy, or dedicated to sacred uses. Specif.: a R. C. Ch. The sin of violating the conditions for a worthy reception of a sacrament. b Robbery from a church; also, that which is stolen. c Alienation to laymen, or to common purposes, of what has been appropriated or consecrated to religious persons or uses." "Sacrilegious" -- "Committing sacrilege; characterized by or involving sacrilege; polluted with sacrilege; as, sacrilegious robbers, depredations, or acts." Repeated in the 1939, 1942, 1944, 1949 printings, among others.

2/48. 1 Funk & Wagnalls' Standard Dictionary of the English Language, which was first copyrighted in 1890, defined sacrilege as follows in the 1895 printing: "1. The act of violating or profaning anything sacred. 2. Eng.Law (1) The larceny of consecrated things from a church; the breaking into a church with intent to commit a felony, or breaking out after a felony. (2) Formerly, the selling to a layman of property given to pious uses." This definition remained unchanged through many printings of that dictionary. The current printing of Funk & Wagnalls' New Standard Dictionary of the English Language, first copyrighted in 1913, carries exactly the same definition of "sacrilege" except that the first definition has been expanded to read: "The act of violating or profaning anything sacred, including sacramental vows ."

Funk & Wagnalls' Standard Dictionary (1895) defined "to profane" as "1. To treat with irreverence or abuse; make common or unholy; desecrate; pollute. 2. Hence, to put to a wrong or degrading use; debase." The New Standard Dictionary adds a third meaning: "3. To vulgarize; give over to the crowd."

2/49. Encyclopaedia Britannica,2d ed., 1782: "Sacrilege" -- "the crime of profaning sacred things, or those devoted to the service of God."

3d ed., 1797: "Sacrilege" -- "the crime of profaning sacred things, or things devoted to God; or of alienating to laymen, for common purposes, what was given to religious persons and pious uses."

8th ed., 1859: "Sacrilege" -- same as 3d ed., 1797.

9th ed., 1886: "Sacrilege" -- A relatively short article the author of which quite apparently had a restricted definition for "sacrilege":

"robbery of churches," "breaking or defacing of an altar, crucifix, or cross," etc.

2/50. Encyclopaedia Britannica (11th ed., 1911), "Sacrilege."

2/51. Schroeder, Constitutional Free Speech (1919), 178-373, makes a lengthy review of "Prosecutions for Crimes Against Religion." The examples in the text are from Schroeder. See also Encyclopaedia of the Social Sciences, "Blasphemy"; Encyclopaedia of Religion and Ethics, "Blasphemy"; Nokes, A History of the Crime of Blasphemy (1928).

2/52. I Yorke, The Life of Lord Chancellor Hardwicke (1913), 80, writes thus of the prosecution of Thomas Woolston for blasphemy:

"The offense, in the first place, consisted in the publication in 1725 of a tract entitled A Moderator between an Infidel and an Apostate,in which the author questioned the historical accuracy of the Resurrection and the Virgin Birth. Such speculations, however much they might offend the religious feeling of the nation, would not now arouse apprehensions in the civil government, or incur legal penalties; but at the time of which we are writing, when the authority of government was far less stable and secure and rested on far narrower foundations than at present, such audacious opinions were considered, not without some reason, as a menace, not only to religion but to the state."

2/53. See, e.g., *Rex v. Boulter*, 72 J.P. 188 (1908); *Bowman v. Secular Society, Ltd.*, [1917] A.C. 406.

2/54. *Reg. v. Ramsay*, 15 Cox's C.C. 231, 238 (1883) (Lord Coleridge's charge to the jury); *Bowman v. Secular Society, Ltd.*, [1917] A.C. 406.

2/55. The latest available statistics of the Bureau of the Census give returns from 256 denominations; 57 other denominations, which did not report, are listed. Bureau of the Census, Religious Bodies: 1936, Vol. I, iii, 7.

2/56. It is not mere fantasy to suggest that the effect of a ban of the "sacrilegious" may be to ban all motion pictures dealing with any subject that might be deemed religious by any sect. The industry's self-censorship has already had a distorting influence on the portrayal of historical figures.

"Pressure forced deletion of the clerical background of Cardinal Richelieu from The Three Musketeers. The [Motion Picture Production] code provision appealed to was the section providing that ministers should not be portrayed as villains."

Note, "Motion Pictures and the First Amendment," 60 Yale L.J. 696, 716, n. 42.

The press recently reported that plans are being made to film a "Life of Martin Luther." N.Y. Times, April 27, 1952, § 2, p. 5, col. 7. Could Luther be sympathetically portrayed and not appear "sacrilegious" to some; or unsympathetically, and not to others?

IN THE MATTER OF JOSEPH BURSTYN INC.

v.

LEWIS A. WILSON, AS COMMISSIONER OF EDUCATION OF THE STATE OF NEW YORK

303 N.Y. 242 (1951)

Court of Appeals of the State of New York

Argued June 1, 1951

Decided October 18, 1951

Ephraim S. London, Clendon H. Lee, Leonard P. Simpson and Seymour M. Burg for appellant.

* * *

LOUGHRAN, Ch. J., LEWIS and CONWAY, JJ., concur with FROESSEL, J.; DESMOND, J., concurs in separate opinion; FULD, J., dissents in opinion in which DYE, J., concurs.

***249** FROESSEL, J.

A license for the exhibition of a motion picture film entitled "The Miracle" together with two other films, described in their combination as a trilogy and called "Ways of Love", was issued to petitioner on November 30, 1950, by the Motion Picture Division of the Department of Education of the State of New York, under the governing statute (Education Law, art. 3, part II). "The Miracle" was produced in Italy as "Il Miracolo", and English subtitles were later added. A prior license had been issued to the original owner of the distribution rights for exhibition, with Italian subtitles alone, but the film was never shown under that license.

The first public exhibition of "The Miracle" as part of the trilogy, "Ways of Love", was shown in New York City on December 12, 1950. It provoked an immediate and substantial public controversy, and the Education Department was fairly flooded with protests against its exhibition. Others expressed a contrary view. In consequence thereof, the Board of Regents of the University of the State of New York (hereinafter called the Regents) proceeded promptly to review the action of its motion picture division. It appointed a subcommittee, and directed a hearing requiring petitioner to show cause why the licenses should not be rescinded and cancelled.

***250** After viewing the film and giving petitioner an opportunity to be heard, its subcommittee reported that there was basis for the claim that the picture is sacrilegious, and recommended that the Regents view the film. Petitioner declined to participate in the hearing other than to appear specially before the subcommittee for the purpose of challenging the jurisdiction of the Regents to cancel the licenses, but its sole stockholder, Joseph Burstyn, appeared as an individual and filed a brief.

Thereupon and on February 16, 1951, after reviewing the picture and the entire record, the Regents unanimously adopted a resolution rescinding and canceling the licenses upon their determination that "The Miracle" is sacrilegious, and not entitled to a license under the law.[*] Thereafter petitioner instituted the present article 78 proceeding to review that determination, and now urges that (1) the Regents were powerless to review the action of its motion picture division or to revoke the licenses; (2) the word "sacrilegious" does not provide a sufficiently definite standard for action; (3) the Regents exceeded their authority; (4) the statute is unconstitutional as in violation of the First and Fourteenth Amendments of the Constitution of the United States in that denial or revocation of a license on account of sacrilege interferes with religious liberty and breaches the wall between Church and State; and (5) the statute is unconstitutional in toto as a prior restraint on the right of free speech guaranteed by the First and Fourteenth Amendments of the Federal Constitution. The Appellate Division unanimously confirmed the determination of the Regents.

First: The principal argument advanced by petitioner is directed toward the claim that the Regents have no power under the statute to rescind a license once issued by the motion picture division, unless upon a charge of fraud in the procurement thereof or subsequent misconduct by the licensee. Any other construction of the statute, it is said, would be inequitable to petitioner, which has spent money relying upon the license as issued. The Regents, on the other hand, contend that they were empowered under the Education Law and our State Constitution to make the determination here challenged.

***251** This issue, then, is one primarily of statutory construction, turning upon the intention of the Legislature as found in the language of the statutes. It is resolved by the answer to the question: Did the Legislature intend that the granting of a license by a subordinate official of the State Education Department should be a determination final and irrevocable, binding on the head of his department, the courts and the public for all time? As we said in *Matter of Equitable Trust Co. v. Hamilton* (226 N.Y. 241, 245) "That is in every case a question dependent for its answer upon the scheme of the statute by which power is conferred."

In considering the statute pattern conferring the power, we should note the framework of fact and circumstance in which the statutes are to be examined, and particularly the nature of the problem with which we are dealing. Motion pictures, by their very nature, present a unique problem. They are primarily entertainment, rather than the expression of ideas, and are engaged in for profit (*Mutual Film Corp. v. Industrial Comm. of Ohio*, 236 U.S. 230; *Mutual Film Co. v. Industrial Comm. of Ohio*, 236 U.S. 247; *Mutual Film Corp. v. Hodges*, 236 U.S. 248). They have universal appeal to literate and illiterate, young and old, of all classes. They may exercise influence for good, but their potentiality for evil, especially among the young, is boundless. As was said in *Pathe Exch., Inc., v. Cobb* (202 App. Div. 450, 457, affd. 236 N.Y. 539), where we sustained the original statute (L. 1921, ch. 715) creating the "motion picture commission" in respect to current events films: "many would cast discretion and self-control to the winds, without restraint, social or moral. There are those who would give unrestrained rein to passion. * * * They appreciate the business advantage of depicting the evil and voluptuous thing with the poisonous charm." A public showing of an obscene, indecent, immoral or sacrilegious film may do incalculable harm, and the State, in making provision against the threat of such harm (Education Law, § 122), may afford protection as broad as the danger presented.

We are thus concerned with a valid exercise of the police power (Mutual Film cases,supra; Note 64 A. L. R. 505, and cases therein cited; *Pathe Exch., Inc., v. Cobb*, supra) and with rights acquired by licensees thereunder. Such rights are not

***252** contractual in the constitutional sense (*People ex rel. Lodes v. Department of Health*, 189 N.Y. 187; 12 Am. Jur., Constitutional Law, § 405; 33 Am. Jur.,

Licenses, §§ 21, 65). This is the general rule notwithstanding the expenditure of money by a licensee in reliance upon the license, although there is authority to the contrary in the case of building permits (33 Am. Jur., Licenses, § 21; People ex rel. *Lodes v. Department of Health*, supra, distinguishing at p. 196, *City of Buffalo v. Chadeayne*, 134 N.Y. 163). Moreover, rights gained under the statute are accepted with whatever conditions or reservations the statute may attach to them. With these precepts in mind, and in the light of the problem with which the Legislature dealt, we may properly turn to a consideration of the statutory scheme.

The original body for the licensing of motion pictures for exhibition in this State was an independent commission created by chapter 715 of the Laws of 1921, its members appointed by the Governor, by and with the advice and consent of the Senate. While the provisions for licensing were similar to those now in the Education Law, there was an essential difference in the scheme embodied therein due to the independent nature of the former commission, which was then expressly given all of the powers now granted to the Regents. In 1926, the functions of the motion picture commission were transferred to the Department of Education and the old commission was abolished (L. 1926, ch. 544; State Departments Law, § 312). In 1927, the present form of the statute was incorporated into the Education Law as article 43 thereof (L. 1927, ch. 153, §§ 28, 29). These changes were significant, as will presently more fully appear.

The Regents are a constitutional body, existing since 1784 (N.Y. Const., art. XI, § 2). They are named as head of the Education Department in the same paragraph as are the three chief elective officers of the State, the Governor, Comptroller and Attorney-General (art. V, § 4). The latter provision of our Constitution empowers the Regents to "appoint and at pleasure remove a commissioner of education to be the chief administrative officer of the department." The mere placing of the motion picture commission in the Department of Education indicates an intention that the Regents should henceforth exercise complete authority over that agency.

***253** Moreover, by explicit language, the Legislature gave to the Regents as head of the Education Department all of the broad powers of control and supervision formerly possessed by the independent commission, leaving to the motion picture division only "the administrative work" of licensing (Education Law, §§ 101, 103, 132). Thus, by section 101 of the Education Law, the Education Department "is charged" with "the exercise of all the functions" of the department, and with "the performance of all" the "powers and duties" transferred from the former independent motion picture commission, "whether in terms vested in such department" or in any "division" thereof (emphasis supplied), and such performance is authorized "by or through" the appropriate officer or division; by the same section the Regents are continued as "the head of the department", as prescribed in the Constitution. The Regents appoint the director, officers and employees of the motion picture division, fix their compensation, assign duties to the division, establish local offices, and "prescribe the powers and duties" (Education Law, §§ 120, 121). The "form, manner and substance" of license applications are prescribed by the Education Department, and not by the motion picture division (Education Law, § 127).

The Regents must review the denial of a license before an unsuccessful applicant, who is given a "right of review by the regents", can avail himself of an article 78 proceeding (Education Law, § 124). A corresponding right of review where a license was issued must be deemed implicit in the broad powers of the board, rendering needless any additional language by way of express grant; when the Legislature intends to withhold the power of review from the head of a department with respect to the finding of an agency of the department, it does so by express language (Labor Law [labor relations], § 702, subd. 9; Workmen's Compensation Law, § 142, subd. 4). Finally, the Regents "have authority to enforce the provisions and purposes" of the statute and to make rules and regulations in "carrying out and enforcing [its] purposes" (Education Law, § 132; emphasis supplied). This latter provision is taken directly from the original statute (§ 15), and, although not embraced in the 1926 enactment transferring the functions of the independent motion picture commission, this precise

***254** authority was expressly given to the Regents by the 1927 amendment (Education Law, former § 1092). The power to enforce embraces the power to correct the action of a subordinate, and one of the specific provisions and purposes of the act is that no sacrilegious films be licensed.

From all of this it is clear that the motion picture division is subject and subordinate to the Education Department and the Regents, and is not independent thereof (cf. *Butterworth v. United States ex rel. Hoe*, 112 U.S. 50, in which an altogether different statute pattern was involved, and where an appeal was expressly authorized from the commissioner to the court, either directly or by means of an original suit in equity). Even such functions as may now be exercised by the director of the division under the statute may be exercised by other officials upon authorization by the Regents (Education Law, §§ 120, 122). Without question, then, the statute constitutes the Regents the main-spring of the entire system therein set up. To deny them the power to correct the action of a subordinate, when the ultimate responsibility rests upon them, would be to set at naught the whole elaborate plan established by the Legislature. Such power is "essential to the exercise" of the powers expressly granted (*Lawrence Constr. Corp v. State of New York*, 293 N.Y. 634, 639).

If petitioner's interpretation of the Education Law were to be adopted, no review either of an administrative or supervisory nature, or through the civil or criminal courts (see Penal Law, § 1141, as amd. by L. 1950, ch. 624; *Hughes Tool Co. v. Fielding*, 188 Misc. 947, affd. 272 App. Div. 1048, affd. 297 N.Y. 1024), of the action of a subordinate granting a license in the first instance is provided by the Legislature. Thus the most indecent, obscene, immoral, sacrilegious or depraved presentation might be made through the medium of motion picture film, provided only there was some slip, inadvertence or mistake on the part of the reviewer, leaving his superiors, the courts, and the public generally powerless to correct the situation. It would simply mean that this statutory plan to protect the public from films forbidden to be licensed for general exhibition under section 122 rests entirely upon the judgment of one or two persons in the motion picture division, whose favorable determination in the first instance is irrevocably binding on the People of the

***255** State of New York. Such intention on the part of the Legislature would seem to be so utterly unreasonable and out of harmony with basic public policy in these matters as to be unthinkable (*People v. Ahearn*, 196 N.Y. 221, 227).

On the other hand, the only reasonable view to be taken is that the Legislature deemed the Constitution and the Education Law vested in the Regents as an independent constitutional body such supervisory powers as sufficiently to protect the public interest against improper action by subordinates, and that the authority thereby granted is therefore sufficiently complete in itself to accomplish the salutary purposes envisioned therein. Once the Legislature placed the power to license in the Department of Education, the Constitution (art. V, § 4) mandated the Board of Regents as its head to exercise it, and there is no legislation even purporting to restrict them from doing so. They are authorized to employ subordinates and to function "by or through" them, but are not thereby divested of their own ultimate responsibility. The action of the motion picture division must thus be regarded as reviewable by the Regents in any case — where the license is refused, on demand of the applicant; where the license is granted, on the Regents' own motion.

Accordingly, we are of the opinion that the Regents have power to review the action of its motion picture division in granting a license to exhibit motion pictures, and rightfully exercised its jurisdiction in this case.

Second: To the claim that the statute delegates legislative power without adequate standards, a short answer may be made. Section 122 of the Education Law provides that a license shall be issued for the exhibition of a submitted film, "unless such film or a part thereof is obscene, indecent, immoral, inhuman, sacrilegious, or is of such character that its exhibition would tend to corrupt morals or incite to crime". Only the word "sacrilegious" is attacked for indefiniteness. The dictionary, however, furnishes a clear definition thereof, were it necessary to seek one, as, e.g., "the act of violating or profaning anything sacred" (Funk & Wagnall's New Standard Dictionary [1937 ed.]). There is no difficulty in recognizing the limits of the criterion thus established, and the courts have had no problem either with the word "sacrilegious" or with its synonym, "profane".

***256** In *Mutual Film Corp. v. Hodges* (236 U.S. 248, supra), the contention that there was an invalid delegation of legislative power was rejected where the statute provided that the censor should approve such films as were found to be "moral and proper and disapprove such as are sacrilegious, obscene, indecent or immoral, or such as tend to corrupt the morals" (p. 257, emphasis supplied). In *Winters v. New York* (333 U.S. 507, 510) it is stated that publications are "subject to control if they are lewd, indecent, obscene or profane" (emphasis supplied). In *Chaplinsky v. New Hampshire* (315 U.S. 568, 571-572) Mr. Justice MURPHY declared for a unanimous court: "There are certain well-defined and narrowly limited classes of speech, the prevention and punishment of which have never been thought to raise any Constitutional problem. These include the lewd and obscene, the profane" (emphasis supplied). Indeed, Congress itself has found in the word "profane" a useful standard for both administrative and criminal sanctions against those uttering profane language or meaning by means of radio (*Dumont Laboratories v. Carroll*, 184 F.2d 153, 156, certiorari denied 340 U.S. 929; U.S. Code, tit. 47, § 303, subd. [m], par. [1], cl. [D]; U.S. Code, tit. 18, § 1464; see, also, Penal Law, § 2072).

Accordingly, the claim that the word "sacrilegious" does not provide a sufficiently definite standard may be passed without further consideration, since it is without substance.

Third: We turn now to the contention that the Regents exceeded their powers.

Petitioner urges that, even if the board had the power, there was no justification for revocation. Of course, as the Appellate Division below, in its opinion, said (278 App. Div. 253, 260): "Under the familiar rule, applicable to all administrative proceedings, we may not interfere unless the determination made was one that no reasonable mind could reach." This rule applies to the courts and not to administrative agencies, as the Regents. (*Matter of Foy Productions. Ltd., v. Graves*, 253 App. Div. 475, affd. 278 N.Y. 498.)

We have all viewed the film in question. The so-called exhibits, which are simply unsworn communications expressing personal opinions, are of little help to us. The principal basis for the charge of sacrilege is found in the picture itself, the

***257** personalities involved, the use of scriptural passages as a background for the portrayal of the characters, and their actions, together with other portions of the script and the title of the film itself. It is featured as a "way of love". At the very outset, we are given this definition: "ardent affection, passionate attachment, men's adoration of God, sexual passion, gratification, devotion".

While the film in question is called "The Miracle", no miracle is shown; on the contrary, we have the picture of a demented peasant girl meeting a complete stranger whom she addresses as "Saint Joseph". At the very beginning of the script, reference is made to "Jesus, Joseph, Mary". "Saint Joseph" first causes her to become intoxicated. Scriptural passages referring to the Holy Sacrament (Luke 22:19), and to the nativity of Christ (Matthew 1:20), are freely employed immediately after she states she is not well. A blackout in the film, in its association with the story, compels the inference that sexual intercourse and conception ensue. "Saint Joseph" abandons her immediately following the seduction, she is later found pregnant, and a mock religious procession is staged in her honor; she is "crowned" with an old washbasin, is thrown out by her former lover, and the picture concludes with a realistic portrayal of her labor pains and the birth in a church courtyard of her child, whom she addresses as "my blessed son", "My holy son".

Christ is the heart and core of the Christian faith. Two personalities most closely related to Him in life were His mother, Mary, and Joseph. They are deeply revered by all Christians. Countless millions over the centuries have regarded their relationship as sacred, and so do millions living today. "The Miracle" not only encroaches upon this sacred relationship and the Biblical presentation thereof in respect to the birth of Christ, but utterly destroys it, associating it, as the Regents found, "with drunkenness, seduction, mockery and lewdness", and, in the language of the script itself, with "passionate attachment * * * sexual passion" and "gratification", as a way of love.

In the light of the foregoing, we conclude, as did the Appellate Division, (1) that we cannot say that the determination complained of "was one that no reasonable mind could reach"; and (2) that the board did not act arbitrarily or capriciously.

***258** Fourth: It is further urged that a license may not be denied or revoked on the ground of sacrilege, because that would require a religious judgment on the part of the censoring authority and thus constitute an interference in religious matters by the State. In this connection, it is also urged that freedom of religion is thereby denied, since one man's sacrilege is another man's dogma, and one may thus be prevented from propagating his own religious views by means of motion pictures. The latter argument is specious when applied to motion pictures offered to the public for general exhibition as a form of entertainment, as we shall hereafter point out. Religious presentations, as ordinarily understood, as well as other educational and scientific films, are exempt (Education Law, § 123). Thus freedom of religion is not impaired in the slightest, as anyone may express any religious or anti[-]religious sentiment he chooses through a proper use of the films.

Nor is it true that the Regents must form religious judgments in order to find that a film is sacrilegious. As hereinbefore indicated, there is nothing mysterious about the standard to be applied. It is simply this: that no religion, as that word is understood by the ordinary, reasonable person, shall be treated with contempt, mockery, scorn and ridicule to the extent that it has been here, by those engaged in selling entertainment by way of motion pictures. As the court below said of the statute in question, "All it purports to do is to bar a visual caricature of religious beliefs held sacred by one sect or another, and such a bar, in our opinion, is not a denial of religious freedom." (278 App. Div. 253, 258.)

Although it is claimed that the law benefits all religions and thus breaches the wall of separation between Church and State, the fact that some benefit may incidentally accrue to religion is immaterial from the constitutional point of view if the statute has for its purpose a legitimate objective within the scope of the police power of the State (*Everson v. Board of Educ.*, 330 U.S. 1; *Cochran v. Louisiana State Bd. of Educ.*, 281 U.S. 370; *Bradfield v. Roberts*, 175 U.S. 291; *People v. Friedman*, 302 N.Y. 75, appeal dismissed for want of substantial Federal question 341 U.S. 907). Cases such as Illinois ex rel. *McCollum v. Board of Educ.* (333 U.S. 203) and *Cantwell v. Connecticut* (310 U.S. 296) are not to the contrary. The former case dealt ***259** with the use of State property for religious purposes (*Matter of Zorach v. Clauson*, 303 N.Y. 161), while the latter held (p. 305) that "a censorship of religion as the means of determining its right to survival is a denial of liberty protected by the" First and Fourteenth Amendments. Yet even in those cases it was recognized that the States may validly regulate the manner of expressing religious views if the regulation bears reasonable relation to the public welfare. Freedom to believe — or not to believe — is absolute; freedom to act is not. "Conduct remains subject to regulation for the protection of society" (*Cantwell v. Connecticut*, supra, p. 304; *American Communications Assn. v. Douds*, 339 U.S. 382, 393).

The statute now before us is clearly directed to the promotion of the public welfare, morals, public peace and order. These are the traditionally recognized objects of the exercise of police power. For this reason, any incidental benefit conferred upon religion is not sufficient to render this statute unconstitutional. There is here no regulation of religion, nor restriction thereof or other interference with religious beliefs except insofar as the picture itself does so, nor is there any establishment of religion or preference of religion or use of State property or funds in aid of religion. There is nothing more than a denial of the claimed right to hurl insults at the deepest and sincerest religious beliefs of others through the medium of a commercial entertainment spectacle.

We are essentially a religious nation (*Church of Holy Trinity v. United States*, 143 U.S. 457, 465), of which it is well to be reminded now and then, and in the McCollum case (supra) the Supreme Court paused to note that a manifestation of governmental hostility to religion or religious teachings "would be at war with our national tradition" (p. 211). The preamble to our State Constitution expresses our gratitude as a people to Almighty God for our freedom. To say that government may not intervene to protect religious beliefs from purely private or commercial attacks or persecution, whatever the underlying motive, and however skillfully accomplished, as distinguished from the assertion of conflicting beliefs, is to deny not only its power to keep the peace, but also the very right to "the free exercise" of religion, guaranteed by the First Amendment. The offering of public gratuitous insult to recognized

***260** religious beliefs by means of commercial motion pictures is not only offensive to decency and morals, but constitutes in itself an infringement of the freedom of others to worship and believe as they choose. Insult, mockery, contempt and ridicule can be a deadly form of persecution — often far more so than more direct forms of action. The prohibition of such conduct comes within the legitimate sphere of State action, and this State has recognized this principle, not only in the Education Law but in other respects as well (see, e.g., Penal Law, art. 186; Civil Rights Law, art. 4). We are not aware that this power has ever been even impliedly denied to the States.

This nation is a land of religious freedom; it would be strange indeed if our Constitution, intended to protect that freedom, were construed as an instrument to uphold those who publicly and sacrilegiously ridicule and lampoon the most sacred beliefs of any religious denomination to provide amusement and for commercial gain.

For the foregoing reasons, we conclude that the challenged portion of the statute in no way violates the provisions of the First Amendment of the Federal Constitution relating to religious freedom.

Fifth: Petitioner finally argues that the statute is unconstitutional in toto; that motion pictures are to be treated as the press generally, and may not be subjected to censorship or prior restraint. While it may not be heard in this respect, inasmuch as it has sought and obtained benefits under the statute, and even now seeks to retain the licenses granted (*Fahey v. Mallonee*, 332 U.S. 245, 255; *Shepherd v. Mount Vernon Trust Co*., 269 N.Y. 234, 244-247), we shall dispose of this argument upon the merits.

The contention urged is made in the face of direct holdings to the contrary (*Mutual Filmcases*, supra; *RD-DR Corp. v. Smith*, 183 F.2d 562 [1950], certiorari denied 340 U.S. 853; *Pathe Exch., Inc., v. Cobb*, 202 App. Div. 450, affd. 236 N.Y. 539, supra; 64 A. L. R. 505).

The rationale of these decisions is that motion pictures are primarily a form of entertainment, a spectacle or show, and not such vehicles of thought as to bring them within the press of the country. On this basis, petitioner's contention that the *Mutual Film* cases (supra) lack authority today, because it was not the Federal Constitution against which the statute was there

***261** tested, is unsound, for the Ohio Constitution guarantees free speech and a free press as does the Federal Constitution. Essentially, what petitioner would have us do is to predict that the Supreme Court will overrule theMutual Film cases and so disregard them here, as well as our own holding in the *Pathe Exchange* case (supra). But such was the position squarely taken in the *RD-DR Corp*. case (supra), where the same arguments were presented as are here urged, and they were unequivocally rejected.

On the same footing is the contention that technical developments have made a difference in the essential nature of motion pictures since the *Mutual Film* decisions. Such development was foreseen in the *Mutual Film* cases (see p. 242), and was realized at the time of the *RD-DR Corp.* case (p. 565), decided a year ago. We have already pointed out that scientific and educational films, among others of kindred nature, are not within the general licensing statute, and are thus not concerned with any problem that might be raised by an attempt to impose general censorship upon such films.

Some comfort is found by petitioner in a statement in *United States v. Paramount Pictures*, Inc. (334 U.S. 131, 166) to the effect that "moving pictures, like newspapers and radio, are included in the press". That was an antitrust case, freedom of the press was not involved, and the statement was pure dictum. Moreover, it may be observed that when certiorari was sought in the *RD-DR Corp.* case (supra), it was denied by the same court; the only Justice voting to grant was the one who wrote that dictum. Were we to rely upon dictum, the concurring remarks of Mr. Justice FRANKFURTER in a subsequently decided free speech case (*Kovacs v. Cooper*, 336 U.S. 77, 96), would be appropriate: "Movies have created problems not presented by the circulation of books, pamphlets, or newspapers, and so the movies have been constitutionally regulated." (Citing the *Mutual Film* cases, supra.) However, dictum is a fragile bark in which to sail the constitutional seas.

The fact is that motion pictures do create problems not presented by other media of communication, visual or otherwise, as already indicated. It should be emphasized, however, that technical developments which increase the force of impact of motion pictures simply render the problem more acute. It does ***262** not avail to argue that there is now greater ability of transmission, when it is precisely that ability which multiplies the dangers already inherent in the particular form of expression.

Whether motion pictures are sui generis or a very special classification of the press becomes a question for the academicians, once it is recognized that there is a danger presented and met by legislation appropriate to protect the public safety, yet narrow enough as not otherwise to limit freedom of expression. If there is any one proposition for which the free speech cases may be cited, from *Schenck v. United States* (249 U.S. 47) to *Dennis v. United States* (341 U.S. 494) and *Breard v. Alexandria* (341 U.S. 622), it is that freedom of speech is not absolute, but may be limited when the appropriate occasion arises. We are satisfied that the dangers present and foreseen at the time of the *Mutual Film* cases (supra) are just as real today.

The order of the Appellate Division should be affirmed, with costs.

DESMOND, J. (concurring).

I concur for affirmance for these reasons:

1. It is not too clear from the statutes that the Legislature, transferring (by L. 1926, ch. 544) motion picture licensing from an independent State Motion Picture Commission to a new Motion Picture Division in the State Department of Education intended, without so saying, that the Board of Regents, as head of the Education Department, should have power to revoke a license granted by the division. However, there is general language in the statute (Education Law, § 132) empowering the Regents to enforce the licensing law, including its prohibition against the licensing of "obscene, indecent, immoral, inhuman, sacrilegious"

films (Education Law, § 122), and it would be an improbable legislative intent that would leave all this solely to a division of the department, with no corrective authority available elsewhere in the State Government. It would be anomalous if the Regents, charged by the statute with enforcing the law, could not correct the errors of their subordinate body.

2. As to whether this film can be considered sacrilegious, our own jurisdiction is limited by the *Miller v. Kling* (291 N.Y. 65) rule which requires us to uphold the administrative body's decision if supported by substantial evidence. In other

***263** words, if reasonable men could regard the picture as sacrilegious, then we cannot say that the Regents' ruling is wrong as matter of law. Reasonable, earnest and religious men in great numbers have said so, although other earnest religious voices express the other view. There was thus fair basis for the Regents' holding.

3. "Sacrilegious", like "obscene" (see *Winters v. New York*, 333 U.S. 507), is sufficiently definite in meaning to set an enforcible standard. That men differ as to what is "sacrilegious" is beside the point — there is nothing in the world which all men everywhere agree is "obscene", yet obscenity laws are universally enforced. Of course, some of the meanings of "sacrilegious" have no possible application to a motion picture, but, according to all the dictionaries and common English usage, the adjective has one applicable meaning, since it includes violating or profaning anything held sacred (see Oxford Dictionary, Vol. 8, pp. 18-19; Webster's New International Dictionary [2d ed.], unabridged, p. 2195; Black's Law Dictionary [deluxe ed.], p. 1574). We thus have a statutory term of broad but ascertainable meaning, and, by settled law, the administrative application thereof must be accepted by the courts "if it has `warrant in the record' and a reasonable basis in law" (*Matter of Mounting & Finishing Co. v. McGoldrick*, 294 N.Y. 104, 108; *Red Hook Cold Storage Co. v. Department of Labor*, 295 N.Y. 1, 9).

4. Motion pictures are, it would seem, not excluded from First Amendment coverage (*United States v. Paramount Pictures*, Inc., 334 U.S. 131, 166) but, since there was a reasonable ground for holding this film "sacrilegious" (in the meaning which the Legislature must have intended for that term), the film was constitutionally "subject to control" (*Ex parte Jackson*, 96 U.S. 727, 736, cited in *Winters v. New York*, supra, p. 510). It fell within the "well-defined and narrowly limited classes of speech, the prevention and punishment of which have never been thought to raise any Constitutional problem" (*Chaplinsky v. New Hampshire*, 315 U.S. 568, 571-572 — italics mine). The *Chaplinsky* decision says that these narrowly limited classes of constitutionally preventable utterances include "the lewd and obscene, the profane, the libelous, and the insulting or `fighting' words — those which by their very utterance inflict injury or

***264** tend to incite an immediate breach of the peace." That covers this case, and should dispose of any claim of violation of the First Amendment. If not, then any prior censorship at all of any motion picture is unconstitutional, and the floodgates are open.

FULD, J. (dissenting).

It may lend perspective to recall that we are here concerned with a motion picture that has passed the rigid scrutiny of a numerous array of critics of undenied religiousness. There is, of course, no suggestion that "The Miracle" is a product of heathen hands. The story was written by a Roman Catholic and the picture produced, directed and acted solely by Roman Catholics. It was filmed in Italy, and first exhibited in Rome, where religious censorship exists. There, the Vatican Newspaper, *L'Osservatore Romano*, in reviewing it, alluded to the story and weighed the artistry of the production without condemning the moving picture or even intimating that there was any impropriety in its being viewed by Catholics. (See *The Commonweal*, March 23, 1951, p. 592.) And thereafter the film passed the United States Customs with no objection registered against it.

In 1949 and again in 1950, successive directors of the motion picture division of the State Education Department licensed the film for state-wide exhibition. It won the approval of the National Board of Review of Motion Pictures. It drew general acclaim from the press and was designated, as part of a trilogy, the best foreign language film of 1950 by the New York Film Critics, an association of critics of the major metropolitan newspapers. Finally, one important Roman Catholic publication, after deploring "these highly arbitrary invocations of a police censorship [that] must ultimately result * * * in great harm to the cause of religion as well as art," noted that the film "is not obviously blasphemous or obscene, either in its intention or execution" (Clancy, The Catholic as Philistine, *The Commonweal*, March 16, 1951, pp. 567-568; also, March 2, 1951, pp. 507-508, and March 23, 1951, pp. 590-592), and all Protestant clergymen who expressed themselves publicly — and they constituted a large number representing various sects — found nothing in the film either irreverent or irreligious.

***265** However, as Judge FROESSEL reminds us, the contrary opinion also found strong voice, eventually reaching the ears of the board of regents. After viewing the film, that body revoked and rescinded the license — some two years after it had been initially granted — invoking as authority therefor section 122 of the Education Law. That statute provides that the motion picture division shall license each moving picture submitted to it unless it is "obscene, indecent, immoral, inhuman, sacrilegious, or is of such character that its exhibition would tend to corrupt morals or incite to crime". The board of regents decided that the film is "sacrilegious," and its decision was confirmed by the Appellate Division.

Laying to one side for the moment the question as to the constitutionality of a statute which sanctions the banning of a moving picture on the ground that it is "sacrilegious," I am of opinion that the regents' action was without legislative warrant.

The controlling statute, the Education Law, is significant both for what it says and for what it leaves unsaid. In section 124, entitled "Review by regents", the legislature expressly gave the regents power to review a determination of the motion picture division denying a license — but it conferred no similar power to review the division's granting of a license. By settled rules of construction, that deliberate omission by the legislature clearly indicates that no such authority was intended. (See, e.g., 2 Sutherland, Statutory Construction [3d ed., 1943], §§ 4915-4917.) And the more one searches the statute, the more clearly does that appear. For example, the statute expressly authorizes the regents to revoke a permit issued for the exhibition of a scientific or educational film (§ 125) and to revoke a motion picture license if it was obtained on a false application or if the licensee tampered with the film or if there is a "conviction for a crime committed by the [film's] exhibition or unlawful possession" (§ 128). But nowhere in the statute is there to be found any general grant of power to the regents to revoke a previously issued license.

This omission is also to be contrasted with the further and explicit grant of such a power of revocation by the same Education Law as regards many other types of licenses issued by the Education Department. (See, e.g., § 6514 [as to doctors]; § 6613 [as to

***266** dentists]; § 6712 [as to veterinarians]; §6804 [as to pharmacists]; § 7108 [as to optometrists]; §7210 [as to engineers]; § 7308 [as to architects]; §7406 [as to certified public accountants]; § 7503 [as to shorthand reporters].) Clearly, the legislature knew how to bestow the power of revocation when that was its purpose.

Even more recent evidence of the legislature's design is at hand. In 1950, the legislature amended the Penal Law to prohibit prosecution, on the ground of obscenity, of a film licensed under the Education Law (L. 1950, ch. 624, amdg. Penal Law, § 1141). That enactment was inspired by *Hughes Tool Co. v. Fielding* (297 N.Y. 1024, affg. 272 App. Div. 1048, affg. 188 Misc. 947). It had there been held that such a criminal prosecution was permissible because the Education Law neither provided for nor allowed any direct review, by the regents or the courts, of a decision of the motion picture division issuing a license. If the legislature had disagreed with that interpretation of the Education Law — clearly indicated at Special Term (188 Misc., at p. 952) — it would undoubtedly have amended the Education Law, not the Penal Law. By depriving the state of the power to prosecute the exhibition of a moving picture once it receives a license, the legislature affirmed, as clearly as it could, that the granting of a license is an act of such implacable finality that it may not be challenged collaterally in a criminal prosecution any more than directly in a civil proceeding.

The legislative scheme so clearly expressed, the board of regents may neither rely upon its status as head of the Education Department to reverse decisions of a subordinate which are not the result of illegality, fraud or vital irregularity (see, e.g., *Butterworth v. Hoe*, 112 U.S. 50, 56, 64; cf. People ex rel. *Finnegan v. McBride*, 226 N.Y. 252, 257; *People ex rel. Chase v. Wemple*, 144 N.Y. 478, 482; *Matter of D & D Realty Corp. v. Coster*, 277 App. Div. 668)[1] nor draw from section 132 of the Education Law — which in over-all manner gives the board "authority to enforce the provisions and purposes of part two

***267** of this article" — an assumption of authority to "review" and "revoke" the grant of a license by the motion picture division. All that section 132 was designed to do, and all that it does, is to authorize enforcement. To construe its general language as authorizing review of the granting of a license is to stretch language beyond all permissible limits and to render superfluous and meaningless the very explicit language of section 124 permitting such review only where a license has been denied.

"A statute must be read and given effect as it is written by the Legislature, not as the court may think it should or would have been written if the Legislature had envisaged all the problems and complications which might arise in the course of its administration. A power not expressly granted by statute is implied only where it is `so essential to the exercise of some power expressly conferred as plainly to appear to have been within the intention of the legislature. The implied power must be necessary, not merely convenient, and the intention of the legislature must be free from doubt.' (*Peo. ex rel. City of Olean v. W. N. Y. & P. T. Co.*, 214 N.Y. 526, 529.)" (*Lawrence Constr. Corp. v. State of New York*, 293 N.Y. 634, 639.)

So, here, the regents' contention that they must have power to review and revoke in order to guard against error by the motion picture division in granting licenses, is not persuasive. The fact is that, in the twenty-five years during which the motion picture division has been in the Department of Education, the regents have never before reviewed the grant of a license or even suggested the existence of such a power. Limited as we are to a determination of what the legislature has done, the argument of alleged necessity has no weight in the face of this long-continued practical construction. For this court now to read into the statute a provision which that body chose not to write into it would constitute an uncalled-for intrusion into the sphere of the legislature. "Freedom to construe is not freedom to amend." (*Sexauer & Lemke v. Burke & Sons Co.*, 228 N.Y. 341, 345; see, also, *Matter of O'Brien v. Tremaine*, 285 N.Y. 233, 238.)

Even if I were to assume, however, that the statute does confer a power to review and revoke, I would still conclude for reversal. In my view, that portion of the statute here involved must fall

***268** before the constitutional guarantee that there be freedom of speech and press. The consistent course of decision by the Supreme Court of the United States in recent years persuades me that the early decision of *Mutual Film Corp. v. Industrial Comm. of Ohio* (236 U.S. 230) — urged as establishing that motion pictures are beyond the First Amendment's coverage — no longer has the force or authority claimed for it.

We are confronted in this case with censorship in its baldest form — a licensing system requiring permission in advance for the exercise of the right to disseminate ideas via motion pictures, and committing to the licensor a broad discretion to decide whether that right may be exercised. Insofar as the statute permits the state to censor a moving picture labelled "sacrilegious," it offends against the First and Fourteenth Amendments of the Federal Constitution, since it imposes a prior restraint — and, at that, a prior restraint of broad and undefined limits — on freedom of discussion of religious matters. And, beyond that, it may well be that it constitutes an attempt to legislate orthodoxy in matters of religious belief, contrary to the constitutional prohibition against laws "respecting an establishment of religion". (Cf. *Everson v. Board of Educ.,* 330 U.S. 1, 15; Illinois ex rel. *McCollum v. Board of Educ.*, 333 U.S. 203, 210.)

The freedoms of the First Amendment are not, I appreciate, absolutes, but insofar as they are qualified, the qualification springs from the necessity of accommodating them to some equally pressing public need. Thus, some limited measure of restraint upon freedom of expression may be justified where the forum is the public street or the public square, where the audience may be a "captive" one, and where breaches of the peace may be imminent as the result of the use, or rather the abuse, of fighting words. (Cf. *Dennis v. United States*, 341 U.S. 494, 503 et seq.; *Feiner v. New York*, 340 U.S. 315, 319; *Niemotko v. Maryland*, 340 U.S. 268; *Terminiello v. Chicago*, 337 U.S. 1; *Chaplinsky v. New Hampshire*, 315 U.S. 568, 571-572; *Cantwell v. Connecticut*, 310 U.S. 296, 308; *Schneider v. State*, 308 U.S. 147, 160.) Here, there is no "captive" audience; only those see the picture who wish to do so, and, then, only if they are willing to pay the price of admission

***269** to the theatre. Moreover, if subject matter furnishes any criterion for the exercise of a restraint, I know of no subject less proper for censorship by the state than the one here involved.

The Supreme Court has "consistently condemned licensing systems which vest in an administrative official discretion to grant or withhold a permit upon broad criteria unrelated to proper regulation of public places." (*Kunz v. New York*, 340 U.S. 290, 294; see, also, *Niemotko v. Maryland*, supra, 340 U.S. 268; *Saia v. New York*, 334 U.S. 558; *Cantwell v. Connecticut*, supra, 310 U.S. 296; *Hague v. C.I.O.*, 307 U.S. 496; *Lovell v. City of Griffin*, 303 U.S. 444.) "The State cannot of course forbid public proselyting or religious argument merely because public officials disapprove the speaker's views. It must act in patent good faith to maintain the public peace, to assure the availability of the streets for their primary purposes of passenger and vehicular traffic, or for equally indispensable ends of modern community life." (See *Niemotko v. Maryland*, supra, 340 U.S. 268, 282, per FRANKFURTER, J., concurring.)

Invasion of the right of free expression must, in short, find justification in some overriding public interest, and the restricting statute must be narrowly drawn to meet an evil which the state has a substantial interest in correcting. (See *Feiner v. New York*, supra, 340 U.S. 315, 319; *Niemotko v. Maryland*, supra, 340 U.S. 268; *Winters v. New York*, 333 U.S. 507, 509; *Cantwell v. Connecticut*, supra, 310 U.S. 296, 307-308; *Thornhill v. Alabama*, 310 U.S. 88, 97-98, 105.) The statute before us is not one narrowly drawn to meet such a need as that of preserving the public peace or regulating public places. On the contrary, it imposes a general and pervasive restraint on freedom of discussion of religious themes in moving pictures, which cannot be justified on the basis of any substantial interest of the state. (Cf. *Kunz v. New York*, supra, 340 U.S. 290; Dennis v. United States, supra, 341 U.S. 494, 508-509.)

Over a century ago, the Supreme Court declared that "The law knows no heresy, and is committed to the support of no dogma". (*Watson v. Jones*, 13 Wall. [U.S.] 679, 728.) Just as clearly, it is beyond the competency of government to prescribe norms of religious conduct and belief. That follows inevitably from adherence to the principles of the First Amendment.

***270** "In the realm of religious faith, and in that of political belief," it has been said (*Cantwell v. Connecticut*, supra, 310 U.S. 296, 310), "sharp differences arise. In both fields the tenets of one man may seem the rankest error to his neighbor. To persuade others to his own point of view, the pleader, as we know, at times, resorts to exaggeration, to vilification of men who have been, or are, prominent in church or state, and even to false statement. But the people of this nation have ordained in the light of history, that, in spite of the probability of excesses and abuses, these liberties are, in the long view, essential to enlightened opinion and right conduct on the part of the citizens of a democracy."

The inherent indefinability, in its present context, of the term "sacrilege" is apparent upon the merest inquiry. At what point, it may be asked, does a search for the eternal verities, a questioning of particular religious dogma, take on the aspect of "sacrilege"? At what point does expression or portrayal of a doubt of some religious tenet become "sacrilegious"? Not even authorities or students in the field of religion will have a definitive answer, and certainly not the same answer. There are more than two hundred and fifty different religious sects in this country, with varying religious beliefs, dogmas and principles. (See *Illinois ex rel. McCollum v. Board of Educ.*, supra, 333 U.S. 203, 227.) With this great contrariety of religious views, it has been aptly observed that one man's heresy is another's orthodoxy, one's "sacrilege," another's consecrated belief. How and where draw the line between permissible theological disputation and "sacrilege"? What is orthodox, what sacrilegious? Whose orthodoxy, to whom sacrilegious? In the very nature of things, what is "sacrilegious" will of necessity differ with the philosophy, the training, the education and the background of the particular censor of the moment; the determination whether a film is "sacrilegious" or not, must necessarily rest in the undiscoverable recesses of the official's mind.

Any possible doubt that the term is essentially vague is dispelled by a reference to the variant and inconsistent definitions ascribed to it by the board of regents and by the Appellate Division and Judge FROESSEL.

***271** Thus, the regents, frowning upon the dictionary definition as "technical",[2] nevertheless assure us that "everyone knows what is meant by this term" and, by way of demonstrating that fact, proceed to define the word as describing a film which "affronts a large segment of the population"; offends the sensibilities by ridiculing and burlesquing anything "held sacred by the adherents of a particular religious faith"; is "offensive to the religious sensibilities of any element of society." (Italics supplied.) Indeed, any semblance of either general meaning or specific content is, I suggest, abandoned by the regents themselves when they assert that, since "anything is only sacrilegious to those persons who hold the concept sacred", the opinions of nonbelievers are "worthless." By such reasoning, the adherents of a particular dogma become the only judges as to whether that dogma has been offended! And, if that is so, it is impossible to fathom how any governmental agency such as the board of regents, composed as it is of laymen of different faiths, could possibly discharge the function of determining whether a particular film is "sacrilegious."

Judge FROESSEL and the Appellate Division state that the statutory proscription against the "sacrilegious" is intended to bar any "visual caricature of religious beliefs held sacred by one sect or another" (opinion of FROESSEL, J., p. 258, italics supplied). Though Judge FROESSEL also defines "sacrilegious" in terms of "attacking" or "insulting" religious beliefs or treating them with "contempt, mockery, scorn and ridicule" — all words of ephemeral and indefinite content — the basic criterion appears to be whether the film treats a religious theme in such a manner as to offend the religious beliefs of any group of persons. If the film does have that effect, and it is "offered as a form of entertainment," it apparently falls within the statutory ban regardless of the sincerity and good faith of the producer of the film, no matter how temperate the treatment of the theme, and no matter how unlikely a public disturbance or breach of the peace.

***272** The drastic nature of such a ban is highlighted by the fact that the film in question makes no direct attack on, or criticism of, any religious dogma or principle, and it is not claimed to be obscene, scurrilous, intemperate or abusive. Nor is there any evidence of any malicious purpose or intention on the part of the producers of the film to revile or even attack Catholic doctrine or dogma, and no suggestion of any reasonable likelihood of a breach of the peace resulting from the film's exhibition.[3] So broad, indeed, is the suggested criterion of "sacrilege" that it might be applied to any fair and temperate treatment of a psychological, ethical, moral or social theme with religious overtones which some group or other might find offensive to its "religious beliefs."

It is claimed that "the courts have had no problem either with the word `sacrilegious' or with its synonym, `profane'" (opinion of FROESSEL, J., supra, p. 255). The cases to which reference is made, however, involved neither the "profane" in religion nor the "sacrilegious," and the simple fact is that the Supreme Court has never had occasion to pass upon either the one term or the other. The context in which the word "profane" appears in the cases cited (*Winters v. New York*, supra, 333 U.S. 507, 510; *Chaplinsky v. New Hampshire*, supra, 315 U.S. 568, 572), as well as the authorities there relied upon (*Cantwell v. Connecticut*, supra, 310 U.S. 296, 309-310; Chafee, *Free Speech in the United States* [1941], pp. 149-150), make it evident that the term was used, not as a synonym for "sacrilegious," but as a substitute for "epithets or personal abuse", for swear words and for the other "insulting or `fighting' words", which "by their very utterance inflict injury or tend to incite an immediate breach of the peace" and "are no essential part of any exposition of ideas". (*Chaplinsky v. New Hampshire*, supra, 315 U.S. 568, 572; see, also, *Cantwell v. Connecticut*, supra, 310 U.S. 296, 310; Chafee, op. cit., p. 150.) In short, the cases cited have nothing whatsoever to do with the

***273** "profane" in religion, and the judges who sat in them were not called upon to give the slightest thought or consideration to the subject with which we are now concerned.

The shortcomings of ambiguous epithets as rigid boundaries for free expression are great enough in temporal and political matters (cf., e.g., *Winters v. New York*, supra, 333 U.S. 507; *Dennis v. United States*, supra, 341 U.S. 494; *Jordan v. De George*, 341 U.S. 223; *Musser v. Utah*, 333 U.S. 95), but they are all the greater when the epithets trench upon areas of religious belief. (See, e.g., *Kunz v. New York*, supra, 340 U.S. 290; *Saia v. New York*, supra, 334 U.S. 558, 561; *Cantwell v. Connecticut*, supra, 310 U.S. 296.) Indeed, the Supreme Court has gone so far as to hold that the First Amendment's guarantee forbids prior restraint of public discussion that even "ridicules" or "denounces" any form of religious belief. (See *Kunz v. New York*, supra, 340 U.S. 290, and see, particularly, concurring opinion of FRANKFURTER, J., reported in 340 U.S., at pp. 285-286.) In a free society "all sects and factions, as the price of their own freedom to preach their views, must suffer that freedom in others." (*Kunz v. New York*, supra, 340 U.S., at p. 301, per JACKSON, J., dissenting; see, also, *Murdock v. Pennsylvania*, 319 U.S. 105, 116.)

Were we dealing with speeches, with handbills, with newspapers or with books, there could be no doubt as to the unconstitutionality of that portion of the statute here under consideration. The constitutional guarantee of freedom of expression, however, is neither limited to the oral word uttered in the street or the public hall nor restricted to the written phrase printed in newspaper or book. It protects the transmission of ideas and beliefs, whether popular or not, whether orthodox or not. A belief does not lose its character as a belief, an idea does not become less of an idea, because, instead of being expressed by the air-borne voice, the printed word or the "still" picture, it is put forward by a "moving" picture. The First Amendment does not ask whether the medium is visual, acoustic, electronic or some yet unheard-of device. It has readily accommodated itself to other products of inventive genius, to other advances in technology, such as the radio and television. If "The Constitution deals with substance, not shadows", if "Its inhibition was levelled at the thing, not the name" (*Cummings v. State of Missouri*, 4 Wall. [U.S.] 277, 325),

***274** then, surely, its meaning and vitality are not to be conditioned upon the mechanism involved. Of course, it may well be that differences in media will give rise to different problems of accommodation of conflicting interests. (See *Kovacs v. Cooper*, 336 U.S.

77, 96, per FRANKFURTER, J., concurring.) But any such accommodation must necessarily be made in the light of fundamental constitutional safeguards.[4]

One reason for denying free expression to motion pictures, we are told, is that the movies are commercial. But newspapers, magazines and books are likewise commercially motivated, and that has never been an obstacle to their full protection under the First Amendment. (See, e.g., *Grosjean v. American Press Co.*, 297 U.S. 233.) Again, it is said, the fact that the moving picture conveys its thought or message in dramatic episodes or by means of a story or in a form that is entertaining, makes the difference. But neither novels, magazines nor comic books are made censorable because they are designed for entertainment or amusement. (See, e.g., *Winters v. New York*, supra, 333 U.S. 507, 510; *Hannegan v. Esquire*, Inc., 327 U.S. 146, 153.) The Supreme Court made that plain in the Winters case, when it declared: "We do not accede to appellee's suggestion that the constitutional protection for a free press applies only to the exposition of ideas. The line between the informing and the entertaining is too elusive for the protection of that basic right. Everyone is familiar with instances of propaganda through fiction. What is one man's amusement, teaches another's doctrine. Though we can see nothing of any possible value to society in these magazines, they are as much entitled to the protection of free speech as the best of literature." (333 U.S., at p. 510.)

Whatever may have been true thirty-six years ago when the *Mutual Film* case (236 U.S. 230), was decided, there is no reason today for casting the motion picture beyond the barriers of protected expression. Learned and thoughtful ***275** writers so opine (see Chafee, *Free Speech in the United States* [1941], pp. 544 et seq.; Ernst, *The First Freedom*, p. 268; Kupferman and O'Brien, *Motion Picture Censorship*, 36 Cornell L. Q. 273; Note, 60 Yale L. J. 696; Note, 49 Yale L. J. 87), and the Supreme Court itself has recently so declared. (See *United States v. Paramount Pictures, Inc.*, 334 U.S. 131, 166; see, also, *Kovacs v. Cooper*, supra, 336 U.S. 77, 102, per BLACK, J., dissenting.) As Chafee put it (op. cit., p. 545), "In an age when `commerce' in the Constitution has been construed to include airplanes and electromagnetic waves, `freedom of speech' in the First Amendment and `liberty' in the Fourteenth should be similarly applied to new media for the communication of ideas and facts. Freedom of speech should not be limited to the air-borne voice, the pen, and the printing press, any more than interstate commerce is limited to stagecoaches and sailing vessels." And, wrote the Supreme Court (*United States v. Paramount Pictures, Inc.*, supra, 334 U.S. 131, 166), "We have no doubt that moving pictures, like newspapers and radio, are included in the press whose freedom is guaranteed by the First Amendment."

Every consideration points that conclusion. The *Mutual Film* case should be relegated to its place upon the history shelf. Rendered in a day before the guarantees of the Bill of Rights were held to apply to the states, and when moving pictures were in their infancy, the decision was obviously a product of the view that motion pictures did not express or convey opinions or ideas. Today, so far have times and the films changed, some would deny protection for the opposite reason, that films are too effective in their presentation of ideas and points of view. The latter notion is as unsupportable as the other and antiquated view; that the moving picture is a most effective mass medium for spreading ideas is, of course, no reason for refusing it protection. If only ineffectual expression is shielded by the Constitution, free speech becomes a fanciful myth. Few would dispute the anomaly of a doctrine that protects as freedom of expression comic books that purvey stories and pictures of "bloodshed and lust" (see *Winters v. New York*, supra, 333 U.S. 507, 510), light and racy magazine reading (see *Hannegan v. Esquire*, Inc., supra,327 U.S. 146, 153) and

*276 loudspeaker harangues (see *Saia v. New York*, supra, 334 U.S. 558), and yet denies that same protection to the moving picture.

Sincere people of unquestioned good faith may, as in this case, find a moving picture offensive to their religious sensibilities, but that cannot justify a statute which empowers licensing officials to censor the free expression of ideas or beliefs in the field of religion. "If there is any fixed star in our constitutional

constellation," the Supreme Court has said (*West Virginia State Bd. of Educ. v. Barnette*, 319 U.S. 624, 642), "it is that no official, high or petty, can prescribe what shall be orthodox in politics, nationalism, religion, or other matters of opinion".

The order of the Appellate Division should be reversed and the determination of the board of regents annulled.

Order affirmed. [See 304 N.Y. 718.]

Footnotes

[*] Education Law, § 122.

[1] There is no substance to the regents' claim that they were merely correcting the "illegal" action of the motion picture division in licensing a "sacrilegious" picture. Since obviously there was at least reasonable doubt as to whether the film was "sacrilegious," the decision of the motion picture division could not be condemned as "illegal."

[2] A typical definition of "sacrilege" is that found in Webster's New International Dictionary (2d ed., 1948): "the crime of stealing, misusing, violating or desecrating that which is sacred, or holy, or dedicated to sacred uses." (See, also, the New Catholic Dictionary [Vatican ed., 1929].)

[3] One writer, associated with the University of Notre Dame, noted (Clancy, op. cit., *The Commonweal*, March 16, 1951, p. 567) that, while some critics have questioned its dramatic validity and others, the director's taste in his choice of theme, "No serious or responsible critic * * * has questioned the sincerity or honesty" of the director's "intention in making the film, an intention abundantly moral * * *."

[4] Whether, for instance, the statute (Education Law, § 122) may be sustained as valid even as a censorship measure insofar as its criterion is the narrow one of "obscenity," is not before us and need not be considered. (Cf. *Chaplinsky v. New Hampshire*, supra, 315 U.S. 568, 572; *Near v. Minnesota ex rel. Olson*, 283 U.S. 697; *Ex parte Jackson*, 96 U.S. 727, 736.)

8

State's Rights

After the *Miracle* decision broke through, courts recognized that in some cases, motion pictures would be protected under the First Amendment's guarantee of freedom of expression. The ruling of *Burstyn v. Wilson* did not eliminate film censorship entirely, but was rather a narrowly drawn decision. Justice Clark signed off with the comment, "We hold only that under the First and Fourteenth Amendments a state may not ban a film on the basis of a censor's conclusion that it is sacrilegious." (*Burstyn v. Wilson*, 343 U.S. 495, 506 (1952), internal quotations omitted).

The next stage of cinema's journey toward broader freedoms would be a series of cases that peeled back layers of regulation.

Like Burstyn and Mayer, Robert and Raymond Hakim, Egyptian born siblings, also made their mark importing continental films for U.S. audiences. The Hakims began their careers as Paramount Picture's Paris-based agents in the 1930s. The following decade they emigrated to America and went into business under their shingle Commercial Pictures. Commercial distributed *Gas Light* (1940), a British film so popular that MGM remade it four years later as a Ingrid Bergman/Charles Boyer vehicle. Commercial's distribution of *La ronde* (1950) met with considerably more resistance. The picture, directed by Max Ophüls, presented a series of interlocking love triangles. Sexual relations seemed to connect everyone in a Viennese neighborhood, housewives with soldiers with prostitutes with university students. New York's Board of Regents threw cold water on the affairs banning the film based on its immorality.

Commercial Pictures called on a pioneering female lawyer to advocate on their behalf. Florence Perlow Shientag (1908-2009) was one of the first women to be admitted to the New York Bar in 1937. By 1943 she became the first woman to serve as an Assistant U.S. Attorney for the Southern District of New York, Criminal Division. She entered private practice in 1953 and was immediately retained by the Hakim brothers.

Shientag was not able to prevail on the state level, but she kept fighting. Appealing to the Supreme Court, *Commercial Pictures* was consolidated with a similar case coming out of Ohio that focused on a film noir remake of Fritz Lang's classic *M* (1931). *M* was bound to be controversial in America—the film warned of mob violence and championed the rule of law, arguing for due process even in the case of a psychopathic child murderer. The Supreme Court combined the cases and overrode New York's and Ohio's censors. Motion pictures could no longer be banned for immorality.

Otto Preminger directed a suggestive screwball comedy entitled *The Moon Is Blue* (1953). The picture revolved around two aging bachelor playboys (William Holden and David Niven) as they vie for the attention of a pretty young woman (Maggie McNamara). The girl fends them off by claiming that she plans to remain a virgin until her wedding night. Her lip service wasn't enough to keep the Kansas censors from crying foul: they banned the film as indecent. Preminger pressured his distributor, United Artists, into releasing the film without a Seal of Approval. The film did solid box office business without a Seal and demonstrated the diminishing influence of the censor's office.

The times were changing and the censor's bureau was quickly becoming an anachronism, out of touch with the direction of American life. Kroger Babb, an exploitation film maven, was able to pack theaters with racy b-movies that could not have been shown even five years earlier. Babb was a marketing man, he promoted an idea or theme; the movies themselves were almost afterthoughts.

Babb arrived on the film scene with *Mom and Dad* (1945), the story of a young girl who gets pregnant, learns about venereal diseases, and gives birth. Forty years later the Library of Congress inducted the low budget sex hygiene film into the National Film Registry. They noted that the picture earned solid box office as third highest grossing film of the 1940s. (See *http://www.loc.gov/ programs/national-film-preservation-board*).

Babb's b-movies brought down New York's censorship code in *Capitol v. Board of Regents* and Pennsylvania's longstanding ordinance in *Hallmark Productions v. Carroll.* But the movies themselves were all wind up with little delivery. They promised titillating scenes but came up just short. Instead it was an innocently titled film called *Garden of Eden* (1954) that went all the way. For the first time in a main-stream theatrically released film, nude bodies were seen on screen.

Garden of Eden was a pseudo-documentary on nudism, a fad that was catching on around America. The picture was not leering, lecherous, dirty, or lewd. It chronicled men, women, and children frolicking at a country resort, swimming, playing volleyball, barbecuing sans clothing. Chicago's film board tried to halt exhibition but was denied. The Northern District Court of Illinois ruled that nudity alone was not per se obscene. Over the course of eight years, from 1952-1960, the layers of state censorship were peeled away. Far from banning films on the basis of sacrilege and immorality, by the end of the decade, even nudity could not be banned outright. Pandora's box had been opened.

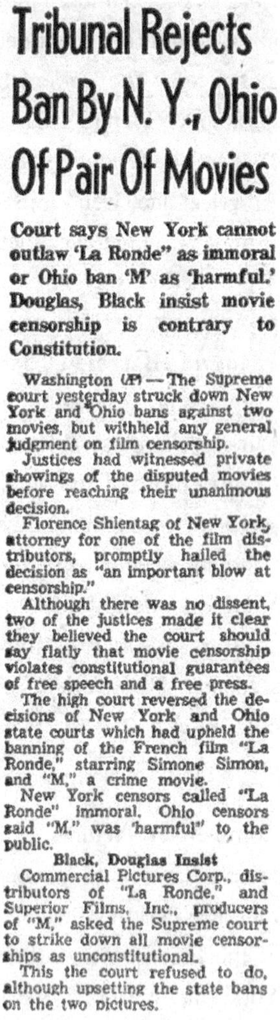

Tribunal Rejects Ban By N. Y., Ohio Of Pair Of Movies

Court says New York cannot outlaw 'La Ronde" as immoral or Ohio ban 'M' as 'harmful.' Douglas, Black insist movie censorship is contrary to Constitution.

Washington (AP)—The Supreme court yesterday struck down New York and Ohio bans against two movies, but withheld any general judgment on film censorship.

Justices had witnessed private showings of the disputed movies before reaching their unanimous decision.

Florence Shientag of New York, attorney for one of the film distributors, promptly hailed the decision as "an important blow at censorship."

Although there was no dissent, two of the justices made it clear they believed the court should say flatly that movie censorship violates constitutional guarantees of free speech and a free press.

The high court reversed the decisions of New York and Ohio state courts which had upheld the banning of the French film "La Ronde," starring Simone Simon, and "M," a crime movie.

New York censors called "La Ronde" immoral. Ohio censors said "M," was 'harmful" to the public.

Black, Douglas Insist

Commercial Pictures Corp., distributors of "La Ronde," and Superior Films, Inc., producers of "M," asked the Supreme court to strike down all movie censorships as unconstitutional.

This the court refused to do, although upsetting the state bans on the two pictures.

The Gazette and Daily,
January 19, 1954

IN THE MATTER OF COMMERCIAL PICTURES CORP.

v.

BOARD OF REGENTS OF THE UNIVERSITY OF THE STATE OF NEW YORK

305 N.Y. 336 (1953)

Court of Appeals of the State of New York

Argued January 7, 1953

Decided May 28, 1953

***338** Florence Perlow Shientag for appellant

***339** FROESSEL, J.

The Motion Picture Division of the State Education Department and the Regents of the University of the State of New York have determined that the motion picture "La Ronde" (revised), produced in France, is not entitled to be licensed for public exhibition, upon the ground that it is "immoral" and "would tend to corrupt morals" within the meaning of section 122 of the Education Law of this State. The Appellate Division has confirmed the determination.

The film from beginning to end deals with promiscuity, adultery, fornication and seduction. It portrays ten episodes, with a narrator. Except for the husband and wife episode, each deals with an illicit amorous adventure between two persons, one of the two partners becoming the principal in the next. The first episode begins with a prostitute and a soldier. Since the former's room is ten minutes walk from their meeting place on the street, and the soldier must hurry back to his barracks, they take advantage of the local environment. She informs him that "civilians" pay, but for "boys like you it's nothing". The cycle continues with the soldier and a parlormaid; the parlormaid and her employer's son; the latter and a young married woman; the married woman and her husband; the husband and a young girl; the girl and a poet; the poet and an actress; the actress and a count, and finally the count and the prostitute. At the very end, the narrator reminds the audience of the author's thesis: "It is the story of everyone".

* * *

***340** ... The issues so presented may be posed thus:

(1) Are motion pictures, as part of the press, altogether exempt from prior restraint or censorship?

(2) Do the words "immoral" and "tend to corrupt morals", in section 122 of the Education Law, viewed in the perspective of their legislative setting, fail to provide a standard adequate to satisfy the requirements of due process?

(3) Has the statute been properly applied herein?

1. Our answer to the first question must be in the negative, as it was in the *Burstyn* case in this court (*Matter of Joseph Burstyn, Inc., v. Wilson*, 303 N.Y. 242, 262; see, also, concurring opinion of DESMOND, J., at pp. 263-264). That question was not reached by the Supreme Court of the United States in *Joseph Burstyn, Inc. v. Wilson* (343 U.S. 495, supra, pp. 502-503, 505-506), and the language employed therein aptly refutes the notion that all media of communication may be grouped under a precise and absolute rule: "To hold that liberty of expression by means of motion pictures is guaranteed by the First and Fourteenth Amendments, however, is not the end of our problem. It does not follow that the Constitution requires absolute freedom to exhibit

every motion picture of every kind at all times and all places...

Insofar, then, as motion pictures tend to present their "own peculiar problems", we think they may properly become the subject of special measures of control. If, as we believe, motion pictures may present a "clear and present danger" of substantive evil to the community (*Schenck v. United States*, 249 U.S. 47, 52), then the Legislature may act to guard against such evil, though in so doing it overrides to a degree the right to free expression (*Poulos v. New Hampshire*, 345 U.S. 395;

* * *

***341** ... The problem of preserving individual rights under the Constitution and still securing to the State the right to protect itself is not always an easy one, and it is sometimes difficult to find the proper balance between them. There is no mathematical formula for accommodating the rights of the individual to the good of the community, and we fully recognize that care must be exercised when preserving one not to suppress the other. But there "is no basis for saying that freedom and order are not compatible. That would be a decision of desperation. Regulation and suppression are not the same, either in purpose or result, and the courts of justice can tell the difference" (*Poulos v. New Hampshire*, supra, p. 408).

***342** Of course it is true that the State may not impose upon its inhabitants the moral code of saints, but, if it is to survive, it must be free to take such reasonable and appropriate measures as may be deemed necessary to preserve the institution of marriage and the home, and the health and welfare of its inhabitants. History bears witness to the fate of peoples who have become indifferent to the vice of indiscriminate sexual immorality—a most serious threat to the family, the home and the State. An attempt to combat such threat is embodied in the sections of the Education Law here challenged...

That a motion picture which panders to base human emotions is a breeding ground for sensuality, depravity, licentiousness and sexual immorality can hardly be doubted. That these vices represent a "clear and present danger" to the body social seems manifestly clear. The danger to youth is self-evident. And so adults, who may react with limited concern to a portrayal of larceny, will tend to react quite differently to a presentation wholly devoted to promiscuity, seductively portrayed in such manner as to invite concupiscence and condone its promiscuous satisfaction, with its evil social consequences. A single motion picture may be seen simultaneously in theaters throughout the State. May nothing be done to prevent countless individuals from being exposed to its vicious effects? To us the answer seems obvious, especially in the light of recent technical developments which render the problem more acute than ever. Now we have commercially feasible three dimensional projection, some forms of which are said to bring the audience "right into the picture". There can be no doubt that attempts will be made to bring the audience right into the bedchamber if it be held that the State is impotent to apply preventive measures...

***343** ... We conclude, therefore, that censorship, as such, is not in every case inimical to the rights of free speech and press guaranteed by the Constitution, so far as motion pictures are concerned...

* * *

***348** ... In summary, we conclude that motion pictures may be censored, upon proper grounds, and that sexual immorality is one such ground. The standard "immoral" and "tend to corrupt morals" embodied in the statute and here applied relates to sexual immorality, and the Regents had the right to find that the motion picture in question falls within the prohibited category.

The order appealed from should be affirmed, with costs.

* * *

DYE, J. (dissenting)

***356** * * * Since the decision in *Joseph Burstyn, Inc. v. Wilson* (343 U.S. 495, supra, revg. 303 N.Y. 242) there is no longer any doubt but that motion picture films enjoy the same constitutional freedom and protection accorded other media of human expression (cf. *United States v. Paramount Pictures*, 334 U.S. 131; *Stromberg v. California*, 283 U.S. 359) and this is so even though motion pictures as such are primarily designed to entertain at exhibitions conducted for private profit and even though motion picture films as such possess "a greater capacity for evil, particularly among the youth of a community, than other modes of expression" (*Burstyn*, supra, p. 502).

* * *

***357** ... Since the courts no longer see any distinction separating motion picture film from the protection accorded other media of communication, it follows as a matter of reason and logic that prior censorship of motion pictures is as to them as it is in other fields of expression, a denial of due process. In saying this we are, of course, mindful of the correlative obligation that in its exercise and enjoyment such right is not unlimited and absolute at all times and under all circumstances (*Chaplinsky v. New Hampshire*, 315 U.S. 568; *Cox v. New Hampshire*, 312 U.S. 569) but that such freedom may properly be restrained when inimical to the public welfare (*Gitlow v. New York*, 268 U.S. 652) and the State may punish its abuse (*Near v. Minnesota*, supra). It is equally well established that before such limitation may be imposed the abuse complained of is to be examined in all cases to determine whether it is of such a nature "as to create a clear and present danger [and] will bring about the substantive evils that Congress has a right to prevent" (*Schenck v. United States*, 249 U.S. 47, 52), which danger should be "apparent and imminent" (*Thornhill v. Alabama*, 310 U.S. 88) such,

***358** for example, as a threat to overthrow the government by unconstitutional means (*Dennis v. United States*, 341 U.S. 494). By the same token, when public safety is involved, its restraint will be approved as a proper exercise of the police power (*Feiner v. New York*, 340 U.S. 315, affg. 300 N.Y. 391; *Kovacs v. Cooper*, 336 U.S. 77) or, to state it differently, there must be present some "overriding public interest" (see dissenting opinion per FULD, J., in *Matter of Joseph Burstyn, Inc., v. Wilson*, supra, p. 269; *Thornhill v. Alabama*, supra), mere fear of possible injury is not enough (*Terminiello v. Chicago*, 337 U.S. 1).

Having in mind these well-recognized principles, it is pertinent to inquire what if anything there is about "La Ronde" that requires denial of constitutional safeguards and the imposition of the sanction of prior restraint. Is it because a showing would offend against some overriding need — would constitute a danger clear and present? We think not.

According to the record, the picture "La Ronde" since its admission through Customs without objection (U.S. Code, tit. 18, § 1462; U.S. Code, tit. 19, §1305) has been exhibited throughout the United States in cities and towns in the States of Arizona, California, Colorado, Connecticut, Delaware, Florida, Kentucky, Louisiana, Maine, Massachusetts, Michigan, Missouri, New Jersey, Oklahoma, Oregon, Texas and Washington, D. C. Nowhere has the showing of "La Ronde" been banned except in New York. While experience elsewhere is not binding on the courts in New York, the opinions of qualified critics may be considered (*United States v. One Book Entitled Ulysses*, 72 F.2d 705). We deem it significant that in the States of Louisiana (La. Rev. Stat., tit. 4, §§301-307) and Massachusetts (Mass. Ann. Laws, ch. 136, §§ 2-4) having censorship laws, though to be sure, not as comprehensive as that in New York, the picture has had an unhampered showing as well as in places where municipal codes are in effect such as Detroit, Michigan; Salem, Oregon and Houston, Texas, to mention a few, a circumstance indicating that in a large segment of society the picture is not offensive per se. Such a showing in other States and cities of this country, where prior restraint was available and not invoked, and elsewhere having no such statutes, all without untoward incident or complaint, is a convincing testimonial

***359** that it is not inimical to the public peace, welfare and safety. On the contrary, we are told that the showing elsewhere has been well received and has elicited favorable acclaim by the premier dramatic critics of eminent publications ...

***360** In addition, it has been shown in the principal cities of most foreign countries and has received special recognition for merit from several motion picture academies as, for instance, in Cuba as the best film of 1951, by the British Film Academy in London as the best film from any source, British or foreign, and in 1952, a nomination for an award at the Hollywood Academy.

* * *

***366** FULD, J. (dissenting).

I agree with Judge DYE and, for myself, would add these words only to underscore what he has written.

That the freedom of expression assured by the First Amendment is not limited to "the air-borne voice, the pen, and the printing press" (Chafee, *Free Speech in the United States* [1941], p. 545), but extends as well to motion pictures, is now beyond dispute. (See *Gelling v. Texas*, 343 U.S. 960; *Joseph Burstyn, Inc. v. Wilson*, 343 U.S. 495.) While I conceive that any legislation imposing a previous restraint on the exhibition of moving pictures is condemned by the Constitution, I do not believe it necessary to invoke that broad principle to reach a decision in this case. Here again, as in Burstyn, the censorship statute must fall because of the lack of a sufficiently definite standard or guide for administrative action.

* * *

I would reverse and annul the determination of the Board of Regents.

SUPERIOR FILMS, INC. [and CLASSIC PICTURES, INC.] v. DEPARTMENT OF EDUCATION OF THE STATE OF OHIO, DIVISION OF FILM CENSORSHIP, HISSONG, SUPT.

159 Ohio St. 315 (1953)
Supreme Court of Ohio
Decided April 29, 1953

***319** * * * The plaintiff in case No. 33265 submits that the question presented is whether "motion pictures, as distinguished from other media of human expression, may be subjected to censorship in advance of publication; or, whether motion pictures, along with such other media, are entitled to protection from all restraint except such as is incident to responsibility for abuse."

On the other hand, the defendant states his basic position as follows:

"The impact of the motion picture, the unrestricted audience, and the subject matter of those films which experience shows have been rejected, taken together present an area of proper interest for Ohio and an area which can be constitutionally regulated. The standards of regulation under this statute have acquired in this court and through administrative experience a definiteness which complies with procedural due process of law. The Division of Film Censorship acted reasonably and within the proper bounds of its discretion in rejecting the motion picture 'M.' * * *

In 1913, the Ohio General Assembly adopted a motion picture censorship act providing for a Board of

***320** Censors to operate under the authority and supervision of the Industrial Commission. Section 871-48, General Code, a part of the act, provided that "it shall be the duty of the Board of Censors to examine and censor as herein provided, of motion picture films to be publicly exhibited and displayed in the state of Ohio."

Section 871-49 provided that "only such films as are in the judgment and discretion of the Board of Censors of a moral, educational or amusing and harmless character shall be passed and approved by such board."

In 1935, the censorship body was designated as the "Division of Film Censorship of the Department of Education" (116 Ohio Laws, 100). In 1943, Section 871-48, General Code, became present Section 154-47, General Code, and Section 871-49, General Code, became present Section 154-47b, General Code (120 Ohio Laws, 481), but the language of the statutes as above quoted has remained practically the same.

In 1914, the constitutionality of the Ohio censorship act, as above noted, was under consideration by the Supreme Court of the United States in the case of *Mutual Film Corp. v. Industrial Commission of Ohio*, 236 U.S., 230, 59 L. Ed., 552, 35 S. Ct., 387, Ann. Cas. 1916C, 296.

* * *

***322** ...The plaintiff asserts that the free speech and press guaranty of the First Amendment to the Constitution of the United States is secured from infringement by the state by the Fourteenth Amendment to that Constitution...

***323** ...and that motion pictures are a mode of expression entitled to the same protection as "speech" and "the press" (*Burstyn, Inc., v. Wilson, Commr.*, supra; *Gelling v. Texas*, 343 U.S., 960, 96 L. Ed., 1359, 72 S. Ct., 1002; *United States v. Paramount Pictures, Inc.*, 334 U.S., 131, 166, 92 L. Ed., 1260, 1297, 68 S. Ct., 915). Upon that premise plaintiff then contends that Sections 154-47 to 154-47i, inclusive, General Code, are an unconstitutional prior restraint upon the exhibition of motion pictures equivalent to prior restraint upon freedom of speech and the press.

* * *

***326** ... It will be noted that in the *Near* case the Supreme Court stated that "the primary requirements of decency may be enforced against obscene publication," and in the case of *Chaplinsky v. New Hampshire*, 315 U.S., 568, 571, 86 L. Ed., 1031, 1034, 62 S. Ct., 766, Justice Murphy, speaking for a unanimous court, said: "There are certain well-defined and narrowly limited classes of speech, the prevention and punishment of which have never been thought to raise any constitutional problem. These include the lewd and obscene, the profane, the libelous, and the insulting or `fighting' words—those which by their very utterance inflict injury or tend to incite an immediate breach of the peace."

***327** In the case of *Commercial Pictures Corp. v. Regents of University of New York*, 114 N.Y. Supp. (2d), 561, decided since the Burstyn case, the court sustained the order of the Regents of the University of New York refusing to license for exhibition a picture film entitled "La Ronde," in connection with which the court, referring to the Burstyn case,said:

"We have no doubt, however, both from the area that was expressly left open in that case by the Supreme Court and from the generally accepted power of a state to deal by its municipal law with matters deemed offensive to public morals that the statute delegating the power of licensing to the Regents remains valid to that extent in a proper case."

* * *

From these expressions of the United States Supreme Court and otherwise, we conclude that, although a motion picture film may not be rejected because of "sacrilegious" expressions or portrayals, there still remains a limited field in which decency and morals may be protected from the impact of an offending motion picture film by prior restraint under proper criteria. There can be no inherent right to publicity

***328** which tends to destroy the very social fabric of the community, and consequently in such instances there is no right of free speech or free press to be infringed. In these times of alarming rise in juvenile delinquency and of increasing criminality in this country, attributed by social agencies, at least in part, to the character of the exhibitions put on in the show houses of the country, criminal prosecution after the fact is a weak and ineffective remedy to meet the problem at hand. In the war against crime and delinquency there must be some effective defensive weapons against immoral publicity, whereby the social fabric may be protected as it is by law from other methods of attack * * *

As we view it, the United States Supreme Court has not ipso facto taken away all community control of moving pictures by censorship, and this court will not do so under the claim of complete unconstitutionality of censorship laws.

The motion picture, "M," as shown by the certificate was rejected for the following reasons, among others:

"1. There is a conviction that the effect of this picture on unstable persons of any age level could lead to a serious increase in immorality and crime.

"2. Presentation of actions and emotions of child killer emphasizing complete perversion without serving any valid educational purpose. Treatment of perversion creates sympathy rather than a constructive plan for dealing with perversion."

* * *

***329** ... The plaintiff claims that the picture is artistic, free from vulgarity and immorality; that its purpose is "to so impress its viewers with the consequences of neglect and apathy that affirmatively moral and righteous attitudes toward the problems dramatized will result"; that it is educational because "it reveals to its audience the sources of five significant contemporary social problems, and then, either proposes a solution, or appeals for public understanding and action"; and that it is not harmful.

The defendant describes the picture as follows:

"This motion picture is filled with brutal crime. Two cold blooded murders are presented, another implied and a third attempted. A schizophrenic killer is treated with sympathy and an underworld boss is depicted as vastly more efficient than the police. Twice, the methods for abducting children on the streets are elaborated."

* * *

It is apparent that the lofty purposes of the picture, as expressed by its producers, would appeal only to a limited number of its viewers, whereas the great majority of a promiscuous audience, including children, would be impressed and affected merely by the exhibitionism and the portrayal of evil conduct in society, which the producers admit is so bad as to need radical correction.

* * *

***333** * * * Our attention is called to the case of *Gelling v. State* of Texas, supra, as being decisive of the instant cases. As disclosed by the per curiam opinion in that case, it was decided on authority of *Joseph Burstyn, Inc., v. Wilson, Commr.*, supra, and *Winters v. New York*, supra, without further statement or reason.

We have already considered the *Burstyn* case. In the *Winters* case, a New York statute made it an offense to publish and distribute publications "principally made up of criminal news, police reports, or accounts of criminal deeds, or pictures, or stories of deeds of bloodshed, lust or crime." In an opinion by Mr. Justice Reed, concurred in by five members of the court, it was held that the statute did not set up a sufficiently definite standard of conduct. ...

***334** * * * In the *Gelling* case, above noted, the appellant was convicted under an ordinance of the city of Marshall, Texas, for exhibiting a picture after being denied a license to do so. The ordinance authorized the licensing board to deny a license to show a motion picture which, in its opinion, was "of such character as to be prejudicial to the best interests of the people of said city." Mr. Justice Frankfurter, concurring in the judgment of reversal, said: "This ordinance offends the due process clause of the Fourteenth Amendment on the score of indefiniteness." This reason for invalidity carries with it the implication that under a proper statute motion pictures may be subjected to reasonable censorship. Conceding that the Marshall ordinance was void for indefiniteness, it does not suggest that the criteria of our licensing statute are insufficient or that it should be stricken down for that reason.

* * *

***335** * * * From the evidence before this court we cannot say that the defendant abused his discretion in refusing to approve the picture film in question. The division, representing the public interest, has made its decision and this court cannot find affirmatively that it was in error in so doing. The prayer of the petition is denied.

* * *

***336** ... TAFT, J., dissenting. I must dissent because bound by the construction put upon the Constitution of the United States by the Supreme Court of the United States. The pronouncements of the law by that court in *Joseph Burstyn, Inc., v. Wilson, Commr.*, 343 U.S., 495, 96 L. Ed., 1098, 72 S. Ct., 777, and the later decision of that court in *Gelling v. Texas*, 343 U.S., 960, 96 L. Ed., 1359, 72 S. Ct., 1002, clearly require the conclusion that the Ohio moving picture censorship statutes are void because of the provisions of the Constitution of the United States. STEWART, J., concurs in the foregoing dissenting opinion.

Joseph Losey's *M* (1951), a film noir-ish re-make of Fritz Lang's cinema classic.

SUPERIOR FILMS, INC. v. DEPARTMENT OF EDUCATION OF OHIO, DIVISION OF FILM CENSORSHIP, HISSONG, SUPERINTENDENT

346 U.S. 587 (1954)

Supreme Court of United States

Argued January 6, 1954

Decided January 18, 1954

***588** PER CURIAM.

The judgments are reversed. *Joseph Burstyn, Inc. v. Wilson*, 343 U.S. 495.

MR. JUSTICE DOUGLAS, with whom MR. JUSTICE BLACK agrees, concurring.

The argument of Ohio and New York that the government may establish censorship over moving pictures is one I cannot accept. In 1925 Minnesota passed a law aimed at suppressing before publication any "malicious, scandalous and defamatory newspaper." The Court, speaking through Chief Justice Hughes, struck down that law as violating the Fourteenth Amendment, which has made the First Amendment applicable to the States. *Near v. Minnesota*, 283 U.S. 697. The "chief purpose" of the constitutional guaranty of liberty of the press, said the Court, was "to prevent previous restraints upon publication." Id., p. 713.

* * * Nor is it conceivable to me that producers of plays for the legitimate theatre or for television could be required to submit their manuscripts to censors on pain of penalty for producing them without approval. Certainly the

***589** spoken word is as freely protected against prior restraints as that which is written. Such indeed is the force of our decision in *Thomas v. Collins*, 323 U.S. 516, 540. The freedom of the platform which it espouses carries with it freedom of the stage.

The same result in the case of motion pictures necessarily follows as a consequence of our holding in *Joseph Burstyn, Inc. v. Wilson*, 343 U.S. 495, 502, that motion pictures are "within the free speech and free press guaranty of the First and Fourteenth Amendments."

Motion pictures are of course a different medium of expression than the public speech, the radio, the stage, the novel, or the magazine. But the First Amendment draws no distinction between the various methods of communicating ideas. On occasion one may be more powerful or effective than another.

* * * Which medium will give the most excitement and have the most enduring effect will vary with the theme and the actors. It is not for the censor to determine in any case. The First and the Fourteenth Amendments say that Congress and the States shall make "no law" which abridges freedom of speech or of the press...In this Nation every writer, actor, or producer, no matter what medium of expression he may use, should be freed from the censor.

R. K. O. RADIO PICTURES, INC.
v.
DEPARTMENT OF EDUCATION OF THE STATE OF OHIO, DIVISION OF FILM CENSORSHIP

162 Ohio St. 263 (1954)
Supreme Court of Ohio
Decided December 1, 1954

***264** LAMNECK, J.

Under Section 3305.04, Revised Code (Section 154-47b, General Code, and former analogous Section 871-49, General Code), "only such films as are, in the judgment and discretion of the Department of Education, of a moral, educational, or amusing and harmless character shall be passed and approved by such department."

* * *

***265** ... On April 29, 1953, this court decided three cases, which were heard together, involving the censoring of two motion pictures. See *Superior Films, Inc., v. Department ofEducation*; *State, ex rel. Classic Pictures, Inc., v. Hissong*, Dir.; *Classic Pictures, Inc., v. Department of Education*; all reported in 159 Ohio St., 315, 112 N. E. (2d), 311. The *Superior Films* case involved the censoring of the motion picture film, "M," which was rejected by the Department of Education "on account of being harmful." The other two cases concerned the motion picture film, "Native Son," which was disapproved as harmful because it "contributes to racial misunderstanding."

The constitutionality of the Ohio Motion Picture Censorship Act was definitely challenged in each of those cases. In the second paragraph of the syllabus of this court's decision, it was held that the constitutional ***266** guaranty of freedom of speech and the press is not violated by Sections 154-47 to 154-47i, General Code (Section 3305.01 et seq., Revised Code), * * *

* * *

***267** ... Five members of the court are of the opinion that the pronouncements of the Supreme Court of the *United States in Burstyn v. Wilson*, supra; *Gelling v. Texas*, 343 U.S., 960, 96 L. Ed., 1359, 72 S. Ct., 1002, and *Superior Films, Inc., v. Department of Education*, supra, are equivalent to a declaration by that court that the censorship provisions of the Ohio Motion Picture Censorship Act, as now drawn, contravene the First and Fourteenth Amendments to the Constitution of the United States.

* * *

***268** ... The majority of this court being of the opinion that the decisions of the Supreme Court of the United States above referred to are equivalent to a declaration by that court that the censorship provisions of the Ohio Motion Picture Censorship Act contravene the First and Fourteenth Amendments to the Constitution of the United States, we must conclude that any censoring order made by the Department of Education pursuant to this act is "unreasonable" and "unlawful" within the meaning of these words as used in Section 3305.07, Revised Code.

Each of the orders complained of is, therefore, vacated and set aside.

Judgments for plaintiffs. * * *

***270** ... In the case of *Superior Films, Inc.* (159 Ohio St., 315), this court held (1) that, although expression by means of motion pictures is included within the freedom of speech and the press guaranty of the First Amendment to the federal Constitution, such Constitution does not guarantee absolute freedom to exhibit motion pictures of every kind at all times and in all places, (2) that constitutional guaranties are not violated by Sections 154-47 to 154-47i, inclusive, General Code, creating a censoring authority with power to examine and censor prior to exhibition motion picture

***271** films and to pass and approve only such films as are of a moral, educational or amusing and harmless character, (3) that the statutory criterion, for the examination and approval by the Ohio censoring authority of motion pictures, that such pictures shall be of a "moral, educational or amusing and harmless character," is sufficiently clear, definite and comprehensive, and (4) that a motion picture film which presented actions and emotions of a child-killer, emphasizing complete perversion, and which was filled with brutal crimes, including two cold-blooded murders, with another implied and a third attempted, was subject to prepublication censorship and of disapproval thereunder.

In the case of *Commercial Pictures Corp. v. Board of Regents*, supra, the Court of Appeals of New York affirmed the judgment of the Appellate Division of the Supreme Court of that state (280 App. Div., 260, 114 N.Y. Supp. [2d], 561) sustaining the order of the Regents of the University of New York in refusing to license for public exhibition a motion picture film entitled "La Ronde" and which dealt with promiscuous illicit sex relations. That court held (1) that a state has a right to exercise its own sovereign powers to determine what motion pictures transgress bounds of decency and sexual morality laid down by common consent, (2) that a statute providing for censorship of motion pictures which transgress the bounds of decency and sexual morality laid down by common consent is a valid exercise of the police power and does not violate constitutional guaranties, and (3) that a motion picture concerned solely with promiscuous illicit sex relations comes within the purview of a statute providing that a motion picture shall not be licensed if it is immoral or is of such character that its exhibition will tend to corrupt morals. * * *

***276** ... The records in two of the instant cases show that before the Department of Education rejected a portion of each of the pictures because of its obscenity and immorality, the plaintiffs' own industry, through the Motion Picture Production Code Administration, had refused to approve the pictures, "Son of Sinbad" and "The French Line," for exhibition. I still maintain that if those portions of the pictures in the instant cases, rejected by the defendant, are in fact obscene and immoral, then the state by statutory action has the authority, in the exercise of its police power, to deny the right of exhibition, and that the Supreme Court of the United States has not passed upon that question as related to the pictures in the instant cases.

In the instant case of *R. K. O. Radio Pictures, Inc.*,

***277** *v. Department of Education*, No. 33931, portions of a picture entitled "Son of Sinbad" were excluded because certain dance scenes have no conceivable purpose except to be sexually stimulating and lust provoking.

In the instant case of *Capitol Enterprises, Inc., v. Department of Education,* No. 33932, parts of a picture entitled "Mom and Dad" were excluded because such portions show in detail and in continuous sequence the birth of a baby by natural means and by Caesarean section, with exposure of the mother. This picture would be unobjectionable if exhibited to medical students for educational purposes, but when it is publicly exposed without restraint as to social maturity, sex or age levels, as is proposed by the plaintiff, it becomes vulgar and shocking to the senses and highly obscene because of the circumstances of time and place.

In the instant case of *R. K. O. Radio Pictures, Inc., v. Department of Education,* No. 33981, the picture called "The French Line" was approved on condition that portions of reel 12 be excluded for the following specific reasons, to wit," obscene movements of body of the dancer, her bathycolpian posing in brief revealing costume, accompanying lust provoking words of her song—all deliberately sexually suggestive." The words of the song and the method of presentation are so vulgar and obscene as to be unfit for publication in a court opinion. * * *

***279** ... The Ohio statute giving the defendant censoring jurisdiction was expressly held valid and constitutional in the case of *Mutual Film Corp. v. Industrial Commission of Ohio,* 236 U.S., 230, 59 L. Ed., 552, 35 S. Ct., 387, Ann. Cas. 1916C, 296. The *Burstyn* case did not expressly overrule the *Mutual Film* case as to the constitutionality of the Ohio statute but held, contrary to the holding of the Ohio Supreme Court in that case, only that motion pictures are within the ambit of protection which the First Amendment, through the Fourteenth, secures to any form of "speech" or to the "press." The court in so holding said that, "to the extent that language in the opinion in *Mutual Film Corp. v. Industrial Comm'r.,* supra, is out of harmony with the views here set forth, we no longer adhere to it."

And, as I have hereinbefore stated, the federal Supreme Court did not pass upon the constitutionality of our statute in the more recent *Superior Films* case (346 U.S., 587). It simply found and held that the specific picture there involved did not offend so as to give the defendant the power to reject it. * * *

HOLMBY PRODUCTIONS, INC. and UNITED ARTISTS CORP.

v.

MRS. FRANCES VAUGHN, MRS. J.R. STOWERS and MRS. BERTHA HALL, constituting The Kansas State Board of Review; HAROLD R. FATZER, Attorney General of the State of Kansas; and DONALD E. MARTIN, County Attorney of Wyandotte County, Kansas

177 Kan. 728 (1955)

Supreme Court of Kansas

Opinion filed April 9, 1955

***729** The opinion of the court was delivered by

ROBB, J.:

This is an appeal from the trial court's order granting a permanent injunction in favor of appellees and enjoining appellants from interference with or penalization of appellees as a result of exhibition of the motion picture, "The Moon is Blue."

* * * Pursuant to G.S. 1949, 51-102 the film was submitted to the Kansas State Board of Review, a creature of the statutes (G.S. 1949, 74-2201). On June 17, 1953, the board disapproved the film for the reasons,

"Sex theme throughout, too frank bedroom dialogue: many sexy words; both dialogue and action have sex as their theme."

The board, after this injunction action was filed, re-examined the film and on September 11, 1953, under authority granted by statute (G.S. 1949, 51-109) again disapproved the film for the reasons,

"... the Board has found that film to be obscene, indecent and immoral, and such as tend to debase or corrupt morals," following in the language of the statute (G.S. 1949, 51-103), which further reads:

"The Board shall examine films, reels, [and] ... spoken dialogue ... and shall approve such films, reels, [and] ... spoken dialogue

***730**... which are moral and proper; and shall disapprove such as are cruel, obscene, indecent or immoral, or such as tend to debase or corrupt morals...."

The injunction action was filed on August 17, 1953, in the district court of Wyandotte county...

The trial court made conclusions of law as follows:

The board's action must be upheld unless it was fraudulent or so arbitrary and capricious as to be, in effect, fraudulent; statutory review of the board's action was not required unless the statute is valid in its present application; motion pictures are protected by the first and fourteenth amendments to the constitution of the United States; the statute providing for censorship is invalid, as repugnant thereto; the board's statements and reasons for its construction of the words of the statute gave each of the words a meaning so broad and vague as to render the statute unconstitutional; and finally, that appellees were entitled to, and the trial court granted, a permanent injunction.

* * *

The only question before us, then, is whether the statutes under consideration are unconstitutional because they are an abridgment or contravention of the first and fourteenth amendments to the constitution of the United States, or because they are couched in language so vague and indefinite as to offend due process.

We will first determine whether the words, "obscene, indecent, or immoral, or such as tend to debase or corrupt morals," are vague and indefinite terms so as to offend due process. We are of the opinion these words have an accepted, definite, and clear meaning.

* * *

In 33 Am. Jur., § 4, p. 17, we find the following:

"Obscenity was indictable at common law, on the ground that what tended to corrupt society amounted to a breach of the peace, and various acts and forms of obscenity are made criminal offenses by statute or ordinance. The word obscenity cannot be said to be a technical term of the law and is not susceptible of exact definition in its judicial uses, although it has been defined in a general sense as meaning offensive to morality or chastity, indecent, or nasty."

* * *

Since the Burstyn case was cited by both appellee and appellant, we feel that reference thereto is appropriate, especially to that part reading as follows:

"Since the term `sacrilegious' is the sole standard under attack here, it is not necessary for us to decide, for example, whether a state may censor motion pictures under a clearly drawn statute designed and applied to prevent the showing of obscene films. That is a very different question from the one now before us. We hold only that under the First and Fourteenth Amendments a state may not ban a film on the basis of a censor's conclusion that it is `sacrilegious.'" (p. 505-506.)

In the *Burstyn* case the court, by the terminology above used, excepted censorship of a film for the reason it was "obscene," which was one of the grounds enumerated by the Kansas board for its disapproval of "The Moon is Blue." In view of what has been said, we are not required to determine how or why our board arrived at its conclusion, or is it necessary here to define other words contained in our censorship statute.

The decree of the trial court is reversed with directions to reinstate the order of the Kansas State Board of Review.

HALLMARK PRODUCTIONS, INC. v. CARROLL

384 Pa. 348 (1956)

Supreme Court of Pennsylvania

Argued January 6, 1956

Decided March 13, 1956

***349** ... Hallmark Productions, Inc., submitted to the Pennsylvania State Board of Censors for approval a motion picture film which presented the story of a dope peddler and the manner in which he enticed innocent people in the use and sale of marijuana cigarettes. The Board concluded that the film was "indecent and immoral and, in the judgment of the Board, tended to debase and corrupt morals," and therefore disapproved it. Court of Common Pleas No. 2 of Philadelphia County reversed the order of the Board and the latter now appeals from that reversal.

No question is here raised as to the merits or demerits of the film or whether the Board of Censors was guilty of an abuse of discretion in refusing to issue a certificate of approval. The sole issue presented is whether the Motion Picture Censorship Act of May 15, 1915, P.L. 534, as amended by the Act of May 8, 1929, P.L. 1655, is unconstitutional, either because it is so vague and indefinite in its terms as to offend the due process clause of the Fourteenth Amendment, or because it abridges freedom of speech in contravention of the First and Fourteenth Amendments to the Constitution of the United States and the free communication of thoughts and opinions in violation of Article I, § 7, of the Constitution of Pennsylvania.

The censorship of motion picture films in this Commonwealth goes back almost to the inception of the industry. The 1915 Act, as amended, provides (§ 6) that "The board [of censors] shall examine or supervise the

***350** examinations of all films, reels, or views to be exhibited or used in Pennsylvania; and shall approve such films, reels, or views which are moral and proper; and shall disapprove such as are sacrilegious, obscene, indecent, or immoral, or such as tend, in the judgment of the board, to debase or corrupt morals." From any elimination or disapproval of a film, reel, or view ordered by the board there is given a right of appeal to the Court of Common Pleas of the proper county.

* * *

***357** The picture involved in the present case was disapproved by the Board of Censors because it was "indecent and immoral and, in the judgment of the Board, tended to debase and corrupt

***358** morals." In view of the foregoing decisions of the Supreme Court, individually and collectively, we are of opinion that these terms must be held subject to the same fatal objections as those which invalidated the statutes held unconstitutional by that Court. It is not necessary for us to consider whether constitutionality of our censorship statute might be effected by amendments that would make its terminology more definite and specific (assuming that greater definiteness is possible in the case of such abstract terms), or whether, however amended and "clearly drawn," any statute censoring motion pictures must be held to be unconstitutional on the theory that motion pictures are as much entitled to the protection of the constitutional guaranty of free speech as is now enjoyed by newspapers, magazines, books, theatrical exhibitions, radio and television scripts. It need hardly be added that even if all pre-censorship of motion picture films were to be held invalid this would not in and of itself affect the right to suppress objectionable films if exhibited, or to punish their exhibitor.

Order affirmed.

* * *

DISSENTING OPINION BY MR. JUSTICE MUSMANNO:

The Majority Opinion is an interesting legal travelogue but it does not decide the issue in this case. It takes the reader on a learned tour of various appellate courts but it does not resolve the appeal before us. The stark question which this litigation presents is a very simple one, namely, "Was the Pennsylvania State Board of Censors, under the law, justified in declining to inflict on the people of this State a monstrosity of a motion picture entitled, "She Should'a Said No!"? To this interrogation the Majority has not answered Yes, and it has not answered No.

Instead of rendering a decision on the proposition calling for a definitive adjudication, this Court has passed sentence of execution on an honorable institution which for forty-one years has protected the good people of Pennsylvania from sacrilegious, obscene, indecent

***360** and immoral pictures and those tending to debase or corrupt morals. * * *

The facts in the present litigation are as follows: On March 20, 1950, the State Board of Censors viewed a film entitled "Wild Weed," and rejected it as being immoral, indecent, not proper, and tending to corrupt and debase morals. The picture was resubmitted on January 24, 1951, with the title changed to "Devil's Weed." It was again rejected for the identical reasons specified the first time. The owners of the pictures now gave to the film the suggestive and odious title, "She Should'a Said No!" and presented it once more to the Board of Censors which detected no change in the odor of the film because of the alteration of name and accordingly refused, as theretofore, to give it a license for distribution.

With a persistence that might have been worthy of a more fragrant product, Hallmark Productions, owners of the picture, protested the Board's decision, and the Board once more re-viewed "She Should'a Said

***361** No!", and once more declared it to be immoral, indecent, not proper and tending to corrupt and debase morals. On July 30, 1953, the Board filed an Adjudication enumerating 22 reasons why it regarded the film unfit for projection in Pennsylvania. It is my opinion that the Board was not only justified in refusing a certificate of license to Hallmark but that in conscience and the faithful fulfillment of its duties the Board could not have done otherwise. Five of the reasons taken from the Board's Adjudication convey a fairly good idea of the indecent and immoral character of "She Should'a Said No!", the film which the Majority of this Court, by its decision, has now allowed to be released for distribution: "FINDINGS OF FACT

"8. The scene of two teenage couples, an open roadster on a hill overlooking Hollywood and being under the influence of the drug; each boy having a girl in his arms and smoking a marijuana cigarette depicts depravity and indecency and is indecent and immoral and, in the judgment of the Board, tends to debase and corrupt morals and teaches a method of crime.

"10. The scene showing the party in Ann's home with Rita and the two men as they smoke marijuana cigarettes and under its influence deport themselves in an obscene manner is indecent and immoral and, in the judgment of the Board, tends to debase and corrupt morals.

"13. The scene showing Rita dancing in an indecent fashion under the influence of the drug after smoking a marijuana cigarette is indecent and immoral and, in the judgment of the Board, tends to debase and corrupt morals.

"14. The statement made by the dope peddler (Markey) is indecent and immoral and, in the judgment of the Board, tends to debase and corrupt morals,

***362** when he says to the girl Ann `ALL THAT ENERGY, BEAUTIFUL — LET'S NOT WASTE IT IN DANCING.'

"15. The scene where the dope peddler (Markey) and Ann leave the room where the party has taken place and where Ann has already smoked her first marijuana cigarette and goes into another room with Markey is indecent and immoral and, in the judgment of the Board, tends to debase and corrupt morals."

The owners of the picture argued that the film serves a good purpose in depicting the evil results of narcotics and that it therefore is a good preachment against crime. The Board, however, saw no merit in this contention: "The evils of drug traffic and addiction shown as the theme of `SHE SHOULD'A SAID NO' are not sufficient of themselves to prevent such crime, or to discourage use of drugs, but rather in detailed dialogue and action show the use of the `weed' leading to use of `heroin, cocaine, opium' excites curiosity toward escape from reality to teenagers, frustrated men and women and weak characters, and actually leads to lives of sin, corruption, horror and murder and is indecent and immoral and, in the judgment of the Board, tends to debase and corrupt morals."

* * *

***364** ... In spite of their apparent revulsion to the film, the Judges of the lower Court were of the opinion that the decision of the Supreme Court of the United States in *Burstyn v. Wilson*, 343 U.S. 495, was determinative of this case and they therefore reversed the order of the Board. They also declared the Pennsylvania Motion Picture Censorship Act to be unconstitutional.

* * *

***366** ... The Majority of this Court overlooks that the Supreme Court, in the *Burstyn* case, specifically pointed out: "Since the term `sacrilegious' is the sole standard under attack here, it is not necessary for us to decide, for example, whether a state may censor motion pictures under a clearly drawn statute designed and applied to prevent the showing of obscene films. That is a very different question from the one now before us."[*] And then so as to remove all possible doubt as to what was intended by the decision, the very last sentence in the Opinion of Justice CLARK, speaking for the majority of the Court, declares: "We hold only that under the First and Fourteenth Amendments a state may not ban a film on the basis of a censor's conclusion that it is 'sacrilegious.'"

* * *

***367** ... The Supreme Court also said in the Burstyn case that: "It does not follow that the Constitution requires absolute freedom to exhibit every motion picture of every kind at all times and at all places... Nor does it follow that motion pictures are necessarily subject to the precise rules governing any other particular method of expression." The Majority Opinion here cites this quotation but declines to apply it to the situation before us. So far as the Majority Opinion is concerned, the vilest motion picture devised may not be censored in Pennsylvania and it may not be kept out of movie houses attended by children. This is indeed a deplorable state of affairs and cannot be passed over with a shrug of robed shoulders.

From time to time one reads in the daily press of raids and arrests made in private clubs because of the showing of lewd, immoral pictures. After the decision of the Majority will have been handed down, those same shameful, shameless, degrading films may be projected anywhere in Pennsylvania publicly, the distributors and exhibitors being subject only, after the showing, to the penalty provided under criminal law. In the meantime, however, grievous harm will have been done. * * *

***368** ... Damage is done at the very first exhibition of the film. There are theatres in Pittsburgh and Philadelphia which accommodate as many as 4,000 patrons for one show. If a picture should last but one day, many thousands would nevertheless have seen it by the time it is withdrawn from circulation. That is why reason dictates that control over immoral films must be found in prevention and not in subsequent punishment.

* * * It is no answer to a demand for motion picture censorship to say that if the people do not like a film they can stay away. How are people to know if a certain production is immoral and indecent? And why should anyone be required to be offended in a theatre with scenes that sting decent eyes and with language that shocks respectable ears? If one is to learn of impurities in water only after he has drunk it, the municipal

***369** authorities have done very little to protect the citizens who make up and maintain the municipality.

...A good citizen not only does not object but is happy for the fact that someone far more skilled than he determines whether the can of peaches he opens or the box of pills he obtains at the drug store is free of poisonous and deleterious ingredients. A worthy member of society, who is just as much concerned about mental purity as he is over bodily cleanliness, is grateful that the government which protects him from contact with physical contagion will also save him from association with moral trash and garbage. No one can sensibly object to the regulation by municipal authorities over the use of public highways, parks, streams, tunnels and buildings. The streets of a city cannot be used for immoral purposes. Why should the avenues of the mind and the soul be polluted with the parading of indecencies and obscenities which can and do sometimes appear in films?

The motion picture industry, made up of responsible companies which have, over the years, earned the respect and the admiration of the American public, is aware of the need for decency on the screen. These companies have of their own volition agreed upon a Production Code * * *

Our Pennsylvania Board of Censors views over a thousand pictures a year. In 1953 it passed on 1144 subjects. It rejected 10 pictures outrightly and in 34 others eliminated 84 scenes. Who can say that he has lost any of his freedom because he was not given the opportunity to see the 10 bad pictures and the 84 outlawed scenes? The virtue in rejection does not lie alone in the discarding of what is improper but in the maintenance of a standard of decency and morality which assures each year the manufacture of less and less undesirable films. But with the elimination of

***371** censorship, the light in the lamps of standardized correctness dims, and, as a consequence, there will not be lacking producers who will be guided only by the beacon of profit which can hardly be depended upon to keep the course of the ship of production traveling within pure waters.

* * *

***373** ...The Pennsylvania Motion Picture Censorship Act is a fortress, armed originally with five cannon to protect the welfare of the people from the forces of immorality and intemperate greed. One of the cannon has been ruled out of action. The other four remain whole and strong and are in excellent firing condition. History has never shown in America a surrender, while artillery of this formidableness was fighting on the side of the right.

With this dissent I serve notice that I oppose hauling down the Flag.

The Devil's Weed (1949), aka *She Shoulda Said 'No'!*, and *Wild Weed* starred Lila Leeds, a former hatcheck girl at Ciro's on the Sunset Strip who gained fame when she was bused for marijuana possession with Robert Mitchum. The exploitation film was produced by Kroger Babb.

IN THE MATTER OF CAPITOL ENTERPRISES, INC.
v.
BOARD OF REGENTS OF THE UNIVERSITY OF THE STATE OF NEW YORK

1 A.D.2d 990 (1956)

Appellate Division of the Supreme Court of the State of New York, Third Department

Decided April 5, 1956

***991** One sequence, to which the licensing division objected, portrays under restrained and controlled conditions, a human birth. The sequence is a biological demonstration, scientific in level and tone. Section 122 of the Education Law requires the division to license a film unless it is "obscene, indecent, immoral, inhuman, sacrilegious". The license was refused here on the ground this sequence, which constitutes a small part of a long narrative film, is "indecent". The prior restraint on the exhibition of motion pictures imposed by New York under this statute has been held to be invalid interference with the constitutional guaranty of freedom of speech and of the press in the refusal of the division to issue a license because a film was thought to be "sacrilegious" (*Joseph Burstyn, Inc., v. Wilson*, 343 U.S. 495), and in another case because the film was thought to be "immoral" (*Superior Films v. Department of Educ.* [*Commercial Pictures Corp. v. Regents of Univ. of State of New York*], 346 U.S. 587). The Supreme Court rendered a similar decision in 1955 in respect of the restraint of exhibition of a film which the Kansas Board had held to be "obscene" (*Holmby Productions v. Vaughn*, 350 U.S. 870). Without passing on the general effect of these decisions on the structure of the New York motion picture censorship law, we hold that this film is not "indecent", in the sense required to justify prior restraint. If the words "obscene" or "indecent" can serve at all as constitutionally valid standards for prior restraint, the words must be given a narrow and restricted interpretation and, so interpreted, the words are clearly not applicable to the film before us. It is questionable whether any area is left open by the decisions of the Supreme Court for the exercise of prior restraint on motion pictures but, even if there is such an area, the State has the "heavy burden" of demonstrating that its statute is operative only in "an exceptional case" (343 U.S. 495, 504, supra). Treating this film as "indecent" and thus refusing it a license does not meet, in our view, the burden the State must meet to justify the exercise of prior restraint. Although the petition asserts that the film is not indecent, the petitioner in its brief in this court, in an effort to reach the ultimate constitutional issue, would stipulate that the film is worse than it is. We are not required to accept this concession for the purpose of reaching a constitutional issue not otherwise presented. In deciding this case, we exercise our own independent judgment as to the film and the validity of the refusal to license it.

The determination of the Board of Regents is annulled and the matter remitted to the license division with a direction to license the film, with $50 costs to the petitioner.

CAPITOL ENTERPRISES, INC., v. CITY OF CHICAGO

260 F.2d 670 (1958)

United States Court of Appeals Seventh Circuit

November 6, 1958

FINNEGAN, Circuit Judge.

Unless a motion picture be first approved by, and a permit secured from, the Commissioner of Police it is unlawful to exhibit it in any public place within the City of Chicago, Illinois. Sections 155-1 to 155-7, Municipal Code of Chicago, contain the details of such prior restraint and among those provisions the following are relevant here:

"155-4. Such permit shall be granted only after the motion picture film for which said permit is requested has been produced at the office of the commissioner of police for examination or censorship.

"If a picture or series of pictures, for the showing or exhibition of which an application for a permit is made, is immoral or obscene, or portrays depravity, criminality, or lack

***671** of virtue of a class of citizens of any race, color, creed, or religion and exposes them to contempt, derision, or obloquy, or tends to produce a breach of the peace or riots, or purports to represent any hanging, lynching or burning of a human being, it shall be the duty of the commissioner of police to refuse such permit; otherwise it shall be his duty to grant such permit.

"In case the commissioner of police shall refuse to grant a permit as hereinbefore provided, the applicant for the same may appeal to the mayor. Such appeal shall be presented in the same manner as the original application to the commissioner of police. The action of the mayor on any application for a permit shall be final.

"155-5. In all cases where a permit for the exhibition of a picture or series of pictures has been refused under the provisions of the preceding section because the same tends towards creating a harmful impression on the minds of children, where such tendency as to the minds of adults would not exist if exhibited only to persons of mature age, the commissioner of police may grant a special permit limiting the exhibition of such picture or series of pictures, to persons over the age of twenty-one years; provided such picture or pictures are not of such character as to tend to create contempt or hatred for any class of law abiding citizens."

Plaintiff, Capitol Enterprises, Inc., a Maryland Corporation, distributor for the motion picture entitled "Mom and Dad" requested a permit, under the Chicago Ordinance, and received this reply from the commanding officer of the Censor Unit, Chicago Police Department: "The motion picture, 'Mom and Dad,' was submitted for censorship by previous owners and agents. It was rejected on four occasions on the ground that it was immoral and obscene, and as such was deemed to be in violation of Section 155-4 of the Municipal Code of Chicago. Your checks * * * are herewith enclosed and returned."

Capitol then appealed, under § 155-4, to the Mayor of Chicago, informing him inter alia that since 1948, "substantial changes [had been] made in the content of the film. A number of the original scenes were eliminated and a number of new scenes * * * inserted * * *." Plaintiff requested a hearing and an opportunity to present evidence. The Mayor responded by letter dated February 18, 1958, stating: "The motion picture has again been reviewed and the decision of the Commissioner of Police is confirmed. Consequently, no permit will be issued for the exhibition of * * * [the] film in the City of Chicago."

"The action of the mayor," under Ordinance § 155-4, "on any application for a permit shall be final." Accordingly, and relying upon diversity of citizenship, plaintiff, on March 25, 1958, commenced suit in the U.S. District Court seeking an order restraining various public officials from preventing it from exhibiting the film; and to have the Ordinance declared unconstitutional. To this complaint bottomed on the First and Fourteenth Amendments to the Constitution, defendants, the City, Mayor and Police Commissioner, filed an answer consisting primarily of general denials. Plaintiff then tendered the movie for viewing by the district judge, moved for summary judgment, and its complaint was dismissed; judgment entered for defendants. Among his findings the trial judge itemized these:

"14. The court further finds that the question of the constitutionality of the ordinance of the City of Chicago involved herein raised in Count 3 of plaintiff's complaint is frivolous.

"15. The court further finds, having viewed the motion picture in evidence as defendants' Exhibit B, that said motion picture is obscene and immoral if exhibited for entertainment and that plaintiff applied

***672** for a license or permit under said ordinance. (Italics ours.)

"16. That the defendants lawfully and properly denied plaintiff a permit or license to exhibit said motion picture."

Our review on the appeal taken by plaintiff from the judgment entered below must be made within the constitutional framework at the federal level. To be sure this Ordinance survived Illinois judicial scrutiny in *American Civil Liberties Union v. City of Chicago*, 1955, 3 Ill.2d 334, 121 N.E.2d 585, but we are not foreclosed from subjecting either the Ordinance or its application to constitutional tests, and, indeed the Supreme Court reversed *Times Film Corporation v. City of Chicago*, 1957, 355 U.S. 35, 78 S.Ct. 115, 2 L.Ed.2d 72, decided under that same ordinance.

We viewed the condemned film which is, of course, the prime exhibit in the record on appeal, and for convenience consider this motion picture divisible into three major parts. The first, and prolix portion animates the theme of the need for sex instruction through a superficial plot, and innocuous acting, depicting a family unit, dominated by a prim mother who denies her nubile teenage daughter any sex knowledge or guidance, a frisky wholesome male sibling, and a weary pliant father. At a high school dance, one evening the young lady encounters a slightly more sophisticated male applicant for the freshman class at a nearby college. A pastoral scene complete with falling leaves and orchestral crescendo symbolizes the transfer of this young uninformed girl from agonized doubt into exaggerated certainty. She is later seen traveling with her mother to Boston for the confinement, and the main plot finally ends on the note of a happy family reunion bound up with tacit understanding engendered by a youngish male high school teacher playing the role of presiding receptive intelligence whose lucidity at first frustrated, finally triumphs at the end of part one.

Wholly disconnected from what has preceded it, part two, introduced as a film within a film, is straightforward instruction on sex. Diagrams are used for explanations of post-insemination stages from embryo to fetus. Following these diagrams there are two separate surgical inserts, one showing a normal delivery, and the other a Caesarian section. Both sequences, focusing on surgical techniques, were apparently photographed at a hospital, and while each shows the birth of a human baby neither departs from its sterile medical environment. Throughout this stage of the film the sound track is devoted solely to inoffensive explanation and instruction.

Venereal disease is the subject of part three and consists primarily of photographs of the human ear, eye, nose and throat, showing the ravages of syphilis. Thousands of young men who served in our armed forces have, without doubt, viewed much stronger versions of this same theme shown in required training films at basic training centers.

Little has been authoritatively written explaining "prior" or "previous" restraint,[1] instead those words are frequently found as part of an incantation used when some censorship determination is judicially annulled. Whether those words work the annulment or if annulment requires such words is difficult of discovery. But, there is a wide chasm between censoring motion pictures before deciding if they can be publicly exhibited and exhibiting a picture to the public for which criminal punishment might be imposed. In the latter situation[2] all the familiar procedural safeguards come into play while in the other instance there are no procedural safeguards and communication is choked off

***673** at the threshold. Submission to compulsory censorship as a condition precedent to public exhibition is undoubtedly more facile unencumbered, as it is, by any procedural safeguards. Complete censorship, as we now have before us, is much like the case of obtaining indictments before a grand jury — no defense counsel is present. There, however, the analogy ends for persons accused of crime are eventually accorded some rights, but in censorship[3] social context may be measured by six or seven persons against, as here, a society of more than approximately 3,620,962 persons, and the applicant for a permit apparently need never be heard, nor is the right to trial by petit jury available.

American Civil Liberties Union v. City of Chicago, 1954, 3 Ill.2d 334, 121 N.E. 2d 585 is used by the defendants as their main authority for resisting reversal of the judgment below. It is true, as respondents' brief shows, the United States Supreme Court did dismiss that appeal, but for the reason, as we ascertained, "for want of a final judgment." 1955, 348 U.S. 979, 75 S.Ct. 572, 99 L.Ed. 763. All this goes further, because that case, *American Civil Liberties Union v. City of Chicago*, was reversed and remanded (3 Ill.2d 334, 353, 121 N.E.2d 585) for trial and when it reached the Illinois trial judge he held the motion picture involved, "The Miracle," obscene; another appeal followed resulting in the opinion reported as *American Civil Liberties Union v. City of Chicago*, 1957, 13 Ill.App.2d 278, 289-290, 141 N.E.2d 56, 62 where the Illinois Appellate Court, First District, First Division, directed "the cause remanded with directions to enter judgment for plaintiffs," and ordered "defendants to issue a permit upon application and payment therefor, and to enjoin them from interfering with the exhibition in Chicago of the motion picture film, The Miracle." Leave to appeal that Appellate Court decision was denied by the Illinois Supreme Court on September 24, 1957. Parenthetically, at least, it might be mentioned that "The Miracle" film is the same one which survived after the review in *Burstyn, Inc., v. Wilson, 1952*, 343 U.S. 495, 497, 72 S.Ct. 777, 96 L.Ed. 1098, and, indeed, this fact precipitated the following passage concerning it, in *American Civil Liberties Union*: "We [the Illinois Supreme Court] may say at once that we do not regard that decision [*Burstyn*] as having completely immunized `the Miracle' against censorship. The sole basis of censorship in that case [*Burstyn*] was that the film was sacrilegious; power to censor upon any other basis was not considered by the Supreme Court * * *. And the court [Supreme Court of the United States] expressly reserved decision on the question `whether a state may censor motion pictures under a clearly drawn statute designed and applied to prevent the showing of obscene films.'" 3 Ill.2d 334, 339, 121 N.E.2d 585, 588.[4]

Two separate appeals, one (*Roth*) from a Federal conviction and the other (*Alberts*) from a California verdict of guilty, were combined for disposition and opinions by a divided court, the majority of which affirmed both convictions and reported as *Roth v. United States*, 1957, 354 U.S. 476, 77 S.Ct. 1304, 1 L.Ed.2d 1498. *Roth*, a New York book dealer, solicited sales through his advertising

***674** circulars sent by mail. He was charged with wilfully, unlawfully and lewdly disseminating obscene matter in violation of the federal obscenity statute — 18 U.S. C. § 1461. Alberts, on the other hand, operated a mail-order business out of Los Angeles where he was convicted in the Municipal Court, Beverly Hills Judicial District, for lewdly keeping for sale obscene and indecent books, and with writing and publishing an obscene advertisement of them, in violation of the California Penal Code. West's Calif. Penal Code Ann., 1955, § 311. "The dispositive question" presented for the majority by Mr. Justice Brennan, was, "whether obscenity is utterance within the area of protected speech and press." 354 U.S. 476, 481, 77 S.Ct. 1304, 1307, 1 L.Ed.2d 1498. Elsewhere in his opinion the Justice stated: "The constitutionality of a criminal obscenity statute is the question in each of these cases. In *Roth*, the primary constitutional question is whether the federal obscenity statute violates the provision of the First Amendment that 'Congress shall make no law * * * abridging the freedom of speech, or of the press * * *' In *Alberts*, the primary constitutional question is whether the obscenity provisions of the California Penal Code invade the freedoms of speech and press as they may be incorporated in the liberty protected from state action by the Due Process Clause of the Fourteenth Amendment." While it was held "that obscenity is not within the area of constitutionally protected speech or press" this certainly cannot be rationally interpreted so that any communication might be rubber stamped "obscene" through the apparatus of preventive censorship. The communication must first be obscene before deprived of its constitutional shelter. *Roth* bristles with explanations and interpretations of "obscene" and "pruriency," but none of them encompasses the film involved here. During the course of his opinion Mr. Justice Brennan concluded at one point: "It is therefore vital that the standards for judging obscenity safeguard the protection of freedom of speech and press for material which does not treat sex in a manner appealing to prurient interest." 1957, 354 U.S. 476, 488, 77 S.Ct. 1304, 1311, 1 L.Ed. 2d 1498.

Value changes that have occurred and are persistently occurring, in this country gradually brought motion pictures to the status of a constitutionally protected medium and consequently early censorship cases serve very little in this modern setting. See e. g. *Burstyn, Inc. v. Wilson*, 1952, 343 U.S. 495, 72 S.Ct. 777, 96 L.Ed. 1098. Judges, no less than legislators should observe, without prejudice, what is going on in our changing society, averting through such alertness treating law as a petrified body of shibboleths. In the past "obscene" was hedged about with all the unreasoning of verbal taboos and the community imagined that word was "invariant under transformation." Coming to terms with change, running throughout the Supreme Court decisions in the previous restraint field during the past years, reveals the penumbra of uncertainty radiating from the use of the word "obscene." And, comparatively recently Mr. Justice Schaefer, speaking for the Illinois Supreme Court, in *American Civil Liberties Union v. City of Chicago*, 1954, 3 Ill.2d 334, 347, 121 N.E.2d 585, 592, interpreted the Ordinance now before us, in this fashion: "* * * [A] motion picture is obscene within the meaning of the ordinance if, when considered as a whole, its calculated purpose or dominant effect is substantially to arouse sexual desires, and if the probabilities of this effect is so great as to outweigh whatever artistic or other merits the film may possess. In making this determination the film must be tested with reference to its effect upon the normal, average person." (Italics supplied.) A good deal of fruitless controversy might arise if our appraisal of this film be construed as meaning we substituted our judgments for those announced by the censors. But the current exigency is nothing new. See e. g. *United*

***675** *States v. Dennett*, 2 Cir., 1930, 39 F.2d 564, 76 A.L.R. 1092.[5] We think the censors' classification of "Mom and Dad" was unwarranted. Struggling to reach by reasoning absolute certainty of what shall be classed as obscene unduly strains the legal machinery. Only by a close study of the facts[6] as they confront judges when a record is made in these cases, can it be determined whether a censor has frustrated an owner, publisher, or exhibitor by an inaccurate classification. After all, censors come to their work with preconceived notions and only an objective comparison of their judgments with the facts allows for legalistic evaluation. Just why they categorized this motion picture as "immoral and obscene" is undisclosed by the City censors and we will not assume what, if anything, in that film caused them to forbid exhibition.

Nothing in the passage we quoted from the Censor Unit's letter to plaintiff indicates whether the meaning ascribed to "obscene" by the Illinois Supreme Court played any part in appraising the film, and obviously if the "four occasions" mentioned in that letter were in 1948, the answer is American Civil Liberties was decided September 20, 1954. On the other hand the Mayor's communication is equally uninformative since it employs the ambiguous phrase "again reviewed" without particularizing whether the reference is to the film or another viewing by the police unit or another review of the four prior decisions. The record before us is barren of any findings of fact by the censors and all it shows is that somebody sometime classed some edition of the film "immoral and obscene." From the district judge's findings it appears "That the said Timothy J. O'Connor [Commissioner of Police] appointed a Censor Board consisting of six persons to aid and assist him in his duties under * * * said ordinance." While § 155-2 authorizes the Commissioner to "cause" films to be inspected, no standards relevant here are provided for the guidance of either the Commissioner or his board other than "immoral and obscene" — incidentally an alternative and construed in 1954 by the Illinois Supreme Court as being synonymous terms. We think the censors' determination in the case before us "is wholly without reasonable basis," borrowing that phrase from *American Civil Liberties Union v. City of Chicago*, 1954, 3 Ill.2d 334, 349, 121 N.E.2d 585. Indeed we are curious as to whether the City censors viewed the identical film that we did. However, in the last cited case the opinion writer also said: "* * [U]pon review of the censors' action, the plaintiff does not carry a burden of proving that the action was arbitrary and unreasonable, but rather that it must affirmatively be made to appear that the film fairly falls within the proscriptive terms of the ordinance." 3 Ill.2d 334, 351, 121 N.E.2d 585, 594. It is our considered judgment and opinion that the subject film is well outside the ambit of the Ordinance.

Capitol Enterprises, Inc., v. Regents of University, 1956, 1 A.D.2d 990, 149 N.Y.S.2d 920, 921-922 is the memorandum decision by the Supreme Court, Appellate Division, of New York reviewing refusal to license, "Mom and Dad," apparently the same film now before us. Annulling the determination of the Board

***676** of Regents, and directing issuance of the license, five New York Judges stated, after viewing the film: "One sequence, to which the licensing division objected, portrays under restrained and controlled conditions, a human birth. A sequence is a biological demonstration, scientific in level and tone * * * we hold that this film is not 'indecent', in the sense required to justify prior restraint. If the words `obscene' or `indecent' can serve at all as constitutionally valid standards for prior restraint, the words must be given a narrow and restricted interpretation and, so interpreted, the words are clearly not applicable to the film before us * * *. In deciding this case, we exercise our own judgment as to the film and the validity of the refusal to license it." Unlike the Chicago Police Commissioner the Regents stated their grounds for refusing the permit.

We have resolved plaintiff's appeal without passing upon the constitutional validity of the Ordinance because it is unnecessary to reach that problem. Even if it be assumed arguendo that the Ordinance survived the constitutional challenge we are of the opinion it was unconstitutionally applied in this instance.[7] Our decision rests on narrow but firm grounds for we are satisfied there was absent any sound basis for outlawing the film and the absence of any reasons by the censors for their classification is a foreboding guise for arbitrary censorship running afoul of the First and Fourteenth Amendments. Nothing has been put forward by the City indicating just what in this film are its inherent evils. A social problem requires defining and that has not been attempted here. Consequently this censorship results in a curb on free expression and it is our view that the trial judge erred; adding the phrase "if exhibited for entertainment"[8] in finding 15 diluted his ultimate conclusion for it manifests doubt, if not reluctance, to permit suppression of the film. Instead of controlling the audience under § 155-5 the Commissioner selected complete restraint, and our decision can only treat with that result.

The judgment appealed is reversed and the cause remanded to the district court with directions to grant the relief prayed for in paragraphs (a) and (c)[9] of plaintiff's complaint.

Judgment reversed and the cause remanded to the district court with directions.

SCHNACKENBERG, Circuit Judge.

I concur in the result reached by Judge FINNEGAN in his opinion and also with all that is said therein which is necessary to said result.

[1] See Kingsley Books, Inc. v. Brown, 1957, 354 U.S. 436, 77 S.Ct. 1325, 1 L.Ed.2d 1469, for the use by a State of an order restraining distribution of obscene booklets, held not to be a "prior restraint."

[2] A potential impact on exhibitors lies in combining the Ordinance with criminal provisions in

Ill.Rev.Stat., 1957, chap. 38, pars. 470-472, §§ 224½-224b.

[3] In *Commercial Pictures Corp. v. Board of Regents*, 1954, 346 U.S. 587, 74 S.Ct. 286, 98 L.Ed. 329, the Supreme Court invalidated censoring based on the test, "immoral."

[4] See however *R.K.O. Radio Pictures v. Department of Education*, 1954, 162 Ohio St. 263, 122 N.E.2d 769,771 for a discussion of Mr. Justice Clark's statement: "it is not necessary for us to decide, for example, whether a state may censor motion pictures under a clearly drawn statute designed and applied to prevent the showing of obscene films." The Ohio Supreme Court was talking about the United States Supreme Court's disposition of its opinion in *Superior Films, Inc., v. Dept. of Education*, 1953, 159 Ohio St. 315, 112 N.E.2d 311, reversed (per curiam) 1954, 346 U.S. 587, 74 S.Ct. 286, 98 L.Ed. 329. See also *Hallmark Productions v. Carroll*, 1956, 384 Pa. 348, 121 A.2d 584.

[5] "We have been referred to no decision where a truthful exposition of the sex side of life, evidently calculated for instruction and for the explanation of relevant facts, has been held to be obscene." Judge Augustus N. Hand speaking for the court in *United States v. Dennett*, 2 Cir., 1930, 39 F.2d 564, 569, 76 A.L.R. 1092.

[6] For example, "The charge in the information is predicated upon a picture story consisting of stills, taken from a moving picture entitled 'The Birth of a Baby.' In addition to the stills, there are two sets of anatomical diagrams * * *. [T]he picture story * * * does not fall within the forbidden class. The picture story was directly based on a film produced under the auspices of a responsible medical group. There is no nudity or unnecessary disclosure. The subject has been treated with delicacy." *People v. Larsen*, Sp.Sess.1938, 5 N.Y.S. 2d 55, 56.

[7] "We agree that the determination that a film or book is obscene must rest on something more than speculation, and that the tendency toward sexual stimulation must be probable and substantial." *American Civil Liberties Union v. City of Chicago*, 1954, 3 Ill.2d 334, 347, 121 N.E.2d 585, 592.

[8] "What is one man's amusement, teaches another's doctrine," taken out of context from *Winters v. People of State of New York*, 1948, 333 U.S. 507, 510, 68 S.Ct. 665, 667, 92 L.Ed. 840.

[9] "(a) That the Court issue an order restraining defendants City of Chicago, Richard J. Daley, as Mayor of said City of Chicago, and Timothy J. O'Connor, as Police Commissioner of said City of Chicago, individually and as acting officers of the City of Chicago, and all police officers, agents, servants and employees acting for and on behalf of the City of Chicago from preventing, hindering or otherwise interfering with the plaintiff, its officers or agents in the exhibition of the film 'Mom and Dad' in the City of Chicago, Illinois."

"(c) That the Court issue an order directed to defendants City of Chicago, Richard J. Daley, Mayor of said City of Chicago, and Timothy J. O'Connor, Police Commissioner of said City of Chicago, commanding defendants to issue forthwith to plaintiff the permit required by the aforesaid municipal ordinance without further submission of the motion picture 'Mom and Dad' for censorship of content."

KINGSLEY INTERNATIONAL PICTURES CORP.
v.
REGENTS OF THE UNIVERSITY OF THE STATE OF NEW YORK

360 U.S. 684 (1959)
Supreme Court of United States
Argued April 23, 1959
Decided June 29, 1959
Appeal from the Court of Appeals of New York

***684** MR. JUSTICE STEWART delivered the opinion of the Court.

* * *

The New York statute makes it unlawful "to exhibit, or to sell, lease or lend for exhibition at any place of amusement for pay or in connection with any business in the state of New York, any motion picture film or reel

***685** ... unless there is at the time in full force and effect a valid license or permit ... The law provides that a license shall issue "unless such film or a part thereof is obscene, indecent, immoral, inhuman, sacrilegious, or is of such a character that its exhibition would tend to corrupt morals or incite to crime. . . ."[2]A recent statutory amendment provides that, "the term `immoral' and the phrase `of such a character that its exhibition would tend to corrupt morals' shall denote a motion picture film or part thereof, the dominant purpose or effect of which is erotic or pornographic; or which portrays acts of sexual immorality, perversion, or lewdness, or which expressly or impliedly presents such acts as desirable, acceptable or proper patterns of behavior."[3]

As the distributor of a motion picture entitled "Lady Chatterley's Lover," the appellant Kingsley submitted that film to the Motion Picture Division of the New York Education Department for a license. Finding three isolated scenes in the film " `immoral' within the intent of our Law," the Division refused to issue a license until the scenes in question were deleted. The distributor petitioned the Regents of the University of the State of New York for a review of that ruling.[4] The Regents upheld the denial of a license, but on the broader ground that "the whole theme of this motion picture is immoral under said law, for that theme is the presentation of adultery as a desirable, acceptable and proper pattern of behavior."

***686** Kingsley sought judicial review of the Regents' determination.[5] The Appellate Division unanimously annulled the action of the Regents and directed that a license be issued. 4 App. Div. 2d 348, 165 N.Y. S. 2d 681. A sharply divided Court of Appeals, however, reversed the Appellate Division and upheld the Regents' refusal to license the film for exhibition. * * *

***687** ... "because its subject matter is adultery presented as being right and desirable for certain people under

***688** certain circumstances." [9] 4 N.Y. 2d, at 369, 151 N. E. 2d, at 208, 175 N.Y.S. 2d, at 55 (concurring opinion).

... the New York Court of Appeals tells us that the relevant portion of the New York Education Law requires the denial of a license to any motion picture which approvingly portrays an adulterous relationship, quite without reference to the manner of its portrayal.

What New York has done, therefore, is to prevent the exhibition of a motion picture because that picture advocates an idea—that adultery under certain circumstances may be proper behavior. Yet the First Amendment's basic guarantee is of freedom to advocate ideas. The State, quite simply, has thus struck at the very heart of constitutionally protected liberty.

It is contended that the State's action was justified because the motion picture attractively portrays a relationship which is contrary to the moral standards, the religious precepts, and the legal code of its citizenry. This

***689** argument misconceives what it is that the Constitution protects. Its guarantee is not confined to the expression of ideas that are conventional or shared by a majority. It protects advocacy of the opinion that adultery may sometimes be proper, no less than advocacy of socialism or the single tax. And in the realm of ideas it protects expression which is eloquent no less than that which is unconvincing.

Advocacy of conduct proscribed by law is not, as Mr. Justice Brandeis long ago pointed out, "a justification for denying free speech where the advocacy falls short of incitement and there is nothing to indicate that the advocacy would be immediately acted on." *Whitney v. California,* 274 U.S. 357, at 376 (concurring opinion).

* * *

Reversed.

MR. JUSTICE BLACK, concurring.

I concur in the Court's opinion and judgment but add a few words because of concurring opinions by several Justices who rely on their appraisal of the movie Lady Chatterley's Lover for holding that New York cannot constitutionally bar it. Unlike them, I have not seen the picture. My view is that stated by MR. JUSTICE DOUGLAS, that prior censorship of moving pictures like prior censorship of newspapers and books violates the First and Fourteenth Amendments. If despite the Constitution, however, this Nation is to embark on the dangerous road of censorship, my belief is that this Court is about the most inappropriate Supreme Board of Censors that could be found. So far as I know, judges possess no special expertise providing exceptional competency to set standards and to supervise the private morals of the Nation. In addition, the Justices of this Court seem especially unsuited to make the kind of value judgments—as to what movies are good or bad for local communities— which the concurring opinions appear to require. We are told that the only way we can decide whether a State or municipality can constitutionally bar movies is for this Court to view and appraise each movie on a case-by-case basis. Under these circumstances, every member of the

***691** Court must exercise his own judgment as to how bad a picture is, a judgment which is ultimately based at least in large part on his own standard of what is immoral. The end result of such decisions seems to me to be a purely personal determination by individual Justices as to whether a particular picture viewed is too bad to allow it to be seen by the public. Such an individualized determination cannot be guided by reasonably fixed and certain standards. Accordingly, neither States nor moving picture makers can possibly know in advance, with any fair degree of certainty, what can or cannot be done in the field of movie making and exhibiting. This uncertainty cannot easily be reconciled with the rule of law which our Constitution envisages.

* * *

MR. JUSTICE FRANKFURTER, concurring in the result.

As one whose taste in art and literature hardly qualifies him for the avant-garde, I am more than surprised, after viewing the picture, that the New York authorities should have banned "Lady Chatterley's Lover." To assume that this motion picture would have offended Victorian

***692** moral sensibilities is to rely only on the stuffiest of Victorian conventions.

* * *

***694** ... [T]here is an evil against which a State may constitutionally protect itself, whatever we may think about the questions of policy involved. The real problem is the formulation of constitutionally allowable safeguards which society may take against evil without impinging upon the necessary dependence of a free society upon the fullest scope of free expression.

* * *

***697** ... MR. JUSTICE DOUGLAS, with whom MR. JUSTICE BLACK joins, concurring.

While I join in the opinion of the Court, I adhere to the views I expressed in *Superior Films v. Department of Education*, 346 U.S. 587, 588-589, that censorship of movies is unconstitutional, since it is a form of "previous restraint" that is as much at war with the First Amendment, made applicable to the States through the Fourteenth, as the censorship struck down in *Near v. Minnesota*, 283 U.S. 697. If a particular movie violates a valid law, the exhibitor can be prosecuted in the usual way. I can find in the First Amendment no room for any censor

***698** whether he is scanning an editorial, reading a news broadcast, editing a novel or a play, or previewing a movie.

* * *

***699** MR. JUSTICE CLARK, concurring in the result * * *

***700**...[I]t is significant to note that in its 14-page opinion that court says again and again, in fact 15 times, that the picture "Lady Chatterley's Lover" is proscribed because of its "espousal" of sexual immorality as "desirable" or as "proper conduct for the people of our State." * * *

***702** ...[A]s my Brother HARLAN points out, "each time such a statute is struck down, the State is left in more confusion." This is true where broad grounds are employed leaving no indication as to what may be necessary to meet the requirements of due process. I see no grounds for confusion, however, were a statute to ban "pornographic" films, or those that "portray acts of sexual immorality, perversion or lewdness." If New York's statute had been so construed by its highest court I believe it would have met the requirements of due process. Instead, it placed more emphasis on what the film teaches than on what it depicts. There is where the confusion enters. For this reason, I would reverse on the authority of *Burstyn.*

MR. JUSTICE HARLAN, whom MR. JUSTICE FRANKFURTER and MR. JUSTICE WHITTAKER join, concurring in the result.

I think the Court has moved too swiftly in striking down a statute which is the product of a deliberate and conscientious effort on the part of New York to meet constitutional objections raised by this Court's decisions respecting predecessor statutes in this field. But although I disagree with the Court that the parts of §§ 122 and 122-a of the NewYork Education Law, 16 N.Y. Laws Ann. § 122 (McKinney 1953), 16 N.Y. Laws Ann. § 122-a (McKinney Supp. 1958), here particularly involved are unconstitutional on their face, I believe that in their application to this film constitutional bounds were exceeded.

* * *

***708**...Because I believe the New York statute was unconstitutionally applied in this instance I concur in the judgment of the Court.

[footnotes omitted]

COMMONWEALTH v. BLUMENSTEIN

396 Pa. 417 (1959)

Supreme Court of Pennsylvania

Argued January 14, 1958

Decided July 2, 1959

***419** OPINION BY MR. JUSTICE BOK

* * *

Defendant was the manager of a drive-in cinema theatre in Lackawanna County and was arrested by state officers for having shown certain films in October, 1956. He was indicted for having unlawfully exhibited obscene motion pictures under the Act of June 24, 1939, P.L. 872, § 528; 18 P.S. § 4528, which reads as follows: "Whoever gives or participates in or being the owner of any premises, or having control thereof, permits within or on said premises, any dramatic, theatrical, operatic, or vaudeville exhibition, or the exhibition of fixed or moving pictures of a lascivious, sacrilegious, obscene, indecent or immoral nature and character, or such as might tend to corrupt morals, is guilty of a misdemeanor. . . ."

* * *

***420** ... The word "sacrilegious" was held unconstitutional by the Supreme Court of the United States in *Burstyn v. Wilson*, 343 U.S. 495, 72 S. Ct. 777 (1952), a motion picture case. The case held that the cinema is within the free speech and press protection of the First and Fourteenth Amendments.

The test of being "lascivious, indecent, immoral or impure" and "tending to corrupt morals" was rejected by the Supreme Court in reversing, per curiam, *Superior Films v. Department of Education of Ohio* and *Commercial Pictures v. Regents of the University*, 346 U.S. 587, 74 S. Ct. 286 (1954), citing *Burstyn*. This case also involved a motion picture.

The remaining words of Section 528 are "lascivious, obscene, and indecent". In the cases of *U.S. v. Clarke, D.C.*, 38 F. 732 (1889) and *U.S. v. Davidson, D.C.* 244 F. 523 (1917) "lascivious" and "lewd" are held to be synonymous, and "lewd" and "obscene" are given as definitions for "indecent": see also *Swearingen v. U.S.*, 161 U.S. 446, 16 S. Ct. 562 (1896); *U.S. v. Ulysses*, 72 F. 2d 705 (1934).

This leaves the single term "obscene" to consider.

* * *

Judgment reversed and defendant discharged.

***423** ... DISSENTING OPINION BY MR. JUSTICE MUSMANNO:

By declaring Section 528 of The Penal Code of 1939 unconstitutional, the Supreme Court has today struck from the hands of every District Attorney in Pennsylvania the last remaining available weapon with which to fight the forces of indecency which for a long time have been trying to capture the moving picture screens of this Commonwealth. In 1956 (in the case of *Hallmark Productions, Inc. v. Carroll*, 384 Pa. 348), this Court dismantled the siege guns of the Motion Picture Censorship Act of 1915 which for 41 years had stopped those invading forces at Pennsylvania's borders. Now, there is nothing left with which to save clean-minded, clean-thinking men, women and children of this State from the vulgarities, obscenities and indecencies which some moving picture producers are determined to inflict on the public for the sake of a greed-soaked dollar.

* * *

***427**...What is the present case about? In December, 1956 and January, 1957, the Court of Quarter Sessions of Lackawanna County heard evidence concerning an alleged indecent motion picture entitled "Undercover Girls." This picture was exhibited at a public theatre. People paid admission to see it. Three members of the State Police saw it and reported to the District Attorney. The District Attorney, undoubtedly assured by the *Hallmark* decision, initiated prosecution against Martin Blumenstein, the exhibitor of "Undercover Girls" under the criminal laws of Pennsylvania, specifically the Act of 1939. Blumenstein was indicted and, at his trial, he agreed to have the case heard by a judge without a jury. The Judge viewed two reels of the motion picture and, after hearing all the evidence, concluded that: "The pictures depicted a series of dancing acts, which were definitely cheap, lewd, obscene and indecent. By their very nature they would corrupt the morals of the immature and the weak, appealing only to those of depraved taste and the lowest of human instincts. To seek and entice dollars through the promotion of lust and immorality manifests the worst kind of greed of money."

***428** The Court found the defendant guilty as indicted and imposed a sentence of $200 fine and imprisonment of three months. The defendant appealed to the Superior Court, which in an excellent opinion by Judge WRIGHT, affirmed the conviction. This Court allowed an allocatur and now this Court reverses the conviction and discharges the defendant.

* * *

***432** The Majority Opinion, which is written almost in telegraphic code, apparently wants to say that the word "obscene" is vague. If that be the intent of the Majority Opinion, I can only say that the word "obscene" today is about as vague as the word "cat." I doubt that there is a newspaper reader, radio listener, or television watcher, no matter how meager his education or how much a stranger to books, who does not know the meaning of the word "obscene." Why the Majority should pretend mystery over so well-known and so generally used a word is a mystery in itself.

* * *

***433** ... It was argued in behalf of Roth and Alberts that the words "obscene," "lewd", "lascivious," "filthy", "obscene" and "indecent" were not sufficiently precise, but the Supreme Court declared: "Many decisions have recognized that these terms of obscenity statutes are not precise. This Court, however, has consistently held that lack of precision is not itself offensive to the requirements of due process. ... [T]he Constitution

***434** does not require impossible standards; all that is required is that the language "conveys sufficiently definite warning as to the proscribed conduct when measured by common understanding and practices..."' These words, applied according to the proper standards for judging obscenity, already discussed, give adequate warning of the conduct proscribed and mark `boundaries sufficiently distinct for judges and juries fairly to administer the law.'"[*]

Summarizing its observations on the statutes involved, the Supreme Court said: "In summary, then, we hold that these statutes, applied according to the proper standard for judging obscenity, do not offend constitutional safeguards against convictions based upon protected material, or fail to give men in acting adequate notice of what is prohibited."

In view of this very clear language and everything else which the Supreme Court said in the Roth case, it completely escapes me how the Majority arrives at the conclusion that the Roth case supports the proposition that Section 528 must die on the guillotine of unconstitutionality.

* * *

***435** ... I must repeat that the Majority does not seem to realize what a serious thing it is to kill a statute enacted by the General Assembly, the sovereign power of the Commonwealth. The Majority completely ignores that this Court has said many times that "all legislation must be construed as intending to favor the public interest." ...

May this Court not presume that it is the intention of the Legislature to favor the public which certainly wishes to see young girls of 16, 15, and 12 protected from the degradation of visual and auditory contact with an immoral picture such as "Undercover Girls" has been proven to be? Who can doubt that many juvenile delinquents have been consciously or unconsciously urged into lurid crime because of being repeatedly exposed to lurid and immoral motion pictures? Children are by nature imitative and when they see

***436** immorality being practiced on so extensive and expansive a medium of expression as the motion picture screen, is it strange if they conclude that there is nothing wrong about doing what is being publicly glorified?

The filth and degeneracy which runs over the screens of many motion picture theatres today is nothing less than appalling. The Saturday Review said of the highly profitable and notorious film entitled "Baby Doll" that it was "one of the most unhealthy and amoral pictures ever made in this country." Time Magazine spoke of it as "just possibly the dirtiest American-made motion picture that has ever been legally exhibited."[4] After this Court knocked out our Motion Picture Censor Board there was no way of keeping this monstrously ugly and degenerate film from the theatres in Pennsylvania and, of course, now that this Court, with today's decision, has destroyed the only remaining protection we have had from cinema monstrosities, there can be no doubt that there will come along other film depravities which will make "Baby Doll" seem like a Sunday School travelogue in comparison.

* * *

***442** Who can deny that the Legislature had this very thing in mind when it enacted the Act here under consideration? ...

While, of course, the law cannot regulate all matters of customs, mores, and taste, the people have the right to expect that their representatives in the Legislature will protect them from what offends against public decency and good morals. ... There are certain inherent rights in parents to protect their children. The community is only a group of parents."

* * *

***444** ... The government inspects food in order to assure the citizen it is free from infectious and contaminative substances; the government inspects medicines and pills to save the citizen from poisoning; the government inspects water to filter out impurities; the government compels inspection of automobiles to save the citizen from faulty brakes or defective lights. The citizen accepts this type of regulation because it helps him to ward off disease, accident, and death. Why should he object to regulation which will preserve his moral health?

The fact of the matter is that the average citizen does not object to motion picture censorship and certainly not to punishment of purveyors of obscenity. On the contrary, he welcomes a regulation which saves him from much of the nausea which passes as entertainment. The one who really protests government supervision of the kind under discussion is the one who makes a business of dealing in media which endangers health. Many who shout for unrestrained exploitation of obscenity shout within the mask of so-called artistic freedom. The commercialized exploiter of cheap, unartistic material can often be found concealed behind a shield of art. He cries for freedom while, as the New York Joint Legislative Committee on Obscene Publications

*445 expressed it, "he openly continues to pander to the lewd and lascivious, seeking only to sensationalize and exploit sex, immorality and perversion for profit."[5]

* * *

There was a time when juries and trial judges conscientiously performing their duty in ascertaining the facts were allowed to use their common sense and appreciation of what is fair and just in deciding what is obscene and what is not obscene. That day is vanishing like the American Indian because recently courts have been fighting windmills over the definition of the simplest words. Any urchin on the street, any illiterate immigrant only in America a few months, any uneducated laborer will tell you the meaning of the word obscene, but there are courts which still cannot define or describe obscenity without employing polysyllabic words enmeshed in complicated verbiage of unending modifications and nuances which finally leave the reader or hearer as confused as one listening to an aboriginal incantation in an equatorial jungle.

* * *

[footnotes omitted]

EXCELSIOR PICTURES CORP. v. CITY OF CHICAGO, ILLINOIS,

182 F.Supp. 400 (1960)

United States District Court N. D. Illinois, E. D.

Decided March 31, 1960

***402** It is not disputed that the motion picture [Garden of Eden] in issue has been viewed by audiences in numerous public theatres throughout the United States and in foreign lands. Up to the end of 1955, it had been viewed by approximately 1,600,000 persons in the United States, Alaska and Hawaiian Islands. Among the cities in the United States in which it has been so exhibited are San Francisco and Los Angeles, California; Washington, D. C.; and, by uncontroverted representation of counsel in open court, New York City, New York.

The Obscenity Issue

The Court has been first presented with the question of whether the film is immoral or obscene within the meaning of the provisions of Sections 155-1 through 155-7 of the Municipal Code of the City of Chicago. Section 155-4 sets forth the following criteria concerning the grounds for denial of a permit to exhibit a motion picture film:

"If a picture or series of pictures, for the showing or exhibition of which an application for a permit is made, is immoral or obscene, or portrays depravity, criminality, or lack of virtue of a class of citizens of any race, color, creed, or religion and exposes them to contempt, derision, or obloquy, or tends to produce a breach of the peace or riots, or purports to represent any hanging, lynching or burning of a human being, it shall be the duty of the commissioner of police to refuse such permit; otherwise it shall be his duty to grant such permit."

* * *

***403** In its function of determining the facts of this case as well as the law, the Court has viewed the film in its entirety and finds that the film does, as plaintiff contends, seek to portray nudism as a healthful and happy way of life. The picture does not expose the private parts of the adult characters. Considered as a whole, its "calculated purpose or dominant effect" is not substantially to arouse sexual desires in "the normal average person." It is not "immoral" or "obscene" within the meaning of the Chicago ordinance.

The Court does not by its ruling purport to encourage the propagandization of nudism in this community. This is not the type of motion picture which the Court, in its personal capacity, would recommend the public to view. But it is not the Court's function to determine legal issues by applying as standards its personal inclinations or its individual proclivities. The Court must apply the definitions which the Illinois Supreme Court has englossed upon the ordinance and which the United States Supreme Court has sustained in like cases.

The mere fact that nudism is not an accepted way of life among the vast majority of persons in the Chicago community, or, indeed, among Americans as a whole, cannot and has not been considered by the Court as controlling. In *Kingsley International Pictures Corp. v. Regents of University of State of New York*, 1959, 360 U.S. 684, 79 S.Ct. 1362, 1364, 3 L.Ed.2d 1512, the Supreme Court of the United States upheld the exhibition of "Lady Chatterley's Lover", a motion picture which portrays adultery. It examined the constitutionality of that

***404** part of a New York statute[1] which that state's highest court had construed as authorizing the denial of a license to exhibit a motion picture "because its subject matter is adultery presented as being right and desirable for certain people under certain circumstances."[2] The Supreme Court there decided[3] that, insofar as the New York statute prohibited the issuance of a license to exhibit "Lady Chatterley's Lover" on that ground,[4] it was unconstitutional. The "opinion of the Court"[5] declared (360 U.S. at page 688, 79 S.Ct. at page 1365):

"It is contended that the State's action was justified because the motion picture attractively portrays a relationship which is contrary to the moral standards, the religious precepts, and the legal code of its citizenry. This argument misconceives what it is that the Constitution protects. Its guarantee is not confined to the expression of ideas that are conventional or shared by a majority. It protects advocacy of the opinion that adultery may sometimes be proper, no less than advocacy of socialism or the single tax. And in the realm of ideas it protects expression which is eloquent no less than that which is unconvincing." (Emphasis supplied.)

The freedoms guaranteed by the First and the Fourteenth Amendments to the United States Constitution are not wholly

***405** unconditional or absolute, and they may not be abused. However, they are not conditioned upon, and may not be construed to have been abused by, the presence or absence of majority endorsement of the views or ideas for the promulgation of which freedom is claimed or sanctions are sought.

This Court further finds that nudity per se is not "immoral" or "obscene" within the meaning of the ordinance. There is hardly an art museum or gallery to which one can go where completely nude statues and pictures are not on constant and prominent exhibition. Many popular books and magazines, far too numerous to list, frequently publish human nudity without offending the law. Certainly, if the advocacy, under certain circumstances, of adultery, which is contrary to moral standards and religious precepts, is protected by our Constitution, then the portrayal, by partial nudity, of nudism as a healthy and happy way of life should be accorded like protection.

Nudism may be unappealing and unattractive to some people. It may be repulsive and vulgar to others. But that does not brand it as "obscene" or "immoral". Whether or not it appeals to or repels an individual's sensitivities is irrelevant when the Court is bound to apply definitions of "obscene" and "immoral" which do not incorporate such subjective standards. This is not to say, however, that nude statues, pictures and representations may not under certain circumstances and by different portrayals be characterized as "obscene".

It is the conclusion of this Court that, because the motion picture "Garden of Eden" may not be denied a license on the ground that it is "obscene" or "immoral" within the meaning of the Chicago ordinance, the denial of that license by the city authorities on that ground (1) constituted a denial of plaintiff's rights to freedom of speech and press guaranteed by the Fourteenth Amendment to the Constitution of the United States to advocate nudism as a healthful and happy way of life, and (2) represents the application of the said ordinance "to a picture to which it cannot be applied without invading the area of constitutionally free expression."[6]

At the Court's suggestion, plaintiff has agreed to limit and restrict the exhibition of the picture to adults only, and not to publicize such exhibition in any manner or form as being authorized by the Court, and it is so ordered.

This memorandum shall stand as the Court's Findings of Fact and Conclusions of Law. Counsel for plaintiff will prepare and submit to the Court a form of Order directing defendants to issue the license.

[Footnotes omitted]

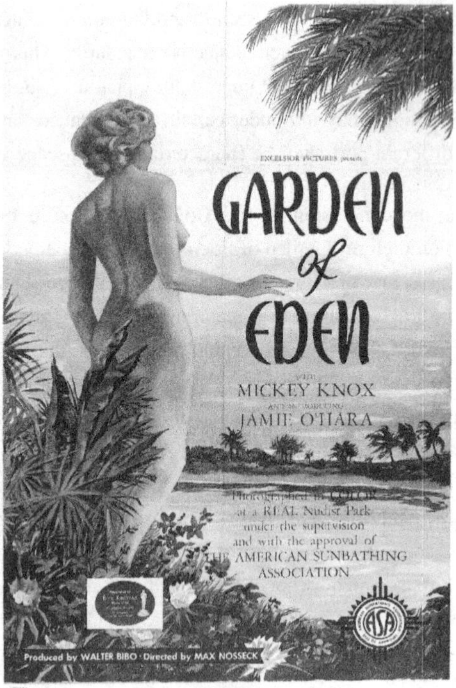

IN THE MATTER OF EXCELSIOR PICTURES CORP. v. REGENTS OF THE UNIVERSITY OF THE STATE OF NEW YORK

2 A.D.2d 941 (1956)

Appellate Division of the Supreme Court of the State of New York, Third Department

November 14, 1956

***942** MEMORANDUM BY THE COURT

We have reviewed the motion picture film Garden of Eden, license for which has been denied by the Motion Picture Division of the State Department of Education on the ground that it is indecent within the scope of the New York licensing statute (Education Law, § 122)...

The specific and limited portions of the film to which the licensing authorities object are exposed portions of human bodies in scenes depicting a nudist colony. There is, however, no full exposure of any adult nude body. The objectionable aspect of the film does not reach a magnitude which, under the limitations with which the Supreme Court has covered over the power of a State to censor films, would warrant prior restraint...In view of the decisions of the Court of Appeals in this area, a majority of the court are of opinion that a decision striking down the entire statute as unconstitutional ought not be entered by an intermediate appellate court.

* * *

9

Due Process, Obscenity & Profanity

In the aftermath of the *Miracle* decision and its progeny, the battle for freedom of the screen continued. Stepping up to the front line of the fight was an independent Chicago-based distributor: Times Film Corporation.

Like Joseph Burstyn, Arthur Mayer, and Robert and Raymond Hakim, Times Film Corp. made their mark by acquiring domestic U.S. distribution rights for notable international films. From the beginning Times Film demonstrated a keen eye and good film sense, picking up a small film that focused on two children in the smoldering ruins of post-World War II Paris entitled *Forbidden Games* (1952). The docudrama was recognized as one of the year's best foreign films by the Academy of Motion Pictures Arts and Sciences.

Times Film stood behind their pictures, using international art cinema to challenge film censors and push for an ever broadening interpretation of First Amendment freedoms. When *The Game of Love* (1954) was refused a permit, Times challenged the city's censorship ordinance. They claimed the words "obscene" and "immoral" were vague and ambiguous, not properly defined in the statute. The 7th circuit shot Times down, finding that *Game of Love* was "supercharged with a current of lewdness." (*Times Film Corp. v. City of Chicago*, 244 F. 2d 432, 436 [7th Cir., 1957]). Next, Times argued that the images in their Brazilian acquisition, *Naked Amazon* (1955), of indigenous Camayura peoples shown nude from the waist down, were not obscene. This time Baltimore's censors banned the picture but the state's court of appeals overturned the Board, permitting the film to play. (See *Maryland State Board of Censors v. Times Film Corp.*, 212 Md. 454 [App. Ct., 1957]).

Empowered by the win, Times Film mounted their boldest challenge yet as they rolled out the release of Walter Kolm-Veltée's cinematic adaptation of the Mozart opera *Don Juan* (1955). *The New York Times* gave the picture a glowing review: "It is doubtful whether Mozart's 'Don Giovanni' has ever been staged more stunningly...sets and costumes of such opulence and color as fairly captivate the eye... So are the beautiful females...To be sure, Mr. Kolm-Veltée has used the music generously to support or enhance most of the action—sometimes with great cleverness." (Bosley Crowther, "Colorful Mozart Don Juan Arrives at the Little Carnegie," in *The New York Times*, March 6, 1956). There was nothing obscene or objectionable in this operatic adaptation to be sure.

But with *Don Juan,* Times Film's legal team of Felix Bilgrey and Abner Mikva took one step too far. They paid Chicago's censors the license fee as the law required but refused to submit the film for approval. Times Film claimed that the law--and any submission requirement--was a prior restraint on the freedom of speech. Here, the Supreme Court disagreed. The requirement of prior submission of a motion picture for approval was not necessarily unconstitutional. (See *Times Film Corp. v. Chicago*, 365 U.S. 43 (1961) and Walter H. Waggoner "Felix Bilgrey, Foe of Censorship of Motion Pictures, Is Dead at 55" in *The New York Times*, January 15, 1980).

Four years later, Times Film tried again, this time they challenged the Maryland film ordinance with French film entitled *Desperate Decision* aka *Revenge at Daybreak* (1952).

Instead of a broadside attack on the very essence of the ordinance, in *Freedman v. Maryland*, Times challenged only the period (i.e., duration) of review. This time the distributor convinced the High Court. The censors had the burden of proving the film was unprotected by the Constitution and they had to demonstrate this in a limited, reasonable, prompt amount of time. Times pushed and finally achieved in narrowing the censor's power to delay distribution.

Along with Times Film, two Chicago theater owners also tested the city's censorship law. In 1933, Abe Teitel purchased a historic venue on Michigan Ave. and renamed it the World Playhouse Theater. With his son, Chuck, the theater became the Midwest's premiere venue for European art films from Ingmar Bergman to François Truffaut. The Teitels suffered some economic setbacks in the late 1960s and briefly exhibited more adult-oriented fare (See "Theater Owner Chuck Teitel Dies" in *Variety*, April 13, 2009). When the World Theater scheduled Michael and Roberta Findlay's S&M-tinged slasher flick, *Body of a Female* (1964), the city's cinema police objected. The Teitels fought the municipal film law all the way to the Supreme Court in *Teitel Film Corp. v. Cusack*. Based on the same theory demonstrated in *Freedman*, the Teitels prevailed: the licensing commission's extended administrative process had become a de facto method of film censorship. The commission's open ended review process was deemed improper.

In addition to due process issues, obscenity and profanity became central issues in the unfolding drama of film and the First Amendment. After nearly one hundred years of relying on the British common law test of obscenity, the U.S. developed its own measure in *Roth v. United States* (1957). This standard was applied to motion pictures in *Jacobellis v. Ohio* (1964), and resulted in perhaps the most memorable one-liner of U.S. jurisprudence (see J. Stewart's concurring opinion, on page 191). The courts also confronted the issue of profanity in Shirley Clarke's jazz-inflected gritty drug drama *The Connection* (1962). Engaging attorney Ephraim London, The Connection Company succeeded in demonstrating to the New York Court of Appeals the difference between using the word "shit" to denote feces (prohibited as indecent) from use of the word "shit" to signify drugs (tolerated as expressive use).

Individual personal rights in America were expanding, and the medium of motion pictures proved to be an influential factor in this cultural evolution. During the 1950s and early 1960s, courts had finally reached a consensus and were liberating the freedom of expression from age-old conventions. Within another decade filmmakers would push their newfound freedom to an extreme that could not abide.

TIMES FILM CORP. v. CITY OF CHICAGO

365 U.S. 43 (1961)

Supreme Court of United States

Argued October 19-20, 1960

Decided January 23, 1961

Appeal from the United States Court of Appeals for the Seventh Circuit

The Municipal Code of Chicago, §155-4, requires submission of all motion pictures for examination or censorship prior to their public exhibition and forbids their exhibition unless they meet certain standards. Petitioner applied for a permit to exhibit a certain motion picture and tendered the required license fee, but the permit was denied solely because petitioner refused to submit the film for examination. Petitioner sued in a Federal District Court for injunctive relief ordering issuance of the permit without submission of the film and restraining the city officials from interfering with its exhibition. It did not submit the film to the court or offer any evidence as to its content. The District Court dismissed the complaint on the ground, inter alia, that neither a substantial federal question nor a justiciable controversy was presented.

* * *

MR. CHIEF JUSTICE WARREN, with whom MR. JUSTICE BLACK, MR. JUSTICE DOUGLAS and MR. JUSTICE BRENNAN join, dissenting.

I cannot agree either with the conclusion reached by the Court or with the reasons advanced for its support. To me, this case clearly presents the question of our approval of unlimited censorship of motion pictures before exhibition through a system of administrative

***51** licensing. Moreover, the decision presents a real danger of eventual censorship for every form of communication, be it newspapers, journals, books, magazines, television, radio or public speeches. The Court purports to leave these questions for another day, but I am aware of no constitutional principle which permits us to hold that the communication of ideas through one medium may be censored while other media are immune. Of course each medium presents its own peculiar problems, but they are not of the kind which would authorize the censorship of one form of communication and not others. I submit that in arriving at its decision the Court has interpreted our cases contrary to the intention at the time of their rendition and, in exalting the censor of motion pictures, has endangered the First and Fourteenth Amendment rights of all others engaged in the dissemination of ideas.

* * *

***63** "The statute involved here does not seek to punish, as a past offense, speech or writing falling within the permissible scope of subsequent punishment. On the contrary, New York requires that permission to communicate ideas be obtained in advance from state officials who judge the content of the words and picture sought to be communicated. This Court recognized many years ago that such a previous restraint is a form of infringement upon freedom of expression to be especially condemned. *Near v. Minnesota ex rel. Olson*, 283 U.S. 697 (1931). * * *

***69** A revelation of the extent to which censorship has recently been used in this country is indeed astonishing. The Chicago licensors have banned newsreel films of Chicago policemen shooting at labor pickets and have ordered the deletion of a scene depicting the birth of a buffalo in Walt Disney's Vanishing Prairie. Gavzer, *Who Censors Our Movies?* Chicago Magazine, Feb. 1956, pp. 35, 39. Before World War II, the Chicago censor denied licenses to a number of films portraying and criticizing life in Nazi Germany including the March of Time's Inside Nazi Germany. Editorials, Chicago DailyTimes, Jan. 20, Nov. 18, 1938. Recently, Chicago refused to issue a permit for the exhibition of the motion picture Anatomy of a Murder based upon the best-selling novel of the same title, because it found the use of the words "rape" and "contraceptive" to be objectionable. *Columbia Pictures Corp. v. City of Chicago* (D. C. N. D. Ill.), 59 C. 1058 (1959) (unreported). The Chicago censor bureau excised a scene in *Street With No Name* in which a girl was slapped

***70** because this was thought to be a "too violent" episode. Life, Oct. 25, 1948, p. 60. It Happened in Europe was severely cut by the Ohio censors who deleted scenes of war orphans resorting to violence. The moral theme of the picture was that such children could even then be saved by love, affection and satisfaction of their basic needs for food. Levy, Case Against Film Censorship, *Films in Review*, Apr. 1950, p. 40 (published by National Board of Review of Motion Pictures, Inc.). The Memphis censors banned *The Southerner* which dealt with poverty among tenant farmers because "it reflects on the south." *Brewster's Millions*, an innocuous comedy of fifty years ago, was recently forbidden in Memphis because the radio and film character Rochester, a Negro, was deemed "too familiar." See Velie, You Can't See That Movie: Censorship in Action,

Collier's, May 6, 1950, pp. 11, 66. Maryland censors restricted a Polish documentary film on the basis that it failed to present a true picture of modern Poland. Levy, Case Against Film Censorship, *Films in Review*, supra, p. 41. *No Way Out*, the story of a Negro doctor's struggle against race prejudice, was banned by the Chicago censor on the ground that "there's a possibility it could cause trouble." The principal objection to the film was that the conclusion showed no reconciliation between blacks and whites. The ban was lifted after a storm of protest and later deletion of a scene showing Negroes and whites arming for a gang fight. *N.Y. Times*, Aug. 24, 1950, p. 31, col. 3; Aug. 31, 1950, p. 20, col. 8. Memphis banned Curley because it contained scenes of white and Negro children in school together. Kupferman and O'Brien, Motion Picture Censorship —The Memphis Blues, 36 Cornell L. J. 273, 276-278. Atlanta barred *Lost Boundaries*, the story of a Negro physician and his family who "passed" for white, on the ground that the exhibition of said picture "will adversely affect the peace, morals and good order" in the

***71** city. *N.Y. Times*, Feb. 5, 1950, § 2, p.5, col. 7. See generally Kupferman and O'Brien, supra; Note, 60 Yale L. J. 696 et seq.; Brief for American Civil Liberties Union as amicus curiae, pp. 14-15. *Witchcraft*, a study of superstition through the ages, was suppressed for years because it depicted the devil as a genial rake with amorous leanings, and because it was feared that certain historical scenes, portraying the excesses of religious fanatics, might offend religion. Scarface, thought by some as the best of the gangster films, was held up for months; then it was so badly mutilated that retakes costing a hundred thousand dollars were required to preserve continuity. The New York censors banned *Damaged Lives*, a film dealing with venereal disease, although it treated a difficult theme with dignity and had the sponsorship of the American Social Hygiene Society. The picture of Lenin's tomb bearing the inscription "Religion is the opiate of the people" was excised from *Potemkin*. From *Joan of Arc* the Maryland board eliminated Joan's exclamation as she stood at the stake: "Oh, God, why hast thou forsaken me?" and from *Idiot's Delight*, the sentence: "We, the workers of the world, will take care of that." *Professor Mamlock* was produced in Russia and portrayed the persecution of the Jews by Nazis. The Ohio censors condemned it as "harmful" and calculated to "stir up hatred and ill will and gain nothing." It was released only after substantial deletions were made. The police refused to permit its showing in Providence, Rhode Island, on the ground that it was communistic propaganda. *Millions of Us*, a strong union propaganda film, encountered trouble in a number of jurisdictions. *Spanish Earth*, a pro-Loyalist documentary picture, was banned by the board in Pennsylvania. Ernst and Lindey,

The Censor Marches On, 96-97, 102-103, 108-111. During the year ending June 30, 1938, the New York board censored, in one way or another, over five percent of the

***72** moving pictures it reviewed. Id., at 81. Charlie Chaplin's satire on Hitler, *The Great Dictator*, was banned in Chicago, apparently out of deference to its large German population. Chafee, supra, at p. 541. Ohio and Kansas banned newsreels considered pro labor. Kansas ordered a speech by Senator Wheeler opposing the bill for enlarging the Supreme Court to be cut from the *March of Time* as "partisan and biased."Id., at 542. An early version of *Carmen* was condemned on several different grounds. The Ohio censor objected because cigarette-girls smoked cigarettes in public. The Pennsylvania censor disapproved the duration of a kiss. Id., at 543. The New York censors forbade the discussion in films of pregnancy, venereal disease, eugenics, birth control, abortion, illegitimacy, prostitution, miscegenation and divorce. Ernst and Lindey, supra, at p. 83. A member of the Chicago censor board explained that she rejected afilm because "it was immoral, corrupt, indecent, against my . . . religious principles." Transcript of Record, p. 172. *Times Film Corp. v. City of Chicago*, 244 F. 2d 432. A police sergeant attached to the censor board explained, "Coarse language or anything that would be derogatory to the government— propaganda" is ruled out of foreign films. "Nothing pink or red is allowed," he added. *Chicago Daily News*, Apr. 7, 1959, p. 3, cols. 7-8. The police sergeant in charge of the censor unit has said: "Children should be allowed to see any movie that plays in Chicago. If a picture is objectionable for a child, it is objectionable period." *Chicago Tribune*, May 24, 1959, p. 8. col. 3. And this is but a smattering produced from limited research. Perhaps the most powerful indictment of Chicago's licensing device is found in the fact that between the Court's decision in 1952 in *Joseph Burstyn, Inc., v. Wilson*, supra, and the filing of the petition for certiorari in 1960 in the present case, not once have the state courts upheld the censor

***73** when the exhibitor elected to appeal. Brief of American Civil Liberties Union as amicus curiae, pp. 13-14.

* * *

MR. JUSTICE DOUGLAS, with whom THE CHIEF JUSTICE and MR. JUSTICE BLACK concur, dissenting.

My view that censorship of movies is unconstitutional because it is a prior restraint and violative of the First Amend*ment has been expressed on prior occasions. Superior Films v. Department of Education*, 346 U.S. 587, 588-

Walter Kolm-Veltée's *Don Juan* (1955) was the final installment of a trilogy of films inspired by the lives of great composers, which included Beethoven in *Eroica* (1949) and *Franz Schubert* (1953).

589 (concurring opinion); *Kingsley Picture Corp. v. Regents*, 360 U.S. 684, 697 (concurring opinion).

While the problem of movie censorship is relatively new, the censorship device is an ancient one. It was recently stated, "There is a law of action and reaction in the decline and resurgence of censorship and control. Whenever liberty is in the ascendant, a social group will begin to resist it; and when the reverse is true, a similar resistance in favor of liberty will occur." Haney, *Comstockery in America* (1960), pp. 11-12.

Whether or not that statement of history is accurate, censorship has had many champions throughout time.

* * *

IN THE MATTER OF THE CONNECTION COMPANY

v.

REGENTS OF THE UNIVERSITY OF THE STATE OF NEW YORK

17 A.D.2d 671 (1962)

Appellate Division of the Supreme Court of the State of New York, Third Department

Decided July 2, 1962

* * * This is a proceeding to review the denial of the Board of Regents for the issuance of a license for the exhibition of the motion picture "The Connection". The sole ground for refusing a license to show the motion picture is premised on obscenity in the use of the word "shit". In most instances the word is not used in its usual connotation but as a definitive expression of the language of the narcotic. At most, the use of the word may be classified as vulgar but it is not obscene, pursuant to section 122 of the Education Law, and the determination of the Board of Regents is annulled. The petitioner further alleges that the licensing section (§ 126) is unconstitutional as the fiscal charge constitutes the imposition of a tax and not a fee. (*People v. Jarvis*, 19 App. Div. 466, 469.) Suffice it to note that the Legislature of this State in 1961 amended the ***672** section by reducing the fees charged so that we must assume, as of now, that the present charges are fair and reasonable. The presumption that the section is constitutional prevails.

Determination of the Board of Regents annulled, with $50 costs to the petitioner.

FREEDMAN v. MARYLAND

380 U.S. 51 (1965)

Supreme Court of United States

Argued November 19, 1964

Decided March 1, 1965

Appeal from the Court of Appeals of Maryland

The Court found the Maryland law to be invalid. The Court decision reflected a concern that the statute provides the danger of "unduly suppressing protected expression." The board was allowed overly broad licensing discretion with a lack of statutory provisions for judicial participation in the the procedure to prohibit a film. The Court established three guidelines as adequate safeguards to protect against the "undue inhibition of protected expression." These guidelines are to: (1) place the burden of proving the film is unprotected expression on the censors, (2) require judicial determination to impose a valid determination, and (3) require prompt determination "within a specified time period."

***52** MR. JUSTICE BRENNAN delivered the opinion of the Court.

Appellant sought to challenge the constitutionality of the Maryland motion picture censorship statute, Md. Ann. Code, 1957, Art. 66A, and exhibited the film "Revenge at Daybreak" at his Baltimore theatre without first submitting the picture to the State Board of Censors as required by §2 thereof.[1] The State concedes that the picture does not violate the statutory standards[2] and

***53** would have received a license if properly submitted, but the appellant was convicted of a §2 violation despite his contention that the statute in its entirety unconstitutionally impaired freedom of expression. The Court of Appeals of Maryland affirmed, 233 Md. 498, 197 A. 2d 232, and we noted probable jurisdiction, 377 U.S. 987. We reverse.

* * *

In the light of the difference between the issues presented here and in *Times Film*, the Court of Appeals erred in saying that, since appellant's refusal to submit the film to the Board was a violation only of §2, "he has restricted himself to an attack on that section

***56** alone, and lacks standing to challenge any of the other provisions (or alleged shortcomings) of the statute." 233 Md., at 505, 197 A. 2d, at 236. Appellant has not challenged the submission requirement in a vacuum but in a concrete statutory context. His contention is that §2 effects an invalid prior restraint because the structure of the other provisions of the statute contributes to the infirmity of §2; he does not assert that the other provisions are independently invalid.

* * *

***60** ... How or whether Maryland is to incorporate the required procedural safeguards in the statutory scheme is, of course, for the State to decide. But a model is not lacking: In *Kingsley Books, Inc. v. Brown*, 354 U.S. 436, we upheld a New York injunctive procedure designed to prevent the sale of obscene books. That procedure postpones any restraint against sale until a judicial determination of obscenity following notice and an adversary hearing. The statute provides for a hearing one day after joinder of issue; the judge must hand down his decision within two days after termination of the hearing. The New York procedure operates without prior submission to a censor, but the chilling effect of a censorship order, even one which requires judicial action for its enforcement, suggests all the more reason for expeditious determination of the question whether a particular film is constitutionally protected.

The requirement of prior submission to a censor sustained in *Times Film* is consistent with our recognition

***61** that films differ from other forms of expression. Similarly, we think that the nature of the motion picture industry may suggest different time limits for a judicial determination. It is common knowledge that films are scheduled well before actual exhibition, and the requirement of advance submission in §2 recognizes this. One possible scheme would be to allow the exhibitor or distributor to submit his film early enough to ensure an orderly final disposition of the case before the scheduled exhibition date—far enough in advance so that the exhibitor could safely advertise the opening on a normal basis. Failing such a scheme or sufficiently early submission under such a scheme, the statute would have to require adjudication considerably more prompt than has been the case under the Maryland statute. Otherwise, litigation might be unduly expensive and protracted, or the victorious exhibitor might find the most propitious opportunity for exhibition past. We do not mean to lay down rigid time limits or procedures, but to suggest considerations in drafting legislation to accord with local exhibition practices, and in doing so to avoid the potentially chilling effect of the Maryland statute on protected expression.

Reversed.

MR. JUSTICE DOUGLAS, whom MR. JUSTICE BLACK joins, concurring.

On several occasions I have indicated my view that movies are entitled to the same degree and kind of protection under the First Amendment as other forms of expression. *Superior Films v. Department of Education*, 346 U.S. 587, 588; *Kingsley Pictures Corp. v. Regents*, 360 U.S. 684, 697; *Times Film Corp. v. Chicago*, 365 U.S. 43, 78.[*] For the reasons there stated, I do not

***62** believe any form of censorship—no matter how speedy or prolonged it may be—is permissible. As I see it, a pictorial presentation occupies as preferred a position as any other form of expression. If censors are banned from the publishing business, from the pulpit, from the public platform—as they are—they should be banned from the theatre. I would not admit the censor even for the limited role accorded him in *Kingsley Books, Inc. v. Brown*, 354 U.S. 436. I adhere to my dissent in that case. Id., at 446-447. Any authority to obtain a temporary injunction gives the State "the paralyzing power of a censor." Id., at 446. The regime of *Kingsley Books* "substitutes punishment by contempt for punishment by jury trial." Id., at 447. I would put an end to all forms and types of censorship and give full literal meaning to the command of the First Amendment.

[footnotes omitted]

TEITEL FILM CORP. v. CUSACK

390 U.S. 139 (1968)

United States Supreme Court

Decided January 29, 1968

Appeal from the Supreme Court of Illinois

Appellants, who were permanently enjoined by the Illinois courts from showing certain motion pictures, challenged the Chicago Motion Picture Censorship Ordinance as unconstitutional on its face and as applied. The ordinance allows 50 to 57 days to complete the administrative process, and there is no provision for a prompt judicial decision by the trial court of the alleged obscenity of the film.

Held: Appellants' constitutional rights were violated, since the requirements of *Freedman v. Maryland*, 380 U.S. 51, that the censor, within a "specified brief period," either issue a license or go to court to restrain showing the film, and that there be "prompt final judicial decision," were not met.

***139** PER CURIAM.

This appeal seeks review of judgments of the Supreme Court of Illinois which affirmed orders of the Circuit Court of Cook County permanently enjoining the appellants from showing certain motion pictures in public places in the City of Chicago, 38 Ill. 2d 53, 230 N. E. 2d 241. The questions presented are whether the Chicago Motion Picture Censorship Ordinance is unconstitutional on its face and as applied, and whether the films involved are obscene.[1]

***140** The Chicago Motion Picture Censorship Ordinance prohibits the exhibition in any public place of "any picture...without first having secured a permit therefor from the superintendent of police." The Superintendent is required "within three days of receipt" of films to "inspect such . . . films . . . or cause them to be inspected by the Film Review Section . . . and within three days after such inspection" either to grant or deny the permit.[2] If the permit is denied the exhibitor may within seven days seek review by the Motion Picture Appeal Board. The Appeal Board must review the film within 15 days of the request for review, and thereafter within 15 days afford the exhibitor, his agent or distributor a hearing. The Board must serve the applicant with written notice of its ruling within five days after close of the hearing. If the Board denies the permit, "the Board, within ten days from the hearing, shall file with the Circuit Court of Cook County an action for an injunction against the showing of the film." A Circuit Court Rule, General Order 3-3, promulgated May 26, 1965, provides that a "complaint for injunction . . . shall be given priority over all other causes. The Court shall set the cause for hearing within five (5) days after the defendant has answered . . . ."[3] However, neither the rule nor any

***141** statutory or other provision assures a prompt judicial decision of the question of the alleged obscenity of the film.

The Illinois Supreme Court held "that the administration of the Chicago Motion Picture Ordinance violates no constitutional rights of the defendants." 38 Ill. 2d, at 63, 230 N. E. 2d, at 247. We disagree. In *Freedman v. Maryland*, 380 U.S. 51, 58-59, we held "...that a noncriminal process which requires the prior submission of a film to a censor avoids constitutional infirmity only if it takes place under procedural safeguards designed to obviate the dangers of a censorship system. ...To this end, the exhibitor must be assured, by statute or authoritative judicial construction, that the censor will, within a specified brief period, either issue a license or go to court to restrain showing the film. . . . [T]he procedure must also assure a prompt final judicial decision, to minimize the deterrent effect of an interim and possibly erroneous denial of a license." (Emphasis supplied.) The Chicago censorship procedures violate these standards in two respects. (1) The 50 to 57 days provided by the ordinance to complete the administrative process before initiation of the judicial proceeding does not satisfy the standard that the procedure must assure "that the censor will, within a specified brief period, either

***142** issue a license or go to court to restrain showing the film." (2) The absence of any provision for a prompt judicial decision by the trial court violates the standard that ". . . the procedure must also assure a prompt final judicial decision . . . ."

Accordingly, we reverse the judgments of the Supreme Court of Illinois and remand the case for further proceedings not inconsistent with this opinion.

It is so ordered.

* * *

JACOBELLIS v. OHIO

378 U.S. 184 (1964)

Supreme Court of United States

Argued March 26, 1963; Reargued April 1, 1964

Decided June 22, 1964

Appeal from the Supreme Court of Ohio

***185** Ephraim London reargued the cause for appellant * * *

Charles H. Keating, Jr. filed a brief for Citizens for Decent Literature, Inc., as amicus curiae, urging affirmance.

MR. JUSTICE BRENNAN announced the judgment of the Court and delivered an opinion in which MR. JUSTICE GOLDBERG joins.

Appellant, Nico Jacobellis, manager of a motion picture theater in Cleveland Heights, Ohio, was convicted on two counts of possessing and exhibiting an obscene film in

***186** violation of Ohio Revised Code (1963 Supp.), § 2905.34.[1] He was fined $500 on the first count and $2,000 on the second, and was sentenced to the workhouse if the fines were not paid...The dispositive question is whether the state courts properly found that the motion picture involved a French film called "Les Amants" ("The Lovers"), was obscene and

***187** hence not entitled to the protection for free expression that is guaranteed by the First and Fourteenth Amendments. We conclude that the film is not obscene and that the judgment must accordingly be reversed.

Motion pictures are within the ambit of the constitutional guarantees of freedom of speech and of the press. *Joseph Burstyn, Inc., v. Wilson*, 343 U.S. 495. But in *Roth v. United States* and *Alberts v. California*, 354 U.S. 476, we held that obscenity is not subject to those guarantees. Application of an obscenity law to suppress a motion picture thus requires ascertainment of the "dim and uncertain line" that often separates obscenity from constitutionally protected expression. *Bantam Books, Inc., v. Sullivan*, 372 U.S. 58, 66; see *Speiser v. Randall*, 357 U.S. 513, 525.[2] It has been suggested that this is a task in which our Court need not involve itself. We are told that the determination whether a particular motion picture, book, or other work of expression is obscene can be treated as a purely factual judgment on which a jury's verdict is all but conclusive, or that in any event the decision can be left essentially to state and lower federal courts, with this Court exercising only a limited review such as that needed to determine whether the ruling below is supported by "sufficient evidence." The suggestion is appealing, since it would lift from our shoulders a difficult, recurring, and unpleasant task. But we cannot accept it. Such an abnegation of judicial

***188** supervision in this field would be inconsistent with our duty to uphold the constitutional guarantees. Since it is only "obscenity" that is excluded from the constitutional protection, the question whether a particular work is obscene necessarily implicates an issue of constitutional law. See *Roth v. United States*, supra, 354 U.S., at 497-498 (separate opinion).

* * *

***189** In other areas involving constitutional rights under the Due Process Clause, the Court has consistently recognized its duty to apply the applicable rules of law upon the basis of an independent review of the facts of each case. E.g., *Watts v. Indiana*, 338 U.S. 49, 51; *Norris v. Alabama*, 294 U.S. 587, 590.[4] And this has been particularly true where rights have been asserted under the First Amendment guarantees of free expression. Thus in *Pennekamp v. Florida*, 328 U.S. 331, 335, the Court stated:

"The Constitution has imposed upon this Court final authority to determine the meaning and application of those words of that instrument which require interpretation to resolve judicial issues. With that responsibility, we are compelled to examine for ourselves the statements in issue and the circumstances under which they were made to see whether or not they...are of a character which the principles of the First Amendment, as adopted by the Due Process Clause of the Fourteenth Amendment, protect."[5]

We cannot understand why the Court's duty should be any different in the present case, where Jacobellis has

***190** been subjected to a criminal conviction for disseminating a work of expression and is challenging that conviction as a deprivation of rights guaranteed by the First and Fourteenth Amendments. Nor can we understand why the Court's performance of its constitutional and judicial function in this sort of case should be denigrated by such epithets as "censor" or "super-censor." In judging alleged obscenity the Court is no more "censoring" expression than it has in other cases "censored" criticism of judges and public officials, advocacy of governmental overthrow, or speech alleged to constitute a breach of the peace. Use of an opprobrious label can neither obscure nor impugn the Court's performance of its obligation to test challenged judgments against the guarantees of the First and Fourteenth Amendments and, in doing so, to delineate the scope of constitutionally protected speech. Hence we reaffirm the principle that, in "obscenity" cases as in all others involving rights derived from the First Amendment guarantees of free expression, this Court cannot avoid making an independent constitutional judgment on the facts of the case as to whether the material involved is constitutionally protected.[6]

***191** The question of the proper standard for making this determination has been the subject of much discussion and controversy since our decision in *Roth* seven years ago. Recognizing that the test for obscenity enunciated there—"whether to the average person, applying contemporary community standards, the dominant theme of the material taken as a whole appeals to prurient interest," 354 U.S., at 489—is not perfect, we think any substitute would raise equally difficult problems, and we therefore adhere to that standard. We would reiterate, however, our recognition in *Roth* that obscenity is excluded from the constitutional protection only because it is "utterly without redeeming social importance," and that "the portrayal of sex, e. g., in art, literature and scientific works, is not itself sufficient reason to deny material the constitutional protection of freedom of speech and press." Id., at 484, 487. It follows that material dealing with sex in a manner that advocates ideas, *Kingsley Int'l Pictures Corp. v. Regents*, 360 U.S. 684, or that has literary or scientific or artistic value or any other form of social importance, may not be branded as obscenity and denied the constitutional protection.[7] Nor may the constitutional status of the material be made to turn on a "weighing" of its social importance against its prurient appeal, for a work cannot be proscribed unless it is "utterly" without social importance. See *Zeitlin v. Arnebergh*, 59 Cal. 2d 901, 920, 383 P. 2d 152, 165, 31 Cal. Rptr. 800,

813 (1963). It should also be recognized that the *Roth* standard requires in the first instance a finding that the material "goes substantially beyond customary limits of candor in description or representation of such matters."

* * *

***192** ... It has been suggested that the "contemporary community standards" aspect of the *Roth* test implies a determination of the constitutional question of obscenity in each case by the standards of the particular local community from which the case arises. This is an incorrect reading of *Roth.* The concept of "contemporary community standards" was first expressed by Judge Learned Hand in *United States v. Kennerley*, 209 F. 119, 121 (D. C. S. D. N. Y. 1913), where he said:

"...should not the word 'obscene' be allowed to indicate the present critical point in the compromise between candor and shame at which the community may have arrived here and now?

* * *

***193** It seems clear that in this passage Judge Hand was referring not to state and local "communities," but rather to "the community" in the sense of "society at large; ... the public, or people in general."[9] Thus, he recognized that under his standard the concept of obscenity would have "a varying meaning from time to time"—not from county to county, or town to town.

We do not see how any "local" definition of the "community" could properly be employed in delineating the area of expression that is protected by the Federal Constitution. MR. JUSTICE HARLAN pointed out in *Manual Enterprises, Inc., v. Day*, supra, 370 U.S., at 488, that a standard based on a particular local community would have "the intolerable consequence of denying some sections of the country access to material, there deemed acceptable, which in others might be considered offensive to prevailing community standards of decency. Cf. *Butler v. Michigan*, 352 U.S. 380."

* * *

***194** Furthermore, to sustain the suppression of a particular book or film in one locality would deter its dissemination in other localities where it might be held not obscene, since sellers and exhibitors would be reluctant to risk criminal conviction in testing the variation between the two places...

It is true that local communities throughout the land are in fact diverse, and that in cases such as this one the Court is confronted with the task of reconciling the rights of such communities with the rights of individuals. Communities vary, however, in many respects other than their toleration of alleged obscenity, and such variances have never been considered to require or justify a varying standard for application of the Federal Constitution. The Court has regularly been compelled, in reviewing criminal convictions challenged under the Due Process Clause of the Fourteenth Amendment, to reconcile the conflicting rights of the local community which brought the prosecution and of the individual defendant. Such a task is admittedly difficult and delicate, but it is inherent in the Court's duty of determining whether a particular conviction worked a deprivation of rights guaranteed by the Federal Constitution. The Court has not shrunk from discharging that duty in other areas, and we see no reason why it should do so here. The Court has explicitly refused to tolerate a result whereby "the constitutional limits of free expression in the Nation

***195** would vary with state lines," *Pennekamp v. Florida*, supra, 328 U.S., at 335; we see even less justification for allowing such limits to vary with town or county lines. We thus reaffirm the position taken in *Roth* to the effect that the constitutional status of an allegedly obscene work must be determined on the basis of a national standard.[10] It is, after all, a national Constitution we are expounding.

We recognize the legitimate and indeed exigent interest of States and localities throughout the Nation in preventing the dissemination of material deemed harmful to children. But that interest does not justify a total suppression of such material, the effect of which would be to "reduce the adult population . . . to reading only what is fit for children." *Butler v. Michigan*, 352 U.S. 380, 383. State and local authorities might well consider whether their objectives in this area would be better served by laws aimed specifically at preventing distribution of objectionable material to children, rather than at totally prohibiting its dissemination.[11] Since the present conviction is based upon exhibition of the film to the public at large and not upon its exhibition to children, the judgment must be reviewed under the strict standard applicable in determining the scope of the expression that is protected by the Constitution.

We have applied that standard to the motion picture in question. "The Lovers" involves a woman bored with her life and marriage who abandons her husband and family for a young archaeologist with whom she has

***196** suddenly fallen in love. There is an explicit love scene in the last reel of the film, and the State's objections are based almost entirely upon that scene. The film was favorably reviewed in a number of national publications, although disparaged in others, and was rated by at least two critics of national stature among the best films of the year in which it was produced. It was shown in approximately 100 of the larger cities in the United States, including Columbus and Toledo, Ohio. We have viewed the film, in the light of the record made in the trial court, and we conclude that it is not obscene within the standards enunciated in *Roth v. United States* and *Alberts v. California*, which we reaffirm here.

Reversed.

* * *

***197** MR. JUSTICE STEWART, concurring.

It is possible to read the Court's opinion in *Roth v. United States* and *Alberts v. California*, 354 U.S. 476, in a variety of ways. In saying this, I imply no criticism of the Court, which in those cases was faced with the task of trying to define what may be indefinable. I have reached the conclusion, which I think is confirmed at least by negative implication in the Court's decisions since *Roth* and *Alberts*,[1] that under the First and Fourteenth Amendments criminal laws in this area are constitutionally limited to hard-core pornography.[2] I shall not today attempt further to define the kinds of material I understand to be embraced within that shorthand description; and perhaps I could never succeed in intelligibly doing so. But I know it when I see it, and the motion picture involved in this case is not that.

MR. JUSTICE GOLDBERG, concurring.

The question presented is whether the First and Fourteenth Amendments permit the imposition of criminal punishment for exhibiting the motion picture entitled

"The Lovers." I have viewed the film and I wish merely to add to my Brother BRENNAN'S description that the love scene deemed objectionable is so fragmentary and fleeting that only a censor's alert would make an audience

***198** conscious that something "questionable" is being portrayed. Except for this rapid sequence, the film concerns itself with the history of an ill-matched and unhappy marriage—a familiar subject in old and new novels and in current television soap operas.

* * *

***199** THE CHIEF JUSTICE, with whom MR. JUSTICE CLARK joins, dissenting.

In this and other cases in this area of the law, which are coming to us in ever-increasing numbers, we are faced with the resolution of rights basic both to individuals and to society as a whole. Specifically, we are called upon to reconcile the right of the Nation and of the States to maintain a decent society and, on the other hand, the right of individuals to express themselves freely in accordance with the guarantees of the First and Fourteenth Amendments. Although the Federal Government and virtually every State has had laws proscribing obscenity since the Union was formed, and although this Court has recently decided that obscenity is not within the protection of the First Amendment,[1] neither courts nor legislatures have been able to evolve a truly satisfactory definition of obscenity. In other areas of the law, terms like "negligence," although in common use for centuries, have been difficult to define except in the most general manner. Yet the courts have been able to function in such areas with a reasonable degree of efficiency. The obscenity problem, however, is aggravated by the fact that it involves the area of public expression, an area in which a broad range of freedom is vital to our society and is constitutionally protected.

Recently this Court put its hand to the task of defining the term "obscenity" in *Roth v. United States*, 354 U.S. 476. The definition enunciated in that case has generated much legal speculation as well as further judicial interpretation by state and federal courts. It has also been relied upon by legislatures. Yet obscenity cases continue to come to this Court, and it becomes increasingly apparent that we must settle as well as we can the question of what constitutes "obscenity" and the question

***200** of what standards are permissible in enforcing proscriptions against obscene matter...

For all the sound and fury that the *Roth* test has generated, it has not been proved unsound, and I believe that we should try to live with it—at least until a more satisfactory definition is evolved. No government—be it federal, state, or local—should be forced to choose between repressing all material, including that within the realm of decency, and allowing unrestrained license to publish any material, no matter how vile. There must be a rule of reason in this as in other areas of the law, and we have attempted in the *Roth* case to provide such a rule.

It is my belief that when the Court said in Roth that obscenity is to be defined by reference to "community standards," it meant community standards—not a national standard, as is sometimes argued. I believe that there is no provable "national standard," and perhaps there should be none. At all events, this Court has not been able to enunciate one, and it would be unreasonable to expect local courts to divine one. It is said that such a "community" approach may well result in material being proscribed as obscene in one community but not in another, and, in all probability, that is true. But communities throughout the Nation are in fact diverse, and it must be remembered that, in cases such as this one, the Court is confronted with the task of reconciling conflicting

***201** rights of the diverse communities within our society and of individuals.

We are told that only "hard core pornography" should be denied the protection of the First Amendment. But who can define "hard core pornography" with any greater clarity than "obscenity"? And even if we were to retreat to that position, we would soon be faced with the need to define that term just as we now are faced with the need to define "obscenity." Meanwhile, those who profit from the commercial exploitation of obscenity would continue to ply their trade unmolested.

In my opinion, the use to which various materials are put—not just the words and pictures themselves—must be considered in determining whether or not the materials are obscene. A technical or legal treatise on pornography may well be inoffensive under most circumstances but, at the same time, "obscene" in the extreme when sold or displayed to children.[2]

* * *

***202** In light of the foregoing, I would reiterate my acceptance of the rule of the *Roth* case: Material is obscene and not constitutionally protected against regulation and proscription if "to the average person, applying contemporary community standards, the dominant theme of the material taken as a whole appeals to prurient interest." 354 U.S., at 489. I would commit the enforcement of this rule to the appropriate state and federal courts, and I would accept their judgments made pursuant to the *Roth* rule, limiting myself to a consideration only of whether there is sufficient evidence in the record upon which a finding of obscenity could be made. If there is no evidence in the record upon which such a finding could be made, obviously the material involved cannot be held obscene. Cf. *Thompson v. City of Louisville*, 362 U.S. 199. But since a mere modicum of evidence may satisfy a "no evidence" standard, I am unwilling to give the important constitutional right of free expression such limited protection. However, protection of society's right to maintain its moral fiber and the effective administration of justice require that this Court not establish itself as an ultimate censor, in each case reading the entire record, viewing the accused material, and making an independent de novo judgment on the question of obscenity. Therefore,

***203** once a finding of obscenity has been made below under a proper application of the *Roth* test, I would apply a "sufficient evidence" standard of review—requiring something more than merely any evidence but something less than "substantial evidence on the record [including the allegedly obscene material] as a whole." Cf. *Universal Camera Corp. v. Labor Board*, 340 U.S. 474. This is the only reasonable way I can see to obviate the necessity of this Court's sitting as the Super Censor of all the obscenity purveyed throughout the Nation.

While in this case, I do not subscribe to some of the State's extravagant contentions, neither can I say that the courts below acted with intemperance or without sufficient evidence in finding the moving picture obscene within the meaning of the *Roth* test. Therefore, I would affirm the judgment.

MR. JUSTICE HARLAN, dissenting.

While agreeing with my Brother BRENNAN'S opinion that the responsibilities of the Court in this area are no different from those which attend the adjudication of kindred constitutional questions, I have heretofore expressed the view that the States are constitutionally permitted greater latitude in determining what is bannable on the score of obscenity than is so with the Federal Government...

The more I see of these obscenity cases the more convinced I become that in permitting the States wide, but not federally unrestricted, scope in this field, while holding the Federal Government with a tight rein, lies the best promise for achieving a sensible accommodation between

***204** the public interest sought to be served by obscenity laws (cf. my dissenting opinion in *Bantam Books, Inc., v. Sullivan*, 372 U.S. 58, 76, 77) and protection of genuine rights of free expression.

...The application of any general constitutional tests must thus necessarily be pricked out on a case-by-case basis, but as a point of departure I would apply to the Federal Government the *Roth* standards as amplified in my opinion in *Manual Enterprises*, supra. As to the States, I would make the federal test one of rationality. I would not prohibit them from banning any material which, taken as a whole, has been reasonably found in state judicial proceedings to treat with sex in a fundamentally offensive manner, under rationally established criteria for judging such material.

On this basis, having viewed the motion picture in question, I think the State acted within permissible limits in condemning the film and would affirm the judgment of the Ohio Supreme Court.

[footnotes omitted]

10

Mainstream Hardcore

Even during the heyday of the censor's power, stag films, blue movies, and sexually-explicit loops were surreptitiously screened in back rooms and men's clubhouses. The oldest surviving American pornographic movie, *A Free Ride* aka *A Grass Sandwich*, was most likely produced in 1915. The black market of obscene cinema has a hidden history, only titles and heavily worn clips remain of *Wonders of the Unseen World* (1927), *Surprise of a Knight* (c. 1920s), *A Stiff Game* (c. 1930s), *The Photographer: Fun and Frolic in the Studio*

(c. 1940s), and *While the Cat's Away* (c. 1950s). Bettie Page achieved a degree of notoriety in recent decades as the alluring icon of soft core simulated S&M role playing, but a harder current was buried even deeper and rarely spoken of.

A 16-year old bleach bottle blonde cigarette girl/stripper took the name "Candy Barr" and appeared in an erotic loop entitled *Smart Alec* (1951). Her epically long sex scene (15 minutes) was shot in a cheap motel room in San Antonio. The film, according to smut scholars, became "the single most popular film of the genre." Candy Barr was the first porn star. (Al Di Lauro and Gerlad Rabkin, *Dirty Movies: An Illustrated History of the Stag Film* (New York: Chelsea House Publishers, 1976), also see Douglas Martin, "Candy Barr, 70, Stripper and Star of 1950's Stag Film, Dies," in *The New York Times*, January 4, 2006). As GIs returned from WWII and more daring films were imported from Europe, sexually explicit loops became more accessible. Still, it would be another two decades before the next performer would break through as an adult cinema icon.

That next performer was a slim, curly haired brunette with girl-next-door qualities. She did have a special skill that was put to use by director Gerard Damiano aka Jerry Gerard in a film entitled *Deep Throat* (1972). *Deep Throat* and its star, Linda Lovelace, became a cultural touchstone, an underground sex film gone mainstream, setting off a fad that the New York Times dubbed the "Porno Chic."

Deep Throat opened at the New Mature World Theater on West 49th Street in New York City on June 12, 1972. The picture built a following of the city's most prominent pundits: Andy Warhol, Gore Vidal, Truman Capote, and Norman Mailer. On the left coast audiences included Johnny Carson, Hugh Hefner, and Jack Nicholson. For a brief moment in time, a filthy film was unavoidable. Then in August, New York's Finest filed charges against the theater and in chilly December 1972, *People v. Mature Enterprises* went to trial.

Three months later, Judge Joel Tyler came down stridently against the film, opining that *Deep Throat* was a "feast of carrion and squalor," "a nadir of decadence" and "a Sodom and Gomorrah gone wild before the fire." (Bruce Weber, "Joel J. Tyler, Judge Who Pronounced *Deep Throat* Obscene, Dies at 90," in *The New York Times*, January 14, 2012). His rant only served to promote the picture further. Even though at one point the film was banned as obscene in 23 states, *Deep Throat* continued to generate box office revenue. When home video arrived, the picture just became bigger.

The problem with prosecuting pornography had been the moving target of the obscenity standard. The Supreme Court endorsed the *Roth* test in 1957. *Roth* was tweaked by

Jacobellis v. Ohio (1964). The standard was changed again with *Memoirs v. Massachusetts* (1966); a final test was endorsed in *Miller v. California* (1973). Justice William Brennan, penned both the *Roth* and *Jacobellis* opinions, vouching for a national standard to weigh obscenity. The plurality of the *Memoirs* decision repudiated that measure for a localized standard. Chief Justice Warren Burger's *Miller* directed the court to look at applicable state law. But even with *Miller*, there was a level of ambiguity. Obscenity law was in flux as the pornography industry was gearing up.

A decade after *Miller* was handed down, the 2nd Circuit provided a level of clarity in *U.S. v. Various Articles of Obscene Merchandise* (1983). The case centered on various hardcore pornographic videocassettes and magazines that had been seized by the government as patently offensive. Among the treasure trove of smut was a VHS of *Deep Throat*. The parties were allowed to introduce evidence probative of contemporary community standards. Judge Walter R. Mansfield approached the subject with less vitriol than Judge Tyler. Mansfield wrote, "While the existence of tolerated enclaves of obscenity does not by itself create a community standard...judicial notice of widespread community availability and patronage of such works may be accepted as circumstantial evidence of contemporary community standards...At some point a work widely available must be considered inferentially acceptable." (*U.S. v. Various Articles of Obscene Merchandise*, 709 F. 2d 132, 137 [2nd Cir, 1983]). Because *Deep Throat* had become so popular it was no longer "patently offensive." The film was recognized for being recognizable.

While porn had broken through to the mainstream, there were still other legal issues to consider. When Bambi Woods put on and took off a white-fringed outfit in *Debbie Does Dallas* (1978), the Cowboys' cheerleaders threw a flag on the play. The issue was not obscenity but trademark infringement and dilution. Here the 2nd Circuit ruled against *Debbie*, concerned that the outfits might unfairly cause confusion about the sponsorship or approval from the NFL team's spirit squad. The balance between First Amendment rights, obscenity, and ancillary intellectual property issues, such as copyright and trademark, remain a fascinating and dynamic area of the law.

A Free Ride (c. 1915)

THE PEOPLE OF THE STATE OF NEW YORK v. MATURE ENTERPRISES, INC.

73 Misc.2d 749 (1973)

Criminal Court of the City of New York, New York County

Decided March 1, 1973

JOEL J. TYLER, J.

We are again thrust into the over explored thicket of obscenity law. The defendant is charged with promotion, or possession with intent to promote, obscene material, knowing the contents and character thereof, all in violation of subdivision 1 of section 235.05 of the Penal Law, a class A misdemeanor.[1] It was tried before the court without a jury.[2]

***750** What is involved is the showing in a public theatre, at a $5 per admission charge, of the film "Deep Throat". The case has engendered some public interest here and elsewhere. However, it is not unique. Many cases dealing with depiction of the same or similar deviate sexual behavior have been reported, but few have had such a full measure of directed publicity.

THE FILM

The film runs 62 minutes. It is in color and in sound, and boasts a musical score. Following the first innocuous scene ("heroine" driving a car), the film runs from one act of explicit sex into another, forthrightly demonstrating heterosexual intercourse and a variety of deviate sexual acts, not "fragmentary and fleeting" as to be de minimis as in *Jacobellis v. Ohio* (378 U.S. 184, 197-198 [1964], GOLDBERG, J.); or 10 minutes out of a 120-minute movie as in "I Am Curious-Yellow" (404 F.2d 196, 203, infra); but here it permeates and engulfs the film from beginning to end. The camera angle, emphasis and close-up zooms were directed, as in *United States v. Kaehler* (12 Cr. L. Rptr. 2383, 2384 [Feb. 7, 1973]), "toward a maximum exposure in detail of the genitalia" during the gymnastics, gyrations, bobbing, trundling, surging, ebb and flowing, eddying, moaning, groaning and sighing, all with ebullience and gusto.

There were so many and varied forms of sexual activity one would tend to lose count of them. However, the news reporters were more adept and counted seven separate acts of fellatio and four of cunnilingus (*Newsweek*, Jan. 15, 1973, p. 50; *New York Times Mag*. Sec., Jan. 31, 1973, p. 28). Such concentration upon the acts of fellatio and cunnilingus overlooked the numerous clear, clinical acts of sexual intercourse, anal sodomy, female masturbation, clear depiction of seminal fluid ejaculation and an orgy scene — a Sodom and Gomorrah gone wild before the fire — all of which is enlivened with the now famous "four letter words" and finally with bells ringing and rockets bursting in climactic ecstasy.

The performance of one sexual act runs almost headlong into the other. One defense witness thought 75% to 80% of the film involved depiction of explicit sexual activity and another viewed it at over 50%. A timekeeper may have clocked a higher percentage. Nothing was faked or simulated; it was as explicit and as exquisite as life. One defense witness said he saw "realism and genuine sexual experience." No imagination was needed, since it was intended to appeal to the imbecile as well.

The defense expert witnesses testified that the film possessed entertainment value and humor. The court in *People ex rel. Hicks v. "Sarong Gals"* (27 Cal. App. 3d 46, 51 [1972])

***751** appropriately answered that tedious and tenuous argument, often but conscientiously made in obscenity cases which have nothing to redeem them: "Presumably, the Romans of the First Century derived entertainment from witnessing Christians being devoured by lions. Given the right audience, the spectacle of a man committing an act of sodomy on another man would provide entertainment value. However, neither this spectacle nor the activities described in the instant case are invested with constitutionally protected values merely because they entertain viewers. However chaotic the law may be in this field, no court has yet adopted such an extreme result."

In passing, it should be noted that the defense "expert" witnesses were unpersuasive in the main. For example, a defense psychologist testified that he would use films like "Deep Throat" as classroom sex educational material not only in colleges but for certain high school students as well.

The alleged "humor" of the film is sick, and designed on a level to appeal especially to those first learning that boys and girls are different. Drama critic Vincent Canby characterizes the jokes as "dumb gags [which] cannot disguise the straight porno intent."[3] This, the defense experts here maintain, helps redeem the film as worthwhile. As to plot, there is none, unless you exclude the sexual activity which is the sole plot. And as to character development, a desirable and necessary concomitant of meaningful film, stage or book, again there is none, unless, of course, one means that the progression (or retrogression) of multiple and varied nymphomania to a singular form (fellatio) is evidence of this attribute.

Oh, yes! There is a gossamer of a story line — the heroine's all-engrossing search for sexual gratification, and when all sexual endeavors fail to gratify, her unique problem is successfully diagnosed to exist in her throat. She then seeks to fill the doctor's prescription by repeated episodes of fellatio, which Nora Ephron euphemistically characterizes as "compensatory behavior" (*Esquire*, Feb., 1973).

The defense experts testified that they see the film legitimatizing woman's need and "life right" (as one put it) for sexual gratification, equal with that of men. They also see in the film the thoughtful lesson that sex should not be unavailingly monolithic

***752** (usual face-to-face relationship)[4], but should take varied forms, with complete sexual gratification as the crowning goal, or as the film seems to advertise in its plebeian fashion — "different strokes for different folks"; or as others, less articulate, might say, "there's more than one way to skin the cat." These unusual and startling revelations are of social value, they say, not only for the bedroom, but necessary as an object lesson for a public forum.

The alleged story lines are the facade, the sheer negligee through which clearly shines the producer's and the defendant's true and only purpose, that is, the presentation of unmistakably hard-core pornography, where "imagination has gone to work in the porno-vineyards" — a quotation by a newsman, and adopted by the defendant in its newspaper advertisements. One defense expert actually but unwittingly, confirms the charade when he says that the "plot" of the film "provides a thread on which the various sequence of sexual acts would be hung."

Movie critic Judith Crist characterizes the production "idiot moviemaking" and the actors "awful" (*New York Magazine*, Feb. 5, 1973, p. 64). I agree, except to add that a female who would readily and with apparent, anxious abandon, submit to the insertion of a glass dildoe container into her vagina, have liquid poured therein and then drink it by means of a tube, as was done here to and by the "superstar", is not a reflection merely upon her thespian ability, but a clinical example of extraordinary perversion, degeneracy and possible amentia.[5] Whatever talent superstar has seems confined to her magnificent appetite and sword-swallowing faculty for fellatio.

In this court's view, the film and its genre have a significant meaning and impact, transcending this case, for all society (including for those who have seen the movie), as noted in the Appendix, attached hereto.

THE LAW

Section 235.05 of the Penal Law, and particularly the definition of "obscene" in subdivision 1 of section 235.00, represent the New York Legislature's attempt to codify the Federal

***753** rules first enunciated in *Roth v. United States* (354 U.S. 476, 489 [1957]), reiterated in *Jacobellis v. Ohio* (378 U.S. 184 [1964]), which also equated "contemporary community standards" with "national" rather than any local standards; and elaborated and summarized in *Memoirs v. Massachusetts* (383 U.S. 413, 418-419 [1966]), (involving the famous "Fanny Hill" book; and, hereinafter, referred to merely asMemoirs); and further elaborated by *Redrup v. New York* (386 U.S. 767 [1967]). (See McKinney's Cons. Laws of N.Y., Practice Commentary, Book 39, Penal Law, p. 89.)

The determination of obscenity involves the "independent" application of three separate tests, all of which must "coalesce" and be directed to the "average person." According to the *Roth-Memoirs* test, material may be deemed obscene if: (a) the dominant theme of the material taken as a whole appeals to prurient interest in sex; (b) it is patently offensive because it affronts contemporary community standards relating to the description or representation of sexual matters, and (c) the material is utterly without redeeming social value.[6]

The tests were adjusted as they apply to sexual deviants by *Mishkin v. New York* (383 U.S. 502 [1966]), and given a different dimension in "close" cases, where "pandering", if found, will move such a case over the brink into the pool of obscenity (*Ginzburg v. United States*, 383 U.S. 463 [1966]), as would the finding of any one of the three added tests in *Redrup* (386 U.S. 767, supra); *People v. Stabile* (58 Misc 2d 905); *Shinall v. Worrell* (319 F.Supp. 485 [1970]).

Clearly, this case does not involve admission to the theatre of minors (Penal Law, §§ 235.20, 235.21; *Jacobellis v. Ohio*, 378 U.S. 184, 195, supra). Nor is there evidence that the film, in some manner, has been foisted upon an unwilling public or individual, in violation of his right to privacy (*Redrup*, supra). Nor is there, nor could there be a claim by defendant of lack of scienter. (*Smith v. California*, 361 U.S. 147 [1959].)

There is a claim, however, that the film here was pandered in violation of the criterion of *Ginzburg* (supra), in that the newspaper ads evidenced an intent to commercially exploit the film for the sake of its prurient appeal, and should be condemned for this among other reasons. There is evidence of pandering here. However, *Ginzburg* is applicable only in "close" cases; and "Deep Throat" is far from a close case; it is a classic case; and, therefore, we need not rely on this prohibition to

***754** legally sanction it. Furthermore, although the advertisements placed in evidence, speak of the film as "The very best porn film ever made" and "Imagination has gone to work in the porno-vineyards"; and courts should "accept [the purveyor's] evaluation at its face value" (Memoirs, 383 U.S. 413, 420, supra), we do not equate that chest thumping with the circumstances of presentation and dissemination condemned in Ginzburg. There is no reason to dwell on this comparatively tenuous element, when there is so much more in the "vine-yards" of this film, offering a direct and clear basis for legal sanction. Accordingly, let us consider: Is the film obscene under the law?

Admittedly, the "guidelines" of *Roth-Memoirs* are distressingly ambiguous. But some would maintain there is merit in ambiguity, to meet the shifts of society's national values and moral imperatives. "The criminal law which deals with imperfect humanity cannot await the perfect definition — nor the perfect society in which, perhaps, no definitions would be necessary." (Hofstadter and Levittan, "No Glory, No Beauty, No Stars — Just Mud", 37 N.Y.S.B.J., 38). We embark to apply the tests to the film, with no trepidations or uncertainty in this particular case.

We begin with the premise, well-established, that motion pictures, as other forms of communication, are equally entitled to constitutional protection under the First Amendment. (*Joseph Burstyn, Inc. v. Wilson*, 343 U.S. 495 [1952]; Kupferman and O'Brien, "Motion Picture Censorship — The Memphis Blues", 36 Cornell L. Rev. 273, 288 [1951].) And they are protected against State abridgment by the Fourteenth Amendment. (*Gitlow v. New York*, 268 U.S. 652 [1925]; *Thomas v. Collins*, 323 U.S. 516 [1945].)

Motion pictures are understood to encompass problems peculiar to that form of expression, not subject to the precise rules governing other communication media. Accordingly, the Constitution does not require "absolute freedom to exhibit every motion picture of every kind at all times and all places." (*Joseph Burstyn, Inc. v. Wilson*, 343 U.S. 495, 502, supra; *Matter of Trans-Lux Distr. Corp. v. Board of Regents*, 14 N.Y. 2d 88, 92 [1964], revd. on other grounds 380 U.S. 259).

We have here a film and not a novel, book or magazine, and this, we believe, adds a different and significant dimension to the question. Stanley Kaufman notes (22 The Public Interest, p. 31, Winter 1971) a discernible difference in the one-to-one relationship of writer and reader "in psychic and social

***755** senses," from the employment of people to enact sexual fantasies on stage and screen before an audience. The stark reality and impact of a movie is undeniably as impressive as the viewing of a true-life situation on the open street. Certainly, to read descriptions of explicit sexual activity as shown in "Deep Throat", or merely to hear them discussed, can never have that same poignancy and cannot create that same lasting impression upon the human mind or appeal to the prurient as does the observation of the acts in a true life situation or on the screen. (*Freedman v. Maryland*, 380 U.S. 51, 61 [1965]; *United States v. A Motion Picture Film Entitled "I Am Curious-Yellow"*, 404 F.2d 196, 203 [1968]; *United States v. A Motion Picture Film Entitled "Pattern of Evil,"* 304 F.Supp. 197, 202 [1969]; *People v. Bercowitz*, 61 Misc 2d 974, 981-983 [1970].)

Because of a film's unique, shocking quality, we cannot disregard its potent visual impact in depicting, as does "Deep Throat", the fellatio, cunnilingus, masturbation, sexual intercourse, and other sexual activity. Such depictions of clearly discernible acts "transcend the bounds of the constitutional guarantee long before a frank description of the same scenes in the written word." (*Landau v. Fording*, 245 Cal. App. 2d 820, 823, affd. 388 U.S. 456 [1967], rehearing den. 389 U.S. 889). Accordingly, the appeal to prurience, the recognition of patent offensiveness, the violation of community standards and absence of social value will be realized more readily and more assuredly with a film than in a writing.

This difference seems to have motivated the Supreme Court in its almost consistent refusal to reject as obscene the written word, such as those in "Tropic of Cancer" (*Grove Press v. Gerstein*, 378 U.S. 577 [1964] and "Fanny Hill" (*Memoirs*, 383 U.S. 413, supra). Since *Redrup v. New York* (386 U.S. 767, supra), the Supreme Court, in seven cases, overruled obscenity convictions involving the publication of novels.[7] As a result, the court in S*tate of Minnesota v. Carlson* (202 N. W. 2d 640, 645 [Sup. Ct. of Minn., 1972], concludes — "Apparently the rulings demonstrate that the printed word, no matter how tawdry, is not obscene."

***756** IT IS HARD-CORE PORNOGRAPHY.

Hard-core pornography was the sole class of material declared impermissible, prior to the adoption of section 235.05 of the Penal Law. (*People v. Richmond County News*, 9 NY 2d 578, 586 [1961]; *People v. Weingarten*, 25 NY 2d 639 [1969].) However, in *Mishkin v. New York* (383 U.S. 502, 506, supra), the court explained that *Roth-Memoirs* criteria expanded the test to include additional classes of material within legal restraint, and apparently, hard-core now remains but one of many conceivable illegalities. (*Redrup v. New York*, supra.)

This court has previously indicated the substantial evidence pointing to the reality that the Supreme Court in *Roth* (354 U.S. 476, supra), and since then, has equated obscenity with hard-core pornography, without expressly saying so, and that *Redrup* lends additional support to the view that that court will limit its condemnations to hard-core only. (*People v. Kirkpatrick*, 64 Misc 2d 1055, 1077-1079 [1970], affd. 69 Misc 2d 212.) In the light of the present position of our forever modulating social standards, it is not farfetched to predict that our high court will eventually and, in fact, expressly say so. It would make more sense than the manifold rules of *Roth-Memoirs*. In fact, at least one jurist apparently believes that the court has already taken this position, when he concludes "that the definition of obscenity contained in section 235.00 of the Penal Law and `hard-core' pornography are synonymous, and it is only this `clearly identifiable class of material * * *' which is proscribed in New York." *(People v. Druss*, N.Y. L. J., Jan. 18, 1973, p. 15, col. 4.)

What is hard-core pornography and its connection with "Deep Throat"?

We know sex is not obscene; *Roth* (354 U.S. 476, 487, supra) tells us that when it says "sex and obscenity are not synonymous". Now, that we know what it is not, then what is obscenity? Admittedly, "obscenity" almost defies meaningful definition. (*Jacobellis v. Ohio*, 378 U.S. 184, 199, supra, Alpert, "Judicial Censorship and Obscene Literature", 52 Harv. L. Rev. 40, 47 [1938].) Is hard-core any more susceptible to exact delineation? Chief Justice WARREN finds both tasks impossible, with the comment — "But who can define 'hard core pornography' with any greater clarity than 'obscenity'" (*Jacobellis*, supra, p. 201)[8].

***757** But yet others find it readily definable and certainly more readily identifiable as a reasonably precise concept, which "theoretically, could unite a strong majority of the Supreme Court", Magrath, The Obscenity Cases: Grapes of Roth, 99 Sup. Ct. Rev. 1, 69 [1966].[9] My learned brother, Judge WILLIAM S. SHEA recently advised that "Hard-core pornography is a specific type of obscenity, it is obscenity in its easiest recognizable form. It contains something more than obscenity in its general or hard to recognize form and that `something' is its depiction of actual sexual activity including intercourse and deviate acts." (*People v. Wrench*, 73 Misc 2d 434.) Also my brother, Judge ARTHUR GOLDBERG (and YEARGIN) agree, that the decisions involving explicit sexual activity represent the distinction to "indicate palpable lines between obscenity and protected expression." (*People v. Bercowitz*, 61 Misc 2d 974, 978 [1970]).[10]

***758** The Report of the Commission on Obscenity and Pornography (*New York Times* Ed. 1970, pp. 22, 425) agrees that explicit sex is the distinguishing feature of hard-core pornography from other obscenity in that it demonstrates "sexual intercourse, depicting vaginal, anal or oral penetration."

They are on good ground and have much support. For example: *Ginzburg v. United States* (383 U.S. 463, 499, supra); *People v. Noroff* (67 Cal. 2d 791, 794, n. 6 [1967]); *Hunt v. Keriakos* (428 F.2d 606 [1970], cert. den. 400 U.S. 929); *Wagonheim v. Maryland St. Bd. of Censors* (255 Md. 297 [1969], affd. sub nom. *Grove Press v. Maryland St. Bd. of Censors*, 401 U.S. 480 [1971]); *State of Wisconsin v. Amato* (49 Wis. 2d 638, 645 [1971], cert. den. 404 U.S. 1063 [1972]); *State of Minnesota v. Carlson* (202 N. W. 2d 640, 647, supra); *People v. Clark* (60 Misc 2d 1073 [1969]); *People v. Morgan* (68 Misc 2d 667 [1971]).

The explicit sexual activity represents the "hard-core" feature of the material, while the "pornography" and its prurient appeal is distinguished by its pervasive hallucinatory quality, its ability to produce physical concomitants of sexual excitement and emotion (Kronhausen, Pornography and The Law, pp. 285-86, 329-301 [1969]). Such material has "the character of the daydream—the product of sheer fantasy." (Margaret Mead, Sex and Censorship in Contemporary Society, New World Writings, p. 19 [1953]). As the Kronhausens noted, life, unlike hard-core, "seldom presents us with a succession of erotic experiences one more stimulating and exciting than the other" (p. 328).

Because of hard-core's ready prurient appeal it is "patently offensive," and its indecency speaks for itself. (Memoirs, 383 U.S. 413, supra; *Womack v. United States*, 294 F.2d 204, 206 [1961], cert. den. 365 U.S. 859). It constitutes "obscenity per se". (*Donnenberg v. State,* 1 Md. App. 591, 600 [1967]; *Morris v. United States*, 259 A. 2d 337, 341 [D.C., 1969]) and condemnable as if res ipsa loquitur, requiring no expert testimony to explain or justify it. (*United States v. Wild,* 422 F.2d 34, 36 [1969], cert. den. 402 U.S. 986; *Womack v. United States,* supra, p. 206; *Hudson v. United States*, 234 A. 2d 903, 906 [D.C., 1967]; *United States v. Young*, 465 F.2d 1096, 1099 [1972]; *People v. Tenga,* N.Y.L.J., Dec. 21, 1972, p. 2, col. 1 [App. Term, 1st Dept.] (England permits

***759** expert testimony only to explain "public good" [i.e., social value] of the material, not "obscene or no" [i.e. prurient appeal, community standards, etc.] *Regina v. Anderson*, 1 Q.B. 304, 313 [1972]).

Since its brazenness is a direct assault upon long-held concepts of national morality and propriety, it is readily recognized throughout the nation by all those not beyond the pale. Apparently, the lay press had no trouble identifying "Deep Throat" as unmistakable hard-core pornography. "It scarcely could be more hard-core," says Thomas Meehan in Saturday Review (p. 80, March, 1973). "The film is solidly hard-core pornography." (*New York Times*, Dec. 30, 1972, p. 22). It is a "hard-core" sex film (*New York Post*, Jan. 3, 1973, p. 10); and it is a "hard-core porno movie" (*Time*, Jan. 15, 1973, p. 46).

What is the purpose and effect of hard-core pornography? Its aim is "to shock, revolt or embarrass" and brutalize (Benjamin Spock, Decent and Indecent [1969], pp. 83-84); "to insult sex, to do dirt on it * * * to insult the human body" and "a vital human relationship" (D.H. Lawrence, Pornography and Obscenity in Sex, Literature and Censorship, pp. 74-79 [1953]); *People v. Bercowitz*, 61 Misc 2d 974, 980-81, supra). I believe Mr. Justice THEODORE R. KUPFERMAN of our Appellate Division would agree. As an attorney, he specialized in censorship and obscenity law. In an enlightening article to the theatrical trade on the law of obscenity (*Variety*, Jan. 5, 1972, p. 12) he points out that a more easily enforced standard "is that while sex is accepted, pornography and obscenity will be recognized in brutalizing or insulting sex."

The United States Supreme Court has never dealt with material so brazenly explicit as the scenes of "Deep Throat", but it has dealt with some cases involving explicit sex activity in films; most, however, dealt with other varities of sexuality. For example, in *Jacobellis v. Ohio* (378 U.S. 184, supra), the first film case since Roth, the Supreme Court considered the film "Les Amants" which it found legally permissible. But there the court found only one "explicit love scene in the last reel of the film" (p. 196), and Justice GOLDBERG further found it "fragmentary and fleeting" as to be de minimis (p. 197-198). And certainly what may have been "explicit" then [1964] may very well be quite different from what we have today or in "Deep Throat".

In *Landau v. Fording* (245 Cal. App. 2d 820, 827, supra), the first case where the Supreme Court found obscenity in a film, the activity there was quite explicit, depicting two males engaged

***760** in "male masturbation, fellatio, oral copulation, voyeurism, nudity, sadism and sodomy". It is plain such activity approached, but did not equal, the explicitness of "Deep Throat". But it had no music or sound, as in "Deep Throat", to sharpen the prurient appeal with grunts, sighs and other sounds of orgasmic pleasure.

The majority of the Second Circuit Court of Appeals, gave its stamp of approval to the film, "I Am Curious--Yellow", in spite of its finding of "sexual intercourse under varying circumstances, some of them quite unusual. There are scenes of oral-genital activity." Judge LUMBARD, in his dissent, explained that "unusual" sexual activity, as fellatio and cunnilingus. (*United States v. A Motion Picture Film Entitled "I Am Curious-Yellow"*, 404 F.2d 196, 198, 203, supra.) But, significantly, when this film finally went to the United States Supreme Court from another jurisdiction, it affirmed the conviction of obscenity. (*Wagonheim v. Maryland St. Bd. of Censors*, 255 Md. 297 [1969], affd. sub nom. *Grove Press v. Maryland St. Bd. of Censors*, 401 U.S. 480 [1971] supra.) Convictions were also obtained in Georgia (*Evans Theatre Corp. v. Slaton*, 227 Ga. 377 [1971], cert. den. 404 U.S. 950); Missouri (*Hoffman v.*

Dickenson Operating Co., 468 S. W. 2d 26); Ohio (*Grove Press v. Flask*, 326 F.Supp. 574, cert. filed, not perfected).

Since the pivotal decision of *Redrup v. New York* (386 U.S. 767, supra), sex movies were the subject of nine Per Curiam reversals by the United States Supreme Court.[11] In those cases in which the sexual activity is reported below, we find much nudity and sexual activity but nowhere do we find actual copulation or oral-genital contact. Where sexual intercourse is depicted, it is usually suggested or simulated. None of the nine

***761** movies even approximate the sexual depictions in "Deep Throat".

When hard-core pornography (and I have yet to see reported anything equal in sexual activity to "Deep Throat") is clearly involved, the United States Supreme Court has affirmed a conviction, as it did in Landau, or denied certiorari, as it did in *Wilhoit v. United States* (279 A. 2d 505 [1971], cert. den. 404 U.S. 994; *State of Wisconsin v. Amato*, 49 Wis. 2d 638 [1971], cert. den. 404 U.S. 1063 [1972]). Many other courts have followed suit. For example: *People v. G. I. Distrs.* (20 N.Y. 2d 104 [1967], cert. den. 389 U.S. 905); *People v. Bercowitz* (61 Misc 2d 974, supra); *United States v. Berger* (325 F.Supp. 249 [1970]); *United States v. Strand Art Theatre Corp.* (325 F.Supp. 256 [1970)]; *People v. Heller*, 29 N.Y. 2d 319 [1971], cert. granted 406 U.S. 916 [pending]); *Slaton v. Paris Adult Theatre I* (228 Ga. 343 [1971], cert. granted 408 U.S. 921 [pending]); *United States v. Young* (465 F.2d 1096 [1972]); *State of Minnesota v. Lebewitz* (202 N.W. 2d 648 [1972]); *United States v. Kaehler* (U.S. Dist. Ct., Iowa, 12 Cr. L. Rptr. 2383 [1973]).

If defendant's counsel had submitted a post trial brief, we are certain he would have mentioned in his support *United States v. 35 MM. Motion Picture Film Entitled "Language of Love"* (432 F.2d 705 [1970]).[12] However, a careful reading of that case will reveal substantive differences between it and the subject film, which the court there found justified the ruling. In "Language of Love," the court noted, "The explicit scenes of sexual activity consist almost exclusively of normal heterosexual relations between adults in private. Female masturbation, cunnilingus (but not fellatio * * *) and one fleeting instance of actual insertion are shown" (supra, p. 707, n. 2, emphasis supplied). "Deep Throat" not only has female masturbation, but numerous depictions of cunnilingus and fellatio, clear and stark, from almost its beginning to its bitter end (for the film's major theme is fellatio); and with one disgusting scene of seminal fluid ejaculation into and about the "superstar's" mouth. "Deep Throat" also boasts of scenes of anal sodomy, an orgy scene, and several scenes of normal heterosexual intercourse, but unlike the other film, it also shows actual insertion in each such scene with purposeful camera focusing close upon the genitals while so engaged.

***762** But the differences are not merely to be found in the number and variety of such activity. Significantly, "Language of Love" was found obscene by a jury; but that was overturned on appeal. And on appeal the court found the described sexual acts with "seemingly interminable" psychological, medical and sociological discussions by doctors and other specialists recognized in their respective fields, making up almost all of the film (supra, p. 707). Further, as indicative of its sex educational purposes, the film includes a demonstration of proper placement of contraceptive devices during the course of a gynecological examination by one of the doctors (supra, p.

707). (Also: *United States v. Stewart,* 336 F.Supp. 299 [1971]; *Haldeman v. United States*, 340 F.2d 59 [1965]). To compare then "Deep Throat" with that film, is not to have seen "Deep Throat", because in the one ("Deep Throat") there lurks behind each elm "the leer of the sensualist" (*Ginzburg v. United States*, 383 U.S. 463, 468). We do not understand our condemnation of "Deep Throat" as running counter to *Kingsley Pictures Corp. v. Regents* (360 U.S. 684 [1959]), which distinguishes the communication of any idea, however deviant from orthodoxy with "the manner of its portrayal" (p. 688). Not only do we hold here that the manner of portrayal, in fact, appeals, and its sole purpose is to appeal, to prurient interest in sex, but we discern no "idea" worthy of protection. As we stated in *People v. Buckley* (65 Misc 2d 917, 922 [1971], affd. 72 Misc 2d 549) "the use of the word 'redeeming' in the social value test is a limiting factor — i.e., the social value of a publication as a whole must at least have a modicum of significance to release it from blame. In *Memoirs* (supra) the Supreme Court held that the social value of Cleland's book, however small it may have been in terms of its literary merit and its depiction of the mores of a particular period, redeemed its prurient-candid sexual references. We find no such qualitative redemption" the court held there as to the publication it was considering. And I find no such qualitative redemption in "Deep Throat" either.

Defendant asks us to be guided by the jury in Binghamton, New York, which acquitted another corporate defendant of the charge of obscenity, involving this film. Counsel appears to urge that surely a jury is far more receptive and attuned to what material does or does not affront community standards, than would a cloistered Judge. An examination of the certified minutes, announcing the verdict in that case, gives reason to ***763** believe that the jury there had possibly a different view of the film than the verdict would imply.[13]

Of course, it is academic that a jury's role stops at the determination of the fact situation. But the determination of obscenity transcends merely fact finding; it is intimately admixed with the determination of constitutional law and that decision is solely for a court, which may not permit the usurpation of that function by a jury. Necessarily, in the determination of the constitutional imperatives, the court must make assessments of the dominant theme, prurient interest, national community standards, redeeming social value and the like. (*Roth v. United States*, 354 U.S. 476, 497-98, supra; *Jacobellis v. Ohio,* 378 U.S. 184, 190, supra; *Memoirs*, 383 U.S. 413, 450, 462, supra; *United States v. 35 MM. Motion Picture Film Entitled "Language of Love"*, 432 F.2d 705, 709-711, supra; *People v. Kirkpatrick*, 64 Misc 2d 1055, 1072, supra.) For this reason courts do, when justified, overturn jury verdicts in this area of law. (*United States v. 35 MM. Motion Picture Film Entitled "Language of Love"*, supra; U*nited States v. A Motion Picture Film Entitled "I Am Curious-Yellow"*, 404 F.2d 196, supra.)

***764** WHEN ALL IS SAID

"Deep Throat" — a nadir of decadence — is indisputably obscene by any legal measurement, and particularly violative of section 235.05 of the Penal Law.

It goes substantially beyond "the present critical point in the compromise between candor and shame at which the [national] community may have arrived here and now." (*United States v. Kennerley*, 209 F. 119, 121 [1913]). It is another manifestation of the refusal to use words as emotional symbols unrelated to the purely physical. There is no effort, by word or conduct, to cut through the imponderable barriers of human understanding to the defense of human integrity. It, in fact, denigrates that integrity of man and particularly, woman, the expert witnesses, notwithstanding. It does this by objectifying and insulting woman, as Anthony Burgess, the author, puts it, by "making woman the sexual instrument come before woman the human being." (*New York Times Book Review*, Jan. 2, 1972, p. 1). Thus it supports the misogynist's view.

Its dominant theme, and in fact, its only theme is to appeal to prurience in sex. It is hard-core pornography with a vengeance. "It creates an abstract paradise in which the only emotion is lust and the only event orgasm and the only inhabitants animated phalluses and vulvae." (Anthony Burgess, supra, speaking of pornography generally, supra, and well applied here). It is neither redeemed nor redeemable, lest it be by the good camera work, editing, clarity, good color and lack of grain, which defense witness, a movie critic, was seemingly impressed with. But that is hardly enough to remove it from the pale of obscenity.[14]

It does, in fact, demean and pervert the sexual experience, and insults it, shamelessly, without tenderness and without understanding of its role as a concomitant of the human condition. Therefore, it does dirt on it; it insults sex and the human body as D. H. Lawrence would describe condemnable obscenity (Sex, Literature and Censorship, pp. 69, 74-79 [1953]). It "focuses predominantly upon what is sexually morbid, grossly perverse and bizarre * * *. It smacks, at times, of fantasy and unreality, of sexual perversion and

***765** sickness". (*People v. Richmond County News*, 9 N.Y. 2d 578, 587 [1961]). Justice STEWART says he knows hard-core pornography when he merely sees it (*Jacobellis v. Ohio*, 378 U.S. 184, 197, supra). We have seen it in "Deep Throat", and this is one throat that deserves to be cut. I readily perform the operation in finding the defendant guilty as charged, as to both cases.

APPENDIX

WHAT IS IT ALL ABOUT?

To accept the defense arguments, that this indisputably obscene film — this feast of carrion and squalor — is constitutionally protected and outside the ambit of prohibition of section 235.05 of the Penal Law would deny, in my view, any validity or meaning to our and all anti-obscenity laws and to the volumes of precedents supporting them. And it would also support the position of those who say that the State has no legitimate power or justification to legislate on matters of morality and particularly sexual morality. To this end, I believe, the defendant's arguments are essentially directed, without expressly saying so.[1]

It is, of course, a predicate of historical truth that the police power extends not only to the preservation of good order but similarly to the preservation of public morals. Such regulation has always been thought to satisfy certain important imperatives in a systematic manner, which is generally considered to be valuable. The State is said to have a legitimate right to legislate in the field of morality, and particularly sexual morality, and this right is deeply part of our law. (*Bear Co. v. Massachusetts*, 97 U.S. 25, 33 [1877]; *Lochner v. New York*, 198 U.S. 45, 53 [1905]; *Roth v. United States*, 354 U.S. 476, 485, 502, supra; *Stanley v. Georgia*, 394 U.S. 557, 566 [1969]; *Poe v. Ullman*, 367 U.S. 497, 545-546 [1961]; Henkin, "Morals and the Constitution: The Sin of Obscenity", 63 Col. L. Rev. 391.[2]

***766** Recognizing then that, historically, the State had, and, the courts say, it still has, a legitimate social interest in this regard, should it continue to exercise the power with respect to all moral issues, particularly as to sexual morality; and if so, should it extend to the private at well as the public area. This debate has plagued and excited the ages, and today's liberality will not resolve it. And, of course, "Deep Throat" is vigorously part of that discussion.

Today's debate is somewhat circumscribed about public, rather than private, morality. Our understanding, cultured by the gentle pressures and experimentation of centuries, has, I believe, refined itself to the point where society will tolerate any conduct in private if noninjurious and not disruptive to others. For this reason many would recommend an end to the crime of consensual sodomy in private, leaving its public prohibition. The willing receipt and possession of obscene material, and the private thoughts generated by it, are now enshrined with the private bedroom, as safe from government encroachment, and now understood to be a basic constitutional right. That, of course, is the court's meaning of *Stanley v. Georgia* (supra), and what it did, I believe, was merely to reflect the consensus of our People as well as good constitutional law.

But it also recognized a verity of the ages — that in all civilized societies, certain things which could be done in private should not, with impunity, be done in public. The court said that in *Stanley*, did it not, when it confirmed the State's power and justification to control "dissemination of ideas inimical to public morality" (394 U.S. 557, 566). And this basic and ancient postulate appears to represent the will of the People, as reflected in the anti-obscenity laws in each of our 50 States and Federal government. (*Roth v. United States*, 354 U.S. 476, 485, supra.) This also appears to be the reason that large forward-thinking citizen organizations, such as the Alliance For A Safer New York (a conglomerate of about 80 New York City civic, religious and labor organizations) can recommend the repeal of almost all laws relating to "victimless crimes," including consensual sodomy, but "has not yet evolved a definite

***767** policy" as to "pornography" (Edwin Kiester, Jr., Crimes With No Victims, 1972, p. 73). It would appear then that the United States Supreme Court (and lower courts accepting its leadership) and our People see a possible social effect of obscenity, but are unconcerned with its private manifestation, where society believes, social effect, if any, is de minimis.

However, there are thoughtful commentators, like Mr. Justice DOUGLAS, who oppose anti-obscenity laws upon the main ground that they see no causal relationship between obscenity and illegal or anti-social conduct. They would go further and divorce the State from all moral concerns (both private and public) not demonstrated to be "brigaded with illegal action." (*Memoirs v. Massachusetts*, 383 U.S. 413, 426, supra). Also: The Report of the Commission on Obscenity and Pornography, 1970. Since no unequivocally scientific relationship has been found, shall we abolish anti-obscenity laws (public morality) to await the behavioral sciences' proof of the connection?[3] The United States Supreme Court has refused to decide the question or even concern itself with the argument. "That function," it says, "belongs to the state legislature." (*Roth v. United States*, 354 U.S. 476, 486, 501, supra; *Beauharnais v. Illinois*, 343 U.S. 250, 266 [1952]).

Without scientific proof, is there not a basis in logic and common experience that the sky-is-the-limit type of pornography, especially the "Deep Throat" kind, has an eroding and corrupting effect on society's moral fabric, which, as aforesaid, we always thought important to enshrine? Our laws are full of inferences and assumptions, requiring no support of "hard" proof, because we "know" by life's experiences, that abstract truth is no less valid, given the proper context, than scientific formulation.

And so, can we not agree with Justice HARLAN when he says (*Roth*, 354 U.S. 476, 502, supra), that assuming there is no

***768** empirical evidence that obscenity causes, in an immediate sense, anti-social conduct, nevertheless "The State can reasonably draw the inference that over a long period of time the indiscriminate dissemination of materials, the essential character of which is to degrade sex, will have an eroding effect on moral standards."

Our armchair nihilists would have us abrogate the anti-obscenity laws with the argument that matters of sex and propriety are subjects best taught in the schools, and the liberty of the adult to see and read what he wishes should not be diminished for the supposed protection of the young. But may we not ask: Where there are no societal restraints, by law and language, will not the parent, the church, the synagogue and the school, being all alone, fail in their effort? Many see the schools, where wholesome disciplines and logical restraints are fast dissipating (and where challenge to authority often and quickly results in the school's surrender) soon joining the permissiveness and cynicism of its surrounding, polluting environment.[4]

Character is shaped by the sum total of the influences and incitations, which ply the sea of the mind. It admittedly begins with consciousness itself. The much respected, the late Justice SAMUEL H. HOFSTADTER of the New York State Supreme Court and my colleague, Judge SHIRLEY R. LEVITTAN agree, with so many others, that books, movies, magazines and all the social stimuli affect us, imperceptibly perhaps when taken singly, but measurably when accepted cumulatively. "It is a poor service to the cause of intellectual freedom and artistic feeling," they said "to pretend that art and literature have no effect on conduct."[5] Irving Kristol, Professor of Urban Values at New York University, cogently speaks of the matter in this fashion (*New York Times* Mag., March 23, 1971, p. 24): "After all, if you believe that no one was ever corrupted by a book, you have also to believe that no one was ever improved by a book (or a play or a movie). You have to believe, in other words, that all art is morally trivial and that, consequently, all education is morally irrelevant. No one, not even a university professor, really believes that."

***769** What then is the resultant quality of character when influenced, over long periods of time, by a suffusion of obscenity? The sages and our common man have never viewed it as having a salutary but rather a negative effect (notwithstanding Justice DOUGLAS and the majority report of the Commission on Obscenity and Pornography). They learned that cheapness breeds cheapness, and filth more filth. They understand that what it does, to again quote Professor Kristol, is "to deprive human beings of their specifically human dimension. That is what obscenity is all about." It relegates the "human dimension" to the debased level of the unfeeling, shameless and loveless beast. Our present-day nihilists fail to understand this connection and its validity in either practical or philosophical terms. What the absolutists seek is not temperance, the logicality of civilized conduct and which our present obscenity laws attempt to achieve, but rather self-indulgence, which is the historic touchstone for intellectual indolence and destruction.

Further, were we to remove indiscriminately, societal safeguards, and permit everyone "to do his thing," what disciplines remain to distinguish the worthy from the gross trash, the dross such as "Deep Throat"?[6] And would not this new liberty of total permissiveness become a "Magna Carta for the pornographer,"[7] to give license to ascend to greater and greater heights of degradation and violence, to depictions and perhaps the glorification of necrophilia and bestiality, and then, whatever? If we are to become inundated, as we are fast becoming, with trash in the arts, in language, in dress and so much more that makes for society's acceptable norms, what enlightened standards would remain to permit us to ascend "from plateau to plateau and finally reach the world of enduring ideas" (*Ginzburg v. United States*, 383 U.S. 463, 492 [1966], dissent, DOUGLAS, J.)? Can there be value in a society where everything has value?

Justice HARLAN, in the aforesaid quote, raises a question which many find cogent and troubling in the light of our new "sexual liberty." What many see in the unrestrained depiction of explicit sexuality and in gross obscenity generally, is the serious and damaging inroads into the tone of society, the mode, the style and quality of life, now and in the future. It hangs

***770** as a pervasive malaise over our moral consciousness. Alexander Bickel (The Public Interest, No. 22, Winter, 1971, p. 26) speaks of it in this fashion: "A man may be entitled to read an obscene book in his room, or expose himself indecently there, or masturbate, or flog himself, if that is possible, or what have you. We should protect his privacy. But if he demands a right to obtain books and pictures he wants in the market, and to foregather in public places — discreet, if you will, but accessible to all — with others who share his tastes, then to grant him his right is to affect the world about the rest of us, and to impinge on other privacies. Even supposing that each of us can, if he wishes, effectively avert the eye and stop the ear (which, in truth, we cannot), what is commonly read and seen and heard and done intrudes upon us all, want it or not."

There it is. "Deep Throat" and all its genre, want it or not, impinges unavoidably on the privacy of each of us, especially the multitudes upon multitudes who have not and will not pay the $5 admission fee or any price.

Further, it pollutes as noxious gas and helps deteriorate the fiber of great city places such as Times Square. It often attracts the unsavory to own, operate and maintain it. In a long investigatory article, dated December 10, 1972, reporters Ralph Blumenthal and Nicholas Gage, (*New York Times*, p. 1) stated "In less than four years, organized crime `families' in New York have made pornography their fastest growing new racket. . . . Racketeers have also discovered that pornography has a major advantage over traditional rackets. Confusing and sometimes contradictory court decisions make distributing pornographic material a lot safer than making book, selling heroin or loan-sharking . . . . Other Mafiosi are known to be investing in film in which sexual acts are part of some kind of story line. The films are often shown in commercial theaters."

These important issues can cause famous liberals, such as Lord Devlin and Professor H. L. A. Hart to fervently and brilliantly differ in public debate.[8] They can also cause liberals

***771** like Drs. Phyllis and Eberhard Kronhausen, D.H. Lawrence, Dr. Benjamin Spock, Morris Ernst, and many others, to decry the brutalization of society, represented by the present proliferating hard-core pornography in films, books and magazines.[9] They can cause such representatives of the liberal press, as The *New York Times*, to editorialize, as it did on April 1, 1969, (p. 46), in this manner: "The explicit portrayal on the stage of sexual intercourse is the final step in the erosion of taste and subtlety in the theater. It reduces actors to mere exhibitionists, turns audiences into voyeurs and debases sexual relationships almost to the level of prostitution.

"It is difficult to see any great principle of civil liberties involved when persons indulging themselves on-stage in this kind of peep-show activity . . . in displaying sodomy and other sexual aberrations, reached the reductio ad obscenum of the theatrical art. While there may be no difference in principle between pornography on the stage, on the screen and on the printed page, there is a difference in immediacy and in direct visual impact when it is carried out by live actors before a (presumably) live audience.

"The fact that the legally enforceable standards of public decency have been interpreted away by the courts almost to the point of no return does not absolve artists, producers or publishers from all responsibility or restraint in pandering to the

***772** lowest possible public taste in quest of the largest possible monetary reward. Nor does the fact that a play, film, article or book attacks the so-called `establishment,' revels in gutter language or drools over every known or unknown form of erotica justify the suspension of sophisticated critical judgment.

"Yet this does seem to be just what has been suspended in the case of many recent works, viz., one current best-seller hailed as a `masterpiece,' which, wallowing in a self-indulgent public psychoanalysis, drowns its literary merits in revolting sex excesses.

"The utter degradation of taste in pursuit of the dollar is perhaps best observed in films, both domestic and foreign, such as one of the more notorious Swedish imports, refreshingly described by one reviewer unafraid of being called a 'square' as 'pseudo-pornography at its ugliest and least titillating and pseudo-sociology at its lowest point of technical ineptitude.'

"Far from providing a measure of cultural emancipation, such descents into degeneracy represent caricatures of art, deserving no exemption from the laws of common decency merely because they masquerade as drama or literature. It is preposterous to banish topless waitresses when there is no bottom to voyeurism on the stage or in the movie houses."

(Certainly, what the editors say of the stage is stark reality as well on the screen.)

These issues can also deeply disturb a thoughtful Judge. And although his views may very well be the unwitting distillation of his social history, which Justice CARDOZO characterized as "the empire of [these] subconscious loyalties,"[10] they cannot be dismissed merely as private notions; for they are imbedded into and built upon ancient and continuing vibrant constitutional verities. So armed, he must, and is expected to exhibit the courage to express and support common moral standards, no less than the courage to express innovation, when law and circumstance require.

As noted, these fundamental issues do not require nor have they resulted in the positioning of the civil libertarians on the one side and the alinement of the philosophical conservatives on the other. Basic here, is not merely the legality of one film, but essentially whether criminal sanctions against promoting (Penal Law § 235.00, subd. 4) obscene material shall be fully lifted, as an acquittal here would certainly and affirmatively imply. On this issue citizens of both persuasions join hands.

***773** As a society we have come upon the crossroads, but we have not as yet crossed the road. To find "Deep Throat", and the rest of its genre, legally viable, will not only cross the road, but would help obliterate it as well. The law, common sense and the history of experience, tell us that this is not in society's best interest, nor do present community standards, whether National or State, demand it.

Footnotes

[1] The defendant was charged with two separate violations, in that, it presented the film involved on August 17, 1972 (Docket No. A54434) and on August 29, 1972 (Docket No. A63354).

[2] The defendant moved in the Supreme Court for a jury trial; the motion was denied, in that the defendant, as a corporation, had no right to a jury trial. (*Mature Enterprises v. Hogan*, N. Y. L. J., Nov. 16, 1972, p. 2, col. 1.)

[3] *New York Times*, Arts and Leisure Sect., p. 1, Jan. 21, 1973. Ellen Willis in the New York Review of Books, Jan. 25, 1973 (pp. 22, 23), characterizes the jokes as "moronic."

[4] One witness further identified it as "the missionary position," enlightening the court with his learned advice that missionaries also had something to do with sex education.

[5] Nora Ephron, in reporting a conversation she had with the female lead (Esquire, Feb. 1973), reports that this "actress" said — "I totally enjoyed myself making the movie and all of a sudden I'm what you call a superstar." Also, one defense witness thought this scene "had humor."

[6] Subdivision 1 of section 235.00 of the Penal Law differs slightly in language but its meaning and intent are the same.

[7] *Childs v. Oregon*, 401 U.S. 1006 (1971); *Hoyt v. Minnesota*, 399 U.S. 524 (1970); *Mazes v. Ohio*, 388 U.S. 453 (1967); *A Quantity of Copies of Books v. Kansas*, 388 U.S. 452 (1967); *Books v. United States*, 388 U.S. 449 (1967); *Corinth Pubs. v. Wesberry*, 388 U.S. 448; *Aday v. United States*, 388 U.S. 447 (1967).

[8] "It is no easier to define hard-core pornography than obscenity. Experience, including that of judicial expertise, demonstrates that any attempt at such formal verbal expression is doomed to failure. * * * Legal definitions reflecting earlier stimuli distort the present when dogmatically applied" (Hofstadter and Levittan, "No Glory, No Beauty, No Stars — Just Mud," 37 N.Y.S.B.J. 40).

[9] Justice STEWART would limit proscription to hard-core, in which he sees "a distinct and easily identifiable class of material in which all of these elements [*Roth-Memoirs* criteria] coalesce." (*Ginzburg v. United States*, 383 U.S. 463, 499, supra). Justice HARLAN agrees, when he says hard-core "does describe something that most judges and others will 'know . . . when [they] see it' * * * and that leaves the smallest room for disagreement between those of varying tastes" (*Memoirs*, 383 U.S. 413, 457, supra). He also expressed this view in *Roth v. United States* (354 U.S. 476, 507-508, supra).

Albert B. Gerber, Esq. specializes in obscenity and pornography litigation, and authored, "Sex, Pornography and Justice" (1965). He consistently opposes anti-obscenity laws. However, he tells us that "where sexual acts and perversions are imitated on stage, it is dubious whether any court for a long time to come will grant the protection of the Constitution." (Wilson Library Bulletin, Feb. 1970, p. 644). Of course, there is nothing simulated or imitated in "Deep Throat"; it is quite real.

[10] D. H. Lawrence, the author of "Lady Chatterly's Lover", understands hard-core pornography "by the insult it offers, invariably, to sex and to the human spirit. Pornography is the attempt to insult sex, to do dirt on it * * * Such material is an * * * insult to the human body, the insult to a vital human relationship. Ugly and cheap they make the human nudity; ugly and degraded they make

the sexual act, trivial and cheap and nasty." And such material he would vigorously have censored. ("Pornography and Obscenity in Sex, Literature and Censorship" [1953], pp. 74-79.)

Mr. Justice STEWART describes it as material "with no pretense of artistic value, graphically depicting acts of sexual intercourse, including various acts of sodomy and sadism, and sometimes involving several participants in scenes of orgy-like character." (*Ginzburg v. United States*, 383 U.S. 463, 499, n. 3 [1966]).

People v. Richmond County News (9 N.Y. 2d 578, 587) tells us that hard-core "focuses predominantly upon what is sexually morbid, grossly perverse and bizarre * * * depicting dirt for dirt's sake, the obscene is the vile, rather than the coarse, the blow to sense, not merely to sensibility. It smacks, at times, of fantasy and unreality, of sexual perversion and sickness".

[11] *Ratner v. California* (388 U.S. 442 [1967]), sex acts not described; *Cobert v. New York* (388 U.S. 443 [1967]), stag film for private home use, sex acts not described; *Schackman v. California* (388 U.S. 454 [1967]), peep show movies for coin-operated machines, sex simulated; *I. M. Amusement Corp. v. Ohio* (389 U.S. 573 [1968]), two nude women acting parts of lesbians, fondling themselves; *Robert-Arthur Mgt. Corp. v. Tennessee* (389 U.S. 578 [1968]), nude women caressing each other in lesbian fashion; *Cain v. Kentucky* (397 U.S. 319 [1970]), nude woman caressing herself, man kisses her stomach, then camera focuses on expression of satisfaction during intercourse, then other similar acts of intercourse; *Bloss v. Michigan* (402 U.S. 938 [1971]), sex acts not described; *Hartstein v. Missouri* (404 U.S. 988 [1971]), nude women gyrating and scenes of physical violence. *California v. Pinkus* (400 U.S. 922 [1971]), stag movie for private home use; woman feigns self-induced sexual satisfaction.

[12] Certiorari was granted for *United States v. Unicorn Enterprises* involving the same film (401 U.S. 907 [1971]), and covered this case as well. However, the writ of certiorari was later dismissed pursuant to agreement of the attorneys (403 U.S. 925 [1971]).

[13] * * *

[14] "This court will not adopt a rule of law which states that obscenity is suppressible but well-written [or a technically well produced] obscenity is not." (*People v. Fritch*, 13 N.Y 2d 119, 126). "A Michelangelo could find no solace from legal restraint if his art be obscene." (*People v. Kirkpatrick*, 64 Misc 2d 1055, 1086, supra).

[1] There are now before the United States Supreme Court three cases which raise basic questions as to all anti-obscenity laws, particularly whether obscene material may be disseminated to consenting adults. (*People v. Kaplan*, 23 Cal. App. 3d Supp. 9, cert. granted 408 U.S. 921; *Paris Adult Theatre I v. Slaton*, 228 Ga. 343, cert. granted 408 U.S. 921; *Alexander v Virginia*, 212 Va. 554, cert. granted 408 U.S. 921.)

[2] In *Poe v. Ullman* (367 U.S. 497, 545-546, supra), HARLAN, J. had this to say in his dissent: "Yet the very inclusion of the category of morality among state concerns indicates that society is not limited in its objects only to the physical well-being of the community, but has traditionally concerned itself with the moral soundness of its people as well. Indeed to attempt a line between public behavior and that which is purely consensual or solitary would be to withdraw from community concern a range of subjects with which every society in civilized times has found it necessary to deal. The laws regarding marriage which provide both when the sexual powers may be used and the legal and societal context in which children are born and brought up, as well as laws forbidding adultery, fornication and homosexual practices which express the negative of the proposition, confining sexuality to lawful marriage, form a pattern so deeply pressed into the substance of our social life that any Constitutional doctrine in this area must build upon that basis. Compare *McGowan v. Maryland*, 366 U.S. 420."

[3] The Report of the Commission on Obscenity and Pornography (*The New York Times* Ed. 1970) claims to prove the absence of this connection. However, the minority report illustrates several instances that the majority's research was inaccurate and the methods used unprofessional. Others refuse to accept the majority's report as convincing proof. Also President Nixon and a majority of the Senate by a vote of 60 to 5 rejected that report. (N.Y. Times, Oct. 14, 1970, p. 30, col. 3.)

John Stuart Mill denied that the State may legislate on moral matters and could only do so "over any member of a civilized community against his will as to prevent harm to others"; and moral harm, he said, is not sufficient to warrant legal forebearance. (On Liberty, ch. I.) Our present day disciples often quote Mill with relish.

[4] In its course "Filmmakers" (for which it charges $60), New York University has as its guest lecturer the executive producer of "Deep Throat", whose subject will be "sensuality, eroticism and the law, and excerpts from Deep Throat are screened" (Bulletin, School of Continuing Education, Spring 1973, p. 35). Is this to be a new art form, with bigger, better and deeper "Deep Throats"?

[5] "No Glory, No Beauty, No Stars — Just Mud," 37 N. Y. S. B. J.

[6] Vincent Canby in his discussion of the merits, or more exactly the demerits, of the film characterized it as "junk" and remained junk, even after seeing it a second time. (N. Y. Times, Jan. 21, 1973, Arts & Leisure Section p. 1.)

[7] Minority Report — Commission on Obscenity and Pornography, supra, p. 456.

[8] Lord Patrick Devlin (The Enforcement of Morals, Oxford Univ. Press 1968 ed.) postulated that what makes a collection of citizens a society is a "shared morality," which acts as "the cement of society" and that any loosening of the cement contributes to its disintegration; that the State should use the law to preserve morality (including sexual morality) as it uses it to safeguard anything else essential to its existence; that there is no theoretical limits to the power of the State to legislate against immorality, and that changes in the moral code must come very slowly where the society sees a needed departure from and finds a substitute for established moral standards. He generally sees no basic differences between private and public morality, when he says — "The suppression of vice is as much the law's business as the suppression of subversive activities; it is no more possible to define a sphere of private morality than it is to define one of private subversive activity" (pp. 13-14).

Professor H. L. A. Hart (Law, Liberty and Morality, Vintage Books, 1963 ed.) agrees that society may use the law to preserve morality, but disagrees that sexual morality is a legitimate State concern, and its enforcement has no "utilitarian reason" or "universal value" as necessary to society's survival. (Also: Louis Henkin: "Morals and the Constitution; The Sin of Obscenity", 63 Colum. L. Rev. 391 [1963]; Basil Mitchell: Law, Morality and Religion in a Secular Society; Oxford Univ. Press, [1970].)

[9] Kronhausen, "Pornography and the Law" [1959]; D.H. Lawrence, "Pornography and Obscenity in Sex, Literature and Censorship" [1953]; Dr. Benjamin Spock, "Decent and Indecent" [1969].

Morris Ernst, the defender of Joyce's "Ulysses," and other material, described as "the noted civil liberties lawyer and a long time opponent of censorship" in a news article appearing in *The New York Times* (Jan. 5, 1970, p. 46, col. 2), is quoted as saying that he would not choose "to live in a society without limits to freedom." Further, "Whereas I defended the book and legitimatized a four-letter word, that doesn't mean that * * * sodomy on the stage or masturbation in the public arena here and the world over." Further, "I deeply resent the idea that the lowest common denominator, the most tawdry magazine, pandering for profit * * * should be able to compete in the marketplace with no restraints."

[10] Benjamin CARDOZO ("The Nature of the Judicial Process, Yale Univ. Press, 1921, p. 175).

DALLAS COWBOYS CHEERLEADERS, INC.
v.
PUSSYCAT CINEMA, LTD. and Michael Zaffarano

604 F.2d 200 (1979)

United States Court of Appeals, Second Circuit

Argued April 6, 1979.

Decided August 14, 1979.

VAN GRAAFEILAND, Circuit Judge:

This is an appeal from orders of the United States District Court for the Southern District of New York granting plaintiff's motions for a preliminary injunction prohibiting Pussycat Cinema, Ltd., and Michael Zaffarano from distributing or exhibiting the motion picture "Debbie Does Dallas." On March 14 this Court granted defendants' motion to stay the injunction and ordered an expedited appeal. The case was argued before us on April 6, following which we dissolved the stay and reinstated the preliminary injunction. We now affirm the orders of the district court.

Plaintiff in this trademark infringement action is Dallas Cowboys Cheerleaders, Inc., a wholly owned subsidiary of the Dallas Cowboys Football Club, Inc. Plaintiff employs thirty-six women who perform dance and cheerleading routines at Dallas Cowboys-football games. The cheerleaders have appeared frequently on television programs and make commercial appearances at such public events as sporting goods shows and shopping center openings. In addition, plaintiff licenses others to manufacture and distribute posters, calendars, T-shirts, and the like depicting Dallas CowboysCheerleaders in their uniforms. These products have enjoyed nationwide commercial success, due largely to the national exposure the Dallas Cowboys Cheerleaders have received through the news and entertainment media. Moreover, plaintiff has expended large amounts of money to acquaint the public with its uniformed cheerleaders and earns substantial revenue from their commercial appearances.

At all the football games and public events where plaintiff's cheerleaders appear and on all commercial items depicting the cheerleaders, the women are clad in plaintiff's distinctive uniform. The familiar outfit consists of white vinyl boots, white shorts, a white belt decorated with blue stars, a blue bolero blouse, and a white vest decorated with three blue stars on each side of the front and a white fringe around the bottom. In this action plaintiff asserts that it has a trademark in its uniform and that defendants have infringed and diluted that trademark in advertising and exhibiting "Debbie Does Dallas."

Pussycat Cinema, Ltd., is a New York corporation which owns a movie theatre in New York City; Zaffarano is the corporation's sole stockholder. In November 1978 the Pussycat Cinema began to show "Debbie Does Dallas," a gross and revolting sex film whose plot, to the extent that there is one, involves a cheerleader at a fictional high school, Debbie, who has been selected to become a "Texas Cowgirl."[1] In order to

***203** raise enough money to send Debbie, and eventually the entire squad, to Dallas, the cheerleaders perform sexual services for a fee. The movie consists largely of a series of scenes graphically depicting the sexual escapades of the "actors". In the movie's final scene Debbie dons a uniform strikingly similar to that worn by the Dallas Cowboys Cheerleaders and for approximately twelve minutes of film footage engages in various sex acts while clad or partially clad in the uniform. Defendants advertised the movie with marquee posters depicting Debbie in the allegedly infringing uniform and containing such captions as "Starring Ex Dallas Cowgirl Cheerleader Bambi Woods" and "You'll do more than cheer for this X Dallas Cheerleader."[2] Similar advertisements appeared in the newspapers.

Plaintiff brought this action alleging trademark infringement under section 43(a) of the Lanham Act (15 U.S.C. § 1125(a)), unfair competition, and dilution of trademark in violation of section 368-d of the New York General Business Law. The district court, in its oral opinion of February 13, 1979, found that "plaintiff ha[d] succeeded in proving by overwhelming evidence the merits of each one of its contentions." Defendants challenge the validity of all three claims.

A preliminary issue raised by defendants is whether plaintiff has a valid trademark in its cheerleader uniform.[3] Defendants argue that the uniform is a purely functional item necessary for the performance of cheerleading routines and that it therefore is not capable of becoming a trademark. We do not quarrel with defendants' assertion that a purely functional item may not become a trademark. See *In re Honeywell, Inc.*, 532 F.2d 180, 182-83 (C.C.P.A.1976). However, we do not agree that all of characteristics of plaintiff's uniform serve only a functional purpose or that, because an item is in part incidentally functional, it is necessarily precluded from being designated as a trademark. Plaintiff does not claim a trademark in all clothing designed and fitted to allow free movement while performing cheerleading routines, but claims a trademark in the particular combination of colors and collocation of decorations that distinguish plaintiff's uniform from those of other squads.[4] Cf. *Socony Vacuum Oil Co. v. Rosen*, 108 F.2d 632, 636 (6th Cir. 1940); *John Wright, Inc. v. Casper Corp.*, 419 F.Supp. 292, 317 (E.D.Pa.1976). It is well established that, if the design of an item is nonfunctional and has acquired secondary meaning,[5] the design may become a trademark even if the item itself is functional. *Ives Laboratories, Inc. v. Darby Drug Co.*, 601 F.2d 631, 642 (2d Cir. 1979); *Truck Equipment Service Co. v. Fruehauf Corp.*, 536 F.2d 1210, 1215 (8th Cir.), cert. denied, 429 U.S. 861, 97 S.Ct. 164, 50 L.Ed.2d 139 (1976). Moreover, when a feature of the construction of the item is arbitrary, the feature may become a trademark even though it serves a useful purpose. *In*

***204** *re Deister Concentrator Co.*, 289 F.2d 496, 506, 48 C.C.P.A. 952 (1961); *Fotomat Corp. v. Cochran*, 437 F.Supp. 1231 (D.Kan.1977). Thus, the fact that an item serves or performs a function does not mean that it may not at the same time be capable of indicating sponsorship or origin, particularly where the decorative aspects of the item are nonfunctional. See *In re Penthouse International Ltd.*, 565 F.2d 679, 681 (Cust. & Pat.App.1977). See also *In re World's Finest Chocolate, Inc.*, 474 F.2d 1012 (Cust. & Pat.App.1973). In the instant case the combination of the white boots, white shorts, blue blouse, and white star-studded vest and belt is an arbitrary design which makes the otherwise functional uniform trademarkable.[6]

Defendants argue that *Sears, Roebuck & Co. v. Stiffel Co.*, 376 U.S. 225, 84 S.Ct. 784, 11 L.Ed.2d 661 (1964), and *Compco Corp. v. Day-Brite Lighting, Inc.*, 376 U.S. 234, 84 S.Ct. 779, 11 L.Ed.2d 669 (1964), preclude a finding that plaintiff's uniform is a trademark. We disagree. In *Sears-Compco* the Court held merely that a state may not, through its law banning unfair competition, undermine the federal patent laws by prohibiting the copying of an article that is protected by neither a federal patent nor a federal copyright. For the Court to have held otherwise would have been to allow states to grant a monopoly to a producer where the federal government had specifically determined that free competition should prevail. This consideration does not apply in a trademark infringement action where the plaintiff does not assert exclusive rights to the sale of a product but merely to a mark indicating its origin or sponsorship. The question presented therefore is one of trademark law, and it is clear that *Sears-Compco* did not redefine the permissible scope of the law of trademarks insofar as it applies to origin and sponsorship. See *Sears, Roebuck & Co. v. Stiffel*, supra, 376 U.S. at 232, 84 S.Ct. 784; *Ives Laboratories, Inc. v. Darby Drug Co.*, supra, at 642 nn. 13-14; *Flexitized, Inc. v. National Flexitized Corp.*, 335 F.2d 774, 781 n. 4 (2d Cir. 1964), cert. denied, 380 U.S. 913, 85 S.Ct. 889, 13 L.Ed.2d 799 (1965); *Rolls-Royce Motors Ltd. v. A & A Fiberglass, Inc.*, 428 F.Supp. 689, 692 (N.D.Ga.1977).

Having found that plaintiff has a trademark in its uniform, we must determine whether the depiction of the uniform in "Debbie Does Dallas" violates that trademark. The district court found that the uniform worn in the movie and shown on the marquee closely resembled plaintiff's uniform and that the public was likely to identify it as plaintiff's uniform. Our own comparison of the two uniforms convinces us that the district court was correct,[7] and defendants do not seriously contend that the uniform shown in the movie is not almost identical with plaintiff's. Defendant's contention is that, despite the striking similarity of the two uniforms, the public is unlikely to be confused within the meaning of section 43(a) of the Lanham Act.

Defendants assert that the Lanham Act requires confusion as to the origin of the film, and they contend that no reasonable person would believe that the film originated with plaintiff. Appellants read the confusion requirement too narrowly. In order to be confused, a consumer need not believe that the owner of the mark actually produced the item and placed it on the market. See *Syntex Laboratories, Inc. v. Norwich Pharmacal Co.*, 437 F.2d 566, 568 (2d Cir. 1971); *Boston Professional Hockey Association v. Dallas Cap & Emblem Mfg., Inc.*, 510 F.2d 1004, 1012 (5th Cir.), cert. denied, 423 U.S. 868, 96 S.Ct. 132, 46

***205** L.Ed.2d 98 (1975). The public's belief that the mark's owner sponsored or otherwise approved the use of the trademark satisfies the confusion requirement. In the instant case, the uniform depicted in "Debbie Does Dallas" unquestionably brings to mind the Dallas Cowboys Cheerleaders. Indeed, it is hard to believe that anyone who had seen defendants' sexually depraved film could ever thereafter disassociate it from plaintiff's cheerleaders. This association results in confusion which has "a tendency to impugn [plaintiff's services] and injure plaintiff's business reputation . . .." See *Coca-Cola Co. v. Gemini Rising, Inc.*, 346 F.Supp. 1183, 1189 (E.D.N.Y.1972). In the Coca-Cola case the defendant had manufactured a poster showing the familiar red and white Coca-Cola design with the word "Cocaine" substituted for "Coca-Cola". As in this case, the defendant there argued that no reasonable purchaser would be confused by the poster; however the court held that a person of average intelligence could believe "that defendant's poster was just another effort . . . by plaintiff to publicize its product," although in a distasteful way. Id. at 1190. In another case, a similarity between the plaintiff's and the defendant's trade slogans was held to confuse the public and "[threaten] injury to the good name of the first user." See *Chemical Corp. of America v. Anheuser-Busch, Inc.*, 306 F.2d 433 (5th Cir. 1962), cert. denied, 372 U.S. 965, 83 S.Ct. 1089, 10 L.Ed.2d 129 (1963). There, the defendant advertised its insecticide by changing plaintiff's slogan "Where there's life, there's Bud" to the slogan "Where there's life, there's bugs." The court's reasoning in upholding the finding of unfair competition is equally applicable here:

The gist of this action is that the plaintiff has a property interest in the slogan, built up at great expense, and that it and its products are favorably known as a result of its use of this property right and that the defendant, with full knowledge of the right and with the purpose of appropriating some of the value engendered in the minds of the public by its use has used, and proposes further to make use of, a deceptively similar slogan in a manner that will bring direct financial loss to the plaintiff, both by reason of confusing the source of the defendant's product, and by reason of the peculiarly unwholesome association of ideas when the word "bugs" was substituted in the slogan for the word "Bud," referring to a food product. Id. at 437.

Plaintiff expects to establish on trial that the public may associate it with defendants' movie and be confused into believing that plaintiff sponsored the movie, provided some of the actors, licensed defendants to use the uniform, or was in some other way connected with the production. The trademark laws are designed not only to prevent consumer confusion but also to protect "the synonymous right of a trademark owner to control his product's reputation." *James Burrough Ltd. v. Sign of the Beefeater, Inc.*, 540 F.2d 266, 274 (7th Cir. 1976) (Markey, C. J.). The district court did not err in holding that plaintiff had established a likelihood of confusion within the meaning of the Lanham Act sufficient to entitle it to a preliminary injunction and that plaintiff had a right to preliminary relief on its claims of unfair competition and dilution.[8] See id. at 274 n. 16.

Defendants assert that the copyright doctrine of "fair use" should be held applicable to trademark infringement actions and that we should apply the doctrine to sanction their use of a replica of plaintiff's uniform. Fair use is "a `privilege in others than the owner of a copyright to use the copyrighted material in a reasonable manner without his consent...'" *Rosemont Enterprises, Inc. v. Random*

***206** *House, Inc.*, 366 F.2d 303, 306 (2d Cir. 1966) (quoting Ball, The Law of Copyright and Literary Property 260 (1944)), cert. denied, 385 U.S. 1009, 87 S.Ct. 714, 17 L.Ed.2d 546 (1967). The fair use doctrine allows adjustments of conflicts between the first amendment and the copyright laws, see *Wainwright Securities Inc. v. Wall Street Transcript Corp.*, 558 F.2d 91, 95 (2d Cir. 1977), cert. denied, 434 U.S. 1014, 98 S.Ct. 730, 54 L.Ed.2d 759 (1978), and is designed primarily to balance "the exclusive rights of a copyright holder with the public's interest in dissemination of information affecting areas of universal concern, such as art, science and industry." Id. at 94. It is unlikely that the fair use doctrine is applicable to trademark infringements;[9] however, we need not reach that question. Although, as defendants assert, the doctrine of fair use permits limited copyright infringement for purposes of parody, see *Berlin v. E. C. Publications, Inc.*, 329 F.2d 541 (2d Cir. 1964),cert. denied, 379 U.S. 822, 85 S.Ct. 46, 13 L.Ed.2d 33 (1965), defendants' use of plaintiff's uniform hardly qualifies as parody or any other form of fair use. See *Walt Disney Productions v. Mature Pictures Corp.*, 389 F.Supp. 1397, 1398 (S.D.N.Y.1975).

Nor does any other first amendment doctrine protect defendants' infringement of plaintiff's trademark. That defendants' movie may convey a barely discernible message[10] does not entitle them to appropriate plaintiff's trademark in the process of conveying that message. See *Interbank Card Association v. Simms*, 431 F.Supp. 131 (M.D.N.C.1977); *Edgar Rice Burroughs, Inc. v. Manns Theatres*, 195 U.S. P.Q. 159 (C.D.Cal.1976); *Coca-Cola Co. v. Gemini Rising, Inc.*, supra, 346 F.Supp. at 1191. Plaintiff's trademark is in the nature of a property right, see *Hanover Milling Co. v. Metcalf*, 240 U.S. 403, 413, 36 S.Ct. 357, 60 L.Ed. 713 (1915); *Alfred Dunhill of London, Inc. v. Dunhill Tailored Clothes, Inc.*, 293 F.2d 685, 692, 49 C.C.P.A. 730 (1961), cert. denied, 369 U.S. 864, 82 S.Ct. 1030, 8 L.Ed.2d 84 (1962), and as such it need not "yield to the exercise of First Amendment rights under circumstances where adequate alternative avenues of communication exist." *Lloyd Corp. v. Tanner*, 407 U.S. 551, 567, 92 S.Ct. 2219, 2228, 33 L.Ed.2d 31 (1972). Because there are numerous ways in which defendants may comment on "sexuality in athletics" without infringing plaintiff's trademark, the district court did not encroach upon their first amendment rights in granting a preliminary injunction. See Walt Disney Productions v. Air Pirates, 581 F.2d 751, 758-59 (9th Cir. 1978); *Reddy Communications, Inc. v. Environmental Action Foundation*, 199 U.S.P.Q. 630, 634 (D.D. C.1977).

For similar reasons, the preliminary injunction did not constitute an unconstitutional "prior restraint". This is not a case of government censorship, but a private plaintiff's attempt to protect its property rights. The propriety of a preliminary injunction where such relief is sought is so clear that courts have often issued an injunction without even mentioning the first amendment. See, e. g., *Gilliam v. American Broadcasting Cos.*, 538 F.2d 14 (2d Cir. 1976); *Edgar Rice Burroughs, Inc. v. Manns Theatres*, supra, 195 U.S.P.Q. 159. The prohibition of the Lanham Act is content neutral, cf. *Schacht v. United States*, 398 U.S. 58, 90 S.Ct. 1555, 26 L.Ed.2d 44 (1970), and therefore does not arouse the fears that trigger the application of constitutional "prior restraint" principles.

The district court's issuance of a preliminary injunction is reversible only for abuse of discretion. *Taylor Wine Co. v. Bully Hill Vineyards, Inc.*, 569 F.2d 731, 732 n. 1 (2d Cir. 1978). A preliminary injunction is proper where the plaintiff establishes possible irreparable harm and either (1)

***207** probable success on the merits or (2) sufficiently serious questions going to the merits to make them a fair ground for litigation and a balance of hardships tipping decidedly in the movant's favor. *Selchow & Righter Co. v. McGraw-Hill Book Co.*, 580 F.2d 25, 27 (2d Cir. 1978). Plaintiff has established a probability of success at trial, and the confusion engendered by defendants' movie would result in irreparable harm to plaintiff were defendants not enjoined from its distribution and exhibition. See *Hills Brothers Coffee, Inc. v. Hills Supermarkets, Inc.*, 428 F.2d 379, 380-81 (2d Cir. 1970); see also *Taylor Wine Co. v. Bully Hill Vineyards, Inc.*, supra, 569 F.2d at 732 n. 1. Accordingly, we affirm the orders of the district court.

Affirmed.

Footnotes

[1] The official appellation of plaintiff's cheerleaders is "Dallas Cowboys Cheerleaders", but the district court found that plaintiff also has a trademark in the names "Dallas Cowgirls" and "Texas Cowgirls" which have been made popular by the media.

[2] Bambi Woods, the woman who played the role of Debbie, is not now and never has been a Dallas Cowboys Cheerleader.

[3] At present plaintiff does not have a registered trademark or service mark in its uniform. However, plaintiff still may prevail if it establishes that it has a common law trademark or service mark. See *Boston Professional Hockey Association v. Dallas Cap & Emblem Mfg., Inc.*, 510 F.2d 1004, 1010 (5th Cir.), cert. denied, 423 U.S. 991, 96 S.Ct. 408, 46 L.Ed.2d 312 (1975); New York General Business Law § 368-d. Whether plaintiff's uniform is considered as a trademark or a service mark, the standards for determining infringement are the same. *West & Co. v. Arica Institute, Inc.*, 557 F.2d 338, 340 n. 1 (2d Cir. 1977).

[4] Plaintiff's design imparts a western flavor appropriate for a Texas cheerleading squad. The design is in no way essential to the performance of cheerleading routines and to that extent is not a functional aspect of the uniform.

[5] Secondary meaning is "[t]he power of a name or other configuration to symbolize a particular business, product or company . . .." *Ideal Toy Corp. v. Kenner Products Division of General Mills Fun Group, Inc.*, 443 F.Supp. 291, 305 n. 14 (S.D.N.Y.1977). There is no dispute in this case that plaintiff's uniform is universally recognized as the symbol of the Dallas Cowboys Cheerleaders.

[6] Although color alone is not capable of becoming a trademark, a combination of colors together with a distinctive arbitrary design may serve as a trademark. *Quabaug Rubber Co. v. Fabiano Shoe Co.*, 567 F.2d 154, 161 (1st Cir. 1977).

[7] To the extent that a finding of likelihood of confusion is based upon a comparison of the two marks, see *Beech-Nut, Inc. v. Warner Lambert Co.*, 346 F.Supp. 547, 550 (S.D.N.Y.1972), aff'd, 480 F.2d 801 (2d Cir. 1973), the appellate court may make an independent judgment as to the similarity of the marks. See *Hills Brothers Coffee, Inc. v. Hills Supermarkets, Inc.*, 428 F.2d 379, 380 (2d Cir. 1970).

[8] Even if plaintiff had not established a likelihood of confusion, it would be entitled to relief under New York General Business Law § 368-d, which permits the enjoining of trademark copying despite the absence of confusion as to source or sponsorship. See *Allied Maintenance Corp. v. Allied Mechanical Trades, Inc.*, 42 N.Y.2d 538, 543-44, 399 N.Y.S.2d 628, 369 N.E.2d 1162 (1977).

[9] Because the primary purpose of the trademark laws is to protect the public from confusion, see *W. E. Basset Co. v. Revlon, Inc.*, 354 F.2d 868, 871 (2d Cir. 1966), it would be somewhat anomalous to hold that the confusing use of another's trademark is "fair use". See also *Truck Equipment Service Co. v. Fruehauf Corp.*, supra, 536 F.2d at 1215.

[10] The question whether "Debbie Does Dallas" is obscene is not before us.

UNITED STATES OF AMERICA

v.

VARIOUS ARTICLES OF OBSCENE MERCHANDISE, SCHEDULE NO. 2102

709 F.2d 132 (1983)

United States Court of Appeals, Second Circuit

Submitted March 16, 1983

Decided May 18, 1983

MANSFIELD, Circuit Judge:

The government appeals from a judgment of the Southern District of New York, entered by Judge Robert W. Sweet after a hearing,[1] upon his opinion holding that various"hard-core" pornographic articles of merchandise (video cassettes and magazines[2]) seized by the government were not

***134** "patently offensive" under contemporary community standards and hence not "obscene" within the meaning of 19 U.S.C. § 1305(a) (1976 & Supp. V 1981) and dismissing the government's complaint under that statute for forfeiture of the merchandise.[3] 565 F.Supp. 7. An earlier opinion by the district court reaching the same result had been remanded because of use of an incorrect legal standard for determining obscenity. *United States v. Various Articles of Obscene Merchandise, Schedule No. 2102*, 678 F.2d 433 (2d Cir.1982) (per curiam). We affirm.

No purpose would be served by describing in detail the seized articles except to say that they unquestionably are examples of hard-core pornography, describing and depicting a wide range of scenes of explicit sex on the part of adults, singly and in groups, including detailed portrayals of genitalia, sexual intercourse, fellatio, and masturbation. The magazines and representative samples of the most pornographic portions of the challenged videotapes were exhibited to the district court and later to ourselves.

In his first dismissal of the complaint the trial judge relied in part on his view that the community standard included a community belief that the right to "free expression ought not to be compromised by government restrictions" such as 19 U.S.C. § 1305. We reversed on the ground that "community tolerance of section 1305 is irrelevant to the determination of obscenity."

On remand, Judge Sweet again found that the articles were not obscene and dismissed the complaint. Relying on a survey of reports described in his prior opinion indicating widespread community availability of and hence community acceptance of pornographic materials, the district judge found that under "contemporary community standards, the movie 'Deep Throat' and the remaining video cassettes and magazines in Schedule 2102, each of which is comparable to 'Deep Throat,' are not patently offensive under contemporary community standards."

In addition, the district court noted that the behavioral psychologist, B.F. Skinner, had recently cited with approval the theologian Paul Tillich for his defense of pornography as "extending sexuality into old age." The remarks of Skinner and Tillich, the judge determined, served to modify the court's prior conclusion that the challenged materials lacked serious literary, artistic, political and scientific value.

DISCUSSION

Although the constitutionality of 19 U.S.C. § 1305 has been upheld, *United States v. 12 200-ft. Reels of Film*, 413 U.S. 123, 93 S.Ct. 2665, 37 L.Ed.2d 500 (1973), determination of what material falls within the term "obscene" does not lend itself easily to the judicial process. Much of the difficulty stems from the vagueness of the

***135** concepts involved, the wide variation in moral attitudes within a heterogeneous population, and the unsuitability of conventional procedures, which rest on "findings of fact" and "conclusions of law," to the task of determining obscenity. Faced with these hurdles the Supreme Court has set forth the standards for determining whether pornographic material is "obscene," as that term is used in § 1305, in *Miller v. California*, 413 U.S. 15, 93 S.Ct. 2607, 37 L.Ed.2d 419 (1973) and its progeny. *United States v. Various Articles of Obscene Merchandise, Schedule No. 2127*, 705 F.2d 41, 43 (2d Cir.1983).

Before a work can be adjudged obscene, the trier of fact must find that (a) "'the average person, applying contemporary community standards' would find that the work, taken as a whole, appeals to the prurient interest;" (b) "the work depicts or describes, in a patently offensive way, sexual conduct specifically defined by the applicable state law;" and (c) "the work, taken as a whole, lacks serious literary, artistic, political, or scientific value."*Miller*, supra, 413 U.S. at 24, 93 S.Ct. at 2614 (citations omitted). Sexually-oriented work is not obscene unless all three elements of the *Miller* test are satisfied. Thus a work, though a valueless piece appealing to the prurient interest, will not be deemed obscene unless it is patently offensive according to contemporary community standards, i.e., in the judgment of the "average person in the community, rather than the most prudish or the most tolerant," *Smith v. United States*, 431 U.S. 291, 304, 97 S.Ct. 1756, 1765, 52 L.Ed.2d 324 (1977). See *Jenkins v. Georgia*, 418 U.S. 153, 161, 94 S.Ct. 2750, 2755, 41 L.Ed.2d 642 (1974); *Miller v. California*, supra, 413 U.S. at 27, 93 S.Ct. at 2616; Lentz, Comparison Evidence in Obscenity Trials, 15 U.Mich.J.L.Ref. 41, 47-48 & n. 9 (1981).

A determination of patent offensiveness requires a two-step inquiry that focuses first on the substantive content of the materials to see whether they depict or describe "hard core" types of sexual conduct that the trier of fact could constitutionally label "patently offensive" according to contemporary community standards, i.e., whether it qualifies as possibly obscene. *Smith v. United States*, supra, 431 U.S. at 301, 97 S.Ct. at 1764. If not, that ends the inquiry. Once this threshold "substantive component" or condition is satisfied, the trier must then determine whether, as a matter of fact, the materials are patently offensive to the average person in the community. *United States v. VariousArticles of Obscene Merchandise, Schedule No. 1769,* 600 F.2d 394, 406 (2d Cir.1979).

The government bears the burden of proving all three elements of obscenity to the satisfaction of the trier of fact, *United States v. 2,200 Paper Back Books*, 565 F.2d 566, 570 (9th Cir.1977), but it is not constitutionally required to introduce evidence of community standards. *Hamling v. United States*, 418 U.S. 87, 104, 94 S.Ct. 2887, 2900, 41 L.Ed.2d 590 (1974). The materials, if "hard core," may speak for themselves, *Paris Adult Theatre I v. Slaton*, 413 U.S. 49, 56 & n. 6, 93 S.Ct. 2628, 2634 & n. 6, 37 L.Ed.2d 446 (1973). While the materials provide the best evidence of their substantive content, they do not supply any information about the community standards by which they are to be judged. *United States v. 2,200 Paper Back*

Books, supra, 565 F.2d at 570. The trier is free to decide that the government has failed to sustain its burden of proving that the materials, although unprotected by virtue of their "hard core" content, are patently offensive to the average member of the community. In order to make that determination he may utilize his own sense of the views of the hypothetical "average person in the community," a flexible concept that requires taking into account such variables as the characteristics of the community,[4] the differing attitudes within it,

***136** the extent to which persons reveal their true opinions, and the nature of the "hard core" material under attack. To arrive at a measure of community tolerance of pornographic material the trial judge may rely upon his own experience in the community and decide as best he can what most people seem to think about such materials. If, on the other hand, he has little or no knowledge of their views, he may turn to opinion proof and, if the government fails to offer such proof, he may be relegated to finding that it has failed to sustain its burden. See, e.g., *United States v. 2,200 Paper Back Books*, supra, 565 F.2d at 570.

The parties may introduce relevant evidence of the prevailing community standard. *Miller*, supra, 413 U.S. at 31 n. 12, 93 S.Ct. at 2619 n. 12; *Hamling v. United States*, supra, 418 U.S. at 106, 94 S.Ct. at 2901. But even if such evidence is adduced, the trier may nonetheless disregard it and rely exclusively on his own knowledge of the views of the average person in the community in making the required determination. *Smith v. United States*, supra, 431 U.S. at 301-02, 97 S.Ct. at 1763-62; *Hamling v. United States*, supra, 418 U.S. at 104, 94 S.Ct. at 2900; *United States v. One Reel of 35mm Color Motion Picture Film Entitled "Sinderella,"* 491 F.2d 956, 959 (2d Cir.1974). Although appellate courts are required to exercise de novo review as to the preliminary substantive requirement that the material be "hard core" pornographic in nature, *Jenkins v. Georgia*, supra, 418 U.S. at 160-61, 94 S.Ct. at 2754-55, the trier's finding that the material is non-obscene is virtually shielded from appellate scrutiny, at least absent evidence that it is so clearly unreasonable as to amount to abuse of discretion. The principal reason for this posture on appeal is that under *Miller* the trier of fact is at liberty to identify and apply community standards as he sees them, unchecked by any definition of the relevant community (except that it may not extend to the entire nation) or by any more precise benchmarks. To this must be added our tradition that it is for the trial judge or jury, not the appellate court, to find the facts, and the dubious assumption that the triers have their fingers on the pornographic pulse in the community, enabling them to determine whether specific material has crossed the line from being tolerated to being patently offensive.

These are indeed difficult concepts for classification as "fact-finding." Although the jury's experience in everyday life equips it to determine what the hypothetical "reasonable man" would do in a given circumstance, judges or jurors lacking experience in the field of pornography and the attitudes of others toward it (often deliberately not revealed) face a greater challenge in making the findings demanded by *Miller*. Note, Community Standards, Class Actions, and Obscenity under *Miller v. California*, 88 Harv.L.Rev. 1838, 1844 (1975).

Applying these principles here, Judge Sweet's findings that all the seized materials on Schedule 2102 satisfied the prurience element and the substantive constitutional "hard core" threshold test for application of the patent offensiveness standard are clearly correct. The controversy arises out of his perception of prevailing community standards.

The government, apparently relying on Judge Sweet's knowledge of community standards, offered no evidence on that element. It now argues that the district judge erred in taking explicit notice of the availability of the same and similar materials in the New York area. We disagree. It is true that the mere availability of similar materials in the Southern District of New York does not demonstrate that they are acceptable to the average member of the community. *Hamling v. United States*, supra, 418 U.S. at 125-26, 94 S.Ct. at 2911-12; *United States v. Various Articles of Obscene Merchandise, Schedule No. 2127*, supra,

***137** at 44; *United States v. One Reel of 35mm Color Motion Picture Film Entitled "Sinderella,"* 491 F.2d 956, 958-59 (2d Cir. 1974); *United States v. Manarite,* 448 F.2d 583, 593 (2d Cir.), cert. denied, 404 U.S. 947, 92 S.Ct. 298, 30 L.Ed.2d 264 (1971). In *Manarite*, we held that evidence of "availability of similar materials is not by itself sufficiently probative of community standards to be admissible in the absence of proof that the material enjoys a reasonable degree of community acceptance." 448 F.2d at 593. However, where the availability and public viewing of the same or comparable materials in the New York area is widespread, as appears to be the case here (e.g., the motion picture "Deep Throat" was exhibited to paying patrons in numerous New York theatres), the trial judge was entitled to draw the inference therefrom that the challenged articles enjoy a "reasonable degree of community acceptance." Id.

Thus, while the existence of enclaves of tolerated obscenity does not by itself create a community standard, *United States v. One Reel of 35mm Color Motion Picture,* supra,491 F.2d at 959, judicial notice of widespread community availability and patronage of such works may be accepted as circumstantial evidence of contemporary community standards. *United States v. 2,200 Paper Back Books*, supra, 565 F.2d at 571; Keller v. State, 606 S.W.2d 931, 933-34 (Tex.Cr.App.1980). At some point a work widely available must be considered inferentially acceptable. Lentz, Comparison Evidence in Obscenity Trials, supra, 15 U.Mich.J.L.Ref. at 67. The weight to be given to wide availability rests with the trier of fact. In the present case the government, which had an opportunity to do so, failed to offer evidence of community standards or to show that the materials were not as widely available as the district court found. "The community cannot, where liberty of speech and press are at issue, condemn that which it generally tolerates." *Smith v. California*, 361 U.S. 147, 171, 80 S.Ct. 215, 228, 4 L.Ed.2d 205 (1959) (Harlan, J., concurring in part and dissenting in part).

We determine obscenity in accordance with the "present critical point in the compromise between candor and shame at which the community may have arrived here and now." *United States v. Kennerley*, 209 F. 119, 121 (S.D.N.Y.1913) (L. Hand, J.). Having reviewed a representative sample of these works and in the absence of contrary evidence of prevailing community standards, we cannot say that the trial court abused its discretion in finding that the articles on Schedule 2102 were not patently offensive under contemporary standards in the New York area.

Nor do we think that the district court's suggestion that the B.F. Skinner speech served to modify its prior conclusion that the materials lack "serious literary, artistic, political and scientific value" was reversible error. While the opinion that all pornography may have value cannot establish the value of each item on the Schedule, see *United States v. Various Articles of Obscene Merchandise*, Schedule No. 2127, supra, at 44, the value vel non of the challenged works is immaterial once the materials are determined not to be patently offensive.

The judgment of the district court is affirmed.

MESKILL, Circuit Judge, concurring in the result:

Judge Sweet described the articles identified in Schedule 2102 as portraying "nudity, sexual intercourse between consenting participants, apparently adults, as well as oral and anal sex, including explicit and detailed pictures of genitalia." *United States v. Various Articles of Obscene Merchandise, Schedule No. 2102*, 81 Civ. 5295, slip op. at 3 (S.D.N.Y. Nov. 3, 1981). He found the material "unpleasant, uncouth, tawdry and undeniably pornographic." Id. at 4. I agree. But, Judge Sweet concluded that the articles are not "obscene" within the meaning

***138** of 19 U.S.C. § 1305(a) (1976 & Supp. V 1981) because they are "not patently offensive under contemporary community standards." *United States v. Various Articles of Obscene Merchandise, Schedule No. 2102*, 81 Civ. 5295, slip op. at 3 (S.D.N.Y. Sept. 29, 1982). I find this conclusion difficult to accept unless the community standards in New York are so low that nothing is obscene. Yet his conclusion is unassailable as a matter of law in the circumstances of this case.

The only issue here is whether the articles identified in Schedule 2102 are "patently offensive" under contemporary community standards, *Miller v. California*, 413 U.S. 15, 24, 93 S.Ct. 2607, 2614, 37 L.Ed.2d 419 (1973), the community in this case being the area encompassed by the Southern District of New York. 81 Civ. 5295, slip op. at 14 (S.D.N.Y. Nov. 3, 1981). On a prior appeal to this Court, a different panel from the one today, a panel of which I was a member, reversed Judge Sweet's finding of non-obscenity because he had relied upon impermissible indicia of community standards. *United States v. Various Articles of Obscene Merchandise, Schedule No. 2102*, 678 F.2d 433, 435 (2d Cir.1982). Although we had not at that time viewed the articles in question, we suggested in remanding the case "that portrayals of some of the activity [Judge Sweet] described would be 'patently offensive' under any standard." Id. at 435. Today, we affirm. In so doing, the majority accords uncommon deference to Judge Sweet's "finding that the material is non-obscene," characterizing it as "virtually shielded from appellate scrutiny, at least absent evidence that it is so clearly unreasonable as to amount to abuse of discretion." Unfortunately, our review is limited to a record devoid of evidence pertaining to community standards. Yet, I do not believe that our hands are tied nearly as tight as the majority thinks. While Judge Sweet surely brings a finely honed sense of community standards to the bench, we are not precluded from testing his assessment of how the average person in the Southern District of New York would react to the allegedly obscene articles.

The question is not whether the community approves of the government's confiscation of these articles; we held in the prior appeal that "the reaction of the community to the wisdom of section 1305 has no bearing on the materials' `patent offensiveness.'" Id. The question is whether the average person in the community would find the articles patently offensive. New York City may be the most sophisticated and cosmopolitan community in the nation, but I cannot imagine its residents to be indifferent to what I witnessed in the screening room. If these articles are acceptable to and tolerated by the average member of the community, I wonder if any form of pornography can be lawfully seized pursuant to section 1305 in the Southern District of New York. Measured against the community standards with which I am familiar, these articles are obscene; they offend my sense of decency and insult the standards of the community that I know. However, I am not a resident of nor as well acquainted with New York City as is Judge Sweet, and I am not well versed in the varieties and types of pornography which circulate there. Consequently, I am ill equipped to question Judge Sweet's assessment. Moreover, the government failed to introduce any evidence pertaining to community standards to facilitate our review. Had this case originated in the District of Connecticut, in a community whose standards are familiar to me, I would not hesitate to reverse; but it did not. I reluctantly concur.

[1] Although the addressees were given notice and chose not to appear, the district court was required to hold a hearing, *United States v. Various Articles of Obscene Merchandise, Schedule No. 1769*, 600 F.2d 394, 398-400 (2d Cir.1979), at which the articles were introduced through a customs agent.

[2] A schedule (No. 2102) identified the articles as follows:

Seizure No.	Merchandise
06979/001	9 Magazines: Horny, Color Orgy #8, 12, Elektra, Sex Deluxe, Color Climax #75, Top Porno, Venus Studio, Wish #3.
06979/002	3 Magazines: Anal Sex #37, Teenager #6, Lust #3.
06979/003	2 Video Cassettes: Jack, The Night Before.
06979/004	4 Magazines: Idol Sex #12, Show Boy # 11, Joy Boy #19, 20.
06979/005	4 Magazines: Chick #132, 144, Tuk # 12, Smile 198.
06979/006	4 Video Cassettes: (a) Insatiable, Star Virgin, Behind the Green Door and one short untitled subject considered to be admissible. (b) Deep Throat, The Opening of Misty Beethoven, Debbie Does Dallas, Joint Venture, Wide World of Spurts. (c) Honeysuckle Rose, Expensive Tastes, 4 short subjects (The Blond, "11," Taboo, High School Memories). (d) The Ecstasy Girls, Inside Desiree Cousteau, Female Athletes.
06979/007	2 Video Cassettes (a) The Autobiography of a Flea, Behind the Green Door, A Dirty Western. (b) Maraschino Cherry, Little Girl Blue, No Title and Flesh Gordon which was considered admissible.

[3] Title 19 U.S.C. §1305(a) provides in relevant part: "All persons are prohibited from importing into the United States from any foreign country...any obscene book, pamphlet, paper, writing, advertisement, circular, print, picture, drawing, or other representation, figure, or image on or of paper or other material ...or other article which is obscene or immoral."

[4] Although the geographical bounds of the "community" as that term is used in *Miller* may not extend to our nation as a whole, *Hamling v. United States*, supra, 418 U.S. at 107, 94 S.Ct. at 2901; *Jenkins v. Georgia*, 418U.S. 153, 157, 94 S.Ct. 2750, 2753, 41 L.Ed.2d 642 (1974), they need not be precisely defined. In this case Judge Sweet properly equated the district in which he sits with the "community." *Hamling v. United States*, supra, 418 U.S. at 104-06, 94 S.Ct. at 2900-01; *United States v. Various Articles of Obscene Merchandise, Schedule No. 1303*, 562 F.2d 185, 188-89 (2d Cir.1977) (obscenity of imported material determined by place of entry), cert. denied, 436 U.S. 931, 98 S.Ct. 2831, 56 L.Ed.2d 776 (1978).

CANDY BARR isn't kidding when she assumes her two-gun stance. This fiery Texan, favorite in Lone Star State, recently proved her ability with shooting irons when she plugged her husband when he tried to break into apartment after a quarrel.

Candy Barr (née Juanita Dale Slusher) was the first true adult-film star.

11

Modern Pornography

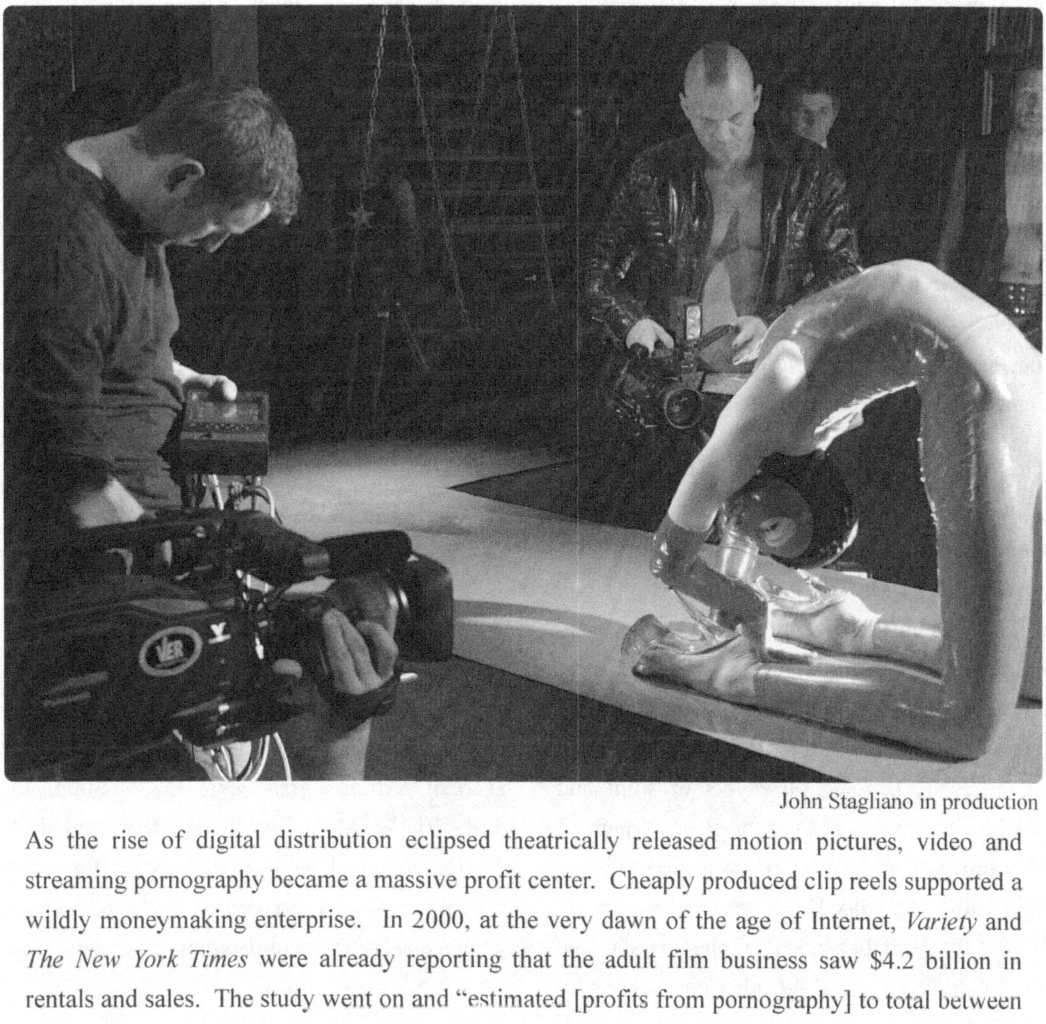

John Stagliano in production

As the rise of digital distribution eclipsed theatrically released motion pictures, video and streaming pornography became a massive profit center. Cheaply produced clip reels supported a wildly moneymaking enterprise. In 2000, at the very dawn of the age of Internet, *Variety* and *The New York Times* were already reporting that the adult film business saw $4.2 billion in rentals and sales. The study went on and "estimated [profits from pornography] to total between $10 billion and $14 billion annually in the United States when you toss in porn networks and pay-per-view movies on cable and satellite, Internet Web sites, in-room hotel movies, phone sex, sex toys and…magazines. (Frank Rich, "Naked Capitalists: There's No Business Like Porn Business" in *The New York Times*, May 20, 2001).

With so much money at stake, a class system arose in the environment of pornography. At one extreme were the polished productions from *Playboy* and *Penthouse*, high-class glamorous and glossy releases; at the other end of the spectrum were the alcohol-fueled reality-based spring break quickies packaged by Joe Francis as *Girls Gone Wild*. A market developed for amateur couples-oriented marital aids as well as more insidious fetish films that demeaned and degraded women.

The control of pornography had been a politically charged issue since the Ulysses S. Grant administration, when the Comstock Law was passed. But as George W. Bush took office, obscenity prosecutions took on renewed prominence. Alberto Gonzales took his post as Attorney General in 2005 and immediately created the Obscenity Prosecution Task Force. The O.P.T.F. targeted purveyors of smut and quickly accumulated an impressive strings of high profile convictions, including Joe Francis, Paul Little aka Max Hardcore, Danilo Simoes Croce, the Brazilian pornographer responsible for *2 Girls 1 Cup*, and 49 other convictions by 2007 (Department of Justice Oversight, Hearing Before the Committee on the Judiciary United States Senate, January 18, 2007, Testimony of Alberto R. Gonzales, p. 20).

One example of the division's work was in a case against Extreme Associates. Extreme was the husband-and-wife team, Rob Zicari aka Rob Black and Janet Romano aka Lizzy Borden. Together, Black and Borden produced videos featuring rough sex play and erotic humiliation. Among the movies they released was *Forced Entry* (2002), which featured simulated rape scenes. Federal prosecutors brought suit in the Western District of Pennsylvania.

At first, Extreme was emboldened by the government investigation. Their web site boasted, "See why the U.S. Government is after us!" (Eric Lichtblau, "Justice Dept. Fights Ruling on Obscenity" in *The New York Times*, February 17, 2005). Extreme prevailed at the district court level, with Judge Gary L. Lancaster opining, "public morality is not a legitimate state interest sufficient to justify infringing on adult, private, consensual, sexual conduct even if that conduct is deemed offensive to the general public's sense of morality." (*U.S. v. Extreme Associates*, 352 F. Supp. 2d 578, 591 [W.D.P.A. 2005]). The Department of Justice appealed, and by the end of the year won a reversal. Extreme was shuttered and its principals, Black and Borden each served a year and a day in prison.

The *Extreme* case showcased the O.P.T.F. at its height. As the Bush regime drew to a close, so did the power and influence of the D.O.J.'s anti-pornography division. The case against John Stagliano exemplified the O.P.T.F.'s diminishing power.

Stagliano, operating under his moniker "Buttman," entered the porn industry as a producer-director-performer in the late 1980s with his company Evil Angel. Stagliano's films were less aggressive than Extreme's or Max Hardcore's. Stagliano also had a sense of playful humor, execplified in the *Buttman Goes to Rio* series (1990-1994) and the *Buttman at Nudes a Poppin'* series (2001-2004), and a sense of style, seen in *Fashionistas* (2002). *Fashionistas* was a rare hardcore-mainstream crossover success; high budget, sexually explicit, and shot on 35mm. The picture was commercially successful and inspired a long running Las Vegas stage show, combining non-explicit fetish and fantasy for couples.

In 2008, the D.O.J. filed obscenity charges against Stagliano and Evil Angel citing several explicit fetish videos. This time the justice department was less prepared, less organized, less funded, and perhaps less interested. Prosecutors could not make their case. Stagliano's attorney, Paul Cambria argued that his client's videos merely depicted "adults putting on a performance…for another adult, who would make that choice if that were his or her cup of tea." (Amanda Hess, "Opening Arguments In *U.S. v. Stagliano*," in *Washington City Paper*, July 13, 2010). After prevailing at trial, Stagliano commented, "This is bad for my autobiography...I was hoping for a better fight than they put on."

Several more obscenity cases remained on the docket, but under the Obama regime, the war on obscenity was re-prioritized and de-prioritized. The following year, 2011, Attorney General Eric Holder folded the Obscenity Prosecution Task Force into the Child Exploitation and Obscenity Section, concentrating more seriously on crimes against children. Obscenity prosecutions have reached a momentary lull, but as soon as a new regime takes power, the balance between freedom and moral control will once again be debated.

In the meantime, as guidance for his clients in the adult industry, Paul Cambira compiled an informal list to help porn producers and distributors avoid what the state may see as actionable obscenity. The so-called "Cambria list" is an itemized catalog of the most controversial, offensive, demeaning and demented, off the wall gonzo sexual acts that are most likely to set off the remaining mechanisms of state censorship. By steering clear of the Cambria list, the next wave of freedom fighters of filth can stay under the state's obscenity radar for the time being.

UNITED STATES OF AMERICA
v.
EXTREME ASSOCIATES, INC.,
Robert Zicari, aka Rob Black; Janet Romano, aka Lizzie Borden

431 F.3d 150 (2005)
United States Court of Appeals, Third Circuit
Argued October 19, 2005
Decided December 8, 2005

Before: SMITH, STAPLETON, and NYGAARD, Circuit Judges.

OPINION

SMITH, Circuit Judge.

This appeal requires us to decide whether the District Court erred by dismissing an indictment brought against Extreme Associates, Inc. and its proprietors under 18 U.S.C. §§ 1461 and 1465, which criminalize the commercial distribution of obscene materials, on the ground that those statutes violate the privacy rights of ExtremeAssociates' customers under the Fifth Amendment doctrine of substantive due process. Because we conclude that the District Court improperly set aside applicable Supreme Court precedent which has repeatedly upheld federal statutes regulating the distribution of obscenity in the face of both First Amendment and substantive due process attacks, we will reverse the judgment of the District Court.

I.

A.

The parties do not dispute the relevant facts. Extreme Associates, Inc. is a California corporation owned and operated by Robert Zicari and Janet Romano.[1] Extreme Associates maintained a website through which it engaged in the business of producing, selling, and distributing obscene video tapes, DVDs, and computer files in interstate commerce.[2]

As part of an investigation, undercover U.S. Postal Inspectors visited the ExtremeAssociates website. The Inspectors found that the website was divided into two sections, one accessible to the general public, and one available to members only. Members were required to register and to pay $89.95 to gain access to the website for ninety days. From the members-only portion of the website, a member, inter alia, could download and view video clips. The general public could order tapes for delivery by mail through the public portion of the website. In the course of the investigation, Postal Inspectors purchased certain videotapes from the public section of the website, whichExtreme Associates delivered through the U.S. mails to undercover addresses. Inspectors also joined the members-only section of the website and downloaded and viewed several video clips.

On August 6, 2003, a federal grand jury returned a ten-count indictment againstExtreme Associates. The first count was a conspiracy charge under 18 U.S.C.

***152** § 371[3] charging Extreme Associates with conspiring to violate 18 U.S.C. §§ 1461[4] and 1465[5] by distributing obscene material through the mails and over the Internet. The remaining counts charged substantive violations of §§ 1461 and 1465 and alleged particular acts of distributing obscene materials in interstate commerce via the mails and the Internet.

On October 9, 2003, Extreme Associates filed a motion to dismiss the indictment on the ground that the "federal obscenity statutes"[6] violate the right to privacy protected by the Due Process Clause of the Fifth Amendment. After briefing and a hearing, the District Court declared the federal statutes regulating the distribution of obscenity unconstitutional as applied to Extreme Associates and dismissed the indictment in a Memorandum and Order on January 20, 2005. The Government appealed the dismissal.

B.

The analytical path taken by the District Court in dismissing the indictment warrants

***153** particular attention. The District Court began by concluding that Extreme Associates had derivative standing to challenge the federal statutes regulating the distribution of obscenity on behalf of its customers. Turning to the merits, the Court noted that in *Stanley v. Georgia*, 394 U.S. 557, 89 S.Ct. 1243, 22 L.Ed.2d 542 (1969), the Supreme Court recognized the First Amendment right of an individual to possess, read, observe, and receive obscene materials in the privacy of that individual's home, and that such a right is "fundamental" under the Constitution. Because the *Stanley* Court also spoke of a privacy right having to do with Stanley's home, the District Court opined that the case "represents a unique intersection between the substantive due process clause's protection of personal liberty and privacy and the First Amendment's protection of an individual's right to receive, and consider, [sic] information and ideas."

The District Court acknowledged that the Supreme Court has refused to strike down the federal statutes regulating the distribution of obscenity, or to recognize, as a corollary to the right recognized in *Stanley*, a First Amendment right to distribute obscene material. The District Court, however, adopted the position advocated by Extreme Associates that *Stanley* and its progeny, i.e., *United States v. Reidel*, 402 U.S. 351, 91 S.Ct. 1410, 28 L.Ed.2d 813 (1971), *United States v. Thirty-Seven (37) Photographs*, 402 U.S. 363, 91 S.Ct. 1400, 28 L.Ed.2d 822 (1973), *United States v. 12 200-Ft. Reels of Super 8mm Film*, 413 U.S. 123, 93 S.Ct. 2665, 37 L.Ed.2d 500 (1973), *United States v. Orito*, 413U.S. 139, 93 S.Ct. 2674, 37 L.Ed.2d 513 (1973), and *Paris Adult Theatre I v. Slaton*, 413U.S. 49. 93 S.Ct. 2628, 37 L.Ed.2d 446 (1973), were decided solely on First Amendment grounds rather than on privacy grounds under the Substantive Due Process Clause. The District Court also agreed with Extreme Associates that the above cases are factually distinguishable from the case at bar in that they dealt either with the importation of obscene material from abroad or involved methods of distribution that were more "public" than the Internet transmissions at issue here.

Noting that Extreme Associates sought to challenge the statutes not on its own behalf but on behalf of the individual privacy rights of its customers, the District Court concluded that because "[n]either the Supreme Court nor the Court of Appeals for the Third Circuit has considered a substantive due process challenge to the federal obscenity statutes by a vendor arguing that the laws place an unconstitutional burden . . . on an individual's fundamental right to possess and view what he pleases in his own home," Extreme Associates' challenge was not precluded by the *Reidel/Orito* line of cases. According to the District Court, the instant case is controlled instead by *Griswold v. Connecticut*, 381 U.S. 479, 85 S.Ct. 1678, 14 L.Ed.2d 510 (1965), *Roe v. Wade*, 410U.S. 113, 93 S.Ct. 705, 35 L.Ed.2d 147 (1973), and their progeny.

Because Extreme Associates based its substantive due process challenge on the existence of a "fundamental" right, the District Court applied strict scrutiny to the federal statutes regulating the distribution of obscenity.[7] The Court concluded that, under such heightened scrutiny, the statutes could not stand as applied to Extreme Associates because they were not narrowly drawn to advance any compelling government interest. Indeed,

***154** the District Court stated that the statutes could not be sustained even under less stringent rational basis review.[8]

The District Court offered two reasons for its ruling. First, the Court concluded that the principal rationale undergirding the federal statutes regulating the distribution of obscenity and the line of Supreme Court decisions upholding them is no longer valid. More specifically, the District Court stated that after the Supreme Court's decision in *Lawrence v. Texas*, 539 U.S. 558, 123 S.Ct. 2472, 156 L.Ed.2d 508 (2003), "the government can no longer rely on the advancement of a moral code, i.e., preventing consenting adults from entertaining lewd or lascivious thoughts, as a legitimate, let alone a compelling, state interest." As such, the District Court indicated that the *Lawrence* decision seriously undermines the validity of the statutes themselves, as well as earlier Supreme Court decisions upholding those statutes on public morality grounds. Applying the above analysis to Extreme Associates' motion to dismiss, the Court concluded that because "upholding the public sense of morality is not even a legitimate state interest that can justify infringing one's liberty interest to engage in consensual sexual conduct in private," such a "historically asserted state interest certainly cannot rise to the level of a compelling interest, as is required" under strict scrutiny.

Second, the District Court held that the Government's alternative asserted interests, i.e., putatively non-morality based interests, were not narrowly advanced by the complete ban on distribution of obscene materials embodied in the federal statutes regulating the distribution of obscenity. The Court stated that, owing to the character of the Internet generally and the particular protective technologies employed by Extreme Associates, the Government's asserted interests of protecting children and unwitting adults from exposure to obscenity could be accomplished by means less restrictive than a total ban on distribution. The Court added that because the latter of the two interests was likely motivated, at least partially, by regard for public morality, it would fail even rational basis review.

In sum, the District Court ruled that because *Lawrence* invalidated the primary rationale for the federal statutes regulating the distribution of obscenity and the Government's cited authority upholding them, and because the Government's remaining asserted interests, even if compelling, were not narrowly advanced by those statutes, the statutes were unconstitutional as applied to Extreme Associates on behalf of its customers. The District Court dismissed the indictment on that basis.

II.

A.

The District Court had original jurisdiction over this criminal action under 18 U.S.C. § 3231. We exercise appellate jurisdiction over the final judgment of a district court under 28 U.S.C. § 1291. Whether the District Court properly dismissed the indictment againstExtreme Associates is a question of law of which our review is plenary. *United States v. Ledesma-Cuesta*, 347 F.3d 527, 530 (3d Cir. 2003);

United States v. DeLaurentis, 230 F.3d 659, 660 (3d Cir. 2000).

***155** B.

As a preliminary matter, we agree with the District Court that Extreme Associates has derivative standing to challenge the constitutionality of the federal statutes regulating the distribution of obscenity on behalf of its customers. The Supreme Court consistently has upheld the ability of vendors to challenge the constitutionality of statutes on their customers' behalf where those statutes are directed at the activity of the vendors. In *Carey v. Population Services International*, 431 U.S. 678, 682-84, 97 S.Ct. 2010. 52 L.Ed.2d 675 (1977), the Court held that a mail-order seller of non-medical contraceptives had standing to argue that a state statute prohibiting the distribution of non-medical contraceptives violated its customers' substantive due process rights to use such contraceptives. Also, in *Craig v. Boren*, 429 U.S. 190, 195, 97 S.Ct. 451, 50 L.Ed.2d 397 (1976), the Court upheld the ability of a beer seller to challenge a state statute on behalf of certain underage customers. The Court noted that "vendors and those in like positions have been uniformly permitted to resist efforts at restricting their operations by acting as advocates of the rights of third parties who seek access to their market or function." Id. Accordingly, Extreme Associates has standing to challenge the federal statutes regulating the distribution of obscenity as violative of the substantive due process rights of its customers.

III.

In its Memorandum, the District Court notes briefly, but never directly addresses, the Government's contention that "because the federal obscenity statutes have withstood constitutional attack for more than thirty-five years, this court lacks the authority to find that they are unconstitutional." The Government's brief on appeal raises the same issue by asserting, essentially, that the District Court erred by granting relief which effectively overturns applicable Supreme Court precedents on the ground that those precedents have been undermined or implicitly overruled by a subsequent Supreme Court decision. We agree with the Government that the District Court was in error, and we conclude that the District Court's violation of the principle articulated below requires reversal.

A.

In *Rodriguez de Quijas v. Shearson/American Express Inc.*, 490 U.S. 477, 484, 109 S.Ct. 1917, 104 L.Ed.2d 526 (1989), the Supreme Court explicitly admonished lower courts that "[i]f a precedent of this Court has direct application in a case, yet appears to rest on reasons rejected in some other line of decisions, the Court of Appeals should follow the case which directly controls, leaving to this Court the prerogative of overruling its own decisions." See also id. (pointing out specifically that the Court of Appeals, "on its own authority," should not have "taken the step of renouncing" a previous Supreme Court decision interpreting the Securities Act, even as the Court itself goes on to overrule the decision in that very case). The Court reiterated its position in *Agostini v. Felton*, 521 U.S. 203, 237, 117 S.Ct. 1997, 138 L.Ed.2d 391 (1997), stating "[w]e do not acknowledge, and we do not hold, that other courts should conclude our more recent cases have, by implication, overruled an earlier precedent." Id. The Court then proceeded to "reaffirm" the precise language quoted above from Rodriguez. Id. The Court explained that "[a]dherence to this teaching by the District Court and Court of Appeals in this litigation does not insulate a legal principle on which they relied from our review to

***156** determine its continued vitality," as lower courts are free to consider the issues and preserve them for the Court even as they obey controlling precedent. Id. at 237-38, 117 S.Ct. 1997. In fact, even as the Court in *Agostini* concluded that its own adherence to the old precedent "would undoubtedly work a `manifest injustice'" in light of later decisions, it emphasized that "the trial court acted within its discretion in entertaining the motion [requesting relief under the newer cases] with supporting allegations, but it was also correct to recognize that the motion had to be denied unless and until this Court reinterpreted the binding precedent." Id. at 236, 238, 117 S.Ct. 1997 (emphasis added).

Our own cases steadfastly apply the *Agostini* doctrine. See United States v. Singletary,268 F.3d 196, 205 (3d Cir.2001) (quoting *Agostini* and indicating that "[w]e have always sought to adhere strictly to that counsel"); *United States v. Abuhouran*, 161 F.3d 206, 215 n. 9 (3d Cir.1998); *Maldonado v. Houstoun*, 157 F.3d 179, 190 (3d Cir.1998); *United States v. Bishop*, 66 F.3d 569, 588 n. 28 (3d Cir.1995); *Swin Resource Sys., Inc. v. Lycoming County*, 883 F.2d 245, 255 (3d Cir.1989). In fact, we emphasized in *Singletary* that even where a lower court's analytical position has merit, the obligation to follow applicable Supreme Court precedent is in no way abrogated:

even if there were merit to *Singletary's* argument that the Supreme Court's [later] decisions have somehow weakened the precedential value of [the older case], we may not precipitate its decline. The Supreme Court itself has admonished lower courts to follow its directly applicable precedent, even if that precedent appears weakened by pronouncements in subsequent decisions. . . .

Singletary, 268 F.3d at 205. We reaffirm our intent to adhere strictly to the principle articulated by the Supreme Court in *Agostini*. It follows that the District Court also was bound by that principle as it considered Extreme Associates' motion to dismiss the indictment.

B.

In this appeal, then, we must decide whether *Reidel's* progeny, which the District Court found to be undermined by Lawrence, was "directly applicable" to Extreme Associates' motion to dismiss the indictment. As an analytical matter, we answer that question in the affirmative. In the broadest and most obvious sense, the Supreme Court has explicitly and repeatedly, in decisions rendered post-*Stanley*,[9] upheld the constitutionality of federal statutes regulating the distribution of obscenity. See *Reidel*, 402 U.S. at 351, 91 S.Ct. 1410; *Thirty-Seven Photographs, 402 U.S.* at 363, 91 S.Ct. 1400; *Orito*, 413 U.S. at 139, 93 S.Ct. 2674; *12 200-Ft. Reels*, 413 U.S. at 123, 93 S.Ct. 2665.

Furthermore, the above cases consistently uphold the constitutionality of the statutes as applied to the right recognized in Stanley. See, e.g., *Thirty-Seven Photographs*, 402 U.S.at 376, 91 S.Ct. 1400; *Orito*, 413 U.S. at 141, 93 S.Ct. 2674. The Court has stated clearly that the right

***157** recognized in *Stanley* to possess obscene material within the home (and, by logical implication, the ability to exercise that right) "does not mean" that there is a correlative right to distribute that material, *Thirty-Seven Photographs*, 402 U.S. at 376, 91 S.Ct. 1400, that it "does not require" the Court to fashion a right to distribute, *Reidel*, 402 U.S. at 356, 91 S.Ct. 1410, and that the *Stanley* "'right to receive' is not a right to the existence of modes of distribution of obscenity, which the State could destroy without serious risk of infringing on the privacy of a man's thoughts; rather, it is a right to a protective zone ensuring the freedom of a man's inner life. . . ." Id. at 359, 91 S.Ct. 1410 (Harlan, J., concurring) (emphasis added).

It bears noting as well that in more than one of the cases following Stanley, the Court heard and rejected the arguments of dissenting Justices that proscribing distribution or private transportation of obscene materials evacuated the Stanley right of any significant meaning. See *Thirty-Seven Photographs*, 402 U.S. at 381, 91 S.Ct. 1400 (Harlan, J., dissenting) (arguing that the right to possess and read obscene material at home "is hollow indeed" without some right to transport it); *Orito*, 413 U.S. at 141, 93 S.Ct. 2674 (Douglas, J., dissenting) (asserting that there is no distinction between private possession and private carriage of obscene material, and arguing that upholding the federal statutes regulating the distribution of obscenity necessitates overruling Stanley).

Most relevant to this appeal, the Supreme Court also has upheld the federal statutes regulating the distribution of obscenity specifically in light of the Court's broader privacy jurisprudence. The District Court stated that Stanley and its progeny do not control the Extreme Associates' motion to dismiss because those cases were all decided merely on the basis that obscenity is not protected under the First Amendment. ExtremeAssociates argues that *Reidel's* progeny dealt only with a "First Amendment concept of privacy." As such, the argument runs, the pivotal obscenity cases ignored substantive due process analysis of the "private possession" right recognized in Stanley and, therefore, did not govern the motion to dismiss.[10] We disagree. It is true that none of the major cases use the phrase "substantive due process" in their holdings, but it is clear — particularly in *Orito* and *Paris Adult Theatre* — that the Court analyzed the federal statutes regulating the distribution of obscenity under both the principles and precedents that, according to the District Court and Extreme Associates, should control this case. Moreover, where such analysis does appear, the Court has found challenges to the statutes under the general constitutional right to privacy unavailing.

In *Orito*, for example, the defendant was prosecuted under §1462 for privately transporting obscene material in interstate commerce (to wit, knowingly carrying obscene materials in his private luggage on a domestic commercial flight). *Orito* "moved to dismiss the indictment on the ground that the statute violated both his First and Ninth Amendment rights." *Orito*, 413 U.S. at 140, 93 S.Ct. 2674 (emphasis added). In dismissing the indictment, the Supreme Court explained that the District Court had misinterpreted not only Stanley, but also Griswold to establish constitutional protection for the "non-public" transportation of obscene material. Id. at 140-41, 93 S.Ct. 2674.

***158** As part of its analysis, the *Orito* Court noted that the Constitution "extends special safeguards to the privacy of the home, just as it protects other special privacy rights such as those of marriage, procreation, motherhood, child rearing, and education." Id. at 142, 93 S.Ct. 2674. To support that assertion, the Court cited, inter alia, *Eisenstadt v. Baird*, 405 U.S. 438, 92 S.Ct. 1029, 31 L.Ed.2d 349 (1972), and *Griswold*. Id. The Court elected, fully conscious of the right recognized in Stanley, to exclude transporting obscene material in interstate commerce from "such special consideration." *Orito*, 413 U.S. at 142, 93 S.Ct. 2674. In upholding the statute at issue, the Court pointed out that the District Court had "erred in striking down 18 U.S.C. §1462 and dismissing the indictment on these 'privacy' grounds." Id. at 141, 93 S.Ct. 2674 (emphasis added). The Court also stated — again, fully conscious of and having made reference to the right articulated in *Stanley* — that in its decision to uphold bans on transporting obscene material within the stream of commerce, "no constitutionally protected privacy is involved." Id. at 143, 93 S.Ct. 2674.

Similarly, in *Paris Adult Theatre*, though the Court dealt with obscenity in a "place of public accommodation" (a theater), much of the Court's analysis dealt squarely with the general constitutional right to privacy as it relates to the Stanley right. The Court first explained the scope of the right in question by indicating that its "prior decisions recognizing a right to privacy guaranteed by the Fourteenth Amendment"[11] referred to a right that "encompasses and protects the personal intimacies of the home, the family, marriage, motherhood, procreation and child rearing." *Paris Adult Theatre*, 413 U.S. at 65, 93 S.Ct. 2628 (emphasis added). To support this proposition, the Court cited *Eisenstadt, Griswold* and *Stanley*. Id. The Court noted the legally operative difference between the *Stanley* right and those deriving from *Griswold* and *Roe*:

The protection afforded by *Stanley* . . . is restricted to a place, the home. In contrast, the constitutionally protected privacy of family, marriage, motherhood, procreation, and child rearing is not just concerned with a particular place, but with a protected intimate relationship. Such protected privacy extends to the doctor's office, the hospital, the hotel room, or as otherwise required to safeguard the right of intimacy involved.

Id. at 66 n. 13, 93 S.Ct. 2628 (citing *Roe* and *Griswold*).

The Court applied the above analysis in reaching its result:

If obscene material . . . carried with it a `penumbra' of constitutionally protected privacy, this Court would not have found it necessary to decide *Stanley* on the narrow basis of the `privacy of the home,' which was hardly more than a reaffirmation that a man's home is his castle. . . . Moreover, we have declined to equate the privacy of the home relied on in *Stanley* with a `zone' of `privacy' that follows a distributor or a consumer of obscene materials wherever he goes.

Paris Adult Theatre, 413 U.S. at 66, 93 S.Ct. 2628 (citing *Stanley, Orito*) (emphasis added). Finally, summarizing the case, the Court indicated it had "reaffirmed [its] holding[]" that "commerce in obscene material is unprotected by any constitutional doctrine of privacy." Id. at 69, 93 S.Ct. 2628 (citing *Orito, Reidel, Thirty-Seven*

***159** *Photographs and 12 200-Ft. Reels*) (emphasis added).

We conclude that the Supreme Court has analyzed and upheld the federal statutes regulating the distribution of obscenity under the constitutional right to privacy embodied collectively in the First, Ninth, and Fourteenth (thus also the Fifth) Amendments, as well as the Griswold line of decisions that the District Court asserted should control this case. The fact that such analysis has never been applied within the precise scenario outlined by the District Court — i.e., use of the talismanic phrase "substantive due process" in the context of a vendor proceeding under derivative standing on behalf of a consumer's right to privately possess obscene material — does not negate the binding precedential value of the Supreme Court cases employing that analysis. The Court's analysis need not be so specific in order to limit a district court's prerogative to overturn an entire category of federal statutes, even as applied to particular defendants, based on speculation about a later decision that fails even to mention those statutes. The Court has considered the federal statutes regulating the distribution of obscenity in the context of the broader constitutional right to privacy and upheld them. That such analysis was conducted absent its constitutional brand name does not negate its precedential value.

In sum, the District Court's Order granting Extreme Associates' motion to dismiss the indictment, as well as Extreme Associates' brief on appeal, deal with the same statutes upheld repeatedly by the Supreme Court. They assert (albeit derivatively) the same right referenced and analyzed in multiple Supreme Court decisions — all of which declined to strike down any part of any statute regulating the distribution of obscenity. Finally, the Supreme Court has analyzed and upheld the constitutionality of the federal statutes regulating the distribution of obscenity specifically in light of the Court's broader right-to-privacy jurisprudence.

C.

We now turn to whether *Reidel* and its progeny, which we find analytically apposite, are meaningfully factually distinguishable from the case at bar. If there is a material factual distinction between the instant case and the putatively controlling precedent, analysis under *Agostini* is wholly inappropriate. Where, as here, an "as applied" constitutional challenge, rather than a facial one, is before the court, this analytical step is of particular importance. The District Court concluded, and Extreme Associates now argues on appeal, that the key cases in the *Reidel* line can be distinguished on their facts inasmuch as (1) none of the key cases address substantive due process privacy rights; (2) certain of the cases dealt exclusively with border and importation issues; and (3) none of the previous obscenity decisions involved transmissions over the Internet. We are unpersuaded by these arguments, however, and we conclude that *Orito* and the other key cases discussed above are sufficiently similar to the instant case to govern it.[12]

First, as discussed at length in section III.B., the District Court Memorandum adopted Extreme Associates' position that

***160** all of the relevant obscenity cases following *Stanley* are distinguishable inasmuch as none of those cases involved a substantive due process privacy challenge against the federal statutes regulating the distribution of obscenity or engaged in such privacy analysis. As we have indicated, we adjudge those assertions to be incorrect, and we need not discuss them further here.

Second, both the District Court and Extreme Associates attempt to distinguish *12 200-Ft. Reels and Thirty-Seven Photographs* on the ground that they deal exclusively with importation and border issues, arguing that such a context necessarily triggers a different analytical framework. This argument is a closer call, but it is also unavailing. Though importation issues do provide the factual backdrop of both cases, both cases engage in standard *Stanley* analysis and are at least generally concerned with Congress's ability, upheld in both cases, to bar transportation of obscene materials in the channels of commerce. See *12 200-Ft. Reels*, 413 U.S. at 128, 93 S.Ct. 2665; *Thirty-Seven Photographs*, 402 U.S. at 376, 91 S.Ct. 1400. At all events, even if we were to grant that *12 200-Ft. Reels* and *Thirty-Seven Photographs* are relevantly distinguishable, *Orito* still deals squarely with *Stanley*, the federal statutes regulating the distribution of obscenity, privacy, and the ability of Congress constitutionally to ban any presence of obscene material in domestic interstate commerce. *Orito* alone provides directly applicable precedent as to the instant appeal.

Finally, Extreme Associates argues that the relevant cases are distinguishable because they "were all decided before the advent of the Internet," suggesting that "the commercial transportation of obscenity considered by the Court [in those cases] was of a more public variety than the Internet commerce at issue here." As such, "[t]he concern for community decency and order that arose in [the other obscenity cases] is irrelevant to this prosecution."[13] We decline to join appellees in that analytical leap. The mere fact, without more, that the instant prosecution involves Internet transmissions is not enough to render an entire line of Supreme Court decisions inapplicable given their analytical and other factual similarities to this case.

Extreme Associates correctly quotes dicta from *Reno v. American Civil Liberties Union*, 521 U.S. 844, 117 S.Ct. 2329, 138 L.Ed.2d 874 (1997), indicating that the Internet is "a unique and wholly new medium of worldwide communication." Id. at 850, 117 S.Ct. 2329 (citing without comment finding of fact 81 from the District Court in that case). In the same case, however, the Court noted that "[t]ransmitting obscenity...whether via the Internet or other means, is already illegal under federal law for both adults and juveniles," and implied that the "Child Decency Act," a statute regulating pornography over the Internet at issue in Reno, might be unnecessary owing to the existing federal statutes regulating the distribution of obscenity. Id. at 878 n. 44, 117 S.Ct. 2329 (citing 18 U.S.C. § 1465). In other words, the Court thus far has not suggested that obscenity law does not apply to the Internet

***161** or even that a new analytical path is necessary in Internet cases. If the Supreme Court wishes to treat all Internet obscenity cases as sui generis for purposes of federal obscenity law analysis, it has not yet said so, "tacitly" or otherwise.[14]

Even clearer is the fact that *Orito* and *Paris Adult Theatre* affirm the power of Congress to "regulate interstate commerce to the extent of forbidding and punishing the use of such commerce as an agency to promote immorality . . . or harm to the people of other states from the state of origin." *Orito*, 413 U.S. at 144 n. 6, 93 S.Ct. 2674; see also id. at 144, 93 S.Ct. 2674 ("Congress may impose relevant conditions . . . on those who use the channels of interstate commerce in order that those channels will not become the means of spreading evil, whether of a physical, moral or economic nature"); id. at 143, 93 S.Ct. 2674 ("[t]hat the transporter has an abstract proprietary power to shield the obscene material from all others and to guard the material with the same privacy as in the home is not controlling"); *Paris Adult Theatre*, 413 U.S. at 58, 93 S.Ct. 2628 ("we hold that there are legitimate state interests in stemming the tide of commercialized obscenity, even assuming it is feasible to enforce effective safeguards against exposure to juveniles and passersby"); id. at 69, 93 S.Ct. 2628 ("commerce in obscene material is unprotected by any constitutional doctrine of privacy") (emphasis added). The Internet is a channel of commerce covered by the federal statutes regulating the distribution of obscenity. Extreme Associates was indicted for engaging in commercial transactions that its own brief on appeal describes as "Internet commerce." This case cannot be meaningfully distinguished merely because it involves the Internet.

IV.

We are satisfied that the Supreme Court has decided that the federal statutes regulating the distribution of obscenity do not violate any constitutional right to privacy. For district and appellate courts in our judicial system, such a determination dictates the result in analogous cases unless and until the Supreme Court expressly overrules the substance of its decision. *Lawrence v. Texas* represents no such definitive step by the Court. It was therefore impermissible for the District Court to strike down the statutes at issue based on speculation that *Orito* and other pivotal obscenity cases "appear[] to rest on reasons rejected in" *Lawrence*. *Agostini*, 521 U.S. at 237, 117 S.Ct. 1997. Even if there were analytical merit to such speculation, an issue on which we do not opine, the constraint on lower courts remains the same. The possibility that Lawrence has "somehow weakened the precedential value of" the *Reidel* line of cases is irrelevant for purposes of ruling on the instant indictment. Singletary, 268 F.3d at 205.

***162** We conclude that directly applicable Supreme Court precedent, upholding the constitutionality of the federal statutes regulating the distribution of obscenity under First Amendment and substantive due process privacy rights, governs this case. The District Court was bound by that authority, as are we, to uphold those statutes as applied to Extreme Associates on behalf of its customers. As such, the District Court erred in striking down the statutes and dismissing the indictment against Extreme Associates.

Accordingly, we will reverse the Order of the District Court and remand the case for further proceedings consistent with this opinion.

Footnotes

[1] We hereinafter refer to Extreme Associates, Inc., Mr. Zicari, and Ms. Romano collectively as "Extreme Associates."

[2] For purposes of the motion to dismiss in the District Court, Extreme Associates stipulated that the material available on its website is legally obscene.

[3] 18 U.S.C. § 371 provides in pertinent part: If two or more persons conspire either to commit any offense against the United States, or to defraud the United States, or any agency thereof in any manner or for any purpose, and one or more of such persons do any act to effect the object of the conspiracy, each shall be fined under this title or imprisoned not more than five years, or both.

[4] [18 U.S.C.] Section 1461 states in relevant part: Every obscene, lewd, lascivious, indecent, filthy or vile article, matter, thing, device, or substance . . . [i]s declared to be nonmailable matter and shall not be conveyed in the mails or delivered from any post office or by any letter carrier. Whoever knowingly uses the mails for the...delivery of anything declared by this section...to be nonmailable...shall be fined under this title or imprisoned not more than five years, or both, for the first such offense, and shall be fined under this title or imprisoned not more than ten years, or both, for each such offense thereafter.

[5] [18 U.S.C.] Section 1465 states in relevant part: Whoever knowingly transports or travels in, or uses a facility or means of, interstate or foreign commerce or an interactive computer service...in or affecting such commerce for the purpose of sale or distribution of any obscene, lewd, lascivious, or filthy book, pamphlet, picture, film, paper, letter, writing, print, silhouette, drawing, figure, image, case, phonograph recording, electrical transcription or other article capable of producing sound or any other matter of indecent or immoral character, shall be fined under this title or imprisoned not more than five years, or both.

[6] Although the Government brought no charges in this case under 18 U.S.C. § 1462, Extreme Associates' Motion to Dismiss attacked

the constitutionality of that statute as well, and the District Court struck it down. We hereinafter refer to §§ 1461, 1462, and 1465 collectively as the "federal statutes regulating the distribution of obscenity" or the "statutes." Section 1462 states in relevant part:

Whoever brings into the United States...or knowingly uses any express company or common carrier or interactive computer service...for carriage in interstate or foreign commerce — (a) any obscene, lewd, lascivious, or filthy book, pamphlet, picture, motion-picture film, paper, letter, writing, print, or other matter of indecent character; or (b) any obscene, lewd, lascivious, or filthy phonograph recording, electrical transcription, or other article or thing capable of producing sound...or [w]hoever knowingly takes or receives, from such express company or other common carrier or interactive computer service...any matter or thing the carriage or importation of which is herein made unlawful — [s]hall be fined under this title or imprisoned for not more than five years, or both, for the first such offense and shall be fined under this title or imprisoned for not more than ten years, or both, for each such offense thereafter.

[7] To survive strict scrutiny, a statute must be narrowly tailored to further a compelling state interest. See, e.g., *Griswold v. Connecticut*, 381 U.S. 479, 497-98, 85 S.Ct. 1678, 14 L.Ed.2d 510 (1965) (Goldberg, J., concurring).

[8] To survive rational basis review, a statute must be rationally related to the advancement of a legitimate state interest. See, e.g., *Griswold*, 381 U.S. at 504, 85 S.Ct. 1678 (White, J., concurring).

[9] Although it does not deal directly with the question, *Stanley* itself, by implication, recognized the constitutionality of the federal statutes regulating the distribution of obscenity even as it recognized the right to possess and observe obscene materials in the home. See *Stanley*, 394 U.S. at 567-68, 89 S.Ct. 1243 (indicating that even if prohibiting obscenity possession is necessary to facilitate the enforcement of statutory schemes prohibiting its distribution, the right to possess materials within the privacy of the home is so important that "its restriction may not be justified by the need to ease the administration of otherwise valid criminal laws.") (emphasis added).

[10] The District Court held, and Extreme Associates argues, further, that certain key cases are meaningfully factually distinguishable. We reject that argument. See section III.C., infra.

[11] *Paris Adult Theatre* dealt with a state statute, so the operative due process provision was that of the Fourteenth Amendment, rather than that of the Fifth Amendment at issue here.

[12] We find especially puzzling the District Court's conclusion that *Orito* is "distinguishable on [its] facts." The District Court concluded that *Orito* was factually distinguishable because the Court in that case "held that the obscenity statutes could be justified as a method of protecting the public morality, a justification no longer valid after *Lawrence*." That observation fails to distinguish *Orito* factually in any way, and, as we discuss below, is analytically irrelevant to the disposition of this case.

[13] We note that Extreme Associates' Internet argument necessarily fails to distinguish three of the counts of the indictment involved in this case. Three counts allege that Extreme Associates distributed obscene materials through the United States mail. Identical conduct was at issue in the case of *United States v. Reidel*, 402 U.S.351, 91 S.Ct. 1410, 28 L.Ed.2d 813 (1971). Seven of the ten counts in the present indictment, however, do pertain to distributing video clips to home computers through the Internet.

[14] Were we to concede that the Supreme Court has or is prepared to analyze obscene Internet transmissions differently because, unlike the acts involved in *Orito* and other cases, such transmissions involve no "physical" transportation of obscenity outside the home, that concession would not save Extreme Associates' motion. The holding in *Orito*, for example, involves two prongs: (1) Congress may regulate obscenity on the basis of the danger that it will not remain private once it physically leaves the home in any way, *Orito*, 413 U.S. at 143, 93 S.Ct. 2674; and (2) irrespective of any such danger, Congress may prevent interstate commerce and the channels thereof from being used to spread evil of a physical, moral or economic nature. Congress may therefore keep all obscene material entirely out of the stream of commerce. Id. at 143-44, 93 S.Ct. 2674. At most, the aforementioned concession regarding the Internet would compromise prong (1). As we discuss below, the second prong stands unscathed for purposes of this appeal and, on its own, would dictate the result.

UNITED STATES OF AMERICA
v.
JOHN STAGLIANO

693 F.Supp.2d 25 (2010)
United States District Court, District of Columbia
Decided February 19, 2010

MEMORANDUM OPINION

RICHARD J. LEON, District Judge.

The defendants—John Stagliano, John Stagliano, Inc., and Evil Angel Productions, Inc.—challenge the constitutionality of four federal statutes that criminalize the interstate trafficking of obscenity. They move to dismiss the Indictment charging them with offenses under 18 U.S.C. § 1462, 18 U.S.C. § 1465, 18 U.S.C. § 1466, and 47 U.S.C. § 223(d). In particular, they contend that these statutes are unconstitutionally vague and overbroad as applied to Internet speech. They also contend that the statutes are unconstitutional in light of recent Supreme Court case law that they say establishes a substantive due process right to sexual privacy broad enough to include the right to distribute obscene materials. Having considered the defendants' arguments, the Court concludes that the federal obscenity statutes charged in the Indictment withstand the

***28** defendants' multi-faceted constitutional challenge. Accordingly, the Court DENIES their respective Motions to Dismiss.

BACKGROUND

The pending Indictment contains seven counts. Counts One and Two charge the defendants with knowingly transporting an obscene motion-picture film in interstate commerce for the purpose of selling or distributing the film, in violation of 18 U.S.C. § 1465.[1] Count Three charges the defendants with knowingly using an interactive computer service for the purpose of distributing in interstate commerce an obscene motion-picture trailer, in violation of 18 U.S.C. § 1465. Counts Four and Five charge the defendants with knowingly using an express company or other common carrier to ship the two films in Counts One and Two from California to a location in Washington, D.C., in violation of 18 U.S.C. §1462.[2] Count Six charges the defendants with knowingly possessing the obscene items in Counts One, Two, and Three with the intent to distribute those items in interstate commerce while engaged in the business of selling obscene material, in violation of 18 U.S.C. §1466.[3] Count Seven charges the defendants with knowingly using an interactive computer service to display an obscene image—that is, the movie trailer identified in Count Three—in a manner available to a person under 18 years of age, in violation of 47 U.S.C. § 223(d).[4]

The FBI obtained the materials that form the basis for these charges in the course of investigating allegations that the defendants produce and distribute certain obscene "hard-core pornography." (Gov't Opposition [# 23] at 1). After placing an

***29** order with the defendants by mailing a form printed from their website, FBI agents in Washington, D.C. received by mail two DVDs—"Milk Nymphos" and "Storm Squirters 2 `Target Practice'"—that allegedly contain obscene movies. (Id. at 1-2). An agent in Washington also downloaded from the defendants' website a free movie trailer—"Fetish Fanatic Chapter 5"—that the government believes to be obscene as well. (Id. at 2). Descriptions of the films are not relevant at this stage, of course, because it is the jury's province to determine whether those films are actually obscene. The issue now before the Court is limited to the legal question of whether the obscenity statutes charged in the Indictment are unconstitutional. The defendants contend that they are. I disagree.

DISCUSSION

The defendants raise a litany of arguments challenging the constitutionality of the federal obscenity statutes charged in this case. First and foremost, they contend that Section 1465 and Section 223(d), both of which incorporate the "community standards" and "as a whole" elements of the obscenity test set forth in *Miller v. California*, 413 U.S. 15, 93 S.Ct. 2607, 37 L.Ed.2d 419 (1973), are unconstitutionally overbroad and vague as applied to Internet speech. Second, they contend that Section 223(d) is a content-based restriction on speech that fails strict scrutiny under the First Amendment. Because of these constitutional defects, the defendants contend, at a minimum, that Counts Three and Seven of the Indictment must be dismissed. Not surprisingly, the defendants do not stop there. In addition to their overbreadth and vagueness claims, they contend that all counts of the Indictment must be dismissed because individuals have a substantive due process right under the Constitution not only to possess and use obscene materials but to produce and distribute those materials as well. Finally, they contend that obscenity prosecutions in the District of Columbia impermissibly burden the right to copyright work that would be protected elsewhere. Unfortunately for the defendants, I am not persuaded by any of these arguments. How so?

I. Overbreadth

The defendants' principal argument, which happens to be their best, is that Section 1465 (charged in Count Three) and Section 223(d) (charged in Count Seven) are unconstitutional as applied to the Internet because the "community standards" and "as a whole" elements of *Miller's* obscenity test render both statutes overbroad. I disagree.

The First Amendment doctrine of overbreadth is an exception to the normal rule governing facial challenges to statutes. *Virginia v. Hicks*, 539 U.S. 113, 118, 123 S.Ct. 2191, 156 L.Ed.2d 148 (2003). To invalidate a law on its face under this doctrine, one need not show that the law is unconstitutional in every instance; rather, one need only show that the "law punishes a `substantial' amount of protected free speech." Id. In that regard, the overbreadth must "be `substantial,' not only in an absolute sense, but also relative to the scope of the law's plainly legitimate applications." Id. at 120, 123 S.Ct. 2191.

Both Section 1465 and Section 223(d) prohibit the use of an interactive computer service to distribute or display "obscene" materials. Beyond dispute is the Supreme Court's repeated admonition "that obscene material is unprotected by the First Amendment. "*Miller*, 413 U.S. at 23, 93 S.Ct. 2607. Of course, courts have long struggled to draw the line between protected expression and unprotected obscenity.

***30** But after years of jurisprudential uncertainty, the Supreme Court in *Miller* finally settled on a three-prong test for determining whether a particular work is obscene: (1) "whether the average person, applying contemporary community standards would find that the work, taken as a whole, appeals to the prurient interest"; (2) "whether the work depicts or describes, in a patently offensive way, sexual conduct specifically defined by the applicable . . . law"; and (3) "whether the work, taken as a whole, lacks serious literary, artistic, political, or scientific value." Id. at 24, 93 S.Ct. 2607 (internal quotation marks omitted). The Supreme Court later refined this test by incorporating the community standards element of the first prong into the second prong and by mandating that the third prong be evaluated using an objective "reasonable person" standard. *Pope v. Illinois*, 481 U.S.497, 500-01, 107 S.Ct. 1918, 95 L.Ed.2d 439 (1987).

Because the challenged statutes incorporate the *Miller* test by virtue of their ban on "obscene" material, it appears, at first blush, that there is an exact congruence between the kind of expression the Constitution permits to be punished and the kind of expression the statutes in fact punish. The statutes criminalize, and the defendants have been charged with, the distribution or display of obscene material, and obscene material "has long been held to fall outside the purview of the First Amendment." *Ashcroft v. American Civil Liberties Union*, 535 U.S. 564, 574, 122 S.Ct. 1700, 152 L.Ed.2d 771 (2002) (ACLU I). For this reason, the Court rejects out of hand the defendants' argument that Section 223(d)(1), which prohibits use of the Internet to display "obscene" material in a manner available to minors,[5] is a content-based regulation that cannot survive strict scrutiny. (See *Evil Angel Productions Mem.* [# 17] at 13-23). Because obscenity, as defined in *Miller*, is a category of speech not protected by the Constitution, statutes like Section 223(d) that regulate obscene materials in a viewpoint neutral way are not subject to strict scrutiny.[6] As such, the Court need only address the defendants central argument that Section 223(d) and Section 1465 are unconstitutional as applied to the Internet because the "community standards" and "as a whole" requirements of *Miller's* obscenity test render both statutes overbroad.

A. "Community Standards" Requirement

The defendants contend that the federal obscenity statutes, which incorporate

***31** the "community standards" test, suppress substantially more speech than is constitutionally permissible when applied to the Internet. Because Internet publishers, unlike those who use mail or telephone, cannot limit the geographic reach of the materials they post on the Internet, those materials are subject to the community standards of the most conservative jurisdictions in the country. Thus, to avoid criminal liability, the publishers must either tailor their speech to conform to those standards or abstain altogether from using the Internet as a medium for their speech. As a consequence, Internet speech that more permissive jurisdictions would surely protect will be unconstitutionally burdened or chilled. (*Evil Angel Productions* [# 17] at 4-8; John Stagliano Inc. [# 20] at 10-12).

Although a majority of Supreme Court justices in a splintered decision in *Ashcroft v. American Civil Liberties Union* (ACLUI) voiced concern that a "community standards" requirement, as applied in Internet prosecutions under the Child Online Protection Act ("COPA"), poses overbreadth problems,[7] those concerns hardly suffice to render the more narrow obscenity statutes unconstitutional as applied to the Internet. Indeed, notwithstanding their concerns, an overwhelming majority of the Supreme Court held inACLU I that "reliance on community standards ... does not by itself render [COPA] substantially overbroad for purposes of the First Amendment."[8] 535 U.S. at 585, 122 S.Ct. 1700

***32** (emphasis in original). The same rationale applies here. If COPA's incorporation of community standards did not by itself render that statute substantially overbroad, then the obscenity statutes' incorporation of community standards does not—standing alone—render those statutes substantially overbroad. Not surprisingly, the defendants offer no argument—nor do they offer any evidence—that would justify holding otherwise.

Indeed, to the extent that the obscenity statutes are overbroad at all— which itself is debatable[9]—it stands to reason that the potential scope of that over-breadth is less extensive than the overbreadth resulting from COPA. After all, COPA threatened greater overbreadth because it regulated far more than obscenity—it regulated "material that is harmful to minors." 47 U.S.C. § 231(a)(1). Regulating a broader range of content "magnif[ies] the impact caused by differences in community standards across the country." ACLUI, 535 U.S. at 578, 122 S.Ct. 1700 (plurality opinion). By contrast, the obscenity statutes are confined to the much

***33** narrower, legal definition of obscenity set forth in *Miller*. Presumably, the only protected speech burdened by those statutes on account of varying community standards are materials that lack serious literary, artistic, political, or scientific value but either do not appeal to the prurient interest or are not patently offensive in some, but not all, jurisdictions.[10] Because the obscenity statutes regulate significantly less content than COPA, the threat of substantial overbreadth due to varying community standards is reduced considerably relative to COPA. Therefore, to the extent that COPA's use of community standards did not—by itself—render that statute substantially overbroad, the Court can safely conclude that the use of community standards in prosecuting obscenity on the Internet does not—by itself—render Section 1465 and Section 223(d) substantially overbroad in violation of the First Amendment. "Surely I cannot do to the obscenity statutes what the Supreme Court was unwilling to do to COPA in the absence of evidence of substantial overbreadth."[11]

B. "As A Whole" Requirement

Of course, the defendants' do not necessarily contend that the "community standards" requirement alone renders the obscenity statutes overbroad. (*Stagliano Mem.* [# 21] at 23). They contend that the "community standards" requirement, coupled with the requirement that the allegedly obscene material be evaluated "as a whole," together renders the obscenity statutes sufficiently overbroad as applied to Internet speech.[12](Id.). In particular,

***34** with respect to the "as a whole" requirement, the defendants claim that the express language of Section 1645 and Section 223(d) permits individual items, such as a "picture" or "image," to be judged, not in context, but by themselves. (*Evil Angel Productions* [# 17] at 12-13; *John Stagliano Inc.* [# 20] at 9). Because a fact finder might consider an individual item obscene in isolation, but not in the context of a surrounding website, the defendants contend that the statutes are overbroad because they suppress or chill speech that would otherwise be protected. I disagree.

Since *Miller*, the Supreme Court has said that the standards announced in that case are applicable to federal legislation and that, to the extent any doubt exists about the constitutionality of a federal obscenity statute, courts are free to construe that statute in line with the *Miller* test. *United States v. 12*

200-Foot Reels of Super 8mm Film, 413 U.S.123, 130 & n. 7, 93 S.Ct. 2665, 37 L.Ed.2d 500 (1973). Both statutes at issue here regulate "obscene" materials. Section 1465 regulates any "obscene ... book, pamphlet, picture, film, paper, letter, writing, print, silhouette, drawing, figure, image, cast, phonograph recording, electrical transcription or other article capable of producing sound." 18 U.S.C. §1465. Similarly, Section 223(d) regulates "any comment, request, suggestion, proposal, image, or other communication that [ ] is obscene." 47 U.S.C. §223(d). By definition, no individual item can be found obscene under *Miller* if taken out of context. The purpose of the "as a whole" requirement is that any allegedly obscene material be judged, not in isolation, but in the context of the work of which they are a part. This point is well demonstrated by *Kois v. Wisconsin*, where the Supreme Court found it unnecessary to evaluate individual pictures "because in the context in which they appeared in the newspaper they were rationally related to an article that itself was clearly entitled to [constitutional] protection." 408 U.S. 229, 231, 92 S.Ct. 2245, 33 L.Ed.2d 312 (1972).

In any event, even if Section 1465 and Section 223(d) could be construed, as the defendants suggest, to permit an individual item to be judged out of context, this Court need not read the statutes that way. Indeed, this Court cannot invalidate an overbroad statute on its face if "a limiting construction or partial invalidation so narrows it as to remove the seeming threat or deterrence to constitutionally protected expression." *Broadrick v. Oklahoma*, 413 U.S. 601, 613, 93 S.Ct. 2908, 37 L.Ed.2d 830 (1973). Fortunately, such a limiting construction is readily available here. Because the obscenity statutes forbid the distribution of items that are obscene and because *Miller* and its progeny define an item as obscene only in relation to the larger work, the Court may reasonably construe the obscenity statutes to require that the listed items be judged, not in isolation, but in the context of the surrounding work. Given this construction, the relevant obscenity statutes do not run afoul of *Miller's* "as a whole" requirement.

Nor are Sections 1462 and 1465, which are charged in Counts One though Five, unconstitutionally overbroad because they include the terms "lewd," "lascivious," "indecent," "filthy," and "vile." The defendants contend that those terms are undefined in the obscenity statutes and that, as a result, the statutes could be used to criminalize constitutionally protected speech that might be lewd or indecent, but not obscene, under the *Miller* test. (*John Stagliano Inc. Mem.* [# 20] at 13-16). The defendants' argument, however, is foreclosed by the reasoning in *United States v. 12 200-Foot Reels of Film* and *Hamling v. United States*. In both cases, the Supreme Court stated that it would construe

***35** the generic terms in Sections 1461 and 1462, which are nearly identical to the terms in Section 1465, in accordance with *Miller's* definition of obscenity. *12 200-Foot Reels of Film,* 413 U.S. at 130 n. 7, 93 S.Ct. 2665; *Hamling v. United States*, 418 U.S. 87, 114, 94 S.Ct. 2887, 41 L.Ed.2d 590 (1974). Because the generic terms of the federal obscenity statutes are appropriately limited by judicial construction, the statutes are not overbroad. As such, the defendants' reliance on cases involving state obscenity statutes that include similar generic terms is entirely misplaced.

II. Vagueness

In addition to overbreadth, the defendants also contend that *Miller's* "as a whole" requirement is unconstitutionally vague because it is unclear how that requirement would apply in the context of the Internet. (*Stagliano Mem.* [#21] at 18-22). Specifically, the defendants point to Justice Kennedy's concurrence in *ACLU I*, where he stated that it was "unclear whether what is to be judged as a whole is a single image on a Web page, a whole Web page, an entire multipage Web site, or an interlocking set of Web sites." *ACLU I*, 535 U.S. at 593, 122 S.Ct. 1700 (Kennedy, J., concurring in the judgment).

Vagueness, of course, is essentially a doctrinal construct of the Fifth Amendment Due Process Clause. A statute is invalid if it "fails to provide a person of ordinary intelligence fair notice of what is prohibited, or is so standardless that it authorizes or encourages seriously discriminatory enforcement." *U.S. v. Williams*, 553 U.S. 285, 128 S.Ct. 1830, 1845, 170 L.Ed.2d 650 (2008). In short, what matters is whether criminal culpability is tied to "wholly subjective judgments without statutory definitions, narrowing context, or settled legal meanings." Id. at 1846.

Since *Miller*, the definition of obscenity and, in particular, the "as a whole" requirement have had a settled legal meaning. Although the defendants contend that the meaning of "as a whole" is unclear as applied to the Internet, the Supreme Court has held that a "lack of precision is not itself offensive to the requirements of due process." *Roth v. United States*, 354 U.S. 476, 491, 77 S.Ct. 1304, 1 L.Ed.2d 1498 (1957). All that is required is sufficient warning: "That there may be marginal cases in which it is difficult to determine the side of the line on which a particular fact situation falls is no sufficient reason to hold the language too ambiguous to define a criminal offense." Id. at 491-92, 77 S.Ct. 1304 (internal quotation marks omitted).

The same reasoning applies here. Even if, as Justice Kennedy suggested in ACLU I, it is less than certain whether the "whole" work is a single image or the entire website, the "as a whole" requirement is no less clear in this case than in countless other cases where courts have applied that requirement in a new factual setting.[13] Far from exposing the defendants

***36** to wholly subjective judgments, *Miller's* definition of obscenity and, in particular, the "as a whole" requirement are sufficiently definite, even in the context of the Internet, to survive yet another constitutional challenge on vagueness grounds. As the Supreme Court itself announced when it decided *Miller*, the obscenity test "provide [s] fair notice to a dealer in [pornographic] materials that his public and commercial activities may bring prosecution." 413 U.S. at 27, 93 S.Ct. 2607. Even though the defendants invite this Court to revisit that determination, I will not do so just because a new medium is in play. As a constitutional matter, I am confident that the relevant obscenity statutes, when read against the backdrop of a long line of Supreme Court cases defining obscenity, provide sufficient guidance to Internet publishers that whatever arguably obscene material they distribute on the Internet will be judged, not in isolation, but in context.

Having determined that Section 1465 and Section 223(d) are not unconstitutionally vague as applied to Internet speech, I will briefly address the defendants' argument that the entire website is the relevant work to be judged in Counts Three and Seven of the Indictment. (*John Stagliano Inc. Mem.* [# 20] at 16-17). Describing the movie trailer as just one small part of the overall Evil Angel website— which includes hundreds of other trailers, information about various Evil Angel productions, a newsletter, customer support and membership information, an on—line store, and links to other websites featuring both erotic and political content—the defendants analogize the website to a magazine, a book of collected works, or a catalogue. (*Stagliano Reply* [# 26] at 3-5). The government argues that the trailer is a single work that should be judged independently. By comparison, it analogizes the website to an on-line store selling individual works with no meaningful connection to one another that would require contextualization. (Gov't Opposition [# 23] at 7-8). The government relies in particular on *United States v. Various Articles of Obscene Merch., Schedule No. 2098*, where the District Court for the Southern District of New York held that each movie on a single video cassette was a separate work entitled to its own independent evaluation. 536 F.Supp. 50, 53 (S.D.N.Y.1981).

Although the relationship between the website and the trailer obviously bear some similarity to the relationship between magazines and articles, books of collected works and the individual works, catalogues and the advertised products, as well as on-line stores and their merchandise, to analogize the website and trailer at issue here to any single kind of work is to lose sight of the fundamental purpose undergirding the "as a whole" requirement. In *Roth v. United States*, the Supreme Court approved a jury instruction that described the requirement this way: "The books, pictures and circulars must be judged as a whole, in their entire context, and you are not to consider detached or separate portions in reaching a conclusion." 354 U.S. at 490, 77 S.Ct. 1304 (internal quotation marks omitted). In short, what is important is that the allegedly obscene material be judged in context. The appropriate context in which to evaluate the trailer here is, at a minimum, the web page on which the trailer was posted. This is not to say that the government must prove that the entire webpage is obscene. The obscenity test, after all, is not quantitative. *Penthouse Int'l, Ltd.*, 610 F.2d at 1368. Rather, the government will have to show that the trailer is obscene in light of the surrounding webpage, not in isolation. During the course of the trial, the Court will address on a case-by-case basis whether

***37** the jury should have access to other pages of the website as well.

III. Substantive Due Process

Having disposed of the defendants' overbreadth and vagueness arguments, I now turn to their more sweeping claim that the entire prosecution should be dismissed because the Constitution creates a substantive due process right to sexual privacy that includes both the right of individuals to possess obscene material and, by extension, the right of publishers to provide that material to willing recipients. As a preliminary matter, I do not believe that Supreme Court precedent can be fairly read to support a First Amendment right to distribute obscene material in public. Indeed, although the Supreme Court has held in *Stanley v. Georgia*, 394 U.S. 557, 89 S.Ct. 1243, 22 L.Ed.2d 542 (1969), that the mere possession of obscene materials in the privacy of one's home is protected by the First Amendment, id. at 568, 89 S.Ct. 1243, subsequent decisions firmly establish that there is no corresponding right to receive or distribute such materials. The Supreme Court has made clear that "the protected right to possess obscene material in the privacy of one's home does not give rise to a correlative right to have someone sell or give it to others." *12 200-Foot Reels of Film*, 413 U.S. at 128, 93 S.Ct. 2665.[14]

Faced with this insurmountable case law, the defendants, like alchemists of old, have conjured up an alternative theory based on evolving developments in the Supreme Court's substantive due process jurisprudence.[15] Relying on a long line of privacy cases beginning with *Griswold v. Connecticut*, 381 U.S. 479, 85 S.Ct. 1678, 14 L.Ed.2d 510 (1965), and culminating with *Lawrence v. Texas*, 539 U.S. 558, 123 S.Ct. 2472, 156 L.Ed.2d 508 (2003), they advance two basic contentions: (1) the sum of these cases establishes a constitutionally protected liberty interest in sexual privacy, which includes the right to possess and the correlative right to distribute or obtain obscene materials; and (2) morality is not a rational, much less compelling, basis for overcoming that liberty interest. (*Evil Angel Productions Mem.* [# 17] at 26-39; *John Stagliano, Inc. Mem.* [# 20] at 20-27; *Stagliano Mem.* [#21] at 13-18). As to both, I disagree.

First, I reject the notion that the liberty interest announced in Lawrence somehow includes a right to obtain or distribute obscenity. The defendants misconstrue

***38** the nature of the liberty interest at stake in that case. What is evident from the Supreme Court's decision is its intent to prevent the state from burdening certain intimate, consensual relationships by criminalizing the private sexual acts that are instrumental to those relationships. In defining the contours of the liberty interest, the Supreme Court made a point to note that the statutes challenged in *Lawrence* "seek to control a personal relationship that ... is within the liberty of persons to choose without being punished as criminals." 539 U.S. at 567, 123 S.Ct. 2472. The defendants, in effect, demean this liberty interest by defining it as a right to sexual privacy, when it is really about the right to form meaningful, personal bonds that find expression in sexual intimacy. As the Supreme Court put it: "When sexuality finds overt expression in intimate conduct with another person, the conduct can be but one element in a personal bond that is more enduring. The liberty protected by the Constitution allows homosexual persons the right to make this choice." Id. The possession and use of obscenity are hardly analogous to the sexual acts that the Lawrence Court found to be so instrumental to the relationships of homosexual persons. Indeed, the liberty interest that the defendants claim pales in comparison to the liberty interest at stake in *Lawrence*. Similarly, the purported right to obtain or distribute obscenity does not remotely approach the fundamental liberty interests implicated in *Griswold v. Connecticut*, 381 U.S. 479, 85 S.Ct. 1678, 14 L.Ed.2d 510 (1965), and *Eisenstadt v. Baird*, 405 U.S. 438, 92 S.Ct. 1029, 31 L.Ed.2d 349 (1972), where the Supreme Court held that the right to decide whether to bear or beget a child includes the right to obtain contraceptives. As a result, I reject the defendants' contention that *Lawrence* and its predecessors created a so-called right to sexual privacy so fundamental and so sweeping that it includes the right to obtain, as well as the correlative right to distribute, obscene materials in the public marketplace, which the post-*Stanley* cases repeatedly rejected. Thus, absent clear support in the constitutional text or in Supreme Court case law, I will neither certify the defendants' gold-toned constitutional concoction, nor conjure one up on my own.

Furthermore, to the extent that *Lawrence* rejects public morality as a legitimate governmental interest, it does so only in the narrow context of private conduct that has no potential to harm others. *Williams v. Morgan*, 478 F.3d 1316, 1322 (11th Cir.2007). The *Lawrence* Court made clear that its holding did not extend to cases that "involve public conduct." *Lawrence*, 539 U.S. at 578, 123 S.Ct. 2472. The obscenity statutes, unlike the statute invalidated in *Lawrence*, do not target purely private activity. To the contrary, they target the public dissemination or the possession for sale of obscene materials. Although public morality may be an insufficient justification for regulating private conduct in some cases, it is certainly a sufficient justification for regulating the sort of public conduct at issue here. Indeed, the Supreme Court has repeatedly upheld obscenity statutes on the basis that the government can "legitimately act ... to protect `the social interest in order and morality.'" *Paris Adult Theatre I v. Slaton*, 413 U.S. 49, 61, 93 S.Ct. 2628, 37 L.Ed.2d 446 (1973) (quoting *Roth*, 354 U.S. at 485, 77 S.Ct. 1304).

Because there is no substantive due process right to sexual privacy that would include the right to obtain or distribute obscene materials and because the government's interest in morality is a sufficient justification for regulating the public dissemination of obscenity, I easily reject the

***39** defendants' substantive due process challenge to the Indictment.

CONCLUSION

The Supreme Court has warned that striking down a statute for overbreadth is "strong medicine" that should be employed "sparingly and only as a last resort." *Broadrick*, 413 U.S. at 613, 93 S.Ct. 2908. Having considered the defendants' overbreadth arguments, I am not convinced that such strong medicine is warranted in this case. Nor am I convinced that the federal obscenity statutes are unconstitutionally vague as applied to Internet speech. Finally, I reject the defendants' most sweeping claim—that the entire Indictment is void because recent developments in Supreme Court case law guarantee the right to produce and distribute obscenity. Absent binding precedent to the contrary, I will not create or enlarge unenumerated constitutional rights of the kind that the defendants seek. Although this case is not the first to attack the constitutionality of federal obscenity statutes, it will not likely be the last. But for now, I see no reason to invalidate what the Supreme Court has repeatedly upheld. There being no convincing basis to set aside the obscenity statutes charged in the Indictment, the Court hereby DENIES the defendants' respective Motions to Dismiss.

ORDER

For the reasons set forth in the Memorandum Opinion, it is this 19th day of February, 2010, hereby

ORDERED that the defendants' respective Motions to Dismiss Indictment [# 17, 20, 21] are DENIED; it is further

ORDERED that defendant John Stagliano's Motion to Join All Other Defendants' Motions [# 21] is GRANTED; it is further

ORDERED that defendant John Stagliano's Motion for Open Public Trial [# 21] remains under advisement; and it is further

ORDERED that, if they choose to do so, the defendants may submit motions for interlocutory appeal no later than five business days from the date of this Order, and the government shall have no more than fourteen days to respond.

SO ORDERED.

Footnotes

[1] Section 1465 specifically provides:

Whoever knowingly produces with the intent to transport, distribute, or transmit in interstate or foreign commerce, or whoever knowingly transports or travels in, or uses a facility or means of, interstate or foreign commerce or an interactive computer service... in or affecting such commerce, for the purpose of sale or distribution of any obscene, lewd, lascivious, or filthy book, pamphlet, picture, film, paper, letter, writing, print, silhouette, drawing, figure, image, cast, phonograph recording, electrical transcription or other article capable of producing sound or any other matter of indecent or immoral character, shall be fined under this title or imprisoned not more than five years, or both.

[2] Section 1462 provides:

Whoever brings into the United States, or any place subject to the jurisdiction thereof, or knowingly uses any express company or other common carrier or interactive computer service...for carriage in interstate or foreign commerce—(a) any obscene, lewd, lascivious, or filthy book, pamphlet, picture, motion-picture film, paper, letter, writing, print, or other matter of indecent character . . . Shall be fined under this title or imprisoned not more than five years, or both...

[3] Section 1466 provides:

(a) Whoever is engaged in the business of producing with intent to distribute or sell, or selling or transferring obscene matter, who knowingly receives or possesses with intent to distribute any obscene book, magazine, picture, paper, film, videotape, or phonograph or other audio recording, which has been shipped or transported in interstate or foreign commerce, shall be punished by imprisonment for not more than 5 years or by a fine under this title, or both.

[4] Section 223(d) provides:

Whoever—(1) in interstate or foreign communications knowingly— . . . (B) uses any interactive computer service to display in a manner available to a person under 18 years of age, any comment, request, suggestion, proposal, image, or other communication that, is obscene or child pornography, regardless of whether the user of such service placed the call or initiated the communication. . . shall be fined under Title 18 or imprisoned not more than two years, or both.

[5] In addition to prohibiting "obscene" material, Section 223(d) also prohibits "child pornography." The defendants raise no facial challenge to this aspect of the statute.

[6] The defendants claim that the Supreme Court has moved away from treating obscenity as "unprotected speech." (*Stagliano Mem.* [# 21] at 10). They point to *R.A.V. v. City of St. Paul* where the Supreme Court made clear that even though certain categories of speech, such as obscenity and defamation, may "be regulated because of their constitutionally proscribable content," those categories are not "entirely invisible to the Constitution." 505 U.S. 377, 383, 112 S.Ct. 2538, 120 L.Ed.2d 305 (1992) (emphasis omitted). The defendants miss the point. *R.A.V.* does not mean that "unprotected" categories of speech like obscenity and defamation can no longer be regulated based on their proscribable content. It stands only for the proposition that those categories cannot "be made the vehicles for content discrimination unrelated to their distinctively proscribable content." Id. at 383-84, 112 S.Ct. 2538 (emphasis added). Thus, for example, "the government may proscribe libel; but it may not make the further content discrimination of proscribing only libel critical of the government." Id.at 384, 112 S.Ct. 2538. The obscenity statutes do not suffer this defect. Even though they regulate constitutionally proscribable content, which is permissible, they do not discriminate on the basis of viewpoint.

[7] For instance, Justice Kennedy, joined by two other justices, acknowledged that the "national variation in community standards constitutes a particular burden on Internet speech." *ACLU I,* 535 U.S. at 597, 122 S.Ct. 1700 (Kennedy, J., concurring in the judgment). Similarly, Justice O'Connor wrote that "given Internet speakers' inability to control the geographic location of their audience, expecting them to bear the burden of controlling the recipients of their speech ... may be entirely too much to ask, and would potentially suppress an inordinate amount of expression." Id. at 587, 122 S.Ct. 1700 (O'Connor, J., concurring in part and concurring in the judgment). In somewhat more colorful language, Justice Breyer pointed out that applying "the community standards of every locality in the United States would provide the most puritan of communities with a heckler's Internet veto affecting the rest of

the Nation." Id. at 590, 122 S.Ct. 1700 (Breyer, J., concurring in part and concurring the in the judgment).

[8] In *United States v. Kilbride*, the Ninth Circuit held that the narrowest reading of the splintered ACLU I decision required the court to accept the view of Justices O'Connor and Breyer "that a national community standard must be applied in regulating obscene speech on the Internet." 584 F.3d 1240, 1254 (9th Cir.2009). I disagree. Eight justices concurred in the judgment that the use of community standards did not "by itself render the statute substantially overbroad." ACLU I, 535 U.S. at 585, 122 S.Ct. 1700. Justice Thomas, joined by Chief Justice Rehnquist and Justice Scalia, did so based on their belief that COPA was sufficiently narrow in application that any variation in community standards did not render the statute substantially overbroad. Id. at 577-84, 122 S.Ct. 1700 (Thomas, J.). The remaining five justices indicated, however, that the possibility of varying community standards raised potential constitutional concerns. Although Justice O'Connor favored a national standard, she nevertheless affirmed the use of community standards because the plaintiffs had failed to demonstrate substantial overbreadth due to excessive variation among local communities. Id. at 586-89, 122 S.Ct. 1700 (O'Connor, J., concurring in part and concurring in the judgment). Unlike Justice O'Connor, however, Justice Breyer concurred, not because of the plaintiffs' failure of proof, but because he read the statutory term "community" to mean the Nation's adult community as a whole. Id. at 589-91, 122 S.Ct. 1700 (Breyer, J., concurring in part and concurring in the judgment). Justice Kennedy, joined by Justices Souter and Ginsburg, affirmed the judgment for much the same reason as Justice O'Connor. See id. at 597-602, 122 S.Ct. 1700 (Kennedy, J., concurring in the judgment). They concluded that it was impossible to "know whether variation in community standards renders [COPA] substantially overbroad without first assessing the extent of the speech covered and the variations in community standards with respect to that speech." Id. at 597, 122 S.Ct. 1700. Of the five justices who found the use of community standards to be constitutionally problematic, only Justice Breyer based his decision on the belief that a national community standard applied. Notwithstanding their concerns, the other four justices were willing to accept the constitutional viability of community standards in the absence of evidence establishing substantial overbreadth based on the amount of speech covered and the degree of variance among communities. Because Justice Breyer disregarded the possibility that local community standards might be constitutional in light of the facts and circumstances of the case and instead imposed a uniform national standard that no other justice thought was necessary, his rationale is not the narrowest, and as a result, it does not control.

[9] Notwithstanding the concerns raised by some of the justices in ACLU I, it is questionable whether the application of community standards renders the obscenity statutes overbroad as applied to the Internet. Because the statutes are limited to the regulation of obscenity, they exceed their plainly legitimate scope only if they burden or chill speech that is actually protected by the First Amendment. In affirming the constitutionality of the "community standards" requirement, the Supreme Court in *Miller* explained that "[i]t is neither realistic nor constitutionally sound to read the First Amendment as requiring that the people of Maine or Mississippi accept public depiction of conduct found tolerable in Las Vegas, or New York City." 413 U.S. at 32, 93 S.Ct. 2607. This point makes sense, however, only if the speech found tolerable in Las Vegas or New York, but regulable in Maine or Mississippi, is not entitled to full First Amendment protection. That more permissive jurisdictions choose not to punish speech that other jurisdictions may constitutionally proscribe does not entitle that speech to protection as a constitutional matter. This point is underscored by the Supreme Court's assurance in *Miller* that, under a national constitution, fundamental First Amendment limitations "do not vary from community to community." Id. at 30, 93 S.Ct. 2607. Furthermore, in rejecting arguments that governmental regulation of obscene speech violates First Amendment norms, the *Miller* Court emphasized that the First Amendment "protects works which, taken as a whole, have serious literary, artistic, political, or scientific value." Id. at 34, 93 S.Ct. 2607. Speech that some jurisdictions could constitutionally prohibit under the *Miller* test but that other jurisdictions would permit due to more permissive community standards necessarily lacks serious literary, artistic, political, and scientific value. Speech that had serious value would obviously be entitled to full constitutional protection in any jurisdiction. Therefore, because the defendants' overbreadth claim involves speech lacking in serious social value, it is doubtful whether that speech is even protected by the First Amendment. At the very least, the constitutional value of that speech is so slight (compared to speech that is found to have serious social value) that any burden imposed upon it does not justify the wholesale invalidation of the obscenity statutes as applied to the Internet.

[10] Unlike the "prurient interest" and "patently offensive" prongs, whether a work lacks serious literary, artistic, political, or scientific value does not depend on varying community standards but is judged by an objective "reasonable person" standard. Pope, 481 U.S. at 500-01, 107 S.Ct. 1918. Thus, to the extent that the same work is constitutionally proscribed in one jurisdiction but permitted in another, the jurisdictions must agree, at a minimum, that the work lacks serious value. If it had serious value, then it could not be prohibited consistent with the Constitution in any jurisdiction.

[11] The defendants' copyright argument, although rather novel, does not justify invalidating the obscenity statutes on their face. First, any burden on a publisher's ability to register a copyright does not itself violate the Constitution because there is no constitutional right to copyright registration. *Darden v. Peters*, 488 F.3d 277, 284 (4th Cir.2007). Second, to the extent that the inability to obtain copyright protection burdens the First Amendment rights of publishers whose works would be protected in one jurisdiction but not in the District of Columbia, the defendants' argument is nothing more than a regurgitation of their claim that *Miller's* "community standards" requirement is overbroad as applied to publishers who cannot control the geographic reach of their allegedly obscene materials. As I have already explained, that fact alone does not warrant invalidating the obscenity statutes charged in the Indictment.

[12] Although the point is not expressed in any detail, the defendants also suggest that the "community standards" requirement violates due process because it allows for selective prosecutions and forum shopping. (Stagliano Mem. [#21] at 7, 20 & n. 26, 23). If the defendants mean that the "community standards" requirement empowers the government to impose the community standards of its preferred jurisdiction on nationwide speech, then this point is simply a restatement of the defendants' overbreadth argument, which the Court has already rejected. If, however, the defendants mean that the "community standards" requirement empowers the government to act unfairly or improperly, then their argument fails because "in the absence of clear evidence to the contrary," courts presume that government agents "properly discharge [] their official duties." *United States v. Armstrong*, 517 U.S. 456, 464, 116 S.Ct. 1480, 134 L.Ed.2d 687 (1996) (internal quotation marks omitted). Speculative fear that the government might abuse its prosecutorial discretion is not grounds for invalidating an otherwise constitutional statute.

[13] See, e.g., *Erznoznik v. City of Jacksonville*, 422 U.S. 205, 212 n. 7, 95 S.Ct. 2268, 45 L.Ed.2d 125 (1975) (noting that "[s]cenes of nudity in a movie, like pictures of nude persons in a book, must be considered as a part of the whole work"); *Kois*, 408 U.S. at 231, 92 S.Ct. 2245 (taking account, not only of the allegedly obscene poem, but also "its placement amid a selection of poems in the interior of a newspaper"); *Penthouse Int'l, Ltd. v. McAuliffe*, 610 F.2d 1353, 1368 (5th Cir.1980) (deciding that magazines are "to be considered as whole works even though made up of separate articles"); *United States v. Various Articles of Obscene Merch., Schedule No. 2098*, 536 F.Supp. 50, 53 (S.D.N.Y.1981) (holding that each film contained on a single video cassette is subject "to its own independent evaluation").

[14] See also *United States v. Orito*, 413 U.S. 139, 141-42, 93 S.Ct. 2674, 37 L.Ed.2d 513 (1973) (rejecting "the idea that some zone of constitutionally protected privacy follows such material when it is moved outside the home area protected by Stanley"); *United States v. Reidel*, 402 U.S. 351, 354-55, 91 S.Ct. 1410, 28 L.Ed.2d 813 (1971) (holding that the right announced in *Stanley* did not apply to those who "are routinely disseminating obscenity through the mails and who have no claim, and could make none, about unwanted governmental intrusions into the privacy of their home").

[15] It is doubtful whether the defendants' substantive due process argument can even be raised to circumvent the post-Stanley line of cases. The Third Circuit held in *United States v. Extreme Associates, Inc.* that even if Lawrence undermined the post-Stanley cases, those cases still control in light of *Agostini v. Felton*, 521 U.S.203, 117 S.Ct. 1997, 138 L.Ed.2d 391 (1997). *Extreme Associates, Inc.*, 431 F.3d 150, 155-56 (3rd Cir.2005). As a result, the Third Circuit rejected a constitutional challenge to the obscenity statutes on the ground that the Supreme Court "has considered the federal statutes regulating the distribution of obscenity in the context of the broader constitutional right to privacy and [has] upheld them." Id. at 159. Whatever the merits of this point, it is academic because the Court is not persuaded that *Lawrence* cast any doubt on the post-*Stanley* cases.

UNITED STATES OF AMERICA

v.

JOHN STAGLIANO

729 F.Supp.2d 215 (2010)

United States District Court, District of Columbia

Decided August 4, 2010

MEMORANDUM OPINION

RICHARD J. LEON, District Judge.

The defendants John Stagliano, John Stagliano, Inc., and Evil Angel Productions, Inc., were charged in a seven-count Indictment with violating several federal obscenity statutes.[1] In essence, the government

***217** accused them of distributing in interstate commerce two obscene movies titled "Milk Nymphos" and "Storm Squirters 2 `Target Practice'" and a movie trailer titled "Fetish Fanatic Chapter 5" that was posted on a website allegedly owned by the defendants.[2] Prior to the trial, the defendants filed a Motion in Limine [# 53] requesting that the Court compel the government, not only to introduce into evidence the entirety of the charged films, but to publish the films in their entirety in open court as part of its case-in-chief. Altogether, the two movies and the trailer take approximately five-and-a-half hours to play in real time. The government opposed the defendants' motion, indicating instead that it would introduce the entire films into evidence but would limit the publication of each film in open court to representative samples accompanied by a summary witness, who would describe the remaining portions. On June 2, 2010, I denied the defendants' motion without further explanation, but left open the question whether the defendants could publish the entire films or, at the very least, whether they could publish the remaining portions of the films as part of their cross-examination of the government's witnesses or as part of their case-in-chief. The defendants promptly filed another motion [# 82], which the government did not oppose, seeking permission to publish the entire films as they deemed appropriate. On July 13, in a ruling from the bench, I articulated the rationale for my earlier decision denying the defendants' first motion, and I announced my decision to deny their second. This Memorandum Opinion sets forth more fully the reasoning for both rulings.

DISCUSSION

I. Motion In Limine To Compel Government To Publish Charged Films

As grounds for their initial Motion in Limine, the defendants contended that the "as a whole" requirement of the obscenity test announced by the Supreme Court in *Miller v. California*, 413 U.S. 15, 93 S.Ct. 2607, 37 L.Ed.2d 419 (1973), required the government to show each work from beginning to end to satisfy its burden of proof. The "as a whole" requirement applies to the first and third prongs of the *Miller* test. Under the first prong, the government must prove beyond a reasonable doubt that, according to contemporary community standards, the charged work, taken as a whole, appeals to the prurient interest. Id. at 24, 93 S.Ct. 2607. Under the third prong, the government must prove beyond a reasonable doubt that the work, again taken as a whole, lacks serious literary, artistic, political, or scientific value. Id. The defendants argued that, unless the government played the entire films to the jury in open court, there would be no "guarantee" that the jurors would actually view the films in their entirety and thus be able to judge them as a whole. Because jury deliberations are generally considered to be sacrosanct, the defendants stressed that "the only way to truly ensure that the jury has viewed the material as a whole would be to require the jury to view the material in open court."

***218** (Defs.' Mot. in Limine [# 53] at 6 (emphasis in original)). A conviction in which the jury failed to view the films in their entirety would, according to the defendants, violate their First Amendment and due process rights, since those films cannot be adjudged obscene without evaluating the prurient appeal and serious literary, artistic, political, and scientific value of the films, taken as a whole.

I denied the defendants' motion because it rested on a non sequitur. Central to the defendants' argument was the premise that jurors cannot properly judge a work as a whole unless they view it in real time from beginning to end. Common sense tells us, however, that a juror need not view every frame of a film or, for that matter, every word of a book or every page or picture in a magazine in order to determine whether a given work, taken as whole, appeals to the prurient interest and lacks serious literary, artistic, political, or scientific value. Thus, quite predictably, the defendants could cite no federal case in which a court required the government to play every frame of film, or read aloud every word of a book or magazine, in open court to ensure that the jury judged it as a whole.

Indeed, the notion that a work need not be viewed in its entirety to be appraised as a whole is entirely consistent with the logic behind the "as a whole" requirement. It is clear from *Miller* and the cases leading to it that the Supreme Court sought to prevent the government from introducing only those portions of a work that, it believed, appealed to the prurient interest or lacked serious literary, artistic, political, or scientific value without giving the jury access to the remainder of the work so that it could evaluate the questionable portions in their proper context. To criminalize an entire work based solely on isolated excerpts taken out of context would, of course, stifle the free expression that the First Amendment was meant to foster. Indeed, in *Roth v. United States*, 354 U.S. 476, 77 S.Ct. 1304, 1 L.Ed.2d 1498 (1957), the Supreme Court expressly rejected an earlier standard for determining obscenity that "allowed material to be judged merely by the effect of an isolated excerpt upon particularly susceptible persons." Id. at 488-89, 77 S.Ct. 1304. The *Roth* Court went on to approve a jury instruction directing that "`[t]he books, pictures and circulars must be judged as a whole, in their entire context, and you are not to consider detached or separate portions in reaching a conclusion.'" Id. at 490, 77 S.Ct. 1304. As I stated in an earlier opinion in this case, "[t]he purpose of the `as a whole' requirement is that any allegedly obscene material be judged, not in isolation, but in the context of the work of which they are a part." *United States v. Stagliano*, 693 F.Supp.2d 25, 34 (D.D.C.2010). In an unpublished opinion that I find persuasive, the Eleventh Circuit explained that the requirement serves two purposes: "(1) it places materials in their proper context so that a jury may properly determine if the material is truly of prurient appeal; and (2) it ensures that any literary, artistic, political, or scientific value endowed in the material by its surrounding context is not lost by viewing the material in isolation." *United States v. Little*, 365 Fed.Appx. 159, 164 (11th Cir. 2010) (per curiam) (unpublished).

The juror's task, therefore, is to view the potentially obscene parts of the work in their proper context and, in so doing, to judge whether the work appeals to the prurient interest and whether it lacks serious literary, artistic, political, or scientific value. Each individual work must be considered as a complete work, not based on isolated portions taken out of context. But that task in no way requires the juror to view every bit of a work. Repetitive sexually-explicit portions that neither alter the

***219** determination of a work's prurient appeal nor add some plausible literary, artistic, political, or scientific value are entirely irrelevant to the "as a whole" analysis. Cf. id. (explaining that "[i]f the website in which material is found does not alter the determination of its prurient appeal or add some redeemable quality to the work, then the website is not necessary for the 'taken as a whole' analysis").

Thus, it was no surprise that the defendants could not cite a single case from the Supreme Court or from our Circuit that requires the jury to watch every frame of a movie or read every word of a book or view every page or picture in a magazine to satisfy the "as a whole" element of the *Miller* test. After all, the jury's duty is to ensure that whatever portions of a given work are thought to make the work obscene are judged, not in isolation, but in the context of the larger work. But to put those portions into context does not necessarily require that the jury view the entire work from beginning to end. The jury may rely, for instance, on summary testimony from witnesses who have viewed the remaining portions of the work and are subject to cross-examination. It is, after all, a common practice in federal court to allow witnesses to summarize evidence at trial that will be available to the jury during its deliberations. Rule 1006 of the Federal Rules of Evidence provides, for instance, that the "contents of voluminous writings, recordings, or photographs which cannot conveniently be examined in court may be presented in the form of a chart, summary, or calculation." Fed.R.Evid. 1006. To provide context, the jury may also rely on other excerpts from the work that either the government or defense presented at trial or that the jury itself viewed during its deliberations.

So long as the government introduces the entire work into evidence for the jury to view as it sees fit during its deliberations, the government need not publish the entire work to the jury in open court to satisfy its burden of proof. In that regard, I am persuaded by an unpublished opinion from the Fourth Circuit, *United States v. Adams*, 337 Fed.Appx. 336, 338-39 (4th Cir.2009) (per curiam) (unpublished), that the government can indeed satisfy its burden by playing representative samples of a charged work in open court with the aid of a witness—subject, of course, to cross-examination—who can put the samples into context by summarizing the portions of the work that are not shown.[3]

The defendants' concern about the inviolability of the jury deliberation process is, to say the least, overblown. It is no per se violation of the defendants' First Amendment and due process rights if the jury deliberates for less than the amount of time it would take to view all three films from beginning to end in real time. For reasons that I just explained,*Miller* does not require that the jury view every frame of the charged films, nor does it require that the jury view each film in real time. Indeed, it would be acceptable as a constitutional matter for the jurors to fast-forward over whatever portions of the film they have reason to believe contain gratuitous

***220** and repetitive sexually-explicit activity that bears little relation to the plot, or that is unnecessary to understand the meaning of the film. So long as the Court properly instructs the jury on the legal requirement that they judge the prurient appeal and literary, artistic, political, and scientific value of the film, taken as a whole, by considering whatever portions of the film are shown at trial in their proper context, the jurors are free to evaluate the evidence in any manner they wish in accordance with those instructions. And, of course, it is well-established that "juries are presumed to follow [the Court's] instructions." *Richardson v. Marsh*, 481 U.S. 200, 211, 107 S.Ct. 1702, 95 L.Ed.2d 176 (1987).

Also unpersuasive is the defendants' claim that allowing the government to play samples of the movies somehow forces the Defendants into a `Catch-22' of choosing between, on the one hand, playing the movies in order to show the jury context and to avoid waiving this issue on appeal, or, on the other hand, choosing to not play the rest of the movies and thereby allow the jury to falsely believe that these excerpts are representative.

(Defs.' Reply to Government's Opp'n to Defs.' Mot. in Limine [# 72] at 6). I fail to see how allowing the government to present its case in the manner that it wishes would necessarily produce a no-win, "Catch-22" situation for the defendants. After all, if the defendants play additional samples of the films as part of their case-in-chief that add context favorable to their case or that demonstrate, for instance, the artistic merit of the film not otherwise evident in the government's samples, then the defendants will obviously benefit. That is hardly a "no-win" alternative. Indeed, it is a potentially winning alternative to the extent that it strengthens the defendants' case.

Accordingly, for all the foregoing reasons, I rejected the defendants' rather unusual effort to dictate how the government would present its case.[4]

II. Defense Motion To Publish The Charged Films In Their Entirety

Even though I denied the defense motion to compel the government to play the charged films in toto, I reserved the question whether the defendants could play the entire films or, at the very least, whether they could play the remaining portions of the films as part of their cross-examination of the government's witnesses or as part of their case-in-chief. The defendants raised essentially two arguments supporting their contention that they were legally entitled to show the entirety of the charged films.

First, they reiterated their argument that *Miller*'s mandate to take the works as a whole required the jurors to view each charged work from beginning to end in real time. Failure to do so, according to the defendants, would violate their First Amendment and due process rights. For the reasons I just explained, however, one need not, as a practical matter, view an entire work in order to take a fair measure of it as a whole—that is, as a complete work. Nor does *Miller*, its progeny, and the case law in our Circuit specifically require a juror to view the entirety of a charged work in order to satisfy the "as a whole" requirement. Because a work

***221** need not be viewed in its entirety to be judged as a complete work, the *Miller* test does not provide a basis for the defendants' claimed entitlement to play the entire charged films on cross-examination or as part of their case-in-chief.

Second, the defendants contended that their Sixth Amendment right to confront the government's witnesses and to put on a defense means that they are entitled to show whatever portions of the films are necessary to cross-examine the government's witnesses or to establish their defense—including, if need be, the entire films. I do not disagree that the defendants may show portions of the films that they can demonstrate are needed to cross-examine the government's witnesses or to establish their defense. The defendants do not have, however, a categorical legal right to show in open court the entirety of the charged films.

Their right to confront opposing witnesses through cross-examination and to put on a defense of their choosing, while robust, is nevertheless constrained by the Court's power and discretion to control the mode by which the parties present evidence. Under Federal Rule of Evidence 611, "the court shall exercise reasonable control over the mode and order of interrogating witnesses and presenting evidence so as to . . . make the interrogation and presentation effective for the ascertainment of the truth [and to] avoid needless consumption of time." Fed.R.Evid. 611. It is no aid to the ascertainment of the truth, nor is it an efficient use of the Court's time, to allow the defendants to play portions of the charged films containing gratuitous scenes of repeated sexually-explicit activity that shed little or no light on the plot or meaning of the films, that add no context to the excerpts already shown by the government, and that no reasonable juror would find to lack prurient appeal or to have serious literary, artistic, political, or scientific value. Accordingly, I declined to permit the defendants to play the entire full-length films as of right. In that respect, I denied their motion.

I did rule, however, that the defendants were permitted to play those portions of the films that they could demonstrate were necessary: (1) to cross-examine a government witness; (2) to put the government's representative samples into context; or (3) to show that the films did not appeal to the prurient interest or that they did not lack serious literary, artistic, political, or scientific value. In short, absent a colorable argument by the defendants that the additional segments they sought to play would actually aid their defense, I refused to allow the segments to be played in open court during the course of the trial, knowing, of course, that the jury would be free to watch the entirety of the charged films during its deliberations.

CONCLUSION

The defendants took a particularly aggressive position regarding the procedural approach to the trial of this case. In effect, they argued that a film—no matter how long or sexually explicit—must be shown to the jury in its entirety in open court to ensure that the jury satisfies *Miller*'s mandate that the film be "taken as a whole" to determine whether it appeals to the prurient interest or lacks serious literary, artistic, political, or scientific value. Implicit in their argument is the flawed premise that a work must actually be viewed in its entirety in order to be judged fairly as a whole. In short, the defendants erroneously conflated the task of reviewing a film from beginning to end in real time with the task of judging the film as a complete work. Because the former is not necessary to accomplish the latter, I rejected

***222** the defendants' argument and accordingly denied both of their motions.

[1] Among the statutes charged in the Indictment were: (1) 18 U.S.C. § 1465, transporting obscene

matters for sale or distribution; (2) 18 U.S.C. § 1462, using a common carrier or interactive computer service to transport obscene matters; (3) 18 U.S.C. § 1466, engaging in the business of selling or transferring obscene matter; and (4) 47 U.S.C. § 223(d), displaying obscene material on the Internet in a manner available to persons under 18.

[2] Ultimately, I dismissed with prejudice Counts 3 and 7 and part of Count 6, all involving the movie trailer, because the FBI's original disc containing the trailer was so defective that it was not sufficiently reliable to be introduced into evidence. As for the remaining counts involving the two full-length movies, I granted the defendants' motion for judgment of acquittal under Rule 29 of the Federal Rules of Criminal Procedure due to the inadequacy of the government's proof linking the defendants to the distribution of the movies into the District of Columbia.

[3] With little argument, the defendants hinted that the government's failure to play the entire films in open court could potentially violate the "best evidence" rule since the jury could base its decision on the summary witness's testimony about the films, rather than on the films themselves. This so-called "best evidence" rule provides that "[t]o prove the content of a writing, recording, or photograph, the original writing, recording, or photograph is required." Fed.R.Evid. 1002. By introducing the original films into evidence in their entirety, the government clearly satisfied that rule. The use of summary witnesses, which is permitted by the Rules, is merely a tool of convenience, not a wholesale substitute for the actual films that are introduced into evidence at trial.

[4] As it turned out, the government showed in open court an approximately 50-minute excerpt from "Milk Nymphos" and a 35-minute excerpt from "Storm Squirters 2 'Target Practice.'" The FBI agent who summarized the remaining portions of each film was thereafter cross-examined by each defense counsel without any attempt, or even a request, to play any other portions of the two films.

Made in United States
North Haven, CT
05 November 2026

21765345R00143